# Taste of Home Comes From the Heart

**Home cooks like you** make *Taste of Home* the world's #1 food and entertaining magazine by sharing their favorite recipes...and you get hundreds in this **keepsake cookbook**.

51

24

10

In every issue, *Taste of Home* magazine serves up a new collection of exciting, never-before-published recipes. But one thing stays the same—each delicious dish comes from the kitchen of a family cook like you. You'll find an entire year's worth of favorites—plus dozens of sensational bonus dishes—in this all-new edition of *Taste of Home Annual Recipes*.

The 22nd installment in our best-selling series, this special cookbook gives you 506 can't-miss dishes your family and friends will ask for again and again. You'll also enjoy tasty new features:

- **Nutrition Facts with Every Recipe**
  With complete nutritional information, it's even easier to make the best choices for your family.
- **Chapter of Child-Pleasing Choices**
  Turn to "Kid-Friendly Foods" (page 262) for an entire chapter of recipes sure to thrill tots and teens.
- **More Stories From Cooks Like You**
  Get to know the people behind the recipes with personal photos, stories and quotes.

And as always, you'll see these helpful recipe icons:
**FAST FIX** = Recipes finished in 30 minutes or less
**EAT SMART** = Recipes lower in calories, fat and sodium
**SLOW COOKER** = Recipes made in a slow cooker
**(5)INGREDIENTS** = Recipes made with 5 or fewer ingredients (excluding water, salt, pepper and canola/olive oil)

With 19 big chapters, gorgeous color photos, helpful hints and two indexes, *Taste of Home Annual Recipes* makes it easy to share the great taste!

## BEST-LOVED RECIPES

From savory main courses and festive party starters to standout sides and tempting desserts, every dish you need for every menu is here in *Taste of Home Annual Recipes*. Take your pick of (from top) colorful Loaded Smashed Taters, hearty Citrus Steak Salad, refreshing Manmosa and hundreds of other favorites.

# Taste of Home
# Annual Recipes 2015

66

142

198

267

### EDITORIAL

Editor-in-Chief **Catherine Cassidy**
Creative Director **Howard Greenberg**
Editorial Operations Director **Kerri Balliet**

Managing Editor/Print & Digital Books **Mark Hagen**
Associate Creative Director **Edwin Robles Jr.**

Editor **Michelle Rozumalski**
Art Director **Maggie Conners**
Contributing Layout Designer **Siya Motamedi**
Editorial Production Manager **Dena Ahlers**
Copy Chief **Deb Warlaumont Mulvey**
Copy Editor **Mary-Liz Shaw**
Contributing Copy Editor **Valerie Phillips**
Copy Desk Intern **Lisa Michel**

Chief Food Editor **Karen Berner**
Food Editors **James Schend; Peggy Woodward, RD**
Recipe Editors **Mary King; Annie Rundle;
Jenni Sharp, RD; Irene Yeh**
Content Operations Manager **Colleen King**
Content Operations Assistant **Shannon Stroud**
Executive Assistant **Marie Brannon**

Test Kitchen & Food Styling Manager **Sarah Thompson**
Test Cooks **Nicholas Iverson (lead), Matthew Hass,
Lauren Knoelke**
Food Stylists **Kathryn Conrad (senior),
Shannon Roum, Leah Rekau**
Prep Cooks **Megumi Garcia, Melissa Hansen,
Bethany Van Jacobson, Sara Wirtz**

Photography Director **Stephanie Marchese**
Photographers **Dan Roberts, Jim Wieland**
Photographer/Set Stylist **Grace Natoli Sheldon**
Set Stylists **Stacey Genaw, Melissa Haberman,
Dee Dee Jacq**

Editorial Business Manager **Kristy Martin**

Editor, *Taste of Home* **Jeanne Ambrose**
Associate Creative Director **Erin Burns**
Art Director, *Taste of Home* **Kristin Bowker**

### BUSINESS

Vice President, Chief Sales Officer **Mark S. Josephson**
Vice President, Business Development & Marketing
**Alain Begun**

General Manager, Taste of Home Cooking School
**Erin Puariea**

Vice President, Digital Experience & E-Commerce
**Jennifer Smith**

### THE READER'S DIGEST ASSOCIATION, INC.

President and Chief Executive Officer
**Bonnie Kintzer**
Vice President, Chief Operating Officer, North America
**Howard Halligan**
Vice President, Enthusiast Brands, Books & Retail
**Harold Clarke**
Vice President, North American Operations
**Philippe Cloutier**
Chief Marketing Officer **Leslie Dukker Doty**
Vice President, Brand Marketing **Beth Gorry**
Vice President, North American Human Resources
**Phyllis E. Gebhardt, SPHR**
Vice President, Consumer Marketing Planning **Jim Woods**

### COVER PHOTOGRAPHY

Photographer **Dan Roberts**
Food Stylist **Kathryn Conrad**
Set Stylist **Stacey Genaw**

© 2014 RDA Enthusiast Brands, LLC
1610 N. 2nd St., Suite 102, Milwaukee WI 53212-3906

International Standard Book Number: 978-1-61765-326-1

International Standard Serial Number: 1094-3463

Component Number: 117400048H00

Printed in U.S.A.
1 3 5 7 9 10 8 6 4 2

# Contents

**PICTURED ON THE COVER** Maple Walnut Cake (p. 179),
Mixed Greens with Lemon Champagne Vinaigrette (p. 23),
Salt-Encrusted Prime Rib (p. 187), Thyme-Roasted Vegetables
(p. 201) and Rustic Garden Herb Biscuits (p. 282).

**PISTACHIO-TURKEY MEATBALLS
IN ORANGE SAUCE**
*PAGE 10*

# Appetizers & Beverages

For a holiday party, after-school snacktime or any occasion at all, try the **small bites and drinks** in this sized-right chapter. You'll find just what you need to serve up **a little refreshment**.

**GRILLED NECTARINE &
CHEESE CROSTINI** *PAGE 7*

**STRAWBERRY-BASIL
COCKTAIL** *PAGE 17*

**TURKEY & SWISS BISCUIT
SLIDERS** *PAGE 13*

## Mushroom & Leek Strudel

Here's a unique, elegant hors d'oeuvre. Use fresh herbs if possible, and feel free to substitute whole-wheat phyllo.

—**LISA DIEHL** EDINA, MN

**PREP:** 50 MIN. + COOLING
**BAKE:** 20 MIN. + STANDING
**MAKES:** 2 STRUDELS (12 SLICES EACH)

- 2 **tablespoons butter, divided**
- 2 **pounds fresh mushrooms, finely chopped, divided**
- 1 **medium leek (white portion only), chopped, divided**
- 2 **garlic cloves, minced**
- ¼ **cup white wine**
- ¼ **cup heavy whipping cream**
- 2 **tablespoons minced fresh parsley**
- 1 **tablespoon minced fresh thyme or 1 teaspoon dried thyme**
- ½ **teaspoon salt**
- ¼ **teaspoon pepper**

**ASSEMBLY**
- 12 **sheets phyllo dough (14x9 inches)**
- ¾ **cup butter, melted**
- 4 **tablespoons grated Parmesan cheese, divided**

**1.** In a large skillet, heat 1 tablespoon butter over medium-high heat. Add half of the mushrooms and leek; cook and stir until mushrooms are lightly browned and leek is tender; remove from pan. Repeat with the remaining butter, mushrooms and leek, adding the garlic during the last minute of cooking. Return all to pan.

**2.** Stir in the wine and heavy whipping cream; cook 1-2 minutes or until liquid is almost evaporated. Stir in the herbs, salt and pepper. Remove from pan; cool completely.

**3.** Preheat oven to 375°. Place one sheet of phyllo dough on a work surface; brush with butter. Layer with five additional phyllo sheets, brushing each layer. (Keep remaining phyllo covered with plastic wrap and a damp towel to prevent it from drying out.)

**4.** Spoon half of the mushroom mixture down the center third of phyllo dough to within 1 in. of ends. Sprinkle filling with 2 tablespoons cheese. Fold up short sides to enclose filling. Roll up jelly-roll style, starting with a long side.

**5.** Transfer to a parchment paper-lined 15x10x1-in. baking pan, seam side down. Brush with additional butter. Repeat with the remaining ingredients. Bake 18-22 minutes or until golden brown.

**6.** Let stand 10 mintues before slicing. Serve warm.

**PER SERVING** *100 cal., 8 g fat (5 g sat. fat), 22 mg chol., 135 mg sodium, 6 g carb., 1 g fiber, 2 g pro.*

SPICY SHRIMP & CRAB COCKTAIL

## Spicy Shrimp & Crab Cocktail

I don't usually eat radishes, but I like them in this shrimp cocktail. Serve it straight up, with tortilla chips or on a bed of butter lettuce.

—**HEIDI KNAAK** LIBERTY, MO

**PREP:** 25 MIN. + CHILLING
**MAKES:** 12 SERVINGS (¾ CUP EACH)

- 2 **medium cucumbers, peeled, seeded and chopped**
- 8 **radishes, halved and thinly sliced (about 2 cups)**
- 2 **cups spicy hot V8 juice (about 16 ounces)**
- 1 **cup Clamato juice**
- ½ **cup finely chopped red onion**
- ½ **cup ketchup**
- 5 **jalapeno peppers, seeded and finely chopped**
- ¼ **cup coarsely chopped fresh cilantro**
- 2 **garlic cloves, minced**
- ½ **teaspoon salt**
- 1 **pound peeled and deveined cooked small shrimp**
- 1 **pound lump crabmeat, drained**
- 2 **medium ripe avocados, peeled and cubed**

In a large bowl, mix the first 10 ingredients. Gently fold in shrimp, crab and avocados. Refrigerate, covered, at least 2 hours or until cold. Serve in martini glasses.

**PER SERVING** *162 cal., 6 g fat (1 g sat. fat), 91 mg chol., 604 mg sodium, 11 g carb., 3 g fiber, 17 g pro.*

MUSHROOM & LEEK STRUDEL

## Cheddar & Onion Beef Sliders

**PREP:** 1¼ HOURS • **COOK:** 10 MIN.
**MAKES:** 8 SERVINGS

- ¼ **cup butter, cubed**
- 1 **medium red onion, halved and thinly sliced**
- 2¼ **teaspoons Montreal steak seasoning, divided**
- 1 **cup dry red wine**
- 1 **pound ground beef**
- 2 **slices cheddar cheese, quartered**
- 8 **dinner rolls, split**

**1.** In a large skillet, heat the butter over medium heat. Add the onion and ¼ teaspoon steak seasoning; cook and stir 6-8 minutes or until the onion is softened. Reduce heat to medium-low; cook 40-45 minutes or until deep golden brown, stirring occasionally. Stir in the wine. Bring to a boil; cook 10-12 minutes or until liquid is almost evaporated.

**2.** In a bowl, combine the beef and remaining steak seasoning, mixing lightly but thoroughly. Shape into eight ½-in.-thick patties.

**3.** In a large nonstick skillet, cook the burgers over medium heat 3-4 minutes on each side or until a thermometer reads 160°; top with cheese during the last 1-2 minutes of cooking. Serve on rolls; top with onion.
**PER SERVING** *320 cal., 17 g fat (8 g sat. fat), 75 mg chol., 499 mg sodium, 20 g carb., 2 g fiber, 15 g pro.*

**GRILLED NECTARINE & CHEESE CROSTINI**

> When my girlfriend and I threw an outdoor party for a bunch of friends, our Cheddar & Onion Beef Sliders went over big. They're great for a quick dinner, too.
> —**KIRK BROOKS** TUCSON, AZ

CHEDDAR & ONION BEEF SLIDERS

---

**EAT SMART** **FAST FIX**

## Grilled Nectarine & Cheese Crostini

We love the summer taste of sweet grilled nectarines and just-picked basil over goat cheese. I can usually find the ingredients we need at our local farmers market.
—**BRANDY HOLLINGSHEAD**
GRASS VALLEY, CA

**START TO FINISH:** 25 MIN.
**MAKES:** 1 DOZEN

- ½ **cup balsamic vinegar**
- 1 **tablespoon olive oil**
- 12 **slices French bread baguette (¼ inch thick)**
- 2 **medium nectarines, halved**
- ¼ **cup fresh goat cheese, softened**
- ¼ **cup loosely packed basil leaves, thinly sliced**

**1.** In a small saucepan, bring vinegar to a boil; cook 10-15 minutes or until the liquid is reduced to 3 tablespoons. Remove from heat.

**2.** Brush oil over both sides of the baguette slices. Grill, uncovered, over medium heat until golden brown on both sides. Grill nectarines 45-60 seconds on each side or until tender and lightly browned. Cool slightly.

**3.** Spread goat cheese over the toasts. Cut the nectarines into thick slices; arrange over cheese. Drizzle with balsamic syrup; sprinkle with basil. Serve immediately.
**PER SERVING** *48 cal., 2 g fat (1 g sat. fat), 5 mg chol., 55 mg sodium, 6 g carb., trace fiber, 1 g pro.* **Diabetic Exchange:** *½ starch.*

CREAMY LEMON MILK SHAKES

EAT SMART FAST FIX

# Tomatillo Salsa

Dare to deviate from the traditional tomato salsa and try this tomatillo-based variation. It's fantastic not only as a snack with tortilla chips, but also as a condiment with a meat entree.
—**LORI KOSTECKI** WAUSAU, WI

**START TO FINISH:** 20 MIN. • **MAKES:** 2¼ CUPS

- 8 **tomatillos, husks removed**
- 1 **medium tomato, quartered**
- 1 **small onion, cut into chunks**
- 1 **jalapeno pepper, seeded**
- 3 **tablespoons fresh cilantro leaves**
- 3 **garlic cloves, peeled**
- 1 **tablespoon lime juice**
- ½ **teaspoon salt**
- ¼ **teaspoon ground cumin**
- ⅛ **teaspoon pepper**
  **Tortilla chips**

**1.** In a large saucepan, bring 4 cups water to a boil. Add the tomatillos. Reduce the heat; simmer, uncovered, for 5 minutes. Drain.

**2.** Place the tomatillos, tomato, onion, jalapeno, cilantro, garlic, lime juice and seasonings in a food processor. Cover and process until blended. Serve with chips.

**NOTE** *Wear disposable gloves when cutting hot peppers; the oils can burn skin. Avoid touching your face.*

**PER SERVING** *19 cal., trace fat (trace sat. fat), 0 chol., 133 mg sodium, 4 g carb., 1 g fiber, 1 g pro.* **Diabetic Exchange:** *Free food.*

FAST FIX

# Creamy Lemon Milk Shakes

Several different recipes inspired the combination of ingredients in my milk shakes. The tart twist of lemon is a wonderful contrast to the creamy sweetness of vanilla ice cream.
—**CAROL GILLESPIE** CHAMBERSBURG, PA

**START TO FINISH:** 10 MIN. • **MAKES:** 4 SERVINGS

- 2 **tablespoons crushed lemon drop candies**
- 1 **teaspoon sugar**
- ½ **small lemon, cut into six slices, divided**
- ½ **cup 2% milk**
- 2 **cups vanilla ice cream**
- 2 **cups lemon sorbet**
- 3 **ounces cream cheese, softened**
- 2 **teaspoons grated lemon peel**
- ½ **teaspoon vanilla extract**

**1.** In a shallow dish, mix crushed lemon drops and sugar. Using 1 or 2 lemon slices, moisten the rims of four glasses; dip rims into candy mixture.

**2.** Place remaining ingredients in a blender; cover and process until smooth. Pour into prepared glasses; serve immediately with remaining lemon slices.

**PER SERVING** *361 cal., 15 g fat (10 g sat. fat), 55 mg chol., 138 mg sodium, 53 g carb., 1 g fiber, 5 g pro.*

TOMATILLO SALSA

MARINATED OLIVE & CHEESE RING

## Marinated Olive & Cheese Ring

We turn Italian meals into celebrations, and the party always starts with an antipasto. This one is almost too pretty to eat.

—**PATRICIA HARMON** BADEN, PA

**PREP:** 25 MIN. + CHILLING • **MAKES:** 16 SERVINGS

- 1 package (8 ounces) cold cream cheese
- 1 package (10 ounces) sharp white cheddar cheese, cut into ¼-inch slices
- ⅓ cup pimiento-stuffed olives
- ⅓ cup pitted Greek olives
- ¼ cup balsamic vinegar
- ¼ cup olive oil
- 1 tablespoon minced fresh parsley
- 1 tablespoon minced fresh basil or 1 teaspoon dried basil
- 2 garlic cloves, minced
- 1 jar (2 ounces) pimiento strips, drained and chopped
  Toasted French bread baguette slices

**1.** Cut cream cheese lengthwise in half; cut each half into ¼-in. slices. On a serving plate, arrange the cheeses upright in a ring, alternating cheddar and cream cheese slices. Place olives in center.

**2.** In a small bowl, whisk the vinegar, oil, parsley, basil and garlic until blended; drizzle over the cheeses and olives. Sprinkle with pimientos. Refrigerate, covered, at least 8 hours or overnight. Serve with baguette slices.

**PER SERVING** *168 cal., 16 g fat (7 g sat. fat), 34 mg chol., 260 mg sodium, 2 g carb., trace fiber, 6 g pro.*

## Sweet & Salty Popcorn

Let kids lend a hand with this crunchy snack. They'll be proud to help—and happy to gobble up the yummy results!

—**DIANE SMITH** PINE MOUNTAIN, GA

**START TO FINISH:** 25 MIN. • **MAKES:** 4 QUARTS

- 10 cups popped popcorn
- 1 cup broken miniature pretzels
- 1 cup candies of your choice, such as Almond Joy pieces or milk chocolate M&M's
- 1 cup chopped dried pineapple
- 10 ounces white candy coating, coarsely chopped

**1.** In a large bowl, combine popcorn, pretzels, candies and pineapple. In a microwave, melt candy coating; stir until smooth. Pour over popcorn mixture; toss to coat.

**2.** Immediately spread onto waxed paper; let stand until set. Break into pieces. Store in airtight containers.

**PER SERVING** *227 cal., 11 g fat (7 g sat. fat), 1 mg chol., 122 mg sodium, 32 g carb., 1 g fiber, 1 g pro.*

## Tangy Strawberry Slush

When summer temperatures rise, cool down with an icy slush. Keep some in the freezer for pop-in guests on a warm evening.

—**LAURA REIGEL** SHEBOYGAN, WI

**PREP:** 10 MIN. + FREEZING • **MAKES:** 26 SERVINGS (¾ CUP EACH)

- 9 cups water, divided
- 3 cups sugar
- 4 individual tea bags
- 1 pint fresh strawberries, stems removed
- 1 cup cranberry juice
- ¾ cup thawed orange juice concentrate
- ¾ cup thawed lemonade concentrate
- 6½ cups lemon-lime soda, chilled

**1.** In a large saucepan, bring 7 cups water and sugar to a boil. Stir until sugar is dissolved. Remove from the heat; cool.

**2.** Meanwhile, in a small saucepan, bring remaining water to a boil. Remove from heat; add the tea bags. Cover and steep for 3-5 minutes. Discard tea bags. Cool. Transfer sugar and tea mixtures to a 4-qt. freezer container.

**3.** In a blender, combine the strawberries, cranberry juice and juice concentrates. Cover and process until pureed. Stir into freezer container; cool. Cover and freeze for 6 hours or overnight.

**4.** To serve, combine ½ cup strawberry mixture and ¼ cup soda in a glass. Serve immediately.

**PER SERVING** *152 cal., trace fat (trace sat. fat), 0 chol., 8 mg sodium, 39 g carb., trace fiber, trace pro.*

TANGY STRAWBERRY SLUSH

PISTACHIO-TURKEY MEATBALLS
IN ORANGE SAUCE

Thanks to the crunch of nuts and an amazing combination of flavors, I always get compliments for Pistachio-Turkey Meatballs in Orange Sauce.
—JEANNE HOLT MENDOTA HEIGHTS, MN

## Pistachio-Turkey Meatballs in Orange Sauce

**PREP:** 25 MIN. • **BAKE:** 20 MIN.
**MAKES:** 4½ DOZEN

- ⅔ cup chopped pistachios
- 2 green onions, finely chopped
- ¼ cup dry bread crumbs
- 1 egg, lightly beaten
- 1 teaspoon grated orange peel
- ½ teaspoon salt
- ⅛ teaspoon pepper
- 1 pound ground turkey
- 1 Italian sausage link (4 ounces), casing removed

**SAUCE**

- 3 tablespoons butter
- 1 tablespoon olive oil
- ¼ cup finely chopped sweet red pepper
- ⅛ teaspoon crushed red pepper flakes
- 2 tablespoons white wine
- 4 teaspoons cornstarch
- 1 cup orange juice
- ½ cup reduced-sodium chicken broth
- 1 tablespoon honey
- ½ teaspoon grated orange peel
- 1 tablespoon minced fresh basil
- 2 tablespoons chopped pistachios

**1.** Preheat oven to 375°. In a large bowl, combine the first seven ingredients. Add turkey and sausage; mix lightly but thoroughly. Shape into 1-in. balls.

**2.** Place the meatballs on greased racks in shallow baking pans. Bake 18-20 minutes or until cooked through.

**3.** In a large skillet, heat butter and oil over medium heat. Add red pepper and pepper flakes; cook and stir 2-3 minutes or until red pepper is tender. Add wine; cook 1 minute longer.

**4.** In a small bowl, whisk cornstarch, orange juice, broth, honey and orange peel until blended. Stir into pan. Bring to a boil; cook and stir 1-2 minutes or until thickened. Stir in the basil and meatballs. Sprinkle with pistachios.

**PER SERVING** *49 cal., 4 g fat (1 g sat. fat), 12 mg chol., 66 mg sodium, 2 g carb., trace fiber, 2 g pro.*

## Manmosa

Are guys on the guest list for your next brunch? Give that ever-popular morning beverage—the mimosa—a masculine twist with just three ingredients.
—MIKE DIETIKER ELBURN, IL

**START TO FINISH:** 5 MIN.
**MAKES:** 2 SERVINGS

- 1 bottle (12 ounces) beer or nonalcoholic beer, chilled
- 1 cup orange juice
- 2 ounces Triple Sec

Divide beer between two tall glasses. Add ½ cup orange juice and 1 ounce Triple Sec to each glass.

**PER SERVING** *229 cal., trace fat (trace sat. fat), 0 chol., 7 mg sodium, 31 g carb., 0 fiber, 1 g pro.*

MANMOSA

My Tuscan Sausage & Bean Dip is a spin-off of a Mexican version I had. The south-of-the-border original was incredibly good, but I decided to try something new. Take it to a party—I'll bet no one else will bring anything like it!

—**MANDY RIVERS** LEXINGTON, SC

TUSCAN SAUSAGE & BEAN DIP

# Tuscan Sausage & Bean Dip

**PREP:** 25 MIN. • **BAKE:** 20 MIN.
**MAKES:** 16 SERVINGS (¼ CUP EACH)

- 1 **pound bulk hot Italian sausage**
- 1 **medium onion, finely chopped**
- 4 **garlic cloves, minced**
- ½ **cup dry white wine or chicken broth**
- ½ **teaspoon dried oregano**
- ¼ **teaspoon salt**
- ¼ **teaspoon dried thyme**
- 1 **package (8 ounces) cream cheese, softened**
- 1 **package (6 ounces) fresh baby spinach, coarsely chopped**
- 1 **can (15 ounces) white kidney or cannellini beans, rinsed and drained**
- 1 **cup chopped seeded tomatoes**
- 1 **cup (4 ounces) shredded part-skim mozzarella cheese**
- ½ **cup shredded Parmesan cheese**
  **Assorted crackers or toasted French bread baguette slices**

**1.** Preheat oven to 375°. In a large skillet, cook sausage, onion and garlic over medium heat until sausage is no longer pink, breaking up sausage into crumbles; drain. Stir in wine, oregano, salt and thyme. Bring to a boil; cook until liquid is almost evaporated.
**2.** Add the cream cheese; stir until melted. Stir in spinach, beans and tomatoes; cook and stir until spinach is wilted. Transfer to a greased 8-in.-square or 1½-qt. baking dish. Sprinkle with cheeses.
**3.** Bake 20-25 minutes or until bubbly. Serve with crackers.
**PER SERVING** *200 cal., 14 g fat (7 g sat. fat), 41 mg chol., 434 mg sodium, 7 g carb., 2 g fiber, 10 g pro.*

# Simple Salmon Dip

This is my go-to appetizer for summer barbecues. The secret is the green chilies—they add just enough heat.
—**SUSAN JORDAN** DENVER, CO

**PREP:** 15 MIN. + CHILLING
**MAKES:** 1¼ CUPS

- 1 **package (8 ounces) reduced-fat cream cheese**
- 2 **tablespoons canned chopped green chilies**
- 1½ **teaspoons lemon juice**
- 2 **green onions, chopped, divided**
- 2 **ounces smoked salmon fillet**
  **Assorted crackers or toasted French bread baguette slices**

**1.** In a small bowl, mix cream cheese, green chilies, lemon juice and half of the green onions. Flake salmon into small pieces; stir into cream cheese mixture. Refrigerate, covered, at least 2 hours before serving.
**2.** Top dip with the remaining green onion. Serve with crackers.
**PER SERVING** *107 cal., 8 g fat (5 g sat. fat), 29 mg chol., 246 mg sodium, 2 g carb., trace fiber, 6 g pro.*

## Did you know?

Smoked salmon is fresh salmon that has undergone a process of either hot or cold smoking. When cold-smoked, salmon is brined or cured in salt and/or sugar before it is smoked at 70-90 degrees. The result, a product called lox, has a delicate flavor and texture. When hot-smoked, salmon is smoked for hours at 120-180 degrees, producing a firm, flaky texture and stronger smoky flavor.

BROWN SUGAR-GLAZED MEATBALLS

## Spiced Apricot Tea

Warm up a chilly fall or winter morning by pouring cups of this fruity spiced tea. It's a wonderful complement to scones, muffins and other breakfast treats.
—**MARY HOUCHIN** LEBANON, IL

**START TO FINISH:** 25 MIN.
**MAKES:** 6 SERVINGS

- 2 **cinnamon sticks (3 inches)**
- 10 **whole cloves**
- 3 **cups water**
- 2 **individual tea bags**
- 3 **cups apricot nectar**
- ⅔ **cup sugar**
- ¼ **cup lemon juice**

**1.** Place cinnamon and cloves on a double thickness of cheesecloth. Gather the corners of cloth to enclose the spices; tie securely with string.
**2.** Place the water and spice bag in a large saucepan; bring to a boil. Remove from heat. Add tea bags; steep, covered, about 5 minutes according to taste. Discard tea and spice bags.
**3.** Add remaining ingredients to tea; heat through, stirring to dissolve sugar. Serve immediately.
**PER SERVING** *159 cal., trace fat (trace sat. fat), 0 chol., 4 mg sodium, 41 g carb., 1 g fiber, 1 g pro.*

## Brown Sugar-Glazed Meatballs

I modeled my glazed pork-and-shrimp meatballs after the filling in Asian wontons. The little sweet-spicy bites always go over well, whether I serve them by themselves as a hearty appetizer or over a bed of hot cooked rice as a main course.
—**LILY JULOW** LAWRENCEVILLE, GA

**PREP:** 35 MIN. • **BAKE:** 15 MIN.
**MAKES:** 3½ DOZEN

- ¾ **pound uncooked small shrimp, peeled, deveined and chopped**
- ½ **cup soft bread crumbs**
- 4 **bacon strips, finely chopped**
- 1 **egg, lightly beaten**
- 1 **tablespoon stone-ground mustard**
- 1½ **teaspoons liquid smoke, optional**
- 1½ **teaspoons smoked paprika**
- 1 **teaspoon salt**
- 1 **garlic clove, minced**
- ¾ **teaspoon dried oregano**
- ½ **to 1 teaspoon hot pepper sauce**
- ½ **teaspoon onion powder**
- 1 **pound ground pork**

**GLAZE**
- ½ **cup packed brown sugar**
- ¼ **cup cider vinegar**
- 4 **teaspoons stone-ground mustard**

**1.** Preheat oven to 350°. In a large bowl, combine the first 12 ingredients. Add pork; mix lightly but thoroughly. With wet hands, shape into 1-in. balls.
**2.** Place meatballs on a greased rack in a shallow baking pan. Bake 14-17 minutes or until meatballs are cooked through. Drain on paper towels.
**3.** Meanwhile, in a large skillet, mix glaze ingredients. Add meatballs; cook over medium heat 8-10 minutes or until meatballs are glazed and heated through, stirring occasionally.
**NOTE** *To make soft bread crumbs, tear bread into pieces and place in a food processor or blender. Cover and pulse until crumbs form. One slice of bread yields ½ to ¾ cup crumbs.*
**PER SERVING** *59 cal., 3 g fat (1 g sat. fat), 23 mg chol., 112 mg sodium, 3 g carb., trace fiber, 4 g pro.*

SPICED APRICOT TEA

TURKEY & SWISS BISCUIT SLIDERS

I enjoy experimenting to create new recipes. I fixed Turkey & Swiss Biscuit Sliders to satisfy my sister's craving when she was pregnant. They did the trick!

—CINDY ESPOSITO BLOOMFIELD, NJ

## Turkey & Swiss Biscuit Sliders

**PREP:** 35 MIN. + RISING • **BAKE:** 10 MIN.
**MAKES:** 16 SERVINGS

- 1 package (¼ ounce) active dry yeast
- ⅔ cup warm buttermilk (110° to 115°)
- 2 tablespoons warm water (110° to 115°)
- 2 cups bread flour
- 3 tablespoons sugar
- 1½ teaspoons baking powder
- ½ teaspoon salt
- ½ cup shortening
- ¾ pound thinly sliced deli smoked turkey
- ½ pound sliced Swiss cheese
  Dijon mustard, optional

**1.** In a small bowl, dissolve yeast in warm buttermilk and water. Place flour, sugar, baking powder and salt in a food processor; pulse until blended. Add shortening; pulse until shortening is the size of peas. While processing, gradually add the yeast mixture and process just until dough forms a ball.

**2.** Turn dough onto a lightly floured surface; knead 8-10 times. Pat or roll to ½-in. thickness; cut with a floured 2-in. biscuit cutter. Place 2 in. apart on greased baking sheets. Let rise until almost doubled, about 30 minutes. Preheat oven to 425°.

**3.** Bake 7-9 minutes or until golden brown. Remove to wire racks to cool slightly. Preheat broiler.

**4.** Split biscuits; place bottoms on greased baking sheets. Layer with turkey and cheese. Broil 3-4 in. from heat 2-3 minutes or until the cheese is melted. Replace tops. If desired, serve with mustard.

**PER SERVING** *198 cal., 11 g fat (5 g sat. fat), 23 mg chol., 306 mg sodium, 14 g carb., trace fiber, 11 g pro.*

## Crab Rangoon Cheese Ball

My whole family loves crab rangoon, so I came up with a healthier version that skips the deep frying. Consider making two—this cheese ball won't last long!

—**BRIDGET MOONEY** CHICAGO, IL

**PREP:** 20 MIN. + CHILLING • **BAKE:** 10 MIN.
**MAKES:** 2 CUPS (48 WONTON CHIPS)

- 1 package (8 ounces) reduced-fat cream cheese
- 1 cup (4 ounces) shredded reduced-fat cheddar cheese
- 1 garlic clove, minced
- 1 teaspoon Worcestershire sauce
- 1 can (6 ounces) lump crabmeat, drained or 6 ounces imitation crabmeat, chopped
- 3 tablespoons minced fresh chives
- 24 wonton wrappers
  Cooking spray
- 1 teaspoon sesame seeds
- ½ teaspoon salt
- ¼ teaspoon pepper

**1.** In a large bowl, beat the cream cheese, cheddar cheese, garlic and Worcestershire sauce until blended. Stir in crab. Shape mixture into a ball; coat with chives. Wrap in plastic wrap; refrigerate at least 1 hour.

**2.** Preheat oven to 350°. Cut wonton wrappers diagonally in half; arrange in a single layer on ungreased baking sheets. Spritz with cooking spray; sprinkle with seeds, salt and pepper. Bake 5-7 minutes or until golden brown. Remove from the pans to wire racks to cool. Serve with cheese ball.

**PER SERVING** *116 cal., 6 g fat (3 g sat. fat), 26 mg chol., 286 mg sodium, 8 g carb., trace fiber, 7 g pro.*

CRAB RANGOON CHEESE BALL

# German Beer Cheese Spread

Bold and smooth, this flavor-packed cheese is great with pretzels, crackers or pumpernickel bread. You could also spread it on bratwursts.

—**ANGELA SPENGLER** MECHANICSBURG, PA

**START TO FINISH:** 15 MIN.
**MAKES:** 2½ CUPS

- 1 **pound sharp cheddar cheese, cut into ½-inch cubes**
- 1 **tablespoon Worcestershire sauce**
- 1½ **teaspoons prepared mustard**
- 1 **small garlic clove, minced**
- ¼ **teaspoon salt**
- ⅛ **teaspoon pepper**
- ⅔ **cup German beer or nonalcoholic beer**
  **Assorted crackers**

**1.** Place the cheddar cheese in a food processor; pulse until finely chopped, about 1 minute.
**2.** Add the Worcestershire sauce, mustard, garlic, salt and pepper. Gradually add the beer, while continuing to process, until the mixture is smooth and spreadable, about 1½ minutes.
**3.** Transfer to a serving bowl or gift jars. Refrigerate, covered, up to 1 week. Serve with crackers.
**PER SERVING** *95 cal., 8 g fat (5 g sat. fat), 24 mg chol., 187 mg sodium, 1 g carb., trace fiber, 6 g pro.*

PUMPKIN SMOOTHIES

# Pumpkin Smoothies

A banana and orange juice bring a burst of fruit and extra nutrition to my simple smoothies. With cinnamon and pie spice, they're perfect for fall and winter.

—**KAREN SIKORA** DAYTON, NV

**START TO FINISH:** 10 MIN.
**MAKES:** 4 SERVINGS

- 1 **can (15 ounces) solid-pack pumpkin**
- 2 **cans (5½ ounces each) evaporated milk**
- 1 **cup orange juice**
- 1 **small banana**
- ⅓ **cup packed brown sugar**
- ½ **teaspoon pumpkin pie spice**
- ¼ **teaspoon ground cinnamon**

Place all ingredients in a blender; cover and process for 30 seconds or until smooth. Pour into chilled glasses; serve immediately.
**PER SERVING** *256 cal., 6 g fat (4 g sat. fat), 25 mg chol., 86 mg sodium, 46 g carb., 5 g fiber, 7 g pro.*

## top tip | Pie Spice Solution

No pumpkin pie spice? For each teaspoon, combine ½ teaspoon cinnamon, ¼ teaspoon ground ginger, ⅛ teaspoon ground nutmeg and ⅛ teaspoon ground cloves or allspice.

GERMAN BEER CHEESE SPREAD

## Chocolate-Mint Popcorn

I wrote a book called *20 New Ways to Enjoy Popcorn*. When I poll friends, they give the highest rating to this recipe.
—**POLLY BRUNNING** THAXTON, VA

**START TO FINISH:** 20 MIN.
**MAKES:** 2 QUARTS

- 8 cups popped popcorn
- 1 package (4 ounces) Junior Mints
- 2 tablespoons butter

**1.** Place the popcorn in a large bowl. In a small saucepan, melt the mints and butter over medium-low heat; stir until smooth. Pour over popcorn; toss to coat.

**2.** Immediately spread the popcorn mixture onto waxed paper; let stand until set. Break into pieces. Store in an airtight container.

**PER SERVING** *145 cal., 9 g fat (3 g sat. fat), 8 mg chol., 143 mg sodium, 17 g carb., 1 g fiber, 1 g pro.*

BACON-WRAPPED SWEET POTATO BITES

CHOCOLATE-MINT POPCORN

## Bacon-Wrapped Sweet Potato Bites

After making little bacon-wrapped sausages for years, I needed a change! I had leftover sweet potatoes and some bacon on hand, so I decided to combine them and added a side of maple syrup for dipping.
—**KELLY WILLIAMS** FORKED RIVER, NJ

**PREP:** 25 MIN. • **BAKE:** 40 MIN.
**MAKES:** ABOUT 2½ DOZEN

- ¼ cup butter, melted
- ½ teaspoon salt
- ½ teaspoon cayenne pepper
- ¼ teaspoon ground cinnamon
- 2 large sweet potatoes (about 1¾ pounds), peeled and cut into 1-inch cubes
- ½ cup packed brown sugar
- 1 pound bacon strips, halved
  Maple syrup, warmed

**1.** Preheat oven to 350°. In a large bowl, mix butter and seasonings. Add potatoes and toss to coat.

**2.** Place brown sugar in a shallow bowl. Wrap one bacon piece around each sweet potato cube; secure with a toothpick. Dip each side in brown sugar. Place on a parchment paper-lined 15x10x1-in. baking pan.

**3.** Bake 40-45 minutes or until bacon is crisp and sweet potato is tender. Serve with maple syrup.

**PER SERVING** *64 cal., 3 g fat (2 g sat. fat), 9 mg chol., 140 mg sodium, 7 g carb., trace fiber, 2 g pro.*

## SLOW COOKER
# Chili Corn Cheese Dip

After trying to come up with a Mexican soup, I ended up with a hearty dip that eats like a meal. My husband and our two young children couldn't get enough! Now it's a popular snack for football game days.

—**SANDRA FICK** LINCOLN, NE

**PREP:** 20 MIN. • **COOK:** 4½ HOURS
**MAKES:** 8 CUPS

- 1 **pound lean ground beef (90% lean)**
- 1 **medium onion, chopped**
- 1 **can (16 ounces) kidney beans, rinsed and drained**
- 1 **can (15 ounces) black beans, rinsed and drained**
- 1 **can (14½ ounces) diced tomatoes in sauce, undrained**
- 1 **cup frozen corn, thawed**
- ¾ **cup water**
- 1 **can (2¼ ounces) sliced ripe olives, drained**
- 3 **teaspoons chili powder**
- ½ **teaspoon dried oregano**
- ½ **teaspoon chipotle hot pepper sauce**
- ¼ **teaspoon garlic powder**
- ¼ **teaspoon ground cumin**
- 1 **package (16 ounces) reduced-fat process cheese (Velveeta), cubed Corn chips or tortilla chips**

**1.** In a large skillet, cook the beef and onion over medium heat 6-8 minutes or until beef is no longer pink and onion is tender, breaking up beef into crumbles; drain.

**2.** Transfer to a 4-qt. slow cooker. Stir in the beans, tomatoes, corn, water, olives, chili powder, oregano, pepper sauce, garlic powder and cumin. Cook, covered, on low 4-5 hours or until heated through.

**3.** Stir in cheese. Cook, covered, on low 30 minutes longer or until cheese is melted. Serve with corn chips.
**PER SERVING** *87 cal., 3 g fat (1 g sat. fat), 12 mg chol., 330 mg sodium, 9 g carb., 2 g fiber, 7 g pro.* **Diabetic Exchanges:** *1 lean meat, ½ starch.*

# Marshmallow-Peanut Popcorn

My brother calls this crunchy combination featuring marshmallows, peanuts and pretzels the perfect popcorn. The taste reminds people of a Big Hunk candy bar.

—**JULIE PEREZ** IDAHO FALLS, ID

**START TO FINISH:** 30 MIN.
**MAKES:** 5 QUARTS

- 15 **cups popped popcorn**
- 2 **cups miniature marshmallows**
- 1 **cup salted peanuts**
- 1 **cup broken pretzel sticks, optional**
- ⅔ **cup sugar**
- ½ **cup butter, cubed**
- ¼ **cup light corn syrup**

**1.** In a large bowl, combine popcorn, marshmallows, peanuts and, if desired, pretzels. In a small saucepan, combine sugar, butter and corn syrup. Bring to a boil; cook and stir 2 minutes. Pour over popcorn mixture; toss to coat.

**2.** Immediately spread onto waxed paper; let stand until set. Break into pieces. Store in airtight containers.
**PER SERVING** *183 cal., 12 g fat (4 g sat. fat), 12 mg chol., 156 mg sodium, 19 g carb., 1 g fiber, 3 g pro.*

CHILI CORN CHEESE DIP

# Mushroom, Walnut & Thyme Cheesecake

Why save cheesecake for dessert? Serve a savory version as a spread with crackers for an extra-special first course.

—ERIKA SZYMANSKI PULLMAN, WA

**PREP:** 35 MIN. + COOLING
**BAKE:** 25 MIN. + CHILLING
**MAKES:** 24 SERVINGS

- 1 cup dry bread crumbs
- ¼ cup butter, melted

**FILLING**

- 1 tablespoon butter
- ½ pound baby portobello mushrooms, chopped
- 1 garlic clove, minced
- ⅓ cup chopped walnuts
- 1 tablespoon minced fresh thyme or 1 teaspoon dried thyme
- 1 teaspoon reduced-sodium soy sauce
- ¼ teaspoon white pepper
- 2 packages (8 ounces each) cream cheese, softened
- ½ cup plain Greek yogurt
- 2 eggs, lightly beaten
  Assorted crackers, baguette slices or sliced apples

**1.** Preheat oven to 325°. In a small bowl, mix bread crumbs and butter. Press onto bottom of a greased 9-in. springform pan. Place pan on baking sheet. Bake 15-17 minutes or until golden brown. Cool on a wire rack.

**2.** In a large skillet, heat butter over medium-high heat. Add mushrooms; cook and stir until tender. Add garlic; cook 1 minute longer. Stir in walnuts; cook until toasted. Stir in thyme, soy sauce and pepper. Remove from heat; cool completely.

**3.** In a large bowl, beat cream cheese until smooth. Beat in yogurt. Add eggs; beat on low speed just until blended. Fold in mushroom mixture. Pour over crust. Return pan to baking sheet.

**4.** Bake 25-30 minutes or until the center of cheesecake is just set and the top appears dull. Cool 10 minutes on a wire rack. Loosen the sides from the pan with a knife. Cool 1 hour longer. Refrigerate overnight.

**5.** Remove the rim from pan. Serve with crackers.

**PER SERVING** *130 cal., 11 g fat (6 g sat. fat), 46 mg chol., 123 mg sodium, 5 g carb., trace fiber, 3 g pro.*

# Strawberry-Basil Cocktail

This cocktail of strawberries and tender basil is very refreshing without being overly sweet. It's our favorite.

—MARY MARLOWE LEVERETTE
COLUMBIA, SC

**START TO FINISH:** 5 MIN.
**MAKES:** 1 SERVING

- 3 fresh strawberries, thinly sliced
- 1 teaspoon minced fresh basil
- ¾ to 1 cup ice cubes
- 2 ounces vodka
- ½ ounce club soda
- 1 teaspoon simple syrup
- 1 teaspoon cranberry juice
  Pinch pepper

In a shaker, muddle the strawberries and basil. Fill the shaker three-fourths full with ice cubes. Add the remaining ingredients; cover and shake 10-15 seconds or until condensation forms on outside of shaker. Strain into a chilled cocktail glass.

**TO MAKE YOUR OWN SIMPLE SYRUP**
*In a small saucepan, combine 2 cups sugar and 1 cup water; bring to a boil over medium heat, stirring to dissolve sugar. Reduce heat; simmer 3 minutes, stirring occasionally. Cool completely. Store, covered, in refrigerator for up to 2 weeks. Use to sweeten cocktails, iced tea or lemonade. Yield: 1⅔ cups.*

**PER SERVING** *162 cal., trace fat (trace sat. fat), 0 chol., 5 mg sodium, 9 g carb., 1 g fiber, trace pro.*

MUSHROOM, WALNUT & THYME CHEESECAKE

**ROASTED BUTTERNUT
TOSSED SALAD**
*PAGE 29*

# Salads
# & Dressings

**Take a fresh look** at lightly mixed greens, tossed veggie blends and hearty dinner entrees. The **extra-special recipes** in this chapter give you mouthwatering new ways to round out menus.

**MOM'S POTATO SALAD**
*PAGE 21*

**CREAM-OF-THE-CROP VEGGIES**
*PAGE 26*

**CITRUS STEAK SALAD**
*PAGE 24*

## EAT SMART
# Colorful Bean Salad

I experimented with many different types of bean dishes before I came up with this one. My husband loves the combination of flavors, colors and textures.

—DALE BENOIT MONSON, MA

**PREP:** 30 MIN. + CHILLING
**MAKES:** 13 SERVINGS (¾ CUP EACH)

- 2 cups fresh or frozen corn, thawed
- 1 can (16 ounces) kidney beans, rinsed and drained
- 1 can (16 ounces) red beans, rinsed and drained
- 1 can (15½ ounces) white kidney or cannellini beans, rinsed and drained
- 1 can (15¼ ounces) lima beans, rinsed and drained
- 1 can (15 ounces) black beans, rinsed and drained
- 1 can (2¼ ounces) sliced ripe olives, drained
- 1 large green pepper, chopped
- 1 small onion, chopped
- ½ cup chili sauce
- ¼ cup olive oil
- ¼ cup red wine vinegar
- 2 garlic cloves, minced
- 2 teaspoons dried oregano
- ½ teaspoon pepper

**1.** In a large bowl, combine the first nine ingredients. In a small bowl, whisk chili sauce, oil, vinegar, garlic, oregano and pepper. Pour over bean mixture; toss to coat.

**2.** Refrigerate for at least 1 hour before serving.

**PER SERVING** *199 cal., 5 g fat (1 g sat. fat), 0 chol., 486 mg sodium, 31 g carb., 8 g fiber, 8 g pro.* **Diabetic Exchanges:** *1½ starch, 1 lean meat, ½ fat.*

GARLIC MAPLE DRESSING

COLORFUL BEAN SALAD

## FAST FIX
# Garlic Maple Dressing

Garlic and maple syrup may seem like an odd pairing, but you'll be amazed at how great they are together in a dressing!

—EMILY TYRA MILWAUKEE, WI

**START TO FINISH:** 5 MIN.
**MAKES:** ¾ CUP (6 SERVINGS)

- ⅓ cup olive oil
- ¼ cup maple syrup
  Juice of 1 medium lemon
- 2 to 3 garlic cloves, minced
- 1 to 2 teaspoons Dijon mustard
- ⅛ teaspoon salt
- ⅛ teaspoon freshly ground pepper

Place all ingredients in a jar with a tight-fitting lid; shake well.

**PER SERVING** *145 cal., 12 g fat (2 g sat. fat), 0 chol., 71 mg sodium, 10 g carb., trace fiber, trace protein.*

**top tip**

# Speeding Up Slow Syrup

When a bottle of syrup is almost empty, it can take awhile for the remaining syrup to pour out. To hasten the process, I run the capped bottle under hot water to heat the liquid. The warmed syrup pours out more quickly.

—VIVIAN T. WESTVILLE, IN

# Whole Wheat Orzo Salad

**START TO FINISH:** 30 MIN.
**MAKES:** 8 SERVINGS

- 2½ cups uncooked whole wheat orzo pasta (about 1 pound)
- 1 can (15 ounces) white kidney or cannellini beans, rinsed and drained
- 3 medium tomatoes, finely chopped
- 1 English cucumber, finely chopped
- 2 cups (8 ounces) crumbled feta cheese
- 1¼ cups pitted Greek olives (about 6 ounces), chopped
- 1 medium sweet yellow pepper, finely chopped
- 1 medium green pepper, finely chopped
- 1 cup fresh mint leaves, chopped
- ½ medium red onion, finely chopped
- ¼ cup lemon juice
- 2 tablespoons olive oil
- 1 tablespoon grated lemon peel
- 3 garlic cloves, minced
- ½ teaspoon pepper

**1.** Cook the orzo according to the package directions. Drain orzo; rinse with cold water.

**2.** Meanwhile, in a large bowl, combine the remaining ingredients. Stir in orzo. Refrigerate until serving.

**PER SERVING** *411 cal., 17 g fat (4 g sat. fat), 15 mg chol., 740 mg sodium, 51 g carb., 13 g fiber, 14 g pro.*

> In 30 minutes, I can toss together the ingredients for Whole Wheat Orzo Salad. It's my go-to recipe and a crowd-pleaser, too.
>
> —MYA ZERONIS PITTSBURGH, PA

WHOLE WHEAT ORZO SALAD

MOM'S POTATO SALAD

# Mom's Potato Salad

This version of a creamy classic is the best I've ever tasted. It was popular when I was growing up, and now I get requests for it whenever we have a family barbecue.

—**SALLY KRAMER** ALOHA, OR

**PREP:** 25 MIN. • **COOK:** 15 MIN. + COOLING
**MAKES:** 6 SERVINGS

- 5 medium red potatoes, cubed
- ½ cup Miracle Whip
- ½ teaspoon salt
- ¼ teaspoon pepper
- 1 garlic clove, minced
- 6 hard-cooked eggs, chopped
- 3 sweet pickles, finely chopped
- 1 jar (2 ounces) diced pimientos, drained
- 2 green onions, chopped
  Paprika

**1.** Place the potatoes in a saucepan and cover with water. Bring to a boil. Reduce heat; cover and simmer for 10-15 minutes or until tender. Drain and cool.

**2.** In a large bowl, combine Miracle Whip, salt, pepper and garlic. Stir in the potatoes, eggs, pickles, pimientos and onions. Sprinkle with paprika. Chill until serving.

**PER SERVING** *225 cal., 11 g fat (2 g sat. fat), 219 mg chol., 555 mg sodium, 23 g carb., 2 g fiber, 8 g pro.*

SOUTHWEST CHICKEN & RICE SALAD

## Southwest Chicken & Rice Salad

Grilled corn adds a subtle smokiness to this colorful, summery medley. With plenty of chicken, it's hearty enough to have as a cool but satisfying dinner on a warm evening.

—**RENEE GAST** STEVENSVILLE, MI

**PREP:** 25 MIN. • **GRILL:** 15 MIN. + CHILLING • **MAKES:** 10 SERVINGS

- 2 medium ears sweet corn
- ¼ cup olive oil, divided
- 2 cups cubed cooked chicken breast
- 1 medium sweet red pepper, julienned
- 2 jalapeno peppers, seeded and minced
- 2 tablespoons minced fresh cilantro
- ¼ cup lime juice
- 1 garlic clove, minced
- 1 teaspoon chili powder
- ¾ teaspoon salt
- ¼ teaspoon pepper
- 1 cup uncooked long grain rice
- 2 medium ripe avocados, peeled and cubed

**1.** Remove and discard the corn husks and silk. Brush 1 tablespoon oil over ears of corn. Grill, covered, over medium heat for 15-20 minutes or until tender. Cut the corn from the cobs.

**2.** In a large bowl, combine chicken, red pepper, jalapenos, cilantro and corn.

**3.** In a small bowl, combine lime juice, garlic, chili powder, salt, pepper and remaining oil; pour over chicken mixture and toss to coat. Cover and refrigerate for 2-3 hours.

**4.** Cook the rice according to the package directions; cool. Just before serving, stir rice and avocados into salad.

**NOTE** *Wear disposable gloves when cutting hot peppers; the oils can burn skin. Avoid touching your face.*

**PER SERVING** *238 cal., 12 g fat (2 g sat. fat), 22 mg chol., 204 mg sodium, 23 g carb., 4 g fiber, 11 g pro.*

FAST FIX

# Avocado & Artichoke Pasta Salad

A squeeze of lime, a sprinkle of cilantro and a little avocado will make this creamy combo tingle your taste buds. Store it in the fridge until serving—if you can keep everyone away from it for that long!

—**CARRIE FARIAS** OAK RIDGE, NJ

**START TO FINISH:** 30 MIN. • **MAKES:** 10 SERVINGS

- 2 cups uncooked gemelli or spiral pasta
- 1 can (14 ounces) water-packed artichoke hearts, drained and coarsely chopped
- 2 plum tomatoes, seeded and chopped
- 1 medium ripe avocado, peeled and cubed
- ¼ cup grated Romano cheese

**DRESSING**
- ¼ cup canola oil
- 2 tablespoons lime juice
- 1 tablespoon minced fresh cilantro
- 1½ teaspoons grated lime peel
- ½ teaspoon kosher salt
- ½ teaspoon freshly ground pepper

**1.** Cook pasta according to package directions. Drain; rinse with cold water.

**2.** In a large bowl, combine the pasta, artichoke hearts, tomatoes, avocado and cheese. In a small bowl, whisk the dressing ingredients. Pour over pasta mixture; toss gently to combine. Refrigerate, covered, until serving.

**PER SERVING** *188 cal., 10 g fat (1 g sat. fat), 3 mg chol., 248 mg sodium, 21 g carb., 2 g fiber, 6 g pro.*

AVOCADO & ARTICHOKE PASTA SALAD

WILD RICE CRAB SALAD

## Mixed Greens with Lemon Champagne Vinaigrette

Here's a tossed salad that has plenty to recommend it. You'll enjoy crunchy toasted walnuts, sweet pomegranate seeds, three kinds of greens and a smooth dressing with just enough zing.

—**RAY UYEDA** MOUNTAIN VIEW, CA

**START TO FINISH:** 15 MIN. • **MAKES:** 10 SERVINGS

- 2 **tablespoons champagne vinegar**
- 2 **teaspoons lemon juice**
- 1 **teaspoon Dijon mustard**
- 1 **shallot, finely chopped**
- ½ **cup olive oil**
- 4 **cups torn leaf lettuce**
- 4 **cups fresh spinach**
- 2 **cups fresh arugula**
- ¾ **cup chopped walnuts, toasted**
- ½ **cup pomegranate seeds**

**1.** In a small bowl, whisk vinegar, lemon juice, mustard and shallot. Gradually whisk in oil.

**2.** In a large bowl, combine the lettuce, spinach and arugula. Pour vinaigrette over salad; toss to coat. Top with walnuts and pomegranate seeds. Serve immediately.

**NOTE** *To toast nuts, spread in a 15x10x1-in. baking pan. Bake at 350° for 5-10 minutes or until lightly browned, stirring occasionally. Or, spread nuts in a dry nonstick skillet and heat over low heat until lightly browned, stirring occasionally.*

**PER SERVING** *169 cal., 17 g fat (2 g sat. fat), 0 chol., 27 mg sodium, 5 g carb., 1 g fiber, 2 g pro.* **Diabetic Exchanges:** *3 fat, 1 vegetable.*

## Wild Rice Crab Salad

Northern Minnesota is known for its abundance of wild rice, and I'm happy to use that versatile ingredient in my recipes. My daughter-in-law shared one for a seafood-filled side dish.

—**LAVERNA M JONES** MOORHEAD, MN

**PREP:** 45 MIN. + CHILLING • **MAKES:** 12 SERVINGS

- 1½ **cups uncooked wild rice**
- 1 **pound cooked fresh or canned crabmeat**
- 2 **cups fresh broccoli florets**
- 2 **cups fresh cauliflowerets**
- ¼ **cup chopped onion**
- 1 **bottle (16 ounces) ranch salad dressing**
- 1 **tablespoon sugar**
- ½ **teaspoon salt**
- ¼ **teaspoon pepper**

**1.** Cook rice according to package directions; drain and rinse in cold water.

**2.** In a large bowl, combine rice, crab, broccoli, cauliflower and onion. Combine ranch salad dressing, sugar, salt and pepper; pour over the salad and toss to coat. Cover and refrigerate for 4 hours before serving.

**PER SERVING** *337 cal., 22 g fat (3 g sat. fat), 44 mg chol., 532 mg sodium, 23 g carb., 2 g fiber, 11 g pro.*

## ? Did you know?

Shellfish are divided into two general categories. Crustaceans (crab, shrimp and lobster) have elongated bodies with jointed external shells, which are periodically shed. Mollusks (clams, oysters, mussels and scallops) have soft, unsegmented bodies; many are covered by a shell.

MIXED GREENS WITH LEMON CHAMPAGNE VINAIGRETTE

# Bountiful Berries

Salads are even better when they burst with the sweet-tart flavor only berries can bring. From tangy cranberries to juicy blueberries, these little gems give any dish an instant upgrade.

CITRUS STEAK SALAD

## (5) INGREDIENTS
## Raspberry Gelatin Ring

Looking for a refreshing contrast to holiday dinner fare? Dress up fruit-filled gelatin with a layer of cream cheese and sour cream.

—**ARDIS ROLLEFSON** JACKSON HOLE, WY

**PREP:** 20 MIN. + CHILLING • **MAKES:** 12 SERVINGS

- 2 **packages (3 ounces each) raspberry gelatin**
- 1½ **cups boiling water**
- 2 **packages (10 ounces each) frozen sweetened raspberries, thawed and drained**
- 2 **cans (8 ounces each) crushed pineapple, undrained**
- ¼ **teaspoon salt**
- 1 **package (8 ounces) cream cheese, softened**
- ½ **cup sour cream**

**1.** In a bowl, dissolve the raspberry gelatin in the boiling water. Stir in raspberries, pineapple and salt. Pour half into an 8-cup ring mold coated with cooking spray; refrigerate for 30 minutes or until firm. Let remaining gelatin mixture stand at room temperature.

**2.** In a bowl, beat the cream cheese and sour cream until smooth. Carefully spread over the gelatin in the mold; top with the remaining gelatin mixture. Refrigerate for 6 hours or until firm.

**PER SERVING** *173 cal., 8 g fat (5 g sat. fat), 27 mg chol., 143 mg sodium, 22 g carb., 1 g fiber, 3 g pro.*

RASPBERRY GELATIN RING

## FAST FIX
## Citrus Steak Salad

Your family will think you spent hours preparing this beautiful entree. The fact that it's a cinch to fix can be your little secret!

—**TASTE OF HOME** TEST KITCHEN

**START TO FINISH:** 25 MIN.
**MAKES:** 4 SERVINGS (1 CUP VINAIGRETTE)

- 6 **tablespoons olive oil**
- ¼ **cup cider vinegar**
- ¼ **cup orange juice**
- 2 **tablespoons minced fresh parsley**
- 2 **tablespoons honey**
- 1 **garlic clove, minced**
- 1 **teaspoon chili sauce**
- ½ **teaspoon salt**
- 8 **cups torn romaine**
- ¾ **pound cooked beef sirloin steak, sliced**
- 2 **cups sliced fresh strawberries**
- 1 **medium red onion, sliced**
- 1 **can (11 ounces) mandarin oranges, drained**
- 1 **cup pecan halves, toasted**
- ½ **cup fresh goat cheese, crumbled**

In a small bowl, whisk the first eight ingredients; set aside. Divide romaine among four plates; top with steak, berries, onion, oranges, pecans and cheese. Serve with vinaigrette.

**PER SERVING** *794 cal., 55 g fat (12 g sat. fat), 113 mg chol., 615 mg sodium, 42 g carb., 8 g fiber, 37 g pro.*

# Blueberry Spinach Salad

When I did a little experimenting with some leftover blueberries, this 10-minute spinach medley was the yummy result.
**—JAN LYSAK-RUIZ** YUCAIPA, CA

**START TO FINISH:** 10 MIN. • **MAKES:** 8 SERVINGS

- ½ **cup olive oil**
- ¼ **cup white balsamic vinegar**
- 2 **teaspoons Dijon mustard**
- 1 **teaspoon sugar**
- ¼ **teaspoon salt**
- 1 **package (10 ounces) fresh spinach, trimmed**
- 1 **cup (4 ounces) crumbled feta cheese**
- 1 **cup fresh blueberries**
- ½ **cup pine nuts, toasted**

**1.** Place the first five ingredients in a jar with a tight-fitting lid; shake well. Refrigerate until serving.
**2.** In a large bowl, combine the spinach, cheese, blueberries and nuts. Just before serving, shake the dressing and drizzle over salad; toss to coat.
**PER SERVING** *229 cal., 20 g fat (4 g sat. fat), 8 mg chol., 269 mg sodium, 8 g carb., 2 g fiber, 6 g pro.*

BLUEBERRY SPINACH SALAD

ROASTED BUTTERNUT SQUASH PANZANELLA

# Roasted Butternut Squash Panzanella

Squash was a hard sell in our house until I served my Italian bread salad. I used pumpkin seeds and cranberries to ramp up the fall flavor and added a zippy horseradish dressing.
**—DEVON DELANEY** WESTPORT, CT

**PREP:** 25 MIN. • **BAKE:** 45 MIN. • **MAKES:** 8 SERVINGS

- 4 **cups cubed sourdough bread**
- 5 **tablespoons olive oil, divided**
- 1 **medium butternut squash (about 3 pounds), peeled and cut into 1-inch cubes**
- ½ **teaspoon each salt, ground ginger, ground cumin and pepper**
- 1 **cup salted shelled pumpkin seeds (pepitas)**
- 1 **cup dried cranberries**
- 4 **shallots, finely chopped (about ½ cup)**

**DRESSING**
- ⅓ **cup red wine vinegar**
- ¼ **cup maple syrup**
- 2 **tablespoons prepared horseradish**
- ½ **teaspoon salt**
- ½ **teaspoon pepper**
- ¼ **teaspoon dried rosemary, crushed**
- ¼ **cup olive oil**

**1.** Preheat oven to 425°. Place bread cubes in a 15x10x1-in. baking pan; toss with 2 tablespoons oil. Bake 10-15 minutes or until toasted, stirring twice.
**2.** Place squash in a greased 15x10x1-in. baking pan. Mix seasonings and remaining 3 tablespoons oil; drizzle over squash and toss to coat. Roast 35-45 minutes or until tender and lightly browned, stirring occasionally.
**3.** In a large bowl, combine bread cubes, squash, pumpkin seeds, dried cranberries and shallots. In a small saucepan, combine the first six dressing ingredients; heat through, stirring to blend. Remove from heat; gradually whisk in oil until blended.
**4.** Drizzle ½ cup dressing over salad and toss to combine. (Save remaining dressing for another use.)
**PER SERVING** *407 cal., 20 g fat (3 g sat. fat), 0 chol., 387 mg sodium, 54 g carb., 8 g fiber, 9 g pro.*

> Persuading kids to eat well can be a challenge. I've found it's easier when I add Cream-of-the-Crop Veggies to my menu.
>
> —LORRAINE CALAND SHUNIAH, ON

CREAM-OF-THE-CROP VEGGIES

## Black-Eyed Pea Salad

This Southern charmer has brought in countless compliments over the years. I love the fact that the bottled Italian dressing keeps the pretty green avocado from turning brown, even if I end up with leftovers—which doesn't happen often!

—NANCY CARIKER BAKERSFIELD, CA

**START TO FINISH:** 10 MIN.
**MAKES:** 4 SERVINGS

- 1 can (15½ ounces) black-eyed peas, rinsed and drained
- 1 large tomato, diced
- 1 medium ripe avocado, peeled and diced
- ⅓ cup chopped green pepper
- 2 green onions, chopped
- 1 tablespoon minced fresh cilantro
- 1 jalapeno pepper, seeded and chopped
- ⅓ cup Italian salad dressing

In a large serving bowl, combine all the ingredients; toss to coat. Serve with a slotted spoon.

**BLACK-EYED PEA CORN SALAD** *Omit the tomato, avocado, green pepper and green onions. Add 2 cups corn and ¼ cup chopped red onion to salad.*

**NOTE** *Wear disposable gloves when cutting hot peppers; the oils can burn skin. Avoid touching your face.*

**PER SERVING** *237 cal., 14 g fat (2 g sat. fat), 0 chol., 562 mg sodium, 22 g carb., 7 g fiber, 7 g pro.*

BLACK-EYED PEA SALAD

## Cream-of-the-Crop Veggies

**PREP:** 20 MIN. • **COOK:** 15 MIN. + CHILLING
**MAKES:** 16 SERVINGS (¾ CUP EACH)

- 3 quarts water
- 4 medium carrots, sliced
- 1½ cups fresh or frozen peas
- 2 small yellow summer squash, halved and cut into ½-inch slices
- 1 pound fresh wax beans, trimmed and cut into 2-inch pieces
- 1 pound fresh green beans, trimmed and cut into 2-inch pieces
- ⅓ cup minced fresh chives
- ⅓ cup mayonnaise
- ⅓ cup creme fraiche or sour cream
- 3 tablespoons thinly sliced fresh basil
- 4 teaspoons snipped fresh dill
- ½ teaspoon salt
- ¼ teaspoon pepper

**1.** In a Dutch oven, bring the water to a boil. Add the carrots and peas; cook, uncovered, 3 minutes. Add the squash; cook 1 minute longer or until crisp-tender. Remove the vegetables and immediately drop into ice water. Drain and pat dry. Repeat with the wax beans and green beans, cooking them separately until crisp-tender, about 3 minutes.

**2.** Place all vegetables in a large bowl. Sprinkle with chives; toss to combine.

**3.** In a small bowl, mix the remaining ingredients. Add to vegetables; toss gently to coat. Refrigerate, covered, 3-4 hours or until cold.

**PER SERVING** *90 cal., 6 g fat (2 g sat. fat), 6 mg chol., 117 mg sodium, 8 g carb., 3 g fiber, 2 g pro.* **Diabetic Exchanges:** *1 vegetable, 1 fat.*

ROASTED SWEET AND GOLD POTATO SALAD

## Roasted Sweet and Gold Potato Salad

Kick potato salad up a notch with this zippy, Tex-Mex version. For an extra festive taste and presentation, I toss in colorful Mexicorn and black beans.
—**JEANNIE TRUDELL** DEL NORTE, CO

**PREP:** 1½ HOURS
**MAKES:** 16 SERVINGS (¾ CUP EACH)

- 2½ pounds Yukon Gold potatoes (about 8 medium)
- 1½ pounds sweet potatoes (about 2 large)
- 2 tablespoons olive oil
- 1 tablespoon ground cumin
- 2 teaspoons chili powder
- 2 teaspoons garlic powder
- 4 thick-sliced bacon strips, chopped
- 4 green onions, sliced
- 1 medium sweet red pepper, finely chopped
- ½ cup minced fresh cilantro
- 2 hard-cooked eggs, chopped
- ¾ cup mayonnaise
- 1 tablespoon chopped chipotle pepper in adobo sauce
- 2 teaspoons sugar
- 1 large ripe avocado, peeled and finely chopped
- 2 tablespoons lime juice

**1.** Peel and cut potatoes and sweet potatoes into ¾-in. cubes. Place in a large bowl; drizzle with oil and sprinkle with seasonings. Toss to coat. Transfer to two greased 15x10x1-in. baking pans. Bake at 450° for 45-55 minutes or until tender, stirring occasionally. Cool slightly.

**2.** In a small skillet, cook the bacon over medium heat until crisp. Remove bacon to paper towels with a slotted spoon; drain.

**3.** In a large bowl, combine the potatoes, bacon, green onions, red pepper, cilantro and eggs. Combine the mayonnaise, chipotle and sugar; pour over potato mixture and toss to coat. In a small bowl, toss avocado with lime juice; gently stir into salad. Serve warm or cold.

**PER SERVING** *236 cal., 14 g fat (2 g sat. fat), 33 mg chol., 145 mg sodium, 24 g carb., 3 g fiber, 4 g pro.* **Diabetic Exchanges:** *2½ fat, 1½ starch.*

FAST FIX ▶
## Honey Mustard Coleslaw

Using packaged shredded cabbage helped me streamline a family slaw recipe. Now it's ready fast—and there's little cleanup!
—**REBECCA ANDERSON** MELISSA, TX

**START TO FINISH:** 10 MIN.
**MAKES:** 5 SERVINGS

- 1 package (14 ounces) coleslaw mix
- ½ cup mayonnaise
- 2 tablespoons honey
- 1 tablespoon cider vinegar
- 1 tablespoon spicy brown mustard
- ½ teaspoon lemon-pepper seasoning
- ⅛ teaspoon celery seed

Place coleslaw mix in a large bowl. Combine the remaining ingredients. Pour over coleslaw mix and toss to coat. Chill until serving.

**PER SERVING** *216 cal., 18 g fat (2 g sat. fat), 8 mg chol., 232 mg sodium, 12 g carb., 2 g fiber, 1 g pro.*

SHIITAKE SALAD WITH SESAME-GINGER VINAIGRETTE

## FAST FIX
# Creamy Pineapple Salad

Guests of all ages will gravitate toward a traditional treat full of marshmallows, pineapple and maraschino cherries. Yum!

—JANICE HENSLEY OWINGSVILLE, KY

**START TO FINISH:** 25 MIN.
**MAKES:** 16 SERVINGS (½ CUP EACH)

- 1 package (8 ounces) cream cheese, softened
- 1 can (14 ounces) sweetened condensed milk
- ¼ cup lemon juice
- 2 cans (20 ounces) pineapple tidbits, drained
- 1½ cups multicolored miniature marshmallows, divided
- 1 carton (8 ounces) frozen whipped topping, thawed
- ½ cup chopped nuts
- ⅓ cup maraschino cherries, chopped

In a large bowl, beat the cream cheese, sweetened condensed milk and lemon juice until smooth. Add the pineapple and 1 cup marshmallows; fold in the whipped topping. Sprinkle with nuts, maraschino cherries and remaining marshmallows. Refrigerate leftovers.

**PER SERVING** *161 cal., 10 g fat (6 g sat. fat), 16 mg chol., 50 mg sodium, 17 g carb., 1 g fiber, 2 g pro.*

CREAMY PINEAPPLE SALAD

## EAT SMART
# Shiitake Salad with Sesame-Ginger Vinaigrette

This Far East favorite combines the Asian flavors I love with crisp, colorful veggies and smoky grilled shiitakes. The mirin for the vinaigrette is sold in the Asian section of well-stocked supermarkets.

—KATHI JONES-DELMONTE ROCHESTER, NY

**PREP:** 25 MIN. • **GRILL:** 10 MIN.
**MAKES:** 4 SERVINGS

- ½ cup mirin (sweet rice wine)
- 6 tablespoons rice vinegar
- 4½ teaspoons reduced-sodium soy sauce
- 1 shallot, minced
- 1 tablespoon minced fresh gingerroot
- 2 teaspoons lemon juice
- 2 teaspoons Sriracha Asian hot chili sauce or 1 teaspoon hot pepper sauce
- 1 teaspoon coarsely ground pepper
- 2 tablespoons olive oil
- 1 tablespoon sesame oil
- **SALAD**
- ½ pound fresh shiitake mushrooms
- 2 teaspoons olive oil
- 4 cups spring mix salad greens
- 4 green onions, chopped
- ⅓ cup thinly sliced radishes
- ⅓ cup thinly sliced fresh carrots
- 1 can (8 ounces) sliced water chestnuts, drained and rinsed
- 2 tablespoons sesame seeds, toasted

**1.** In a small saucepan, bring mirin to a boil. Reduce the heat; simmer, uncovered, for 5-7 minutes or until slightly thickened. Transfer to a small bowl; cool to room temperature. Whisk in vinegar, soy sauce, shallot, ginger, lemon juice, chili sauce, pepper and oils; set aside.

**2.** Place shiitake mushrooms in a small bowl; drizzle with oil and toss to coat. Transfer to a grill wok or basket. Grill, uncovered, over medium heat for 6-8 minutes or until tender, stirring frequently.

**3.** In a large bowl, combine the salad greens, green onions, radishes, carrots and water chestnuts. Add half of the vinaigrette; toss to coat. Divide among four plates; top salad with mushrooms. Drizzle with the remaining vinaigrette and sprinkle with sesame seeds.

**NOTE** *Look for mirin in the Asian condiments section.*

**PER SERVING** *289 cal., 15 g fat (2 g sat. fat), 0 chol., 365 mg sodium, 31 g carb., 5 g fiber, 5 g pro.* **Diabetic Exchanges:** *3 fat, 2 starch.*

ROASTED BUTTERNUT TOSSED SALAD

**EAT SMART** **FAST FIX**
## Broccoli Slaw with Lemon Dressing

**START TO FINISH:** 15 MIN.
**MAKES:** 10 SERVINGS

- ½  cup sour cream
- 3  tablespoons lemon juice
- 2  tablespoons mayonnaise
- 1  tablespoon white wine vinegar
- 2  teaspoons grated lemon peel
- 1  teaspoon Dijon mustard
- ½  teaspoon salt
- ¼  teaspoon freshly ground pepper
- 1  package (12 ounces) broccoli coleslaw mix
- 2  large red apples, julienned

In a large bowl, mix the first eight ingredients. Add the coleslaw mix and apples; toss to coat. Refrigerate, covered, until serving.

**PER SERVING** *79 cal., 4 g fat (2 g sat. fat), 9 mg chol., 152 mg sodium, 9 g carb., 2 g fiber, 1 g pro.* **Diabetic Exchanges:** *1 fat, ½ starch.*

BROCCOLI SLAW WITH LEMON DRESSING

**EAT SMART**
## Roasted Butternut Tossed Salad

With the autumn appeal of butternut squash and dried cranberries, this easy but special medley is the perfect salad for a Thanksgiving dinner menu.

**—KATIE WOLLGAST** FLORISSANT, MO

**PREP:** 20 MIN. + COOLING • **BAKE:** 20 MIN.
**MAKES:** 8 SERVINGS

- 4  cups cubed peeled butternut squash (about 1 pound)
- 1  large onion, chopped
- 1  tablespoon honey
- ½  teaspoon salt
- ½  teaspoon garlic powder
- ¼  teaspoon pepper
- 1  package (6 ounces) fresh baby spinach
- 2  cups coarsely chopped iceberg lettuce
- ½  cup shredded fat-free cheddar cheese
- 6  tablespoons reduced-fat poppy seed salad dressing, divided
- ½  cup seasoned stuffing cubes
- ½  cup dried cranberries

- ¼  cup slivered almonds, toasted
- 4  bacon strips, cooked and crumbled

**1.** Preheat oven to 400°. In a large bowl, toss squash and onion with honey, salt, garlic powder and pepper. Transfer to a 15x10x1-in. baking pan coated with cooking spray. Bake 20-25 minutes or until vegetables are tender, stirring once. Cool slightly.

**2.** In another bowl, combine spinach, lettuce, cheese and squash mixture. Just before serving, drizzle with 4 tablespoons dressing; toss to coat. Divide salad among eight plates; top with stuffing cubes, berries, nuts and bacon. Drizzle with remaining dressing.

**NOTE** *To toast nuts, spread in a 15x10x1-in. baking pan. Bake at 350° for 5-10 minutes or until lightly browned, stirring occasionally. Or, spread in a dry nonstick skillet and heat over low heat until lightly browned, stirring occasionally.*

**PER SERVING** *165 cal., 4 g fat (1 g sat. fat), 5 mg chol., 453 mg sodium, 28 g carb., 4 g fiber, 7 g pro.* **Diabetic Exchanges:** *2 starch, ½ fat.*

**PAT'S KING OF STEAKS
PHILLY CHEESE STEAK**
PAGE 33

# Soups & Sandwiches

Whether your family craves a **casual dinner** on a busy weeknight or a **comforting lunch** on a weekend, look here. This chapter features scrumptious choices that are guaranteed to please.

**SWEET & SOUR PORK WRAPS**
*PAGE 37*

**SLOW-COOKED CHICKEN CHILI**
*PAGE 40*

**BURGER AMERICANA**
*PAGE 39*

FAST FIX

# Shrimp Egg Drop Soup

Who knew that making egg drop soup at home could be so easy? Three basic steps and 30 minutes are all you'll need.

**—TASTE OF HOME TEST KITCHEN**

**START TO FINISH:** 30 MIN. • **MAKES:** 4 SERVINGS

- 4 teaspoons cornstarch
- ½ teaspoon soy sauce
- ⅛ teaspoon ground ginger
- 1½ cups water, divided
- 2 cans (14½ ounces each) chicken broth
- 1½ cups frozen home-style egg noodles
- 1 cup frozen broccoli florets, thawed and coarsely chopped
- ½ cup julienned carrot
- 1 egg, lightly beaten
- ½ pound cooked medium shrimp, peeled and deveined

**1.** In a small bowl, combine cornstarch, soy sauce, ginger and ½ cup cold water; set aside.

**2.** In a large saucepan, combine the chicken broth and remaining water. Bring to a simmer; add the egg noodles. Cook, uncovered, for 15 minutes. Add broccoli and carrot; simmer 3-4 minutes longer or until noodles are tender.

**3.** Drizzle the beaten egg into hot soup, stirring constantly. Stir cornstarch mixture and add to the pan. Bring to a boil; cook and stir for 2 minutes or until slightly thickened. Add shrimp; heat through.

**PER SERVING** *241 cal., 4 g fat (1 g sat. fat), 196 mg chol., 1,050 mg sodium, 30 g carb., 2 g fiber, 18 g pro.*

SHRIMP EGG DROP SOUP

BUFFALO CHICKEN WRAPS

FAST FIX

# Buffalo Chicken Wraps

For such a simple wrap, this one packs a punch! It comes from the ranch dressing, bacon strips and spicy buffalo wing sauce.

**—SARAH GOTTSCHALK** RICHMOND, IN

**START TO FINISH:** 30 MIN. • **MAKES:** 8 SERVINGS

- 1½ pounds chicken tenderloins
- 1 cup buffalo wing sauce, divided
- 8 lettuce leaves
- 8 flour tortillas (10 inches), warmed
- 16 bacon strips, cooked
- 1 small green pepper, cut into strips
- ½ cup ranch salad dressing

**1.** In a large skillet, bring the chicken and ½ cup buffalo wing sauce to a boil. Reduce heat; cover and simmer for 10-12 minutes or until the meat is no longer pink. Remove from heat; cool slightly. Shred chicken with two forks.

**2.** Place a lettuce leaf on each tortilla; spoon about ½ cup chicken mixture down the center. Top with bacon and green pepper. Drizzle with ranch dressing and remaining buffalo wing sauce; roll up.

**PER SERVING** *449 cal., 18 g fat (4 g sat. fat), 66 mg chol., 1,749 mg sodium, 35 g carb., 6 g fiber, 30 g pro.*

**top tip**

## Tender Tortillas

If your flour tortillas are a little too stiff to roll up, wrap them in a damp, microwave-safe paper towel and warm them in the microwave for a few seconds until they are soft and pliable.

**—KAREN ANN BLAND** GOVE, KS

## FAST FIX ▶
## Pat's King of Steaks Philly Cheese Steak

Here's the ultimate cheese steak, an iconic Philadelphia sandwich. It's a best-seller at Pat's King of Steaks Restaurant.

**—FRANK OLIVIERI** PHILADELPHIA, PA

**PREP/TOTAL TIME:** 20 MIN. • **MAKES:** 4 SERVINGS

- 1 large onion, sliced
- ½ pound sliced fresh mushrooms, optional
- 1 small green pepper, sliced, optional
- 1 small sweet red pepper, sliced, optional
- 6 tablespoons canola oil, divided
- 1½ pounds beef ribeye steaks, thinly sliced
- 4 crusty Italian rolls, split
  Process cheese sauce
  Ketchup, optional

**1.** In a large skillet, saute onion and, if desired, mushrooms and peppers in 3 tablespoons oil until tender. Remove and keep warm. In the same pan, saute the beef in the remaining oil in batches for 45-60 seconds or until the meat reaches desired doneness.

**2.** On each roll bottom, layer beef, onion mixture, cheese and, if desired, ketchup. Replace tops.

**PER SERVING** *714 cal., 49 g fat (12 g sat. fat), 101 mg chol., 299 mg sodium, 31 g carb., 2 g fiber, 36 g pro.*

FOUR-CHEESE FRENCH ONION SOUP

## Four-Cheese French Onion Soup

This beef broth is slightly sweet—not too salty like other versions I've had. Serve the cheesy soup as your first course on a special occasion or as a main dish with a green salad.

**—GAIL VAN OSDELL** ST. CHARLES, IL

**PREP:** 25 MIN. • **COOK:** 50 MIN. • **MAKES:** 8 SERVINGS

- ⅓ cup butter, cubed
- 2 tablespoons olive oil
- 12 cups thinly sliced onions
- 2 teaspoons salt
- 1 teaspoon sugar
- ¼ cup all-purpose flour
- 2 cartons (32 ounces each) reduced-sodium beef broth
- 1½ cups white wine or additional reduced-sodium beef broth
- 8 slices French bread (½-inch thick)
- 1⅓ cups shredded Swiss cheese
- ⅔ cup shredded cheddar cheese
- ½ cup shredded part-skim mozzarella cheese
- 2 tablespoons grated Parmesan cheese

**1.** In a Dutch oven, melt the butter with oil. Add the onions, salt and sugar; cook over medium heat for 15-20 minutes or until lightly browned, stirring frequently.

**2.** Sprinkle flour over onion mixture; stir until blended. Gradually stir in beef broth and wine. Bring to a boil; cook and stir for 2 minutes. Reduce heat; cover and simmer for 30 minutes, stirring occasionally.

**3.** Place bread slices on an ungreased baking sheet. Broil 3-4 in. from the heat for 3-5 minutes on each side or until lightly browned; set aside. Combine the cheeses.

**4.** Ladle soup into ovenproof bowls. Top each with a slice of toast; sprinkle with cheese mixture. Place bowls on a baking sheet. Broil for 2-3 minutes or until cheese is lightly golden.

**PER SERVING** *388 cal., 21 g fat (12 g sat. fat), 56 mg chol., 1,293 mg sodium, 29 g carb., 3 g fiber, 15 g pro.*

PAT'S KING OF STEAKS
PHILLY CHEESE STEAK

OVER-THE-RAINBOW MINESTRONE

FAST FIX

## Toasted Sausage Cacciatore Sammies

To make these filling sandwiches even heftier, use chunky spaghetti sauce.
—*TASTE OF HOME* TEST KITCHEN

**START TO FINISH:** 30 MIN.
**MAKES:** 4 SERVINGS

- 1 loaf frozen garlic bread
- 3 Italian sausage links, chopped
- 1 medium eggplant, cubed
- ½ pound sliced fresh mushrooms
- 1 medium onion, halved and thinly sliced
- 1 jar (14 ounces) spaghetti sauce
- ½ teaspoon Italian seasoning
- 6 slices provolone cheese

**1.** Bake garlic bread according to the package directions. Meanwhile, cook the sausage, eggplant, mushrooms and onion in a large skillet over medium heat until meat is no longer pink.

**2.** Stir in spaghetti sauce and Italian seasoning; heat through. Spoon over cut sides of garlic bread and top with cheese. Cut into slices.

**PER SERVING** *360 cal., 22 g fat (9 g sat. fat), 43 mg chol., 865 mg sodium, 28 g carb., 4 g fiber, 17 g pro.*

TOASTED SAUSAGE
CACCIATORE SAMMIES

My Over-the-Rainbow Minestrone is vegetarian-friendly and bursting with color. Feel free to substitute a different kind of pasta for the rotini.
—**CRYSTAL SCHLUETER** NORTHGLENN, CO

SLOW COOKER

## Over-the-Rainbow Minestrone

**PREP:** 20 MIN. • **COOK:** 6 HOURS 20 MIN.
**MAKES:** 10 SERVINGS (3¾ QUARTS)

- 4 stalks Swiss chard (about ½ pound)
- 2 tablespoons olive oil
- 1 medium red onion, finely chopped
- 6 cups vegetable broth
- 2 cans (14½ ounces each) fire-roasted diced tomatoes, undrained
- 1 can (16 ounces) kidney beans, rinsed and drained
- 1 can (15 ounces) garbanzo beans or chickpeas, rinsed and drained
- 1 medium yellow summer squash or zucchini, halved and cut into ¼-inch slices
- 1 medium sweet red or yellow pepper, finely chopped
- 1 medium carrot, finely chopped
- 2 garlic cloves, minced
- 1½ cups uncooked spiral pasta
- ¼ cup prepared pesto

**1.** Cut the stems from the chard; chop stems and leaves separately. Reserve leaves for adding later. In a large skillet, heat the oil over medium heat. Add the onion and chard stems; cook and stir 3-5 minutes or until tender. Transfer to a 6-qt. slow cooker.

**2.** Stir in vegetable broth, tomatoes, beans, squash, pepper, carrot and garlic. Cook, covered, on low 6-8 hours or until vegetables are tender.

**3.** Stir in the pasta and reserved chard leaves. Cook, covered, on low 20-25 minutes longer or until pasta is tender. Top servings with pesto.

**PER SERVING** *231 cal., 7 g fat (1 g sat. fat), 2 mg chol., 1,015 mg sodium, 34 g carb., 6 g fiber, 9 g pro.*

## FAST FIX ▶
# Cajun Popcorn Shrimp Sandwiches

I serve these zippy pitas with additional hot sauce for dipping. Tweak the amount of that ingredient and the seasoning in the pockets if you'd like to alter the heat level.

—**KENT WHITAKER** ROSSVILLE, GA

**START TO FINISH:** 30 MIN.
**MAKES:** 4 SERVINGS

- 2 **tablespoons butter, melted**
- 1 **teaspoon garlic powder**
- ¼ to ½ **teaspoon Cajun seasoning**
- 3½ **cups frozen breaded popcorn shrimp**
- ½ **cup mayonnaise**
- 1 **tablespoon hot pepper sauce**
- 1 **teaspoon sweet pickle relish**
- ½ **teaspoon prepared mustard**
- 8 **pita pocket halves, warmed**
- 1 **cup shredded lettuce**
- 8 **thin slices tomato**

**1.** In a bowl, combine butter, garlic powder and Cajun seasoning. Toss with the shrimp. Prepare shrimp according to the package directions for baking.
**2.** Combine the mayonnaise, pepper sauce, relish and mustard. Spread into warmed pitas. Fill pitas with shrimp, lettuce and tomato slices.
**PER SERVING** *668 cal., 40 g fat (8 g sat. fat), 96 mg chol., 1,139 mg sodium, 58 g carb., 3 g fiber, 18 g pro.*

CAJUN POPCORN
SHRIMP SANDWICHES

## ⑤ INGREDIENTS | SLOW COOKER 🍲
# Shredded Turkey Sandwiches

An envelope of onion soup mix, some butter and beer are all you need to give slow-cooked turkey breast terrific flavor.

—**JACKI KNUTH** OWATONNA, MN

**PREP:** 15 MIN. • **COOK:** 7 HOURS
**MAKES:** 24 SERVINGS

- 2 **boneless skinless turkey breast halves (2 to 3 pounds each)**
- 1 **bottle (12 ounces) beer or nonalcoholic beer**
- ½ **cup butter, cubed**
- 1 **envelope onion soup mix**
- 24 **French rolls, split**

**1.** Place turkey in a 5-qt. slow cooker. Combine the beer, butter and soup mix; pour over meat. Cover and cook on low for 7-9 hours or until the meat is tender.
**2.** Shred the meat and return to the slow cooker; heat through. Serve on French rolls.
**PER SERVING** *294 cal., 7 g fat (3 g sat. fat), 57 mg chol., 476 mg sodium, 31 g carb., 1 g fiber, 24 g pro.* **Diabetic Exchanges:** *3 lean meat, 2 starch, ½ fat.*

AUTUMN CHILI

FAST FIX

## Ham & Cheese Bagels

I came up with these bagels one day when I needed a quick but wholesome lunch. Now they're my go-to sandwiches.

**—NITA GRAFFIS** DOVE CREEK, CO

**START TO FINISH:** 30 MIN.
**MAKES:** 6 SERVINGS

- 4 teaspoons butter, softened
- 6 plain bagels, split
- 6 slices deli ham
- 6 slices cheddar cheese
- 2 ounces cream cheese, softened
- ⅛ teaspoon salt
- ⅛ teaspoon pepper
- 1 large tomato, sliced
- 1 medium ripe avocado, peeled and sliced

**1.** Spread butter over the cut sides of bagels. Place buttered sides up on an ungreased baking sheet. Broil 4-6 in. from the heat for 3-4 minutes or until lightly browned. Set aside bagel tops.
**2.** On the bottom of each bagel, place a slice of ham and cheddar cheese. Broil 3-4 minutes longer or until the cheese is melted.
**3.** Meanwhile, spread the bagel tops with cream cheese; sprinkle with salt and pepper. Layer bottom halves with tomato and avocado. Replace tops.
**PER SERVING** *427 cal., 21 g fat (11 g sat. fat), 56 mg chol., 791 mg sodium, 41 g carb., 4 g fiber, 20 g pro.*

## Autumn Chili

When I was growing up in the North, we always ate our chili over rice. But after I married my husband, who is from Texas, I began serving it with chopped onions, shredded cheese and, of course, a side of corn bread! A little baking cocoa lends richness without adding sweetness.

**—AUDREY BYRNE** LILLIAN, TX

**PREP:** 10 MIN. • **COOK:** 2 ¼ HOURS
**MAKES:** 4 SERVINGS

- 1 pound ground beef
- 1 large onion, chopped
- 2 cans (16 ounces each) kidney beans, rinsed and drained
- 2 cans (14½ ounces each) diced tomatoes, undrained
- 1 can (8 ounces) tomato sauce
- 1 medium green pepper
- 3 tablespoons chili powder
- 1 tablespoon ground cumin
- 2 garlic cloves, minced
- 1 teaspoon baking cocoa
- 1 teaspoon dried oregano
- 1 teaspoon Worcestershire sauce, optional
  Salt and pepper to taste

**1.** In a large saucepan, cook the beef and onion over medium heat until the meat is no longer pink, breaking meat into crumbles; drain.
**2.** Add the remaining ingredients; bring to a boil. Reduce the heat; cover and simmer for 2 hours, stirring occasionally.
**PER SERVING** *540 cal., 16 g fat (6 g sat. fat), 86 mg chol., 1,026 mg sodium, 58 g carb., 18 g fiber, 43 g pro.*

HAM & CHEESE BAGELS

> We always fix Sweet & Sour Pork Wraps for our annual family party, and they're a hit every year. The cabbage and cilantro give them great texture and flavor.
>
> **—ANDREW DEVITO** HARTFORD, CT

**SWEET & SOUR PORK WRAPS**

## Sweet & Sour Pork Wraps

**PREP:** 15 MIN. • **COOK:** 6 HOURS
**MAKES:** 8 SERVINGS (2 WRAPS EACH)

- 1 boneless pork shoulder butt roast (3 to 4 pounds)
- 1 medium onion, chopped
- 1 cup water
- 1 cup sweet-and-sour sauce
- ¼ cup sherry or chicken broth
- ¼ cup reduced-sodium soy sauce
- 1 envelope onion soup mix
- 1 tablespoon minced fresh gingerroot
- 3 garlic cloves, minced
- 16 flour tortillas (6 inches), warmed
- 4 cups shredded cabbage
- ¼ cup minced fresh cilantro

**1.** Place the roast and onion in a 6-qt. slow cooker. In a small bowl, whisk water, sweet-and-sour sauce, sherry, soy sauce, soup mix, ginger and garlic until blended; pour over pork. Cook, covered, on low 6-8 hours or until the meat is tender.

**2.** When cool enough to handle, shred pork with two forks. To serve, spoon about ⅓ cup pork mixture onto the center of each tortilla. Top with ¼ cup cabbage; sprinkle with cilantro. Fold bottom of tortilla over filling; fold both sides to close.

**PER SERVING** *523 cal., 23 g fat (6 g sat. fat), 101 mg chol., 1,357 mg sodium, 42 g carb., 1 g fiber, 36 g pro.*

## Lemon Chicken & Rice Soup

Here's my attempt at duplicating one of my favorite restaurant soups at home in my slow cooker. The recipe is low-calorie, low-fat and gluten-free, too.

**—KRISTIN CHERRY** BOTHELL, WA

**PREP:** 35 MIN. • **COOK:** 4¼ HOURS
**MAKES:** 12 SERVINGS (4 QUARTS)

- 2 tablespoons olive oil
- 2 pounds boneless skinless chicken breasts, cut into ½-inch pieces
- 5 cans (14½ ounces each) reduced-sodium chicken broth
- 8 cups coarsely chopped Swiss chard, kale or spinach
- 2 large carrots, finely chopped
- 1 small onion, chopped
- 1 medium lemon, halved and thinly sliced
- ¼ cup lemon juice
- 4 teaspoons grated lemon peel
- ½ teaspoon pepper
- 4 cups cooked brown rice

**1.** In a large skillet, heat 1 tablespoon oil over medium-high heat. Add half of the chicken; cook and stir until browned. Transfer to a 6-qt. slow cooker. Repeat with the remaining oil and chicken.

**2.** Stir the chicken broth, vegetables, lemon slices, lemon juice, peel and pepper into chicken. Cook, covered, on low 4-5 hours or until chicken is tender. Stir in rice; heat through.

**PER SERVING** *203 cal., 5 g fat (1 g sat. fat), 42 mg chol., 612 mg sodium, 20 g carb., 2 g fiber, 20 g pro.* **Diabetic Exchanges:** *2 lean meat, 1 starch, 1 vegetable, ½ fat.*

**LEMON CHICKEN & RICE SOUP**

## FAST FIX ▶
# Mexican Grilled Cheese Sandwiches

Spice up a classic using Mexican cheese blend, peppers and salsa. These toasty sandwiches are perfect for busy weeknights.

—*TASTE OF HOME* TEST KITCHEN

**START TO FINISH:** 25 MIN. • **MAKES:** 4 SERVINGS

- 1 **medium sweet yellow pepper, chopped**
- 1 **medium green pepper, chopped**
- 2 **teaspoons olive oil**
- 8 **slices rye bread**
- 2 **tablespoons mayonnaise**
- 1 **cup fresh salsa, well drained**
- ¾ **cup shredded Mexican cheese blend**
- 2 **tablespoons butter, softened**

**1.** In a small skillet, saute the peppers in oil until tender. Spread four bread slices with mayonnaise. Layer with peppers, salsa and cheese. Top with remaining bread. Butter outsides of sandwiches.

**2.** In a small skillet over medium heat, toast sandwiches for 2-4 minutes on each side or until cheese is melted.

**PER SERVING** *402 cal., 22 g fat (10 g sat. fat), 36 mg chol., 892 mg sodium, 39 g carb., 4 g fiber, 11 g pro.*

GOLDEN POTATO SOUP

MEXICAN GRILLED CHEESE SANDWICHES

# Golden Potato Soup

Requests pour in for this chunky soup whenever family members are having an event or heading off to deer camp. If you're in the mood for a bowlful of comfort food, this is the one for you!

—**SHELLY WOODS** BLISSFIELD, MI

**PREP:** 25 MIN. • **COOK:** 25 MIN. • **MAKES:** 8 SERVINGS (2¾ QUARTS)

- 6 **cups cubed Yukon Gold potatoes**
- 2 **cups water**
- 1 **cup sliced celery**
- 1 **cup sliced carrots**
- ½ **cup chopped onion**
- 2 **teaspoons dried parsley flakes**
- 2 **teaspoons chicken bouillon granules**
- 1 **teaspoon salt**
- ½ **teaspoon pepper**
- ¼ **cup all-purpose flour**
- 2 **cups whole milk, divided**
- 1 **package (16 ounces) process cheese (Velveeta), cubed**
- 1 **cup cubed fully cooked ham**
- ⅓ **cup real bacon bits**

**1.** In a Dutch oven, combine the first nine ingredients. Bring to a boil over medium heat. Reduce heat; cover and simmer for 12-14 minutes or until potatoes are tender.

**2.** Meanwhile, in a small bowl, combine flour and ¼ cup milk until smooth; add to the soup. Bring to a boil; cook and stir for 2 minutes or until thickened. Stir in the cheese and remaining milk until cheese is melted. Add ham and bacon; heat through.

**PER SERVING** *401 cal., 19 g fat (11 g sat. fat), 57 mg chol., 1,666 mg sodium, 36 g carb., 3 g fiber, 22 g pro.*

# Rich Clam Chowder

When I discovered a clam chowder recipe I liked several years ago, I changed it a bit to tweak the flavor. The new version also makes more than 20 servings, so it's great for larger get-togethers.
—**TERESA DASTRUP** MERIDIAN, ID

**PREP:** 45 MIN. • **COOK:** 25 MIN.
**MAKES:** 22 SERVINGS (1 CUP EACH)

- 6 cups diced peeled red potatoes
- 3 large onions, finely chopped
- 6 celery ribs, finely chopped
- 3 cups water
- 6 cans (6½ ounces each) minced clams
- 1½ cups butter, cubed
- 1½ cups all-purpose flour
- 8 cups half-and-half cream
- ¼ cup red wine vinegar
- 2 tablespoons minced fresh parsley
- 3 teaspoons salt
- ¼ teaspoon pepper

**1.** In a stockpot, combine the potatoes, onions, celery and water. Drain the clams, reserving the juice; set clams aside. Add the juice to the potato mixture. Bring to a boil. Reduce heat; cover and simmer for 10 minutes or until the potatoes are tender.

**2.** Meanwhile, in a large saucepan, melt the butter over medium heat. Whisk in flour. Cook and stir for 5 minutes or until lightly browned. Gradually stir in the cream. Bring to a boil; cook and stir for 2 minutes or until thickened. Gradually stir into potato mixture.

**3.** Add the vinegar, parsley, salt, pepper and clams. Cook 5-10 minutes longer or until heated through.

**PER SERVING** *318 cal., 21 g fat (14 g sat. fat), 85 mg chol., 675 mg sodium, 20 g carb., 1 g fiber, 8 g pro.*

RICH CLAM CHOWDER

Burger Americana is a true red-white-and-blue tradition. Keep it simple or stack the grilled beef patty sky-high with the toppings of your choice: cheese, bacon, onion, tomato, coleslaw, whatever!
—**SUSAN MAHANEY** NEW HARTFORD, NY

BURGER AMERICANA

**FAST FIX**
# Burger Americana

**START TO FINISH:** 25 MIN. • **MAKES:** 4 SERVINGS

- ½ cup seasoned bread crumbs
- 1 egg, lightly beaten
- ½ teaspoon salt
- ½ teaspoon pepper
- 1 pound ground beef
- 1 tablespoon olive oil
- 4 sesame seed hamburger buns, split
  Toppings of your choice

**1.** In a large bowl, combine seasoned bread crumbs, egg, salt and pepper. Add beef; mix lightly but thoroughly. Shape into four ½-in.-thick patties. Press a shallow indentation in the center of each with your thumb. Brush both sides of patties with oil.

**2.** Grill burgers, covered, over medium heat or broil 4 in. from heat 4-5 minutes on each side or until a thermometer reads 160°. Serve on buns with toppings.

**PER SERVING** *429 cal., 20 g fat (6 g sat. fat), 123 mg chol., 796 mg sodium, 32 g carb., 1 g fiber, 28 g pro.*

SLOW-COOKED CHICKEN CHILI

## SLOW COOKER
# Slow-Cooked Chicken Chili

Lime juice gives this chunky chili a tangy twist, while canned tomatoes and beans make preparation a breeze. I toast tortilla strips and serve them on the side.

—**DIANE RANDAZZO** SINKING SPRING, PA

**PREP:** 25 MIN. • **COOK:** 4 HOURS
**MAKES:** 6 SERVINGS

- 1  **medium onion, chopped**
- 1  **each medium sweet yellow, red and green pepper, chopped**
- 2  **tablespoons olive oil**
- 3  **garlic cloves, minced**
- 1  **pound ground chicken**
- 2  **cans (14½ ounces each) diced tomatoes, undrained**
- 1  **can (15 ounces) white kidney or cannellini beans, rinsed and drained**
- ¼  **cup lime juice**
- 1  **tablespoon all-purpose flour**
- 1  **tablespoon baking cocoa**
- 1  **tablespoon ground cumin**
- 1  **tablespoon chili powder**
- 2  **teaspoons ground coriander**
- 1  **teaspoon grated lime peel**
- ½  **teaspoon salt**
- ½  **teaspoon garlic pepper blend**
- ¼  **teaspoon pepper**
- 2  **flour tortillas (8 inches), cut into ¼-inch strips**
- 6  **tablespoons reduced-fat sour cream**

**1.** In a large skillet, saute onion and peppers in oil for 7-8 minutes or until crisp-tender. Add garlic; cook 1 minute longer. Add chicken; cook and stir over medium heat for 8-9 minutes or until meat is no longer pink.
**2.** Transfer to a 3-qt. slow cooker. Stir in the tomatoes, beans, lime juice, flour, baking cocoa, cumin, chili powder, coriander, lime peel, salt, garlic pepper and pepper.
**3.** Cover and cook on low for 4-5 hours or until heated through.
**4.** Place tortilla strips on a baking sheet coated with cooking spray. Bake at 400° for 8-10 minutes or until crisp. Serve chili with sour cream and tortilla strips.
**PER SERVING** *356 cal., 14 g fat (3 g sat. fat), 55 mg chol., 644 mg sodium, 39 g carb., 8 g fiber, 21 g pro.*

FAST FIX
# Peanut Chicken Pockets

A friend shared her yummy recipe for chicken pita pockets with me years ago, and they win raves every time I fix them.

—**ESTHER DAVIS** CHELAN, WA

**START TO FINISH:** 30 MIN.
**MAKES:** 4 SERVINGS

- 2  **cups cubed cooked chicken**
- 2  **celery ribs, chopped**
- ¼  **cup chopped cucumber**
- ¼  **cup bean sprouts**
- ¼  **cup chopped peanuts**
- ¼  **cup mayonnaise**
- 2  **green onions, chopped**
- 1  **tablespoon minced fresh parsley**
- 1  **tablespoon lemon juice**
- ¼  **teaspoon salt**
- ¼  **teaspoon pepper**
- 4  **pita breads (6 inches), halved**
- 8  **lettuce leaves**
- 8  **tomato slices**

In a large bowl, combine the first 11 ingredients. Line the pita halves with lettuce leaves and tomato slices. Spoon chicken mixture into pitas.
**PER SERVING** *474 cal., 22 g fat (4 g sat. fat), 67 mg chol., 669 mg sodium, 40 g carb., 3 g fiber, 29 g pro.*

PEANUT CHICKEN POCKETS

## Bacon-Beef Barley Soup

This hearty soup goes over especially well with hungry guys. I ladle it over mashed potatoes for a complete dinner.

**—CATHY PETERSON** MENOMINEE, MI

**PREP:** 40 MIN. • **COOK:** 7 HOURS
**MAKES:** 7 SERVINGS

- 4 bacon strips, chopped
- 1½ pounds beef stew meat, cut into ½-inch pieces
- 1 medium onion, chopped
- 4 medium red potatoes, cut into ½-inch cubes
- 1½ cups fresh baby carrots, cut in half lengthwise
- 1 cup frozen corn
- ¼ cup medium pearl barley
- 2 cans (14½ ounces each) beef broth
- 1 can (14½ ounces) diced tomatoes with basil, oregano and garlic, undrained
- 1 jar (12 ounces) home-style beef gravy
- ½ teaspoon pepper
  Mashed potatoes, optional

**1.** In a large skillet, cook the bacon over medium heat until crisp. Using a slotted spoon, remove to paper towels to drain. Cook the beef and onion in the bacon drippings until the meat is browned; drain.
**2.** In a 5-qt. slow cooker, layer the potatoes, carrots, corn and barley. Top with the beef mixture and bacon. Combine the broth, tomatoes, gravy and pepper; pour over top (do not stir).
**3.** Cover and cook on low for 7-9 hours or until the meat and vegetables are tender. Stir before serving. Serve over mashed potatoes if desired.
**PER SERVING** *319 cal., 10 g fat (3 g sat. fat), 68 mg chol., 1,218 mg sodium, 32 g carb., 4 g fiber, 26 g pro.*

## Slow Cooker Smarts

Unless your recipe instructs otherwise, do not lift the lid of a slow cooker while it cooks. Every time you lift the lid, you add 15 to 30 minutes of cooking time.

## Creamy Root Veggie Soup

On chilly nights, we fill a Dutch oven with parsnips, celery root, onion and garlic for a smooth, creamy treat that warms us up from head to toe. Bacon and thyme are great garnishes.

**—SALLY SIBTHORPE** SHELBY TOWNSHIP, MI

**PREP:** 15 MIN. • **COOK:** 1 HOUR
**MAKES:** 8 SERVINGS

- 4 bacon strips, chopped
- 1 large onion, chopped
- 3 garlic cloves, minced
- 1 large celery root, peeled and cubed (about 5 cups)
- 6 medium parsnips, peeled and cubed (about 4 cups)
- 6 cups chicken stock
- 1 bay leaf
- 1 cup heavy whipping cream
- 2 teaspoons minced fresh thyme
- 1 teaspoon salt
- ¼ teaspoon white pepper
- ¼ teaspoon ground nutmeg
  Additional minced fresh thyme

**1.** In a Dutch oven, cook the bacon over medium heat until crisp, stirring occasionally. Remove with a slotted spoon; drain on paper towels. Cook and stir the onion in bacon drippings 6-8 minutes or until tender. Add garlic; cook 1 minute longer.
**2.** Add celery root, parsnips, chicken stock and leaf. Bring to a boil. Reduce heat; cook, uncovered, 30-40 minutes or until the vegetables are tender. Remove leaf.
**3.** Puree soup using an immersion blender. Or, cool slightly and puree in batches in a blender; return to pan. Stir in whipping cream, 2 teaspoons thyme, salt, pepper and nutmeg; heat through. Top servings with bacon and additional thyme.
**PER SERVING** *295 cal., 17 g fat (9 g sat. fat), 50 mg chol., 851 mg sodium, 30 g carb., 6 g fiber, 8 g pro.*

**CURRIED FRIED RICE
WITH PINEAPPLE**
*PAGE 53*

# Side Dishes & Condiments

Enhance menus with dishes that are **every bit as special** as your entree. The veggie casseroles, stuffed potatoes, sandwich toppings and other **tasty accompaniments** in this chapter make it easy!

**BACON-WRAPPED CORN**
*PAGE 44*

**LOADED SMASHED TATERS**
*PAGE 51*

**SWEET ONION & RED BELL PEPPER TOPPING** *PAGE 49*

SAVORY MEDITERRANEAN ORZO

# Bacon-Wrapped Corn

All year long, we look forward to the wonderful summer treat of fresh-picked corn on the cob. And it tastes even better wrapped with strips of bacon, sprinkled with chili powder and popped on the grill. The tender kernels are so flavorful, you can skip the added butter and salt.

—LORI BRAMBLE OMAHA, NE

**START TO FINISH:** 30 MIN.
**MAKES:** 8 SERVINGS

- 8 **large ears sweet corn, husks removed**
- 8 **bacon strips**
- 2 **tablespoons chili powder**

**1.** Wrap each ear of corn with a bacon strip; place on a piece of heavy-duty foil. Sprinkle with chili powder. Wrap securely, twisting the ends to make handles for turning.

**2.** Grill the wrapped corn, covered, over medium heat 20-25 minutes or until the corn is tender and the bacon is cooked, turning once.

**PER SERVING** *210 cal., 14 g fat (5 g sat. fat), 15 mg chol., 199 mg sodium, 18 g carb., 3 g fiber, 5 g pro.*

**EAT SMART**
# Savory Mediterranean Orzo

In the mood for something a bit different? Consider orzo pasta. It has a shape that's similar to rice and is easy to prepare in this Mediterranean dish. To make the recipe vegetarian, substitute reduced-sodium vegetable broth for the chicken broth.

—KRISTI SILK FERNDALE, WA

**PREP:** 25 MIN. • **BAKE:** 20 MIN.
**MAKES:** 12 SERVINGS (⅔ CUP EACH)

- 4 **cups reduced-sodium chicken broth**
- 1 **package (16 ounces) orzo pasta**
- 1 **medium onion, finely chopped**
- 2 **tablespoons olive oil**
- 4 **garlic cloves, minced**
- 2 **cups (8 ounces) crumbled feta cheese, divided**
- 1 **package (10 ounces) frozen chopped spinach, thawed and squeezed dry**
- 1 **jar (7½ ounces) roasted sweet red peppers, drained and chopped**
- 1 **small yellow summer squash, finely chopped**
- ½ **teaspoon salt**
- ½ **teaspoon pepper**

**1.** In a large saucepan, bring broth to a boil. Stir in orzo; cook over medium heat for 6-8 minutes. Remove from the heat.

**2.** In a small skillet, saute the onion in oil until tender. Add the garlic; cook 1 minute longer. Stir into orzo mixture. Stir in 1 cup feta cheese, spinach, red peppers, squash, salt and pepper.

**3.** Transfer to a greased 13x9-in. baking dish; sprinkle with remaining feta cheese. Bake at 350° for 20-25 minutes or until heated through.

**PER SERVING** *233 cal., 6 g fat (2 g sat. fat), 10 mg chol., 554 mg sodium, 33 g carb., 3 g fiber, 10 g pro.* **Diabetic Exchanges::** *2 starch, 1 vegetable, 1 fat.*

BACON-WRAPPED CORN

# Pumpkin & Cauliflower Garlic Mash

I wanted healthier alternatives to some of our favorite foods. This smooth, garlicky side makes a light but yummy replacement for the usual mashed potatoes. Your family won't miss them!

—**KARI WHEATON** SOUTH BELOIT, IL

**START TO FINISH:** 25 MIN.
**MAKES:** 6 SERVINGS

- 1 **medium head cauliflower, broken into florets (about 6 cups)**
- 3 **garlic cloves**
- ⅓ **cup spreadable cream cheese**
- 1 **can (15 ounces) solid-pack pumpkin**
- 1 **tablespoon minced fresh thyme**
- 1 **teaspoon salt**
- ¼ **teaspoon cayenne pepper**
- ¼ **teaspoon pepper**

**1.** Place 1 in. of water in a large saucepan; bring to a boil. Add the cauliflower and garlic cloves; cook, covered, 8-10 minutes or until tender. Drain; transfer to a food processor.
**2.** Add remaining ingredients; process until smooth. Return to the pan; heat through, stirring occasionally.
**PER SERVING** *87 cal., 4 g fat (2 g sat. fat), 9 mg chol., 482 mg sodium, 12 g carb., 4 g fiber, 4 g pro.* **Diabetic Exchanges:** *1 vegetable, ½ starch, ½ fat.*

PUMPKIN & CAULIFLOWER GARLIC MASH

# Spiced Cranberry-Orange Chutney
We like this bright, tangy medley over Brie or cream cheese as a spread for crackers.
—**CRYSTAL SCHLUETER** NORTHGLENN, CO

**PREP:** 20 MIN. • **COOK:** 10 MIN.
**MAKES:** 10 SERVINGS

- ½ **cup water**
- ¼ **cup dried cranberries**
- 1 **unpeeled medium orange, seeded and finely chopped (about 1¼ cups)**
- ½ **cup sugar**
- 1 **tablespoon lemon juice**
- ¼ **teaspoon ground cinnamon**
  **Dash ground ginger**
  **Dash ground cloves**
- 8 **ounces Brie or cream cheese**
- ¼ **cup chopped pecans, toasted**
  **Assorted crackers**

**1.** Preheat oven to 400°. In a small saucepan, bring the water to a boil. Stir in the cranberries; remove from heat and let stand 5 minutes.
**2.** Drain the cranberries, reserving 1 tablespoon soaking liquid. Return the cranberries and reserved liquid to the pan. Stir in the orange, sugar, lemon juice and spices; bring to a boil. Reduce the heat; simmer, uncovered, 5-10 minutes or until orange is tender and liquid is almost evaporated, stirring occasionally.
**3.** Place the Brie cheese in a 9-in. pie plate. Bake 8-10 minutes or just until softened.
**4.** Spoon the chutney over warm cheese; sprinkle with pecans. Serve warm with crackers.
**PER SERVING** *147 cal., 8 g fat (4 g sat. fat), 23 mg chol., 143 mg sodium, 14 g carb., 1 g fiber, 5 g pro.*

ZUCCHINI & SWEET CORN SOUFFLE

# Spicy Refried Beans

Start the fiesta by spicing up canned beans with jalapeno, cheese and seasonings. Serve a basket of tortilla chips for scooping.
—*TASTE OF HOME* TEST KITCHEN

**START TO FINISH:** 15 MIN. • **MAKES:** 2 CUPS

- 1 **small onion, chopped**
- 1 **jalapeno pepper, seeded and chopped**
- 1 **garlic clove, minced**
- 2 **teaspoons vegetable oil**
- 1 **can (16 ounces) refried beans**
- 2 **tablespoons water**
- 1 **teaspoon hot pepper sauce**
- ¼ **teaspoon ground cumin**
- ¼ **teaspoon chili powder**
- ⅛ **teaspoon cayenne pepper**
- ½ **cup shredded Monterey Jack cheese**

In a large skillet, saute the onion, jalapeno and garlic in oil for 2-3 minutes or until tender. Stir in the beans, water, hot pepper sauce, cumin, chili powder and cayenne. Cook and stir over medium-low heat until heated through. Transfer to a serving bowl; sprinkle with cheese.
**NOTE** *Wear disposable gloves when cutting hot peppers; the oils can burn skin. Avoid touching your face.*
**PER SERVING** *95 cal., 4 g fat (2 g sat. fat), 11 mg chol., 212 mg sodium, 10 g carb., 3 g fiber, 5 g pro.*

# Zucchini & Sweet Corn Souffle

As novice gardeners, my husband and I sowed zucchini seeds—15 hills' worth! This yummy souffle was a well-used recipe.
—**CAROL ELLERBROEK** GLADSTONE, IL

**PREP:** 40 MIN. + STANDING • **BAKE:** 45 MIN. • **MAKES:** 10 SERVINGS

- 2 **medium zucchini (about 1½ pounds), shredded**
- 2½ **teaspoons salt, divided**
- 6 **eggs**
- 2 **medium ears sweet corn, husks removed**
- 6 **tablespoons butter**
- 2 **green onions, chopped**
- 6 **tablespoons all-purpose flour**
- ¼ **teaspoon pepper**
- 1¼ **cups 2% milk**
- ½ **cup shredded Swiss cheese**

1. Place the zucchini in a colander over a plate; sprinkle with 1 teaspoon salt and toss. Let stand 30 minutes. Rinse and drain well; blot dry with paper towels. Meanwhile, separate eggs; let stand at room temperature 30 minutes. Grease a 2½-qt. souffle dish; dust lightly with flour.
2. Preheat oven to 350°. Place the corn in a large saucepan; add water to cover. Bring to a boil. Reduce the heat; cook, covered, 3-5 minutes or until crisp-tender; drain. Cool slightly. Cut corn from cobs and place in a large bowl.
3. In a large skillet, heat the butter over medium-high heat. Add green onions and zucchini; cook and stir until tender. Stir in the flour, pepper and remaining salt until blended; gradually stir in milk. Bring to a boil, stirring constantly; cook and stir 1-2 minutes or until the sauce is thickened. Add to corn; stir in cheese.
4. Stir a small amount of the hot zucchini mixture into egg yolks; return all to bowl, stirring constantly. Cool slightly.
5. In a large bowl, beat egg whites on high speed until stiff but not dry. With a rubber spatula, gently stir a fourth of the egg whites into the zucchini mixture. Fold in remaining egg whites. Transfer to prepared dish.
6. Bake 45-50 minutes or until top is puffed and center appears set. Serve immediately.
**PER SERVING** *178 cal., 12 g fat (7 g sat. fat), 152 mg chol., 599 mg sodium, 10 g carb., 1 g fiber, 8 g pro.*

SPICY REFRIED BEANS

# Lemon-Butter Brussels Sprouts

**START TO FINISH:** 25 MIN. • **MAKES:** 4 SERVINGS

- 1 **pound fresh or frozen Brussels sprouts, thawed**
- 3 **tablespoons olive oil**
- 2 **garlic cloves, minced**
- ¼ **cup white wine**
- ½ **cup chicken broth**
- 4 **teaspoons lemon juice**
- ½ **teaspoon dried thyme**
- ¼ **teaspoon salt**
- ¼ **teaspoon pepper**
- 2 **tablespoons butter**
- 1 **teaspoon grated lemon peel**
  **Minced fresh parsley, optional**

**1.** Cut the Brussels sprouts in half. In a large skillet, heat oil over medium heat. Add the sprouts and garlic; cook and stir 5 minutes or until sprouts begin to brown.

**2.** Add the wine, stirring to loosen browned bits from pan. Stir in broth, lemon juice, thyme, salt and pepper. Bring to a boil. Reduce heat; simmer, covered, 8-10 minutes or until sprouts are tender.

**3.** Stir in the butter and lemon peel until butter is melted. If desired, sprinkle with parsley.

**PER SERVING** *207 cal., 16 g fat (5 g sat. fat), 16 mg chol., 340 mg sodium, 12 g carb., 5 g fiber, 4 g pro.*

> Lots of people say they don't like green veggies. Lemon-Butter Brussels Sprouts win over even the biggest skeptics.
> —**JENN TIDWELL** FAIR OAKS, CA

LEMON-BUTTER BRUSSELS SPROUTS

SWEET AND SAVORY STUFFING

## Sweet and Savory Stuffing

With bits of bacon, apple and sage, this easy stuffing is chock-full of delightful flavors and textures. It's great for holidays, but you'll be tempted to have it on other days, too!

—**SHARON FERRANTE** MIFFLINTOWN, PA

**PREP:** 20 MIN. • **BAKE:** 30 MIN. • **MAKES:** 7 CUPS

- ½ **pound bacon strips, diced**
- ½ **cup chopped sweet onion**
- 5 **cups unseasoned stuffing cubes**
- 1 **large tart apple, finely chopped**
- 2 **tablespoons minced fresh parsley**
- 1 **teaspoon rubbed sage**
- ½ **teaspoon salt**
- ½ **teaspoon pepper**
- 1¼ to 1¾ **cups chicken broth**

**1.** In a large skillet, cook the bacon and onion over medium heat until bacon is crisp. Transfer to a large bowl. Add the stuffing cubes, apple, parsley, sage, salt and pepper. Stir in enough broth to reach desired moistness.

**2.** Transfer to a greased 8-in. square baking dish. Bake, uncovered, at 350° for 30-35 minutes or until golden brown.

**PER SERVING** *238 cal., 13 g fat (4 g sat. fat), 18 mg chol., 708 mg sodium, 26 g carb., 2 g fiber, 7 g pro.*

## top tip · Super Use for Sprouts

I shake steamed Brussels sprouts in a mixture of ¾ cup flour, ¼ cup grated Parmesan and pepper to taste. Then I dunk them in beaten egg and back into the flour mixture. After refrigerating them for about an hour, I fry them in oil until golden.

—**RUTH C.** GLENDALE HEIGHTS, IL

SUMMER SQUASH CASSEROLE

## Tex-Mex Summer Squash Casserole

Mild-flavored yellow squash gets a big boost when you add jalapenos, green chilies, red onion and salsa.

—**TOMMY LOMBARDO** EUCLID, OH

**PREP:** 15 MIN. • **BAKE:** 40 MIN. + STANDING
**MAKES:** 10 SERVINGS

- 7 **medium yellow summer squash, sliced (about 10 cups)**
- 2¼ **cups (9 ounces) shredded cheddar cheese, divided**
- 1 **medium onion, chopped**
- 1 **can (4 ounces) chopped green chilies**
- 1 **can (4 ounces) diced jalapeno peppers, drained**
- ¼ **cup all-purpose flour**
- ½ **teaspoon salt**
- ¾ **cup salsa**
- 4 **green onions, sliced**
- ¼ **cup chopped red onion**

**1.** Preheat oven to 400°. In a large bowl, combine squash, ¾ cup cheese, onion, chilies and jalapenos. Sprinkle with flour and salt; toss to combine.
**2.** Transfer to a greased 13x9-in. baking dish. Bake, covered, 30-40 minutes or until squash is tender.
**3.** Spoon salsa over the top; sprinkle with the remaining 1½ cups cheese. Bake, uncovered, 10-15 minutes longer or until golden brown. Let stand 10 minutes. Top with green and red onions before serving.
**PER SERVING** *143 cal., 8 g fat (5 g sat. fat), 27 mg chol., 420 mg sodium, 12 g carb., 2 g fiber, 8 g pro.*

---

**⑤INGREDIENTS**

## Strawberry Jam in a Jiffy

I love slathering a little butter and this amazing strawberry jam on a piping hot piece of cornbread. Scrumptious!

—**MICHELLE ROBERTS** GREENDALE, WI

**PREP:** 20 MIN. + STANDING
**COOK:** 10 MIN. + STANDING
**MAKES:** 4½ CUPS

- 4 **cups fresh strawberries, hulled**
- 4 **cups sugar**
- ¾ **cup water**
- 1 **package (1¾ ounces) powdered fruit pectin**

**1.** Rinse five 1-cup freezer-safe containers and lids with boiling water. Dry thoroughly. Thoroughly crush the strawberries, 1 cup at a time, to measure exactly 2 cups; transfer to a large bowl. Stir in the sugar; let the mixture stand 10 minutes, stirring occasionally.
**2.** In a small saucepan, mix the water and pectin; bring to a boil over high heat, stirring constantly. Boil 1 minute longer. Add to the strawberry mixture, stirring until the sugar is dissolved, about 3 minutes. (A few sugar crystals may remain.)
**3.** Immediately fill all containers to within ½ in. of the tops. Wipe off the top edges of containers; immediately cover with lids. Let stand at room temperature 24 hours.
**4.** Jam is now ready to use. Refrigerate up to 3 weeks or freeze containers up to 12 months. Thaw frozen jam in the refrigerator before serving.
**PER SERVING** *91 cal., trace fat (trace sat. fat), 0 chol., trace sodium, 23 g carb., trace fiber, trace pro.*

---

**FAST FIX**

## Green Onion Tartar Sauce

Here's a traditional sauce worth making from scratch. It brings an extra-special touch to meals in just 10 minutes, and my guests are always impressed by the homemade taste. You may never want to buy the bottled version again!

—**ROGER SLIVON** GENESEE DEPOT, WI

**START TO FINISH:** 10 MIN.
**MAKES:** ¾ CUP

- ½ **cup mayonnaise**
- 2 **green onions, finely chopped**
- 1 **whole dill pickle, finely chopped**
- 2 **tablespoons sour cream**
- 1 **teaspoon minced fresh parsley**
- 1 **teaspoon cider vinegar**
- ½ **teaspoon sugar**
- ¼ **teaspoon dried tarragon**
- ⅛ **teaspoon pepper**

In a small bowl, combine all ingredients. Refrigerate tartar sauce until serving.
**PER SERVING** *74 cal., 8 g fat (1 g sat. fat), 5 mg chol., 106 mg sodium, 1 g carb., trace fiber, trace pro.*

---

SWEET ONION & RED BELL PEPPER TOPPING

**EAT SMART** **SLOW COOKER**

## Sweet Onion & Red Bell Pepper Topping

As soon as spring Vidalia onions hit the market, I get busy preparing this topping. It's great on everything from hot dogs and bruschetta to cream cheese and crackers.

—**PAT HOCKETT** OCALA, FL

**PREP:** 15 MIN. • **COOK:** 4 HOURS
**MAKES:** 16 SERVINGS (¼ CUP EACH)

- 4 **large sweet onions, thinly sliced (about 8 cups)**
- 4 **large sweet red peppers, thinly sliced (about 6 cups)**
- ½ **cup cider vinegar**
- ¼ **cup packed brown sugar**
- 2 **tablespoons honey**
- 2 **tablespoons canola oil**
- 2 **teaspoons celery seed**
- ¾ **teaspoon crushed red pepper flakes**
- ½ **teaspoon salt**

In a 5- or 6-qt. slow cooker, combine all ingredients. Cook, covered, on low 4-5 hours or until the vegetables are tender. Serve with a slotted spoon.
**PER SERVING** *76 cal., 2 g fat (trace sat. fat), 0 chol., 84 mg sodium, 14 g carb., 2 g fiber, 1 g pro.* **Diabetic Exchange:** *1 starch.*

# Popular Potatoes

From the grill, oven or stovetop, a spud-filled side dish is guaranteed to please everyone at the table. You just can't miss when you prepare the winning potato recipes here.

COCONUT TWICE-BAKED SWEET POTATOES

**(5)INGREDIENTS FAST FIX**
## Parmesan & Garlic Fries

A generous amount of Parmesan cheese and minced garlic take plain fries to a whole new level. Ketchup is strictly optional!
—*TASTE OF HOME* TEST KITCHEN

**START TO FINISH:** 20 MIN. • **MAKES:** 5 SERVINGS

- 5 **cups frozen French-fried potatoes**
- 2 **tablespoons olive oil**
- 3 **to 4 garlic cloves, minced**
- ¼ **teaspoon salt**
- ¼ **cup grated Parmesan cheese**

**1.** Preheat oven to 450°. Place the potatoes in a large bowl. Mix the oil, garlic and salt; toss with potatoes. Arrange in a single layer on a large baking sheet.
**2.** Bake 15-20 minutes or until golden brown, stirring once. Sprinkle with cheese; toss lightly. Serve immediately.
**PER SERVING** *199 cal., 11 g fat (2 g sat. fat), 4 mg chol., 524 mg sodium, 18 g carb., 2 g fiber, 4 g pro.*

PARMESAN & GARLIC FRIES

**EAT SMART**
## Coconut Twice-Baked Sweet Potatoes

Savor a taste of the tropics with these coconut-topped potatoes. Maple syrup, ginger, nuts and adobo sauce lend even more flavor.
—**NANCY SOBEL** BAY SHORE, NY

**PREP:** 30 MIN. • **BAKE:** 20 MIN. • **MAKES:** 8 SERVINGS

- 4 **medium sweet potatoes**
- ½ **cup coconut milk**
- 1 **tablespoon maple syrup**
- 1 **teaspoon minced fresh gingerroot**
- 1 **teaspoon adobo sauce**
- ½ **teaspoon salt**
- ¼ **cup chopped pecans**
- ¼ **cup flaked coconut**

**1.** Scrub and pierce potatoes; place on a microwave-safe plate. Microwave, uncovered, on high for 10-12 minutes or until tender, turning once.
**2.** When cool enough to handle, cut each potato in half lengthwise. Scoop out the pulp, leaving thin shells. In a large bowl, mash the pulp with coconut milk. Stir in the syrup, ginger, adobo sauce and salt. Spoon into potato shells.
**3.** Place potatoes on a baking sheet. Sprinkle with pecans and coconut. Bake at 350° for 20-25 minutes or until heated through.
**PER SERVING** *137 cal., 7 g fat (4 g sat. fat), 0 chol., 175 mg sodium, 18 g carb., 2 g fiber, 2 g pro.* **Diabetic Exchanges:** *1 starch, 1 fat.*

**LOADED SMASHED TATERS**

## FAST FIX ▶
# Grilled Potatoes with Sour Cream Sauce

Seasoned grilled spuds are great all by themselves. But pairing them with a rich, zippy sour cream sauce creates a standout side dish that will complement a variety of entrees.

**—CRAIG CARPENTER** CORAOPOLIS, PA

**START TO FINISH:** 30 MIN. • **MAKES:** 5 SERVINGS

- 2 **tablespoons olive oil**
- 1 **tablespoon barbecue seasoning**
- 2 **garlic cloves, minced**
- 2 **teaspoons lemon juice**
- 1½ **pounds small potatoes, quartered**

**SAUCE**
- ⅔ **cup ranch salad dressing**
- 4 **teaspoons bacon bits**
- 2 **teaspoons minced chives**
-   **Dash hot pepper sauce**

**1.** In a large bowl, combine the oil, barbecue seasoning, garlic and lemon juice. Add the potatoes; toss to coat. Place on a double thickness of heavy-duty foil (about 28 in. x 18 in.). Fold foil around the potato mixture and seal tightly.

**2.** Grill, covered, over medium heat for 20-25 minutes or until potatoes are tender.

**3.** In a small bowl, combine the sauce ingredients. Serve with potatoes.

**NOTE** *This recipe was tested with McCormick's Grill Mates Barbecue Seasoning. Look for it in the spice aisle.*

**PER SERVING** *365 cal., 23 g fat (4 g sat. fat), 7 mg chol., 879 mg sodium, 37 g carb., 3 g fiber, 4 g pro.*

# Loaded Smashed Taters

My husband loves these taters with a steak, and even my young daughter is a fan! I use baby Yukon Golds because the skins are thin and easy to mash. Sometimes I load them up even more by adding garlic and chives.

**—ANDREA QUIROZ** CHICAGO, IL

**PREP:** 20 MIN. • **COOK:** 20 MIN. • **MAKES:** 8 SERVINGS

- 2½ **pounds baby Yukon Gold potatoes**
- 1 **cup 2% milk, warmed**
- ½ **cup spreadable garlic and herb cream cheese**
- 3 **tablespoons butter, softened**
- 1 **pound bacon strips, cooked and crumbled**
- 1 **cup (4 ounces) shredded cheddar cheese**
- ½ **cup shredded Parmesan cheese**
- 3 **green onions, chopped**
- ⅓ **cup oil-packed sun-dried tomatoes, chopped**
- 2 **teaspoons dried parsley flakes**
- ¼ **teaspoon salt**
- ¼ **teaspoon pepper**

**1.** Place the potatoes in a large saucepan; add water to cover. Bring to a boil. Reduce heat; cook, uncovered, 15-20 minutes or until tender.

**2.** Drain the potatoes; return to the pan. Lightly mash the potatoes, gradually adding the warm milk, cream cheese and butter to reach the desired consistency. Stir in bacon, cheddar cheese, Parmesan cheese, green onions, sun-dried tomatoes, parsley, salt and pepper.

**PER SERVING** *379 cal., 24 g fat (13 g sat. fat), 63 mg chol., 682 mg sodium, 27 g carb., 2 g fiber, 15 g pro.*

**GRILLED POTATOES WITH SOUR CREAM SAUCE**

## Zucchini & Cheese Casserole

My daughter and I are big fans of zucchini, and this cheesy casserole is packed!

—**RACHELLE STRATTON** ROCK SPRINGS, WY

**PREP:** 20 MIN. • **BAKE:** 25 MIN. + STANDING
**MAKES:** 6 SERVINGS

- 4 **tablespoons butter, divided**
- 6 **small zucchini, chopped (about 7 cups)**
- 1 **large onion, chopped**
- 1½ **cups crushed Rice Chex**
- 1 **cup (4 ounces) shredded Colby-Monterey Jack cheese**
- 2 **eggs, lightly beaten**
- 1 **teaspoon salt**
- ¼ **teaspoon pepper**

**1.** Preheat oven to 350°. In a large skillet, heat 2 tablespoons butter over medium-high heat. Add the zucchini and onion; cook and stir 10-12 minutes or until crisp-tender. Transfer to a bowl; cool slightly.

**2.** In a microwave, melt the remaining butter. Drizzle over the cereal and toss to coat.

**3.** Stir cheese, eggs, salt and pepper into zucchini mixture; transfer to a greased 8-in.-square baking dish. Sprinkle with cereal mixture.

**4.** Bake, uncovered, 25-30 minutes or until heated through. Let stand 10 minutes before serving.

**PER SERVING** *260 cal., 15 g fat (10 g sat. fat), 99 mg chol., 778 mg sodium, 23 g carb., 2 g fiber, 9 g pro.*

**⑤ INGREDIENTS** **EAT SMART** **FAST FIX**

## Carrots and Snow Peas

Here's my all-time-favorite side dish. Sherry brings an amazing spark to the veggies, which are easy to prepare.

—**CHERYL DONNELLY** ARVADA, CO

**START TO FINISH:** 25 MIN.
**MAKES:** 4 SERVINGS

- 1¾ **cups sliced fresh carrots**
- 2 **tablespoons butter**

ZUCCHINI & CHEESE CASSEROLE

- 2¾ **cups fresh snow peas**
- 1 **shallot, minced**
- ¼ **teaspoon salt**
- 1 **tablespoon sherry or chicken broth**

In a large skillet or wok, stir-fry the carrots in butter for 3 minutes. Add the snow peas, shallot and salt; stir-fry 2 minutes longer or until vegetables are crisp-tender. Stir in the sherry; heat through.

**PER SERVING** *129 cal., 6 g fat (4 g sat. fat), 15 mg chol., 231 mg sodium, 15 g carb., 5 g fiber, 4 g pro.* **Diabetic Exchanges:** *2 vegetable, 1 fat.*

**⑤ INGREDIENTS**

## Honeyed Cranberries

Love cranberries but want to balance the tartness? This recipe featuring honey and orange flavor does just that. It makes a wonderful addition to holiday menus.

—**JAMES SCHEND** PLEASANT PRAIRIE, WI

**PREP:** 15 MIN.+ STANDING
**COOK:** 5 MIN. + CHILLING
**MAKES:** 8 SERVINGS

- 1 **medium orange**
- ½ **cup honey**
- 2 **tablespoons water**
- 1 **cup fresh cranberries**
- ½ **cup sugar**

**1.** Using a citrus zester, remove the peel from the orange in long narrow strips (save the fruit for another use). In a large saucepan, combine honey, water and peel; cook and stir over medium heat just until simmering (do not boil). Cool 20 minutes.

**2.** Transfer to a small bowl; stir in the cranberries. Refrigerate, covered, 8 hours or overnight.

**3.** Drain cranberries, allowing berries to stand 15 minutes. Discard orange peel and cooking liquid.

**4.** Place the sugar in a small bowl. Add cranberries, a few at a time, and toss to coat. Transfer to a parchment-paper lined baking sheet. Let stand until completely dry, about 30 minutes. Store, covered, at room temperature for up to 3 days.

**PER SERVING** *60 cal., trace fat (0 saturated fat), 0 cholesterol, 1 mg sodium, 16 g carb., 1 g fiber, trace pro.*

PANZANELLA PASTA

FAST FIX ▸
## Panzanella Pasta

We toss traditional panzanella ingredients such as ripe tomatoes, peppers and olives with whole wheat spaghetti for a hearty pasta dinner. My children are especially fond of the crunchy croutons.

—**ASHLEY PIERCE** BRANTFORD, ON

**START TO FINISH:** 30 MIN.
**MAKES:** 12 SERVINGS (1 CUP EACH)

- 4 **ounces uncooked whole wheat spaghetti**
- 2 **tablespoons plus ½ cup olive oil, divided**
- 6 **cups cubed French bread (1-inch pieces)**
- ⅓ **cup red wine vinegar**
- 2 **tablespoons Dijon mustard**
- 1 **teaspoon salt**
- ½ **teaspoon coarsely ground pepper**
- 4 **cups cherry tomatoes, halved**
- 2 **medium sweet yellow or orange peppers, chopped**
- ½ **cup pitted Greek olives**
- ½ **cup loosely packed basil leaves, torn**
- 8 **ounces feta or part-skim mozzarella cheese, cut into ½-inch cubes**

**1.** Cook spaghetti according to the package directions. In a large skillet, heat 2 tablespoons oil over medium-high heat. Add the bread cubes; cook and stir 3-4 minutes or until toasted. Remove from heat.

**2.** In a large bowl, whisk the vinegar, mustard, salt, pepper and remaining oil until blended. Add the tomatoes, peppers, olives and basil; toss lightly.

**3.** Drain spaghetti and add to tomato mixture. Add bread cubes and cheese; toss to combine. Serve immediately.
**PER SERVING** *297 cal., 18 g fat (5 g sat. fat), 17 mg chol., 739 mg sodium, 28 g carb., 3 g fiber, 7 g pro.*

FAST FIX ▸
## Curried Fried Rice with Pineapple

Popular in Thai restaurants, this is a special fried rice called Khao Pad. It has a bit of heat that contrasts with a little sweetness.

—**JOANNA YUEN** SAN JOSE, CA

**START TO FINISH:** 30 MIN.
**MAKES:** 8 SERVINGS

- 4 **tablespoons canola oil, divided**
- 2 **eggs, beaten**
- 1 **small onion, finely chopped**
- 2 **shallots, finely chopped**
- 3 **garlic cloves, minced**
- 4 **cups cold cooked rice**
- 1 **can (8 ounces) unsweetened pineapple chunks, drained**
- ½ **cup lightly salted cashews**
- ½ **cup frozen peas**
- ⅓ **cup minced fresh cilantro**
- ¼ **cup raisins**
- 3 **tablespoons chicken broth**
- 2 **tablespoons fish sauce**
- 1½ **teaspoons curry powder**
- 1 **teaspoon sugar**
- ¼ **teaspoon crushed red pepper flakes**

**1.** In a large skillet or wok, heat 1 tablespoon oil over medium-high heat; add the eggs. As eggs set, lift the edges, letting the uncooked portion flow underneath. When eggs are completely cooked, remove to a plate and keep warm.

**2.** In the same pan, stir-fry onion and shallots in remaining oil until tender. Add garlic; cook 1 minute longer. Stir in the rice, pineapple, cashews, peas, cilantro, raisins, broth, fish sauce, curry, sugar and pepper flakes; heat through. Chop egg into small pieces; add to rice mixture.

**PER SERVING** *286 cal., 13 g fat (2 g sat. fat), 53 mg chol., 413 mg sodium, 36 g carb., 2 g fiber, 7 g pro.*

CURRIED FRIED RICE WITH PINEAPPLE

**GRILLED EGGPLANT PITA PIZZAS**
*PAGE 74*

# Main Dishes

When it comes to mealtime, the **memorable main courses** in this chapter play a starring role. You'll find winning choices for busy weekdays, holidays and **everything in between**.

**GUINNESS CORNED BEEF
AND CABBAGE**
PAGE 71

**WALKING TACOS**
PAGE 63

**GRILLED BROWN SUGAR-
MUSTARD CHICKEN**
PAGE 65

## SLOW COOKER
# Slow Cooker Tropical Pork Chops

**PREP:** 15 MIN. • **COOK:** 3 HOURS • **MAKES:** 4 SERVINGS

- 2 jars (23½ ounces each) mixed tropical fruit, drained and chopped
- ¾ cup thawed limeade concentrate
- ¼ cup sweet chili sauce
- 1 garlic clove, minced
- 1 teaspoon minced fresh gingerroot
- 4 bone-in pork loin chops (¾ inch thick and 5 ounces each)
- 1 green onion, finely chopped
- 2 tablespoons minced fresh cilantro
- 2 tablespoons minced fresh mint
- 2 tablespoons slivered almonds, toasted
- 2 tablespoons finely chopped crystallized ginger, optional
- ½ teaspoon grated lime peel

**1.** In a 3-qt. slow cooker, combine the first five ingredients. Add pork, arranging chops to sit snugly in fruit mixture. Cook, covered, on low 3-4 hours or until meat is tender (a thermometer inserted in pork should read at least 145°).
**2.** In a small bowl, mix the remaining ingredients. To serve, remove pork chops from slow cooker. Using a slotted spoon, serve fruit over pork. Sprinkle with herb mixture.
**NOTE** *To toast nuts, place in a dry nonstick skillet and heat over low heat until lightly browned, stirring occasionally.*
**PER SERVING** *572 cal., 13 g fat (4 g sat. fat), 69 mg chol., 326 mg sodium, 91 g carb., 3 g fiber, 24 g pro.*

Mixed fruit and a twist of lime bring a taste of paradise to Slow Cooker Tropical Pork Chops.
—ROXANNE CHAN ALBANY, CA

ASIAN SNAPPER WITH CAPERS

HOT & SPICY TURKEY LEGS

# Hot & Spicy Turkey Legs

Who doesn't love a good turkey leg at a street fair? You don't have to wait for the next fair when you can make your own drumsticks at home. Just marinate, bake and enjoy!
—*TASTE OF HOME* TEST KITCHEN

**PREP:** 10 MIN. + MARINATING • **BAKE:** 1½ HOURS
**MAKES:** 4 SERVINGS

- 4 turkey drumsticks (1½ pounds each)
- ⅔ cup Louisiana-style hot sauce
- ⅓ cup canola oil
- 1 tablespoon reduced-sodium soy sauce
- 1 tablespoon chili powder
- 2 teaspoons ground mustard
- 1 teaspoon garlic powder
- 1 teaspoon poultry seasoning
- 1 teaspoon onion powder
- 1 teaspoon celery salt
- ½ teaspoon white pepper
- ½ teaspoon hot pepper sauce, optional

**1.** Divide the drumsticks between two large resealable bags. In a bowl, whisk the remaining ingredients until blended. Add ¾ cup marinade to drumsticks, dividing evenly between the bags. Seal bags and turn to coat. Refrigerate 8 hours or overnight. Cover and refrigerate remaining marinade.
**2.** Preheat oven to 375°. Remove the drumsticks from the marinade to a foil-lined 15x10x1-in. baking pan; discard the marinade in bags.
**3.** Bake, covered, 45 minutes. Uncover; bake 45-60 minutes longer or until a thermometer reads 175°, basting occasionally with reserved marinade.
**PER SERVING** *937 cal., 50 g fat (13 g sat. fat), 343 mg chol., 587 mg sodium, 2 g carb., 1 g fiber, 113 g pro.*

## Italian Sausage and Spinach Pie

My mother gave me her meat pie recipe, which I tweaked a bit. It makes a hearty supper with a side of pasta.

—TERESA JOHNSON PERU, IL

**PREP:** 25 MIN. • **BAKE:** 50 MIN. + STANDING • **MAKES:** 8 SERVINGS

- 1 pound bulk Italian sausage
- 1 medium onion, chopped
- 6 eggs
- 2 packages (10 ounces each) frozen chopped spinach, thawed and squeezed dry
- 4 cups (16 ounces) shredded mozzarella cheese
- 1 cup ricotta cheese
- ½ teaspoon garlic powder
- ¼ teaspoon pepper
  Pastry for double-crust pie (9 inches)
- 1 tablespoon water

**1.** In a large skillet, brown sausage and onion over medium heat 6-8 minutes or until sausage is no longer pink, breaking sausage into crumbles; drain.

**2.** Separate 1 egg; reserve the yolk for brushing the pastry. In a large bowl, whisk remaining eggs and egg white. Stir in sausage mixture, spinach, mozzarella cheese, ricotta cheese, garlic powder and pepper.

**3.** Preheat oven to 375°. On a lightly floured surface, roll one half of pastry dough to a ⅛-in.-thick circle; transfer to a 9-in. deep-dish pie plate. Trim pastry even with rim. Add sausage mixture. Roll the remaining dough to a ⅛-in.-thick circle. Place over filling. Trim, seal and flute edge.

**4.** In a small bowl, whisk the water and reserved egg yolk; brush over pastry. Cut slits in top.

**5.** Bake 50 minutes or until golden brown. Let stand 10 minutes before serving.

**PASTRY FOR DOUBLE-CRUST PIE (9 INCHES)** *Combine 2½ cups all-purpose flour and ½ tsp. salt; cut in 1 cup cold butter until crumbly. Gradually add ⅓ to ⅔ cup ice water, tossing with a fork until dough holds together when pressed. Divide dough in half and shape into disks; wrap in plastic wrap and refrigerate 1 hour.*

**PER SERVING** *608 cal., 40 g fat (19 g sat. fat), 248 mg chol., 787 mg sodium, 33 g carb., 1 g fiber, 28 g pro.*

ITALIAN SAUSAGE AND SPINACH PIE

ASIAN SNAPPER WITH CAPERS

**EAT SMART** **FAST FIX**

## Asian Snapper with Capers

If you've never had red snapper and like the flavors of the Far East, consider giving this simple but special entree a try. The sauteed fish fillets will bring a little Asian-style excitement to dinnertime with fresh ginger, capers and soy sauce. The bonus is that you'll be sitting down to eat in only 20 minutes.

—MARY ANN LEE CLIFTON PARK, NY

**START TO FINISH:** 20 MIN. • **MAKES:** 4 SERVINGS

- 4 red snapper fillets (6 ounces each)
- 4½ teaspoons Mongolian Fire oil or sesame oil
- ¼ cup apple jelly
- 3 tablespoons ketchup
- 2 tablespoons capers, drained
- 1 tablespoon lemon juice
- 1 tablespoon reduced-sodium soy sauce
- 1 teaspoon grated fresh gingerroot

**1.** In a large skillet, cook red snapper fillets in oil over medium heat for 3-5 minutes on each side or until fish flakes easily with a fork; remove and keep warm.

**2.** Stir the apple jelly, ketchup, capers, lemon juice, soy sauce and ginger into the skillet. Cook and stir for 2-3 minutes or until slightly thickened; serve sauce with fish fillets.

**PER SERVING** *275 cal., 7 g fat (1 g sat. fat), 60 mg chol., 494 mg sodium, 17 g carb., trace fiber, 34 g pro.* **Diabetic Exchanges:** *4 lean meat, 1 starch, 1 fat.*

GRILLED MAPLE PORK CHOPS

**⑤ INGREDIENTS**

# Grilled Maple Pork Chops

Chops on the grill are hard to beat. Dress them up with a tangy maple marinade, and you have something extra special!
—**NICHOLAS KING** DULUTH, MN

**PREP:** 5 MIN + MARINATING. • **GRILL:** 15 MIN.
**MAKES:** 4 SERVINGS

- 6 **tablespoons maple syrup**
- 6 **tablespoons balsamic vinegar**
- ¾ **teaspoon salt**
- ¾ **teaspoon coarsely ground pepper**
- 4 **boneless pork loin chops (1½ inch thick and 12 ounces each)**

**1.** In a small bowl, whisk the maple syrup, vinegar, salt and pepper until blended. Pour ½ cup marinade into a large resealable plastic bag. Add the pork chops; seal bag and turn to coat. Refrigerate 1 hour. Reserve remaining marinade for basting.
**2.** Drain chops, discarding marinade in bag. Moisten a paper towel with cooking oil; using long-handled tongs, rub on grill rack to coat lightly.
**3.** Grill the chops, covered, over medium heat or broil 4 in. from heat 13-17 minutes or until a thermometer reads 145°, turning occasionally and basting with the reserved marinade during the last 5 minutes. Let stand 5 minutes before serving.
**PER SERVING** *509 cal., 19 g fat (7 g sat. fat), 164 mg chol., 339 mg sodium, 15 g carb., trace fiber, 65 g pro.*

# Salad-Topped Flatbread Pizzas

The crisp veggies on these pies are so refreshing, and the vinaigrette adds zing.
—**JULIE MERRIMAN**
SEATTLE, WA

**PREP:** 45 MIN. • **BAKE:** 10 MIN.
**MAKES:** 6 SERVINGS

- 1 **pound turkey or pork Italian sausage links, casings removed**
- 2 **tablespoons olive oil, divided**
- 2 **large onions, halved and sliced**
- ¼ **teaspoon pepper, divided**
- 6 **naan flatbreads**
- 1 **package (8 ounces) reduced-fat cream cheese, softened**
- ½ **cup reduced-fat red wine vinaigrette, divided**
- 1½ **cups (6 ounces) shredded part-skim mozzarella cheese**
- 3 **cups shredded lettuce**
- 1 **medium cucumber, thinly sliced**
- 1 **large tomato, seeded and chopped**
- ½ **medium red onion, thinly sliced**

**1.** In a large skillet, cook the sausage links over medium heat 6-8 minutes or until no longer pink, breaking into crumbles. Remove sausage with a slotted spoon; drain on paper towels. Remove drippings from pan.

**2.** Preheat oven to 425°. Heat 1 tablespoon oil in same skillet. Add onions and ⅛ teaspoon pepper; cook and stir 4-5 minutes or until softened. Reduce heat to medium-low; cook 15-20 minutes or until golden brown, stirring occasionally. Stir in sausage; remove from heat.
**3.** Lightly brush remaining oil on both sides of flatbreads. Place on ungreased baking sheets; bake 4-6 minutes on each side or until golden brown.
**4.** In a small bowl, beat cream cheese and ¼ cup vinaigrette until blended. Spread onto breads; top with sausage mixture. Sprinkle with cheese. Bake 6-9 minutes or until cheese is melted.
**5.** Meanwhile, in a large bowl, combine the lettuce, cucumber, tomato and red onion. Add the remaining vinaigrette and pepper; toss to coat. Divide salad among pizzas; serve immediately.
**PER SERVING** *510 cal., 28 g fat (11 g sat. fat), 76 mg chol., 1,308 mg sodium, 41 g carb., 3 g fiber, 25 g pro.*

# Did you know?

Cutting into an onion creates and releases a gas that reacts with the natural water in your eye to produce sulfuric acid. This causes the stinging sensation that makes you cry.

SALAD-TOPPED FLATBREAD PIZZA

EASY CHICKEN TAMALE PIE

Easy Chicken Tamale Pie takes advantage of convenience items such as a packaged corn bread mix. I can go fishing while my slow cooker does most of the work!
—**PETER HALFERTY** CORPUS CHRISTI, TX

**SLOW COOKER**
## Easy Chicken Tamale Pie

**PREP:** 20 MIN. • **COOK:** 7 HOURS
**MAKES:** 8 SERVINGS

- 1 **pound ground chicken**
- 1 **teaspoon ground cumin**
- 1 **teaspoon chili powder**
- ½ **teaspoon salt**
- ¼ **teaspoon pepper**
- 1 **can (15 ounces) black beans, rinsed and drained**
- 1 **can (14½ ounces) diced tomatoes, undrained**
- 1 **can (11 ounces) whole kernel corn, drained**
- 1 **can (10 ounces) enchilada sauce**
- 2 **green onions, chopped**
- ¼ **cup minced fresh cilantro**
- 1 **package (8½ ounces) corn bread/muffin mix**
- 2 **eggs, lightly beaten**
- 1 **cup (4 ounces) shredded Mexican cheese blend**

**Optional toppings: sour cream, salsa and minced fresh cilantro**

**1.** In a large skillet, cook the chicken over medium heat 6-8 minutes or until no longer pink, breaking into crumbles. Stir in cumin, chili powder, salt and pepper.
**2.** Transfer the chicken to a 4-qt. slow cooker. Stir in black beans, tomatoes, corn, enchilada sauce, green onions and cilantro. Cook, covered, on low 6-8 hours or until heated through.
**3.** In a small bowl, combine muffin mix and eggs; spoon over the chicken mixture. Cook, covered, on low 1 to 1½ hours longer or until a toothpick inserted into the corn bread layer comes out clean.
**4.** Sprinkle with cheese; let stand, covered, 5 minutes. If desired, serve with toppings.
**PER SERVING** *359 cal., 14 g fat (5 g sat. fat), 110 mg chol., 1,021 mg sodium, 40 g carb., 5 g fiber, 20 g pro.*

## Reuben-Style Pizza
I love a traditional Reuben sandwich and thought, why not make it into a pizza?
—**TRACY MILLER** WAKEMAN, OH

**PREP:** 20 MIN. • **BAKE:** 15 MIN.
**MAKES:** 6 SERVINGS

- 1 **tube (13.8 ounces) refrigerated pizza crust**
- 4 **ounces cream cheese, softened**
- 1 **can (10¾ ounces) condensed cheddar cheese soup, undiluted**
- ¼ **cup Thousand Island salad dressing**
- 2 **cups cubed pumpernickel bread**
- 2 **tablespoons butter, melted**
- ½ **pound sliced deli corned beef, coarsely chopped**
- 2 **cups sauerkraut, rinsed and well drained**
- 1½ **cups (6 ounces) shredded Swiss cheese**

**1.** Preheat oven to 425°. Unroll and press the dough onto the bottom of a greased 15x10x1-in. baking pan. Bake 6-8 minutes or until the edges are lightly browned.
**2.** Meanwhile, in a small bowl, beat cream cheese, soup and salad dressing until blended. In another bowl, toss bread cubes with melted butter.
**3.** Spread cream cheese mixture over crust; top with corned beef, sauerkraut and cheese. Sprinkle with bread cubes. Bake 12-15 minutes or until the crust is golden and the cheese is melted.
**PER SERVING** *539 cal., 28 g fat (14 g sat. fat), 84 mg chol., 1,939 mg sodium, 48 g carb., 4 g fiber, 24 g pro.*

REUBEN-STYLE PIZZA

EASY STUFFED SHELLS

## Easy Stuffed Shells

One day when we had unexpected guests, I improvised and threw together stuffed shells using a jar of spaghetti sauce, frozen meatballs and shredded cheese. The easy pasta bake is now a family favorite.

—DOLORES BETCHNER CUDAHY, WI

**PREP:** 20 MIN. • **BAKE:** 40 MIN.
**MAKES:** 12 SERVINGS

- 36 uncooked jumbo pasta shells
- 1 jar (24 ounces) spaghetti sauce
- 36 frozen fully cooked Italian meatballs (½ ounce each), thawed
- 2 cups (8 ounces) shredded part-skim mozzarella cheese

1. Preheat oven to 350°. Cook pasta shells according to package directions; drain and rinse in cold water.
2. Spread ½ cup sauce into a greased 13x9-in. baking dish. Fill each shell with a meatball; place over the sauce. Top with remaining sauce and cheese.
3. Bake, covered, 35 minutes. Uncover; bake 3-5 minutes longer or until bubbly and cheese is melted.

**PER SERVING** *334 cal., 17 g fat (8 g sat. fat), 45 mg chol., 711 mg sodium, 30 g carb., 3 g fiber, 16 g pro.*

## Crumb-Coated Ranch Chicken

How do you get so much flavor out of a five-ingredient recipe? Ranch dressing! It transforms plain chicken breasts into an entree worthy of special occasions.

—LADONNA REED PONCA CITY, OK

**PREP:** 10 MIN. • **BAKE:** 30 MIN.
**MAKES:** 4 SERVINGS

- ⅔ cup ranch salad dressing
- 2 cups coarsely crushed cornflakes
- 1 tablespoon Italian seasoning
- 1 teaspoon garlic powder
- 4 boneless skinless chicken breast halves (6 ounces each)

1. Preheat oven to 400°. Place the salad dressing in a shallow bowl. In a separate shallow bowl, mix cornflakes, Italian seasoning and garlic powder. Dip the chicken into the dressing, then into the cornflake mixture, patting to help the coating adhere.

2. Place chicken on a greased baking sheet. Bake 30-35 minutes or until a thermometer reads 165°.

**PER SERVING** *608 cal., 27 g fat (5 g sat. fat), 132 mg chol., 750 mg sodium, 42 g carb., 1 g fiber, 49 g pro.*

SLOW COOKER

## Slow-Roasted Lemon Dill Chicken

This citrusy main course is a little lighter and fresher-tasting than the slow cooker dishes I typically find. Keep your dinner fuss-free by adding a side of buttery noodles or a tossed green salad.

—LORI LOCKREY PICKERING, ON

**PREP:** 20 MIN.
**COOK:** 4 HOURS + STANDING
**MAKES:** 6 SERVINGS

- 2 medium onions, coarsely chopped
- 2 tablespoons butter, softened
- ¼ teaspoon grated lemon peel
- 1 broiler/fryer chicken (4 to 5 pounds)
- ¼ cup chicken stock
- 4 sprigs fresh parsley
- 4 fresh dill sprigs
- 3 tablespoons lemon juice
- 1 teaspoon salt
- 1 teaspoon paprika
- ½ teaspoon dried thyme
- ¼ teaspoon pepper

1. Place onions in bottom of a 6-qt. slow cooker. In a small bowl, mix the butter and lemon peel.
2. Tuck the wings under the chicken; tie the drumsticks together. With your fingers, carefully loosen the skin from chicken breast; rub the butter mixture under the skin. Secure the skin to the underside of breast with toothpicks. Place chicken over the onions, breast side up. Add the chicken stock, parsley and dill.
3. Drizzle the lemon juice over the chicken; sprinkle with seasonings. Cook, covered, on low 4-5 hours (a thermometer inserted into thigh should read at least 180°).
4. Remove chicken from slow cooker; tent with foil. Let stand 15 minutes before carving.

**PER SERVING** *366 cal., 23 g fat (8 g sat. fat), 127 mg chol., 542 mg sodium, 1 g carb., trace fiber, 37 g pro.*

CHERRY BALSAMIC PORK LOIN

SLOW COOKER

## Cherry Balsamic Pork Loin

After trying a terrific cherry topping for Brie cheese, I just had to make one for pork.

—SUSAN STETZEL
GAINESVILLE, NY

**PREP:** 20 MIN.
**COOK:** 3 HOURS + STANDING
**MAKES:** 8 SERVINGS (1⅓ CUPS SAUCE)

- 1 boneless pork loin roast (3 to 4 pounds)
- 1 teaspoon salt
- ½ teaspoon pepper
- 1 tablespoon canola oil
- ¾ cup cherry preserves
- ½ cup dried cherries
- ⅓ cup balsamic vinegar
- ¼ cup packed brown sugar

1. Sprinkle roast with salt and pepper. In a large skillet, heat oil over medium-high heat. Brown roast on all sides.
2. Transfer to a 6-qt. slow cooker. In a small bowl, mix the preserves, dried cherries, vinegar and brown sugar until blended; pour over the roast. Cook, covered, on low 3-4 hours or until tender (a thermometer inserted into pork should read at least 145°).
3. Remove roast from slow cooker; tent with foil. Let stand 15 minutes before slicing. Skim fat from cooking juices. Serve pork with sauce.

**PER SERVING** *359 cal., 10 g fat (3 g sat. fat), 85 mg chol., 128 mg sodium, 34 g carb., trace fiber, 33 g pro.*

FLANK STEAK WITH CILANTRO &
BLUE CHEESE BUTTER

## Flank Steak with Cilantro & Blue Cheese Butter

My kids are big fans of flank steak, and I love enhancing it with the honey-sweetened marinade and tangy blue cheese butter in this recipe. What a treat from the grill!

—**GWEN WEDEL** AUGUSTA, MI

**PREP:** 15 MIN. + MARINATING • **GRILL:** 15 MIN. • **MAKES:** 8 SERVINGS

- ½ **cup canola oil**
- ¼ **cup cider vinegar**
- ¼ **cup honey**
- 1 **tablespoon reduced-sodium soy sauce**
- ½ **teaspoon paprika**
- 1 **beef flank steak (2 pounds)**

**BLUE CHEESE BUTTER**
- ¾ **cup crumbled blue cheese**
- 3 **tablespoons butter, softened**
- 1 **green onion, finely chopped**
- 1 **tablespoon minced fresh cilantro**
- ⅛ **teaspoon salt**
- ⅛ **teaspoon pepper**

**1.** In a large resealable plastic bag, combine the first five ingredients. Add the steak; seal the bag and turn to coat. Refrigerate 2-4 hours.

**2.** Drain beef, discarding marinade. Grill steak, covered, over medium heat or broil 4 in. from heat 6-8 minutes on each side or until the meat reaches desired doneness (for medium-rare, a thermometer should read 145°; medium, 160°; well-done, 170°). Let steak stand 5 minutes before thinly slicing across the grain.

**3.** In a small bowl, beat blue cheese butter ingredients until blended. Serve steak with butter.

**PER SERVING** *283 cal., 19 g fat (8 g sat. fat), 74 mg chol., 302 mg sodium, 3 g carb., trace fiber, 24 g pro.*

EAT SMART

## Pork Tenderloin with Sweet Potato Ragout

Apples and sweet potatoes always make me think of autumn. I often use them for a ragout served with tender slices of pork.

—**GREG FONTENOT** THE WOODLANDS, TX

**PREP:** 1 HOUR • **GRILL:** 20 MIN.
**MAKES:** 6 SERVINGS (3 CUPS RAGOUT)

- 2 **tablespoons olive oil**
- 1 **large onion, chopped**
- 2 **garlic cloves, minced**
- 1 **large navel orange**
- ¼ **cup packed brown sugar**
- ¼ **cup balsamic vinegar**
- ⅛ **teaspoon plus ½ teaspoon salt, divided**
- 1 **can (15¾ ounces) cut sweet potatoes in syrup, undrained**
- 1 **can (14½ ounces) diced tomatoes, undrained**
- 2 **medium tart apples, peeled and chopped**
- 2 **pork tenderloins (¾ pound each)**
- ½ **teaspoon pepper**

**1.** In a large skillet, heat oil over medium heat. Add onion; cook and stir 4-5 minutes or until softened. Reduce heat to medium-low; cook 20-25 minutes or until golden brown, stirring occasionally. Add garlic; cook 1 minute longer.

**2.** Finely grate peel from orange. Cut orange crosswise in half; squeeze juice from orange. Stir brown sugar, vinegar, ⅛ teaspoon salt, peel and juice into onion mixture. Bring to a boil; cook 6-8 minutes or until liquid is almost evaporated.

**3.** Stir in sweet potatoes, tomatoes and apples. Return to a boil. Reduce heat; simmer, uncovered, 20-25 minutes or until apples are tender and liquid is almost evaporated, stirring occasionally.

**4.** Sprinkle the pork with pepper and remaining salt. Grill pork, covered, over medium heat 18-22 minutes or until a thermometer reads 145°, turning occasionally. Let stand 5 minutes before slicing. Serve with ragout.

**PER SERVING** *344 cal., 9 g fat (2 g sat. fat), 64 mg chol., 436 mg sodium, 42 g carb., 5 g fiber, 25 g pro.*

PORK TENDERLOIN WITH SWEET POTATO RAGOUT

WALKING TACOS

## Slow Cooker Mushroom Chicken & Peas

Some wonderfully fresh mushrooms I found a[t] market inspired my slow-cooked chicken. Roun[d] a basket of warm-from-the-oven breadsticks or rol[ls]

—**JENN TIDWELL** FAIR OAKS, CA

**PREP:** 10 MIN. • **COOK:** 3 HOURS 10 MIN. • **MAKES:** 4 SERVIN[GS]

- 4 **boneless skinless chicken breast halves (6 ounces each)**
- 1 **envelope onion mushroom soup mix**
- 1 **cup water**
- ½ **pound sliced baby portobello mushrooms**
- 1 **medium onion, chopped**
- 4 **garlic cloves, minced**
- 2 **cups frozen peas**

**1.** Place the chicken in a 3-qt. slow cooker. Sprinkle with soup mix, pressing to help seasonings adhere. Add water, mushrooms, onion and garlic.

**2.** Cook, covered, on low 3-4 hours or until the chicken is tender (a thermometer inserted into chicken should read at least 165°). Stir in peas; cook, covered, 10 minutes longer or until heated through.

**PER SERVING** *292 cal., 5 g fat (1 g sat. fat), 94 mg chol., 566 mg sodium, 20 g carb., 5 g fiber, 41 g pro.* **Diabetic Exchanges:** *5 lean meat, 1 starch, 1 vegetable.*

Walking Tacos are perfect for family game or movie nights. The ingredients go right into the chip bags!

—**BEVERLY MATTHEWS** PASCOS, WA

## Walking Tacos

**PREP:** 10 MIN. • **COOK:** 30 MIN. • **MAKES:** 5 SERVINGS

- 1 **pound ground beef**
- 1 **envelope reduced-sodium chili seasoning mix**
- ¼ **teaspoon pepper**
- 1 **can (10 ounces) diced tomatoes and green chilies**
- 1 **can (15 ounces) Ranch Style beans (pinto beans in seasoned tomato sauce)**
- 5 **packages (1 ounce each) corn chips**
  **Toppings: shredded cheddar cheese, sour cream and sliced green onions**

**1.** In a large skillet, cook the beef over medium heat 6-8 minutes or until no longer pink, breaking into crumbles; drain. Stir in chili seasoning mix, pepper, tomatoes and beans; bring to a boil. Reduce heat; simmer, uncovered, 20-25 minutes or until thickened, stirring occasionally.

**2.** Just before serving, cut open corn chip bags. Add beef mixture and toppings as desired.

**PER SERVING** *530 cal., 28 g fat (6 g sat. fat), 56 mg chol., 1,017 mg sodium, 44 g carb., 6 g fiber, 24 g pro.*

SLOW COOKER MUSHROOM CHICKEN & PEAS

PEPPERONI-SAUSAGE STUFFED PIZZA

## Pepperoni-Sausage Stuffed Pizza

For 30 years, friends have been telling me to open a pizzeria that serves this pie!

**—ELIZABETH WOLFF**
CARMEL, IN

**PREP:** 45 MIN. + RISING
**BAKE:** 40 MIN. + STANDING
**MAKES:** 12 SERVINGS

- 1 package (¼ ounce) active dry yeast
- 1¼ cups warm water (110° to 115°)
- 2 tablespoons olive oil
- 1½ teaspoons salt
- 1 teaspoon sugar
- 3½ to 4 cups all-purpose flour
**FILLING**
- 2½ cups (10 ounces) shredded part-skim mozzarella cheese, divided
- 2½ cups (10 ounces) shredded white cheddar cheese, divided
- 2 tablespoons all-purpose flour
- 2 teaspoons dried oregano
- 2 teaspoons dried basil
- ½ teaspoon crushed red pepper flakes
- 1 pound bulk Italian sausage, cooked and crumbled
- ½ pound sliced fresh mushrooms
- 1 package (3½ ounces) sliced pepperoni
- 1 can (15 ounces) pizza sauce
  Grated Parmesan cheese, optional

**1.** In a small bowl, dissolve yeast in warm water. In a large bowl, combine the oil, salt, sugar, yeast mixture and 1 cup flour; beat on medium speed until smooth. Stir in enough remaining flour to form a stiff dough.

**2.** Turn dough onto a floured surface; knead until smooth and elastic, about 6-8 minutes. Place in a greased bowl, turning once to grease the top. Cover with plastic wrap and let rise in a warm place until doubled, about 1 hour.

**3.** Preheat oven to 425°. Grease a 13x9-in. baking pan. Punch down dough; divide into three portions. On a lightly floured surface, combine two portions of dough; roll into a 15x11-in. rectangle. Transfer to prepared pan, pressing onto bottom and up sides of pan. Top with 2 cups mozzarella cheese and 2 cups cheddar cheese. Sprinkle with the flour, seasonings, sausage, mushrooms and pepperoni.

**4.** Roll out the remaining dough into a 13x9-in. rectangle. Place dough over the filling, crimping the edges to seal; prick the top with a fork. Sprinkle with remaining cheeses. Bake on a lower oven rack 10 minutes.

**5.** Reduce oven setting to 375°. Spread sauce over cheese. Bake 30-35 minutes longer or until edges are lightly browned. Let stand 10 minutes before cutting. If desired, sprinkle with Parmesan cheese.

**PER SERVING** *481 cal., 27 g fat (13 g sat. fat), 72 mg chol., 1,115 mg sodium, 36 g carb., 2 g fiber, 24 g pro.*

## Salmon & Dill Sauce with Lemon Risotto

I love the classic combo of lemon and fish. Risotto rounds out the menu perfectly.

**—AMANDA REED** NASHVILLE, TN

**PREP:** 20 MIN. • **COOK:** 30 MIN.
**MAKES:** 4 SERVINGS

**SAUCE**
- ½ cup mayonnaise
- ¼ cup sour cream
- 1 tablespoon chopped green onion
- 1 tablespoon lemon juice
- 1½ teaspoons snipped fresh dill or ½ teaspoon dill weed
**RISOTTO**
- 3 to 3½ cups chicken broth
- 2 tablespoons olive oil
- 1 shallot, finely chopped
- 1 cup uncooked arborio rice
- 1 garlic clove, minced
- 2 teaspoons grated lemon peel
- ¼ teaspoon pepper
**SALMON**
- 4 salmon fillets (6 ounces each)
- ½ teaspoon salt
- ¼ teaspoon pepper
- 2 tablespoons olive oil

**1.** In a small bowl, mix the sauce ingredients. Refrigerate, covered, until serving.

**2.** In a small saucepan, bring broth to a simmer; keep hot. In a large saucepan, heat oil over medium heat. Add shallot; cook and stir 1-2 minutes or until tender. Add the rice and garlic; cook and stir 1-2 minutes or until rice is coated.

**3.** Stir in ½ cup hot broth. Reduce heat to maintain a simmer; cook and stir until the broth is absorbed. Add the remaining broth, ½ cup at a time, cooking and stirring until the broth has been absorbed after each addition, the rice is tender but firm to the bite and the risotto is creamy. Remove from heat; stir in lemon peel and pepper.

**4.** Meanwhile, sprinkle the fillets with salt and pepper. In a large skillet, heat oil over medium heat. Add fillets; cook 6-8 minutes on each side or until fish just begins to flake easily with a fork. Serve with sauce and risotto.

**PER SERVING** *815 cal., 54 g fat (10 g sat. fat), 109 mg chol., 1,273 mg sodium, 44 g carb., 1 g fiber, 34 g pro.*

SALMON & DILL SAUCE WITH LEMON RISOTTO

GRILLED BROWN SUGAR-MUSTARD CHICKEN

## Ham & Cheese Potato Casserole

This convenient recipe makes two creamy casseroles. Have one tonight and put the other in the freezer for a busy weeknight in the future. It's like having money in the bank when things get hectic!

—**KARI ADAMS** FORT COLLINS, CO

**PREP:** 15 MIN. • **BAKE:** 50 MIN. + STANDING
**MAKES:** 2 CASSEROLES (5 SERVINGS EACH)

- 2 cans (10¾ ounces each) condensed cream of celery soup, undiluted
- 2 cups (16 ounces) sour cream
- ½ cup water
- ½ teaspoon pepper
- 2 packages (28 ounces each) frozen O'Brien potatoes
- 1 package (16 ounces) process cheese (Velveeta), cubed
- 2½ cups cubed fully cooked ham

**1.** Preheat oven to 375°. In a large bowl, mix soup, sour cream, water and pepper until blended. Stir in potatoes, cheese and ham.
**2.** Transfer mixture to two greased 11x7-in. baking dishes. Bake, covered, 40 minutes. Uncover; bake 10-15 minutes longer or until bubbly. Let stand 10 minutes before serving.
**FREEZE OPTION** *Cover and freeze unbaked casseroles. To use, partially thaw in the refrigerator overnight. Remove from refrigerator 30 minutes before baking. Preheat oven to 375°. Bake casseroles as directed, increasing time as necessary to heat through and for a thermometer inserted into center to read 165°.*
**PER SERVING** *474 cal., 26 g fat (14 g sat. fat), 92 mg chol., 1,555 mg sodium, 36 g carb., 4 g fiber, 20 g pro.*

## Cooked Ham on Hand

We often have ham on holidays. I cube the leftovers and pop them into the freezer. Then I just pull out cooked ham whenever I want to add it to casseroles, scrambled eggs, soups or other dishes.

—**PEG SCHAEFER** NEWARK, DE

---

(5)INGREDIENTS **EAT SMART** **FAST FIX**

## Grilled Brown Sugar-Mustard Chicken

When I was in college, I came up with this easy chicken. Now it's a mealtime staple.

—**KENDRA DOSS**
COLORADO SPRINGS, CO

**START TO FINISH:** 20 MIN.
**MAKES:** 8 SERVINGS

- ½ cup yellow or Dijon mustard
- ⅓ cup packed brown sugar
- ½ teaspoon ground allspice
- ¼ teaspoon crushed red pepper flakes
- 8 boneless skinless chicken thighs (about 2 pounds)

**1.** In a large bowl, mix mustard, brown sugar, allspice and pepper flakes. Remove ¼ cup mixture for serving. Add chicken to remaining mixture; toss to coat.
**2.** Grill the chicken, covered, over medium heat or broil 4 in. from heat 6-8 minutes on each side or until a thermometer reads 170°. Serve with reserved mustard mixture.
**PER SERVING** *224 cal., 9 g fat (2 g sat. fat), 76 mg chol., 597 mg sodium, 13 g carb., 1 g fiber, 22 g pro.* **Diabetic Exchanges:** *3 lean meat, 1 starch.*

---

(5)INGREDIENTS **FAST FIX**

## Smothered Burritos

Here's a quick Mexican dinner. For milder burritos, reduce the amount of salsa verde.

—**KIM KENYON** GREENWOOD, MO

**START TO FINISH:** 25 MIN.
**MAKES:** 4 SERVINGS

- 1 can (10 ounces) green enchilada sauce
- ¾ cup salsa verde
- 1 pound ground beef
- 4 flour tortillas (10 inches)
- 1½ cups (6 ounces) shredded cheddar cheese

**1.** Preheat oven to 375°. In a small bowl, mix sauce and salsa verde.
**2.** In a large skillet, cook beef over medium heat 8-10 minutes or until no longer pink, breaking into crumbles; drain. Stir in ½ cup sauce mixture.
**3.** Spoon ⅔ cup beef mixture across the center of each tortilla; top with 3 tablespoons cheese. Fold bottom and sides of tortilla over filling; roll up.
**4.** Place in a greased 11x7-in. baking dish. Pour remaining sauce mixture over top; sprinkle with remaining cheese. Bake, uncovered, 10-15 minutes or until cheese is melted.
**PER SERVING** *624 cal., 33 g fat (15 g sat. fat), 115 mg chol., 1,470 mg sodium, 44 g carb., 2 g fiber, 36 g pro.*

## Indiana-Style Corn Dogs

Among the best parts of the many fairs and festivals in Indiana are the corn dogs. My family adores them, so this recipe is a popular one in our house.
**—SALLY DENNEY** WARSAW, IN

**PREP:** 20 MIN. • **COOK:** 5 MIN./BATCH
**MAKES:** 12 TO 16 CORN DOGS

- 1  **cup all-purpose flour**
- ½  **cup yellow cornmeal**
- 1  **tablespoon sugar**
- 1  **tablespoon baking powder**
- 1  **teaspoon salt**
- ½  **teaspoon ground mustard**
- ¼  **teaspoon paprika**
   **Dash of pepper**
- 1  **egg, lightly beaten**
- 1  **cup evaporated milk**
   **Oil for deep-fat frying**
- 12  **to 16 wooden skewers**
- 12  **to 16 hot dogs**

**1.** In a bowl, whisk the first eight ingredients. Whisk in egg and milk just until blended. Transfer batter to a tall drinking glass.
**2.** In an electric skillet, heat oil to 375°. Insert skewers into the hot dogs. Dip hot dogs into the batter; allow excess batter to drip off. Fry, a few at a time, 2-3 minutes or until golden brown, turning occasionally. Drain on paper towels. Serve immediately.
**PER SERVING** *258 cal., 19 g fat (7 g sat. fat), 43 mg chol., 703 mg sodium, 13 g carb., 1 g fiber, 8 g pro.*

I serve Summer Garden Fish Tacos with quinoa and black beans for a complete meal. Peppers, green onions and purple carrots make fun, colorful toppings.
**—CAMILLE PARKER** CHICAGO, IL

SUMMER GARDEN FISH TACOS

INDIANA-STYLE CORN DOGS

## Summer Garden Fish Tacos

**PREP:** 20 MIN. • **GRILL:** 20 MIN.
**MAKES:** 4 SERVINGS

- 1  **medium ear sweet corn, husk removed**
- 1  **poblano pepper, halved and seeds removed**
- 4  **tilapia fillets (4 ounces each)**
- ⅛  **teaspoon salt**
- 1  **yellow summer squash, halved lengthwise**
- 1  **medium heirloom tomato, chopped**
- ⅓  **cup chopped red onion**
- 3  **tablespoons coarsely chopped fresh cilantro**
- 1  **teaspoon grated lime peel**
- 3  **tablespoons lime juice**
- 8  **taco shells, warmed**
- ½  **medium ripe avocado, peeled and sliced**

**1.** Moisten a paper towel with cooking oil; using long-handled tongs, rub it on the grill rack to coat lightly. Grill corn and pepper, covered, over medium heat 10-12 minutes or until tender, turning occasionally. Cool slightly.
**2.** Meanwhile, sprinkle fish with salt. Grill fish and squash, covered, over medium heat 7-9 minutes or until fish just begins to flake easily with a fork and squash is tender, turning once.
**3.** Cut corn from cob and place in a bowl. Chop pepper and squash; add to corn. Stir in tomato, onion, cilantro, lime peel and juice. Serve fish in shells; top with corn mixture and avocado.
**NOTE** *Wear disposable gloves when cutting hot peppers; the oils can burn skin. Avoid touching your face.*
**PER SERVING** *278 cal., 10 g fat (2 g sat. fat), 55 mg chol., 214 mg sodium, 26 g carb., 5 g fiber, 25 g pro.* **Diabetic Exchanges:** *3 lean meat, 1½ starch, 1 vegetable, ½ fat.*

## White Pizza with Roasted Tomatoes

My grandma taught me to cook with fresh, simple ingredients. Ricotta brings out the sweetness of the tomatoes in this pizza.

—**DEBBIE ROPPOLO** SAN MARCOS, TX

**PREP:** 45 MIN. + ROASTING • **BAKE:** 25 MIN.
**MAKES:** 8 SERVINGS

- 4 plum tomatoes (about 1 pound), cut lengthwise into ½-inch slices and seeded
- ¼ cup olive oil
- 1 teaspoon sugar
- ½ teaspoon salt

**CRUST**
- 2 tablespoons olive oil
- 1 large onion, finely chopped (about 1 cup)
- 2 teaspoons dried basil
- 2 teaspoons dried thyme
- 1 teaspoon dried rosemary, crushed
- 1 package (¼ ounce) active dry yeast
- 1 cup warm water (110° to 115°)
- 5 tablespoons sugar
- ¼ cup olive oil
- 1½ teaspoons salt
- 3¼ to 3¾ cups all-purpose flour

**TOPPING**
- 1 cup ricotta cheese
- 3 garlic cloves, minced
- ½ teaspoon salt
- ½ teaspoon Italian seasoning
- 2 cups (8 ounces) shredded part-skim mozzarella cheese

**WHITE PIZZA WITH ROASTED TOMATOES**

**1.** Preheat oven to 250°. In a bowl, toss the tomatoes with oil, sugar and salt. Transfer to a greased 15x10x1-in. baking pan. Roast 2 hours or until tomatoes are soft and slightly shriveled.

**2.** For crust, in a large skillet, heat oil over medium-high heat. Add onion; cook and stir 3-4 minutes or until tender. Stir in herbs. Cool slightly.

**3.** In a small bowl, dissolve the yeast in the warm water. In a large bowl, combine sugar, oil, salt, yeast mixture and 1 cup flour; beat on medium speed until smooth. Stir in the onion mixture and enough remaining flour to form a soft dough (dough will be sticky).

**4.** Turn the dough onto a floured surface; knead until smooth and elastic, about 6-8 minutes. Place in a greased bowl, turning once to grease the top. Cover with plastic wrap and let rise in a warm place until almost doubled, about 1½ hours.

**5.** Preheat oven to 400°. Grease a 15x10x1-in. baking pan. Punch down dough; roll to fit bottom and ½ in. up sides of pan. Cover; let rest 10 minutes. Bake 10-12 minutes or until edges are lightly browned.

**6.** In a small bowl, mix ricotta, garlic, salt and Italian seasoning. Spread over crust; top with roasted tomatoes and mozzarella. Bake 12-15 minutes or until crust is golden and cheese is melted.
**PER SERVING** *503 cal., 25 g fat (7 g sat. fat), 29 mg chol., 911 mg sodium, 54 g carb., 3 g fiber, 17 g pro.*

**SLOW COOKER**
## Slow Cooker Short Ribs

These short ribs are an easy alternative to the traditionally braised ones. You don't have to pay any attention to these once you get them in the slow cooker.

—**REBEKAH BEYER** SABETHA, KS

**PREP:** 30 MIN. • **COOK:** 6¼ HOURS
**MAKES:** 6 SERVINGS

- 3 pounds bone-in beef short ribs
- ½ teaspoon salt
- ½ teaspoon pepper
- 1 tablespoon canola oil
- 4 medium carrots, cut into 1-inch pieces
- 1 cup beef broth
- 4 fresh thyme sprigs
- 1 bay leaf

**SLOW COOKER SHORT RIBS**

- 2 large onions, cut into ½-inch wedges
- 6 garlic cloves, minced
- 1 tablespoon tomato paste
- 2 cups dry red wine or beef broth
- 4 teaspoons cornstarch
- 3 tablespoons cold water
    Salt and pepper to taste

**1.** Sprinkle short ribs with salt and pepper. In a large skillet, heat oil over medium heat. Brown ribs in batches on all sides; transfer to a 4- or 5-qt. slow cooker. Add carrots, broth, thyme and bay leaf to ribs.

**2.** Add onions to same skillet; cook and stir over medium heat 8-9 minutes or until tender. Add garlic and tomato paste; cook 1 minute longer. Stir in wine. Bring to a boil; cook 8-10 minutes or until liquid is reduced by half. Add to slow cooker. Cook, covered, on low 6-8 hours or until meat is tender.

**3.** Remove the beef and vegetables; keep warm. Transfer the cooking juices to a small saucepan; skim fat. Discard thyme and bay leaf. Bring the juices to a boil. Mix the cornstarch and water until smooth; gradually stir into pan. Return to a boil; cook and stir 1-2 minutes or until thickened. Season with salt and pepper to taste. Serve ribs and vegetables with sauce.
**PER SERVING** *250 cal., 13 g fat (5 g sat. fat), 55 mg chol., 412 mg sodium, 12 g carb., 2 g fiber, 20 g pro.*

## Deluxe Baked Macaroni and Cheese

Add diced ham and tomatoes to cheesy macaroni. You'll have great comfort food!

**—KATHY YAROSH**
APOPKA, FL

**PREP:** 30 MIN. • **BAKE:** 25 MIN.
**MAKES:** 12 SERVINGS

- 1 package (16 ounces) elbow macaroni
- ¼ cup all-purpose flour
- 2 cups 2% milk
- ½ cup heavy whipping cream
- 1 package (8 ounces) process cheese (Velveeta), cubed
- 1 cup (4 ounces) shredded cheddar cheese
- ⅔ cup whipped cream cheese
- ¼ cup grated Parmesan cheese
- 1 can (14½ ounces) diced tomatoes, drained
- 1½ cups cubed fully cooked ham
- 1 cup (8 ounces) sour cream
- 1 teaspoon Dijon mustard

**TOPPING**
- 1½ cups soft bread crumbs
- ¼ cup grated Parmesan cheese
- 2 tablespoons butter, melted

**1.** Preheat oven to 350°. Cook the macaroni according to the package directions. In a Dutch oven, whisk flour, milk and cream until smooth. Bring to a boil; cook and stir 2 minutes or until thickened.

**2.** Stir in the cheeses until melted. Add the tomatoes, ham, sour cream and mustard. Drain macaroni; add to cheese mixture and toss to coat.

**3.** Transfer to a greased 13x9-in. baking dish. In a small bowl, mix the topping ingredients; sprinkle over the top. Bake, uncovered, 25-30 minutes or until bubbly and the bread crumbs are lightly browned.

**NOTE** *To make soft bread crumbs, tear bread into pieces and place in a food processor or blender. Cover and pulse until crumbs form. One slice of bread yields ½ to ¾ cup crumbs.*

**PER SERVING** *441 cal., 23 g fat (14 g sat. fat), 85 mg chol., 734 mg sodium, 39 g carb., 2 g fiber, 19 g pro.*

⑤ INGREDIENTS

## Broccoli Chicken Casserole

Kids and adults alike enjoy this creamy dinner, which requires just five simple ingredients. Sometimes I toss dried cranberries into the stuffing.

**—JENNIFER SCHLACHTER** BIG ROCK, IL

**PREP:** 15 MIN. • **BAKE:** 30 MIN.
**MAKES:** 6 SERVINGS

- 1 package (6 ounces) chicken stuffing mix
- 2 cups cubed cooked chicken
- 1 cup frozen broccoli florets, thawed
- 1 can (10¾ ounces) condensed broccoli cheese soup, undiluted
- 1 cup (4 ounces) shredded cheddar cheese

**1.** Preheat oven to 350°. Prepare stuffing mix according to package directions, using 1½ cups water.

**2.** In large bowl, combine chicken, broccoli and soup; transfer to a greased 11x7-in. baking dish. Top with stuffing; sprinkle with cheese. Bake, covered, 20 minutes. Uncover; bake 10-15 minutes or until heated through.

**PER SERVING** *315 cal., 13 g fat (6 g sat. fat), 66 mg chol., 1,025 mg sodium, 25 g carb., 2 g fiber, 23 g pro.*

## Caprese Chicken

**PREP:** 10 MIN. + MARINATING
**BAKE:** 20 MIN. • **MAKES:** 4 SERVINGS

- ⅔ cup Italian salad dressing
- 2 teaspoons chicken seasoning
- 2 teaspoons Italian seasoning
- 4 boneless skinless chicken breast halves (6 ounces each)
- 2 tablespoons canola oil
- ½ pound fresh mozzarella cheese, cut into 4 slices
- 2 medium tomatoes, sliced
- 1 tablespoon balsamic vinegar or balsamic glaze
  Torn fresh basil leaves

**1.** In a large resealable plastic bag, combine the Italian salad dressing, chicken seasoning and Italian seasoning. Add the chicken; seal the bag and turn to coat. Refrigerate 4-6 hours. Drain the chicken, discarding the marinade.

**2.** Preheat oven to 450°. In an ovenproof skillet, heat the oil over medium-high heat. Brown the chicken on both sides. Transfer the skillet to the oven; bake 15-18 minutes or until a thermometer reads 165°.

**3.** Top the chicken with cheese and tomato. Bake 3-5 minutes longer or until the cheese is melted. Drizzle with vinegar; top with basil.

**NOTE** *This recipe was tested with McCormick's Montreal Chicken Seasoning. Look for it in the spice aisle.*

**PER SERVING** *525 cal., 34 g fat (11 g sat. fat), 139 mg chol., 761 mg sodium, 5 g carb., 1 g fiber, 45 g pro.*

## top tip
## Fresh Take on Mozzarella

Fresh mozzarella is softer and more moist than most of the commercially produced kind. Featuring a mild, delicate and somewhat milky flavor, fresh mozzarella is usually shaped into balls and stored in brine. After purchase, fresh mozzarella should be refrigerated in the brine and eaten within a few days.

DELUXE BAKED MACARONI AND CHEESE

The classic Italian salad of mozzarella, tomatoes and basil inspired my Caprese Chicken. We've made it on the grill but think it's best straight from the oven.
—**DANA JOHNSON** SCOTTSDALE, AZ

CAPRESE CHICKEN

LEMON-GARLIC CREAM FETTUCCINE

# Lemon-Garlic Cream Fettuccine

I've been serving my creamy fettuccine pasta for many years. Pair it with a tossed green salad for a complete dinner.
—**ANNE MILLER** GLENFIELD, NY

**PREP:** 25 MIN. • **COOK:** 15 MIN. • **MAKES:** 4 SERVINGS

- 3 teaspoons grated lemon peel
- 2 teaspoons minced fresh parsley
- 2 garlic cloves, minced
- 8 ounces uncooked fettuccine
**SAUCE**
- ¼ cup butter
- 1 small onion, chopped
- 2 garlic cloves, minced
- 1 teaspoon grated lemon peel
- ½ cup heavy whipping cream
- ¼ teaspoon salt
- ⅛ teaspoon pepper
- 4 ounces cream cheese, cubed
- 2 tablespoons lemon juice
- 2 plum tomatoes, chopped
- 2 teaspoons minced fresh parsley
  Grated Parmesan cheese, optional

**1.** In a small bowl, mix lemon peel, parsley and garlic. Cook fettuccine according to package directions; drain.
**2.** For sauce, in a large skillet, heat butter over medium-high heat. Add onion; cook and stir 2-3 minutes or until tender. Add the garlic and lemon peel; cook 1 minute longer. Stir in cream, salt and pepper. Whisk in cream cheese until melted. Remove from heat; cool slightly. Stir in lemon juice.
**3.** Add the pasta, tomatoes and parsley to skillet; toss to combine. Serve immediately with lemon peel mixture and, if desired, Parmesan cheese.
**PER SERVING** *518 cal., 34 g fat (21 g sat. fat), 102 mg chol., 346 mg sodium, 46 g carb., 3 g fiber, 11 g pro.*

# Sweet Potato & Fontina Pizza

My husband, a huge pizza fan, was the main inspiration for this different but delicious pie. It brings nutrient-rich sweet potatoes into an everyday meal and gets everyone asking for another cheesy, yummy slice.
—**LIBBY WALP** CHICAGO, IL

**PREP:** 20 MIN. • **BAKE:** 15 MIN. • **MAKES:** 6 SERVINGS

- 1 medium sweet potato (about 10 ounces)
- 2 tablespoons water
- ¼ teaspoon salt
- ⅛ teaspoon coarsely ground pepper
- 1 tube (13.8 ounces) refrigerated pizza crust
- 1 cup (4 ounces) shredded part-skim mozzarella cheese
- 1 cup (4 ounces) shredded fontina cheese
- 2 tablespoons olive oil, divided
- 1 teaspoon minced fresh rosemary or ¼ teaspoon dried rosemary, crushed
- 1 teaspoon minced fresh thyme or ¼ teaspoon dried thyme
- ¼ cup grated Parmesan cheese

**1.** Preheat oven to 450°. Grease a 12-in. pizza pan. Peel and cut the sweet potato into ¼-in. slices. Cut each slice into ½-in.-wide strips; place in a microwave-safe dish. Add the water. Microwave, covered, on high 3-4 minutes or until potato is almost tender. Drain; sprinkle with salt and pepper.
**2.** Unroll and press the dough to fit prepared pan. If desired, pinch the edge to form a rim. Sprinkle with mozzarella and fontina cheeses; drizzle with 1 tablespoon oil.
**3.** Top with the potato; sprinkle with herbs. Drizzle with the remaining oil; sprinkle with Parmesan cheese. Bake on lowest oven rack 12-15 minutes or until the crust is golden and the cheese is melted.
**PER SERVING** *374 cal., 16 g fat (7 g sat. fat), 35 mg chol., 819 mg sodium, 39 g carb., 2 g fiber, 17 g pro.*

SWEET POTATO & FONTINA PIZZA

GUINNESS CORNED
BEEF AND CABBAGE

A friend of my mother's gave her the recipe for Guinness Corned Beef and Cabbage. It's become a favorite in our house for birthday parties and St. Patrick's Day.
—**KARIN BRODBECK** RED HOOK, NY

## Guinness Corned Beef and Cabbage

**PREP:** 20 MIN. • **COOK:** 8 HOURS • **MAKES:** 9 SERVINGS

- 2 **pounds red potatoes, quartered**
- 1 **pound carrots, cut into 3-inch pieces**
- 2 **celery ribs, cut into 3-inch pieces**
- 1 **small onion, quartered**
- 1 **corned beef brisket with spice packet (3 to 3½ pounds)**
- 8 **whole cloves**
- 6 **whole peppercorns**
- 1 **bay leaf**
- 1 **bottle (12 ounces) Guinness stout or reduced-sodium beef broth**
- ½ **small head cabbage, thinly sliced**
  **Prepared horseradish**

**1.** In a 6-qt. slow cooker, combine potatoes, carrots, celery and onion. Add corned beef (discard spice packet or save for another use).
**2.** Place the cloves, peppercorns and bay leaf on a double thickness of cheesecloth. Gather corners of cloth to enclose seasonings; tie securely with string. Place in slow cooker. Pour stout over top.
**3.** Cook, covered, on low 8-10 hours or until the meat and vegetables are tender, adding cabbage during the last hour of cooking. Discard spice bag.
**4.** Cut the beef diagonally across the grain into thin slices. Serve beef with vegetables and horseradish.
**PER SERVING** 374 cal., 20 g fat (7 g sat. fat), 104 mg chol., 1,256 mg sodium, 25 g carb., 4 g fiber, 22 g pro.

## Pulled Pork with Ginger Sauce

Here in the capital of South Carolina, it verges on sacrilegious to make a pulled-pork sauce without using mustard. But my family loves this Asian-inspired ginger version. Wonderful in a sandwich, the slow-cooked meat is great over rice, too.
—**MARY MARLOWE LEVERETTE** COLUMBIA, SC

**PREP:** 15 MIN. • **COOK:** 7 HOURS • **MAKES:** 6 SERVINGS

- 2 **medium onions, chopped**
- 1 **boneless pork shoulder butt roast (3 pounds), trimmed**
- 1 **teaspoon salt**
- ½ **teaspoon pepper**
- 1 **cup ketchup**
- 3 **tablespoons lemon juice**
- 2 **tablespoons Worcestershire sauce**
- 2 **tablespoons honey**
- 4 **teaspoons butter, melted**
- 1 **teaspoon ground coriander**
- 1 **teaspoon minced fresh gingerroot**
  **Hamburger buns, split**
  **Thinly sliced green onions**

**1.** Place onions in a 4- or 5-qt. slow cooker. Sprinkle roast with salt and pepper; add to slow cooker. Cook, covered, on low 6-8 hours or until pork is tender.
**2.** Remove pork and onions; cool slightly. Discard cooking juices or save for another use. Shred pork with two forks. Return pork and onions to slow cooker. In a small bowl, whisk ketchup, lemon juice, Worcestershire sauce, honey, butter, coriander and ginger. Stir into pork mixture.
**3.** Cook, covered, on low 1 hour longer. Serve on buns; top with green onions.
**PER SERVING** 479 cal., 25 g fat (10 g sat. fat), 141 mg chol., 1,115 mg sodium, 23 g carb., 1 g fiber, 39 g pro.

PULLED PORK WITH GINGER SAUCE

CUMIN-CHILI SPICED FLANK STEAK

## EAT SMART
# Turkey Sausage-Stuffed Acorn Squash

Finding lighter recipes that will please the whole family can be a challenge. We all like this fun-to-eat stuffed squash.

—MELISSA BIRDSONG WALESKA, GA

**PREP:** 30 MIN. • **BAKE:** 50 MIN.
**MAKES:** 8 SERVINGS

- 4 **medium acorn squash (about 1½ pounds each)**
- 1 **cup cherry tomatoes, halved**
- 1 **pound Italian turkey sausage links, casings removed**
- ½ **pound sliced fresh mushrooms**
- 1 **medium apple, peeled and finely chopped**
- 1 **small onion, finely chopped**
- 2 **teaspoons fennel seed**
- 2 **teaspoons caraway seeds**
- ½ **teaspoon dried sage leaves**
- 3 **cups fresh baby spinach**
- 1 **tablespoon minced fresh thyme**
- ¼ **teaspoon salt**
- ⅛ **teaspoon pepper**
- 8 **ounces fresh mozzarella cheese, chopped**
- 1 **tablespoon red wine vinegar**

**1.** Preheat oven to 400°. Cut squash lengthwise in half; remove and discard seeds. Using a sharp knife, cut a thin slice from the bottom of each half to allow them to lie flat. Place in a shallow roasting pan, hollow side down; add ¼ in. of hot water and halved tomatoes. Bake, uncovered, 45 minutes.

**2.** Meanwhile, in a large skillet, cook the sausage, mushrooms, apple, onion and dried seasonings over medium heat 8-10 minutes or until sausage is no longer pink, breaking up sausage into crumbles; drain. Add the spinach, thyme, salt and pepper; cook and stir 2 minutes. Remove from heat.

**3.** Carefully remove the squash from roasting pan. Drain the cooking liquid, reserving tomatoes. Return squash to pan, hollow side up.

**4.** Stir cheese, vinegar and reserved tomatoes into sausage mixture. Spoon into squash cavities. Bake 5-10 minutes longer or until heated through and the squash is easily pierced with a fork.

**PER SERVING** *302 cal., 10 g fat (5 g sat. fat), 43 mg chol., 370 mg sodium, 42 g carb., 7 g fiber, 15 g pro.* **Diabetic Exchanges:** *2½ starch, 2 medium-fat meat.*

# Cumin-Chili Spiced Flank Steak

Here's a complete steak dinner, including broiled peppers and a homemade salsa.

—YVONNE STARLIN HERMITAGE, TN

**PREP:** 40 MIN. • **COOK:** 15 MIN.
**MAKES:** 4 SERVINGS

- 2 **small sweet red peppers, cut into 2-inch strips**
- 1 **small sweet yellow pepper, cut into 2-inch strips**
- 2 **cups grape tomatoes**
- 1 **small onion, cut into ½-inch wedges**
- 2 **jalapeno peppers, halved and seeded**
- 2 **tablespoons olive oil, divided**
- ¾ **teaspoon salt, divided**
- ¾ **teaspoon pepper, divided**
- 2 **teaspoons ground cumin**
- 1 **teaspoon chili powder**
- 1 **beef flank steak (1½ pounds)**
- 2 **to 3 teaspoons lime juice**
    **Hot cooked couscous**
    **Lime wedges**

**1.** Preheat broiler. Place the first five ingredients in a greased 15x10x1-in. baking pan. Toss with 1 tablespoon oil, ¼ teaspoon salt and ¼ teaspoon pepper. Broil 4 in. from the heat 10-12 minutes or until vegetables are tender and begin to char, turning once.

**2.** Meanwhile, mix the cumin, chili powder and remaining oil, salt and pepper; rub over both sides of steak. Grill, covered, over medium heat or broil 4 in. from heat 6-9 minutes on each side or until the meat reaches the desired doneness (for medium-rare, a thermometer should read 145°; medium, 160°; well-done, 170°). Let stand 5 minutes.

**3.** For the salsa, chop broiled onion and jalapenos; place in a small bowl. Stir in tomatoes and lime juice. Thinly slice steak across the grain; serve with salsa, broiled peppers, couscous and lime wedges.

**NOTE** *Wear disposable gloves when cutting hot peppers; the oils can burn skin. Avoid touching your face.*

**PER SERVING** *359 cal., 20 g fat (6 g sat. fat), 81 mg chol., 562 mg sodium, 10 g carb., 3 g fiber, 35 g pro.*

TURKEY SAUSAGE-STUFFED ACORN SQUASH

## top tip
# Sausage Selections

For Turkey Sausage-Stuffed Acorn Squash (above left), feel free to use pork or chicken sausage in place of the turkey variety called for in the recipe.

## Roast Pork Loin with Rosemary Applesauce

I served this for my husband's birthday. The tender roast is so comforting paired with the made-from-scratch applesauce.
—ANGELA LEMOINE HOWELL, NJ

**PREP:** 15 MIN. + MARINATING
**BAKE:** 55 MIN. + STANDING
**MAKES:** 8 SERVINGS (3 CUPS APPLESAUCE)

- ¼ cup olive oil
- 2 tablespoons salt
- 4 teaspoons garlic powder
- 4 teaspoons minced fresh rosemary or 1½ teaspoons dried rosemary, crushed
- 2 teaspoons pepper
- 1 boneless pork loin roast (2 to 3 pounds), halved

**APPLESAUCE**
- ¼ cup butter, cubed
- 6 medium Golden Delicious apples, peeled and chopped (about 5 cups)
- 1 to 2 teaspoons ground cinnamon
- 2 teaspoons brown sugar
- 1½ teaspoons minced fresh rosemary or ½ teaspoon dried rosemary, crushed
- ½ teaspoon salt
- 1 cup water

**1.** In a large resealable plastic bag, combine the first five ingredients. Add the pork; seal the bag and turn to coat. Refrigerate 8 hours or overnight.
**2.** Preheat oven to 350°. Place pork on a rack in a shallow roasting pan, fat side up. Roast 55-65 minutes or until a thermometer reads 145°.
**3.** Meanwhile, in a large skillet, heat the butter over medium heat. Add the apples, cinnamon, brown sugar, rosemary and salt; cook 8-10 minutes or until the apples are tender, stirring occasionally.
**4.** Stir in the water; bring to a boil. Reduce the heat; simmer, uncovered, 10 minutes or until the apples are very soft. Remove from heat; mash apples to desired consistency.
**5.** Remove the roast from oven; tent with foil. Let stand 10 minutes before slicing. Serve with warm applesauce.
**PER SERVING** *287 cal., 16 g fat (6 g sat. fat), 72 mg chol., 1,418 mg sodium, 15 g carb., 2 g fiber, 22 g pro.*

## EAT SMART SLOW COOKER
## Simple Poached Salmon

Healthy and simple to prepare, salmon is one of my favorite entrees. I often pop it into the slow cooker with some veggies.
—ERIN CHILCOAT CENTRAL ISLIP, NY

**PREP:** 10 MIN. • **COOK:** 1½ HOURS
**MAKES:** 4 SERVINGS

- 2 cups water
- 1 cup white wine
- 1 medium onion, sliced
- 1 celery rib, sliced
- 1 medium carrot, sliced
- 2 tablespoons lemon juice
- 3 fresh thyme sprigs
- 1 fresh rosemary sprig
- 1 bay leaf
- ½ teaspoon salt
- ¼ teaspoon pepper
- 4 salmon fillets (1¼ inches thick and 6 ounces each)
  Lemon wedges

**1.** In a 3-qt. slow cooker, combine the first 11 ingredients. Cook, covered, on low 45 minutes.
**2.** Carefully place the salmon fillets in the liquid; add additional warm water (120° to 130°) to cover fillets if needed. Cook, covered, 45-55 minutes or just until fish flakes easily with a fork (a thermometer inserted into fish should read at least 145°). To serve, remove fish from cooking liquid. Serve with lemon wedges.
**PER SERVING** *272 cal., 16 g fat (3 g sat. fat), 85 mg chol., 115 mg sodium, 1 g carb., trace fiber, 29 g pro.* **Diabetic Exchange:** *4 lean meat.*

## Grilled Pork Tenderloin & Veggies

Marinate the pork for this meal overnight and enjoy fuss-free prep the next day.
—MARIE PARKER MILWAUKEE, WI

**PREP:** 15 MIN. + MARINATING
**GRILL:** 30 MIN. • **MAKES:** 4 SERVINGS

- ¾ cup orange juice
- ½ cup olive oil
- ¼ cup lime juice
- 4 garlic cloves, minced
- 2 teaspoons dried oregano
- 1 teaspoon grated lime peel
- 1 teaspoon ground cumin
- ½ teaspoon salt
- ½ teaspoon pepper
- 2 pork tenderloins (1 pound each)
- 8 small carrots, halved lengthwise
- 2 medium zucchini, sliced lengthwise

**1.** In a small bowl, whisk the first nine ingredients until blended. Pour ½ cup marinade into a large resealable plastic bag. Add the tenderloins; seal the bag and turn to coat. Refrigerate 8 hours or overnight. Cover and refrigerate remaining marinade.
**2.** Drain pork, discarding marinade in the bag. Grill tenderloins, covered, over medium heat 18-22 minutes or until a thermometer reads 145°, turning and basting occasionally with ¼ cup of reserved marinade during the last 10 minutes of grilling. Let stand 5 minutes before slicing.
**3.** Toss the carrots and zucchini with the remaining reserved marinade. Grill, covered, over medium heat 4-6 minutes on each side or until crisp-tender. Serve pork with vegetables.
**PER SERVING** *446 cal., 21 g fat (4 g sat. fat), 126 mg chol., 465 mg sodium, 17 g carb., 4 g fiber, 47 g pro.*

GRILLED PORK TENDERLOIN & VEGGIES

BLUE RIBBON BEEFY BURRITOS

# Blue Ribbon Beefy Burritos

I have a son who lives in Mexico. Whenever I make these burritos, I think of him.

**—MARINA CASTLE** CANYON COUNTRY, CA

**PREP:** 40 MIN. • **BAKE:** 15 MIN.
**MAKES:** 8 SERVINGS

- 1½ **pounds ground beef**
- 1 **bottle (8 ounces) taco sauce**
- 1 **tablespoon Worcestershire sauce**
- 1½ **teaspoons onion powder**
- 1 **teaspoon paprika**
- ½ **teaspoon garlic powder**
- ½ **teaspoon salt, divided**
- ¼ **teaspoon pepper**
  **Juice of ½ lemon**
- 1 **can (2¼ ounces) sliced ripe olives, drained, optional**
  **Oil for frying**
- ¾ **pound potatoes (about 2 medium), peeled and cut into ½-in. cubes**
- 8 **flour tortillas (10 inches), warmed**
- 4 **cups (16 ounces) shredded Mexican cheese blend**

**1.** Preheat oven to 400°. In a large skillet, cook ground beef over medium heat 8-10 minutes or until no longer pink, breaking into crumbles; drain. Stir in the taco sauce, Worcestershire sauce, onion powder, paprika, garlic powder, ¼ teaspoon salt and pepper. Add lemon juice and, if desired, olives.
**2.** In an electric skillet, heat 1 in. of oil to 375°. Working in batches, fry the potatoes 3-4 minutes or until golden brown, stirring occasionally. Remove with a slotted spoon; drain on paper towels. Sprinkle with remaining salt.

**3.** Stir the potatoes into the ground beef mixture. Place ⅔ cup mixture near the center of each flour tortilla; top with ½ cup cheese. Fold bottom and sides of the tortilla over the filling and roll up.
**4.** Wrap each burrito in foil; place on a baking sheet. Bake 15-18 minutes or until heated through.
**FREEZE OPTION** *Cool the filling before making the burritos. After wrapping the burritos in foil, freeze in a resealable plastic freezer bag. To use burritos, partially thaw overnight in the refrigerator. Reheat the foil-wrapped burritos on a baking sheet in a preheated 350° oven 25-30 minutes or until heated through. Or, to reheat one burrito, remove the foil and rewrap the burrito in paper towel; place on a microwave-safe plate. Microwave on high for 3-4 minutes or until heated through, turning once. Let stand 20 seconds.*
**PER SERVING** *682 cal., 37 g fat (17 g sat. fat), 103 mg chol., 1,166 mg sodium, 44 g carb., 7 g fiber, 34 g pro.*

# Grilled Eggplant Pita Pizzas

We grow eggplant and like to use it for a meatless pizza. Grilling is a simple way to add robust flavor to the crust, veggies and garlic. The hardest part? Waiting to pick the harvest from our garden!

**—JUDITH BARRETT** CHELSEA, AL

**PREP:** 20 MIN. + STANDING • **GRILL:** 20 MIN.
**MAKES:** 4 PIZZAS

- 2 **small eggplants**
- 1 **teaspoon salt**
- 1 **large sweet red pepper, halved and sliced**
- 1 **medium onion, halved and sliced**
- 12 **garlic cloves, halved**
- 3 **tablespoons olive oil, divided**
- ¼ **teaspoon pepper**
- 4 **whole pita breads**
- 1 **large tomato, seeded and chopped**
- ¾ **cup shredded fresh mozzarella cheese**
- ¼ **cup pitted ripe olives, coarsely chopped**
- ½ **teaspoon crushed red pepper flakes, optional**
- 1 **cup loosely packed basil leaves, coarsely chopped**

**1.** Cut eggplants into ¾-in. slices. Place in a colander over a plate; sprinkle with salt and toss. Let stand 30 minutes.
**2.** Meanwhile, in a bowl, toss the red pepper, onion and garlic with 1 tablespoon oil. Transfer to a grill wok or open grill basket; place on grill rack. Grill, uncovered, over medium-high heat 8-12 minutes or until vegetables are crisp-tender and slightly charred, stirring frequently.
**3.** Rinse and drain eggplants; blot dry with paper towels. Brush eggplants with 1 tablespoon oil; sprinkle with pepper. Grill, covered, over medium heat 4-5 minutes on each side or until tender. Cut each slice into quarters.
**4.** Brush both sides of pita breads with the remaining oil. Grill, covered, over medium-low heat 1-2 minutes or until bottoms are lightly browned. Remove from grill.
**5.** Layer the grilled sides of pitas with grilled vegetables, tomato, cheese and olives. If desired, sprinkle with pepper flakes. Return to grill; cook, covered, 3-4 minutes or until cheese is melted. Sprinkle with basil.
**PER SERVING** *428 cal., 17 g fat (5 g sat. fat), 17 mg chol., 721 mg sodium, 59 g carb., 12 g fiber, 14 g pro.*

GRILLED EGGPLANT PITA PIZZAS

SLOW COOKER RED BEANS & SAUSAGE

## Slow Cooker Red Beans & Sausage

A native of Louisiana, I love to indulge in my favorite comfort food: red beans. Putting on a nice pot of them for Sunday dinner goes back generations in my family. Dig in with some hot buttered corn bread.
—**LISA BOWIE** LAS VEGAS, NV

**PREP:** 30 MIN. • **COOK:** 8 HOURS
**MAKES:** 8 SERVINGS (2¾ QUARTS)

- 1 **pound dried red beans**
- 1 **tablespoon olive oil**
- 1 **pound fully cooked andouille sausage links, cut into ¼-inch slices**
- 1 **large onion, chopped**
- 1 **medium green pepper, chopped**
- 2 **celery ribs, finely chopped**
- 3 **teaspoons garlic powder**
- 3 **teaspoons Creole seasoning**
- 2 **teaspoons smoked paprika**
- 2 **teaspoons dried thyme**
- 1½ **teaspoons pepper**
- 6 **cups chicken broth**
  **Hot cooked rice**

**1.** Rinse and sort the beans; soak according to the package directions.
**2.** In a large skillet, heat oil over medium-high heat. Brown sausage. Remove with a slotted spoon. Add the onion, green pepper and celery to the skillet; cook and stir 5-6 minutes or until crisp-tender.

**3.** In a 5- or 6-qt. slow cooker, combine beans, sausage, vegetables and seasonings. Stir in broth. Cook, covered, on low 8-10 hours or until beans are tender.
**4.** Remove 2 cups of the bean mixture to a bowl. Mash gently with a potato masher. Return to slow cooker; heat through. Serve with rice.
**NOTE** *The following spices may be substituted for 3 teaspoons Creole seasoning: ¾ teaspoon each salt, garlic powder and paprika; and ⅛ teaspoon each ground cumin, dried thyme and cayenne pepper.*
**PER SERVING** *283 cal., 14 g fat (4 g sat. fat), 77 mg chol., 1,534 mg sodium, 43 g carb., 27 g fiber, 25 g pro.*

## Mediterranean Baked Chicken with Lemon

While visiting our daughters in Ohio, we cooked a wonderful Lebanese meal featuring this chicken. Garlic potatoes and homemade baklava completed the menu.
—**SHIRLEY GLAAB** HATTIESBURG, MS

**PREP:** 20 MIN. + MARINATING
**BAKE:** 35 MIN. • **MAKES:** 8 SERVINGS

- 1 **cup olive oil**
- ½ **cup lemon juice**
- 6 **garlic cloves, minced**
- 1 **teaspoon salt**
- 1 **teaspoon dried thyme**
- ½ **teaspoon pepper**
- ¼ **teaspoon ground allspice**
- ¼ **teaspoon ground nutmeg**
- 8 **boneless skinless chicken breast halves (6 ounces each)**
- 3 **medium lemons, thinly sliced**

**SPICE BLEND**
- 2 **teaspoons paprika**
- ½ **teaspoon garlic salt**
- ½ **teaspoon lemon-pepper seasoning**
- ¼ **teaspoon ground allspice**
- ⅛ **teaspoon ground cinnamon**

**1.** In a small bowl, whisk the first eight ingredients until blended. Pour 1 cup marinade into a large resealable plastic bag. Add chicken; seal bag and turn to coat. Refrigerate 1 hour. Cover and refrigerate remaining marinade.
**2.** Preheat oven to 350°. Arrange the lemon slices in two greased 11x7-in. baking dishes. Drain the chicken, discarding the marinade in bag. Place chicken over lemon slices. Mix spice blend ingredients; sprinkle over the chicken. Drizzle with the reserved marinade. Bake, covered, 35-40 minutes or until a thermometer reads 165°.
**PER SERVING** *385 cal., 26 g fat (4 g sat. fat), 94 mg chol., 469 mg sodium, 4 g carb., 1 g fiber, 34 g pro.*

MEDITERRANEAN BAKED CHICKEN WITH LEMON

**ZUCCHINI & CHEESE DROP BISCUITS**
*PAGE 82*

# Breads, Rolls & Muffins

When the **heavenly aroma** wafts from the oven as these golden loaves, buns and other goodies bake, you know you're in for a treat. Then the time comes for a taste, and it's **sheer bliss!**

**BREAD MACHINE DINNER ROLLS** *PAGE 81*

**LEMON BLUEBERRY BISCUITS** *PAGE 83*

**CRANBERRY SWIRL LOAF** *PAGE 87*

## Cream Cheese Bran Muffins

Bran muffins become indulgent when you add a rich cream cheese center. There's no need to slather on butter!

**—JEANNETTE MACK** RUSHVILLE, NY

**PREP:** 15 MIN. + STANDING • **BAKE:** 20 MIN.
**MAKES:** 1 DOZEN

- 1 cup All-Bran
- ½ cup 2% milk
- 1 cup (8 ounces) sour cream
- 1 egg, lightly beaten
- 1 package (16.6 ounces) date quick bread mix
- 1 package (3 ounces) cream cheese

**1.** In a large bowl, combine cereal and milk; let stand for 10 minutes. Stir in sour cream and egg. Stir in bread mix just until moistened.

**2.** Fill greased or paper-lined muffin cups about three-fourths full. Cut cream cheese into 12 cubes; gently press one cube into the center of each muffin cup just until covered with batter (cups will be full).

**3.** Bake at 400° for 18-20 minutes or until a toothpick inserted near the center comes out clean. Cool for 5 minutes before removing from pan to a wire rack. Serve warm. Refrigerate leftovers.

**PER SERVING** *241 cal., 8 g fat (4 g sat. fat), 40 mg chol., 201 mg sodium, 37 g carb., 3 g fiber, 5 g pro.*

ITALIAN TOMATO ROLLS

CREAM CHEESE BRAN MUFFINS

## Italian Tomato Rolls

Friends and family are always surprised when I tell them these tender, chewy rolls are made with pizza sauce. For even more flavor, I mix in a little dried basil.

**—MARGARET PETERSON** FOREST CITY, IA

**PREP:** 30 MIN. + RISING • **BAKE:** 10 MIN.
**MAKES:** 15 ROLLS

- 1 package (¼ ounce) active dry yeast
- 1 teaspoon plus 2 tablespoons sugar, divided
- ¼ cup warm water (110° to 115°)
- 1 cup pizza sauce
- ¼ cup plus 2 tablespoons butter, melted, divided
- 1 egg
- 1 teaspoon salt
- ¾ teaspoon dried basil
- 3 to 4 cups all-purpose flour

**1.** In a large bowl, dissolve the yeast and 1 teaspoon sugar in warm water; let stand for 5 minutes. Add the pizza sauce, ¼ cup butter, egg, salt, basil, 2 cups flour and remaining sugar; beat until smooth. Stir in enough remaining flour to form a firm dough.

**2.** Turn dough onto a floured surface. Knead until smooth and elastic, about 6-8 minutes. Place in a greased bowl, turning once to grease top. Cover and let rise in a warm place until doubled, about 1½ hours.

**3.** Punch dough down. Turn onto a lightly floured surface; divide into 15 pieces. Shape each into a 2-in. ball. Place 2 in. apart on greased baking sheets. Cover and let rise until doubled, about 30 minutes.

**4.** Bake at 400° for 10-12 minutes or until golden brown. Remove from the pans to wire racks. Brush with the remaining butter.

**PER SERVING** *150 cal., 5 g fat (3 g sat. fat), 26 mg chol., 240 mg sodium, 22 g carb., 1 g fiber, 4 g pro.* **Diabetic Exchanges:** *1½ starch, 1 fat.*

## Did you know?

Yeast is a microorganism that becomes activated when combined with warm water and sugar. It produces carbon dioxide gas, which helps give bread its light, airy texture.

# Lemon Meringue Muffins

Lemon meringue pie is one of my favorite desserts, so I couldn't wait to try these.

—**NANCY KEARNEY** MASSILLON, OH

**PREP:** 25 MIN. • **BAKE:** 25 MIN.
**MAKES:** 1 DOZEN

- 6 **tablespoons butter, softened**
- 1 **cup sugar, divided**
- 2 **eggs**
- ½ **cup plain yogurt**
- 2 **tablespoons lemon juice**
- 1 **tablespoon grated lemon peel**
- ¼ **teaspoon lemon extract**
- 1⅓ **cups all-purpose flour**
- ½ **teaspoon baking powder**
- ½ **teaspoon baking soda**
- 2 **egg whites**

**1.** Preheat oven to 350°. In a large bowl, cream butter and ⅔ cup sugar until light and fluffy. Add eggs, one at a time, beating well after each addition. Beat in yogurt, juice, peel and extract.

**2.** In another bowl, whisk the flour, baking powder and baking soda. Add to the creamed mixture; stir just until moistened. Fill greased or paper-lined muffin cups three-fourths full. Bake 17-19 minutes or until a toothpick inserted in the center comes out clean. Remove from the oven. Increase oven setting to 400°.

**3.** Meanwhile, in a small bowl, beat egg whites on medium speed until soft peaks form. Gradually add remaining sugar, 1 tablespoon at a time, beating on high after each addition until sugar is dissolved. Continue beating until stiff glossy peaks form.

**4.** Spread or pipe the meringue onto the muffins. Bake 6-8 minutes longer or until meringue is golden brown.

**5.** Cool 5 minutes before removing from pan to a wire rack. Serve warm. Refrigerate leftovers.

**PER SERVING** *188 cal., 7 g fat (4 g sat. fat), 52 mg chol., 135 mg sodium, 28 g carb., trace fiber, 4 g pro.* **Diabetic Exchanges:** *2 starch, 1 fat.*

DILL AND CHIVE BREAD

# Dill and Chive Bread

A chive and onion spread is such an easy way to give plain dough a boost. I like to let my bread machine do most of the work, and then I enjoy the results!

—**DAWN HIGGS** EAST MOLINE, IL

**PREP:** 15 MIN. • **BAKE:** 3 HOURS
**MAKES:** 1 LOAF (16 SLICES)

- ¾ **cup water (70° to 80°)**
- ½ **cup spreadable chive and onion cream cheese**
- 2 **tablespoons sugar**
- 2 **teaspoons dill weed**
- 1¼ **teaspoons salt**
- 3 **cups all-purpose flour**
- 1 **package (¼ ounce) active dry yeast**

In bread machine pan, place all ingredients in the order suggested by the manufacturer. Select the basic bread setting. Choose crust color and loaf size if available. Bake according to the bread machine directions (check the dough after 5 minutes of mixing; add 1 to 2 tablespoons of water or flour if needed).

**PER SERVING** *121 cal., 3 g fat (2 g sat. fat), 8 mg chol., 219 mg sodium, 20 g carb., 1 g fiber, 3 g pro.* **Diabetic Exchanges:** *1 starch, ½ fat.*

LEMON MERINGUE MUFFINS

CHEDDAR CHEESE
BATTER BREAD

## Cheddar Cheese Batter Bread

As a dairy farmer, I like to promote our products whenever I can. This cheddar-filled loaf was a winner at our state fair.

—JEANNE KEMPER BAGDAD, KY

**PREP:** 30 MIN. + RISING • **BAKE:** 25 MIN. + COOLING
**MAKES:** 2 LOAVES (16 SLICES EACH)

- 2 packages (¼ ounce each) active dry yeast
- ¾ cup warm water (110° to 115°)
- 3 cups (12 ounces) shredded cheddar cheese
- ¾ cup shredded Parmesan cheese
- 2 cups warm 2% milk (110° to 115°)
- 3 tablespoons sugar
- 1 tablespoon butter, melted
- 2 teaspoons salt
- 6 to 6½ cups all-purpose flour
- 1 egg white, beaten
- 1 tablespoon water

**TOPPING**
- ½ cup finely shredded cheddar cheese
- 1 garlic clove, minced
- ½ teaspoon sesame seeds
- ½ teaspoon poppy seeds
- ½ teaspoon paprika
- ¼ teaspoon celery seed

**1.** In a large bowl, dissolve the yeast in warm water. Add cheeses, milk, sugar, butter, salt and 3 cups flour. Beat on medium speed for 3 minutes. Stir in enough remaining flour to form a firm dough.
**2.** Do not knead. Cover and let rise in a warm place until doubled, about 1½ hours.
**3.** Stir dough down; transfer to two greased 9x5-in. loaf pans. Cover and let rise until doubled, about 30 minutes.
**4.** Preheat oven to 375°. In a small bowl, combine egg white and water. In another bowl, combine topping ingredients. Brush loaves with egg white mixture; sprinkle with topping. Bake 25-30 minutes or until golden brown. Remove from pans to wire racks to cool.
**PER SERVING** *155 cal., 5 g fat (3 g sat. fat), 17 mg chol., 266 mg sodium, 21 g carb., 1 g fiber, 7 g pro.* **Diabetic Exchanges:** *1½ starch, 1 fat.*

## Banana Mocha-Chip Muffins

**PREP:** 20 MIN. • **BAKE:** 20 MIN. • **MAKES:** 2 DOZEN

- 5 teaspoons instant coffee granules
- 5 teaspoons hot water
- ¾ cup butter, softened
- 1¼ cups sugar
- 1 egg
- 1⅓ cups mashed ripe bananas
- 1 teaspoon vanilla extract
- 2¼ cups all-purpose flour
- 1½ teaspoons baking powder
- ½ teaspoon baking soda
- ½ teaspoon salt
- 1½ cups semisweet chocolate chips

**1.** In a small bowl, dissolve the coffee granules in hot water. In a large bowl, cream butter and sugar until light and fluffy. Add egg; beat well. Beat in the bananas, vanilla and coffee mixture. Combine the flour, baking powder, baking soda and salt; add to creamed mixture just until moistened. Fold in chocolate chips.
**2.** Fill paper-lined muffin cups two-thirds full. Bake at 350° for 18-20 minutes or until a toothpick inserted in muffin comes out clean. Cool for 5 minutes before removing from pans to wire racks. Serve warm.
**PER SERVING** *198 cal., 9 g fat (6 g sat. fat), 24 mg chol., 145 mg sodium, 29 g carb., 1 g fiber, 2 g pro.*

BANANA MOCHA-CHIP
MUFFINS

Banana Mocha-Chip Muffins boast two of my favorites—chocolate and java. The fruit's a bonus!
—MELISSA WILLIAMS TAYLORVILLE, IL

SOUTHWESTERN CORN BREAD

## Southwestern Corn Bread

I put a Tex-Mex twist on my grandma's corn bread. The flavored butter is an added treat and keeps in the fridge for about a week.

—**ELIZABETH CHARPIOT** SANTA ROSA, CA

**PREP:** 20 MIN. • **BAKE:** 25 MIN.
**MAKES:** 15 SERVINGS (½ CUP BUTTER)

- 2 cups all-purpose flour
- 2 cups yellow cornmeal
- ½ cup sugar
- 4 teaspoons baking powder
- 1 teaspoon baking soda
- 1 teaspoon salt
- 1 teaspoon dried minced garlic
- 1 teaspoon dried minced onion
- 1 teaspoon paprika
- 1 teaspoon chili powder
- 2 cups buttermilk
- ½ cup canola oil
- 2 eggs
- 1 jar (7 ounces) roasted sweet red peppers, drained, patted dry and chopped
- 1 cup frozen corn, thawed
- ¼ cup minced chives

**CHILI HONEY-LIME BUTTER**
- ½ cup butter, softened
- 1 tablespoon lime juice
- 1 tablespoon honey
- 1 teaspoon chili powder
- 1 teaspoon grated lime peel

**1.** In a large bowl, combine the first 10 ingredients. In a small bowl, whisk the buttermilk, oil and eggs. Stir into dry ingredients just until moistened. Fold in the red peppers, corn and chives.

**2.** Transfer to a greased 13-in. x 9-in. baking dish. Bake at 400° for 23-28 minutes or until a toothpick inserted near the center comes out clean. Remove to a wire rack.

**3.** In a small bowl, combine the butter, lime juice, honey, chili powder and lime peel. Serve with warm corn bread.

**PER SERVING** *317 cal., 15 g fat (5 g sat. fat), 46 mg chol., 488 mg sodium, 40 g carb., 2 g fiber, 6 g pro.*

## Bread Machine Dinner Rolls

Ever since my dad tried one of these dinner rolls, he's raved about them. He even offers samples to family and friends!

—**REBECAH LYTLE** OCALA, FL

**PREP:** 25 MIN. + RISING • **BAKE:** 10 MIN. • **MAKES:** 2 DOZEN

- 1 cup water (70° to 80°)
- ¼ cup butter, cubed
- 1 egg
- 1¼ teaspoons salt
- 3¼ cups bread flour
- ¼ cup sugar
- 3 tablespoons nonfat dry milk powder
- 1 package (¼ ounce) quick-rise yeast

**EGG WASH**
- 1 egg
- 4 teaspoons water

**1.** In bread machine pan, place the first eight ingredients in the order suggested by manufacturer. Select dough setting. Check dough after 5 minutes of mixing; add 1-2 tablespoons water or flour if needed.

**2.** When the cycle is completed, turn dough onto a lightly floured surface. Divide and shape into 24 balls. Roll each into an 8-in. rope; tie into a loose knot. Tuck ends under.

**3.** Place 1½ in. apart on greased baking sheets. Cover with a kitchen towel; let rise in a warm place until doubled, about 30 minutes. Preheat oven to 400°.

**4.** For egg wash, in a small bowl, whisk egg and water; brush over rolls. Bake 8-9 minutes or until golden brown. Remove from pans to wire racks; serve warm.

**NOTE** *We recommend you do not use a bread machine's time-delay feature for this recipe.*

**PER SERVING** *98 cal., 2 g fat (1 g sat. fat), 14 mg chol., 147 mg sodium, 16 g carb., 1 g fiber, 3 g pro.*

BREAD MACHINE DINNER ROLLS

# Best-Loved Biscuits

Who can resist the flaky, buttery goodness of homemade biscuits? Treat family and friends to any of the delightful variations here.

## Flaky Cheddar-Chive Biscuits

Yes, you *do* have time to bake! These fresh-from-the oven treats are ready to serve in less than half an hour.

—**BETSY KING** DULUTH, MN

**START TO FINISH:** 25 MIN. • **MAKES:** 10 BISCUITS

- 2¼ cups all-purpose flour
- 2½ teaspoons baking powder
- 2 teaspoons sugar
- ½ teaspoon baking soda
- ½ teaspoon salt
- ½ cup cold butter, cubed
- 1 cup (4 ounces) shredded cheddar cheese
- 3 tablespoons minced fresh chives
- 1 cup buttermilk

**1.** Preheat oven to 425°. In a large bowl, whisk the first five ingredients. Cut in butter until mixture resembles coarse crumbs; stir in cheese and chives. Add buttermilk; stir just until moistened. Turn onto a lightly floured surface; knead gently 8-10 times.

**2.** Pat or roll dough to ¾-in. thickness; cut with a floured 2½-in. biscuit cutter. Place 2 in. apart on a greased baking sheet. Bake 10-12 minutes or until golden brown. Serve warm.

**PER SERVING** *236 cal., 13 g fat (8 g sat. fat), 37 mg chol., 440 mg sodium, 24 g carb., 1 g fiber, 6 g pro.*

ZUCCHINI & CHEESE DROP BISCUITS

## Zucchini & Cheese Drop Biscuits

Put homegrown zucchini to scrumptious use in golden brown goodies. Three kinds of cheese, bits of sun-dried tomatoes and flecks of basil add even more flavor and appeal.

—**KEITH MESCH** MT. HEALTHY, OH

**PREP:** 25 MIN. + STANDING • **BAKE:** 25 MIN. • **MAKES:** 1 DOZEN

- ¾ cup shredded zucchini
- 1¼ teaspoons salt, divided
- 2½ cups all-purpose flour
- 1 tablespoon baking powder
- ½ cup cold butter, cubed
- ½ cup shredded cheddar cheese
- ¼ cup shredded part-skim mozzarella cheese
- ¼ cup shredded Parmesan cheese
- 2 tablespoons finely chopped oil-packed sun-dried tomatoes, patted dry
- 2 tablespoons minced fresh basil or 2 teaspoons dried basil
- 1 cup 2% milk

**1.** Preheat oven to 425°. Place the zucchini in a colander over a plate; sprinkle with ¼ teaspoon salt and toss. Let stand 10 minutes. Rinse and drain well. Squeeze zucchini to remove excess liquid. Pat dry.

**2.** In a large bowl, whisk the flour, baking powder and remaining salt. Cut in the butter until mixture resembles coarse crumbs. Stir in zucchini, cheeses, tomatoes and basil. Add milk; stir just until moistened.

**3.** Drop by ⅓ cupfuls into a greased 13x9-in. baking pan. Bake 22-26 minutes or until golden brown. Serve warm.

**PER SERVING** *205 cal., 11 g fat (7 g sat. fat), 29 mg chol., 482 mg sodium, 22 g carb., 1 g fiber, 6 g pro.*

FLAKY CHEDDAR-CHIVE BISCUITS

## Lemon Blueberry Biscuits

Here's a recipe featuring the wonderful combination of lemon and blueberries. You won't want to skip the yummy glaze on top!
—*TASTE OF HOME* TEST KITCHEN

**PREP:** 30 MIN. • **BAKE:** 15 MIN. • **MAKES:** 1 DOZEN

- 2 **cups all-purpose flour**
- ½ **cup sugar**
- 2 **teaspoons baking powder**
- ½ **teaspoon baking soda**
- ¼ **teaspoon salt**
- 1 **cup (8 ounces) lemon yogurt**
- 1 **egg**
- ¼ **cup butter, melted**
- 1 **teaspoon grated lemon peel**
- 1 **cup fresh or frozen blueberries**

**GLAZE**
- ½ **cup confectioners' sugar**
- 1 **tablespoon lemon juice**
- ½ **teaspoon grated lemon peel**

**1.** Preheat oven to 400°. In a large bowl, whisk the first five ingredients. In another bowl, whisk the yogurt, egg, melted butter and lemon peel until blended. Add to flour mixture; stir just until moistened. Fold in blueberries.

**2.** Drop by ⅓ cupfuls 1 in. apart onto a greased baking sheet. Bake 15-18 minutes or until light brown.

**3.** In a small bowl, combine the glaze ingredients; stir until smooth. Drizzle over warm biscuits.

**NOTE** *If using frozen blueberries, use without thawing to avoid discoloring the dough.*

**PER SERVING** *193 cal., 5 g fat (3 g sat. fat), 29 mg chol., 223 mg sodium, 35 g carb., 1 g fiber, 4 g pro.*

BUTTERMILK ANGEL BISCUITS

## Buttermilk Angel Biscuits

These slightly sweet favorites are great with jam in the morning. After cutting out the dough, I fold over one side of each circle about a third of the way for a more traditional look.
—**CAROL HOLLADAY** DANVILLE, AL

**PREP:** 30 MIN. + STANDING • **BAKE:** 10 MIN. • **MAKES:** 2 DOZEN

- 2 **packages (¼ ounce each) active dry yeast**
- ¼ **cup warm water (110° to 115°)**
- 5¼ to 5½ **cups self-rising flour**
- ⅓ **cup sugar**
- 1 **teaspoon baking soda**
- 1 **cup shortening**
- 1¾ **cups buttermilk**

**1.** In a small bowl, dissolve yeast in warm water. In a large bowl, whisk 5¼ cups flour, sugar and baking soda. Cut in shortening until mixture resembles coarse crumbs. Stir in buttermilk and yeast mixture to form a soft dough (dough will be sticky).

**2.** Turn onto a floured surface; knead gently 8-10 times, adding additional flour if needed. Roll the dough to ¾-in. thickness; cut with a floured 2½-in. biscuit cutter. Place 2 in. apart on greased baking sheets. Let stand at room temperature 20 minutes. Preheat oven to 450°.

**3.** Bake 8-12 minutes or until golden brown. Serve warm.

**PER SERVING** *180 cal., 8 g fat (2 g sat. fat), 1 mg chol., 386 mg sodium, 23 g carb., 1 g fiber, 3 g pro.*

LEMON BLUEBERRY BISCUITS

**top tip**

## Reduce Rolling

To save time, I pat or roll biscuit dough into a rectangle and cut out square biscuits with a pizza cutter. Because there are no little leftover pieces, the dough needs to be rolled out only once.
—**KONNIE L.** GROVE, OK

STREUSEL-TOPPED PLUM MUFFINS

I made Streusel-Topped Plum Muffins by adapting a recipe that called for cherries. My husband and I loved the change and used the homegrown fruit from our farm.
—**BETTY TIMMRECK** EAU CLAIRE, WI

## Streusel-Topped Plum Muffins

**PREP:** 25 MIN. • **BAKE:** 20 MIN.
**MAKES:** 15 MUFFINS.

- ½ cup butter, softened
- 1 cup sugar
- 2 eggs
- 1 teaspoon almond extract
- ½ teaspoon vanilla extract
- 2 cups all-purpose flour
- 2 teaspoons baking powder
- ½ teaspoon salt
- ½ cup heavy whipping cream
- 1½ cups chopped fresh plums

**TOPPING**

- 3 tablespoons brown sugar
- 2 tablespoons all-purpose flour
- 1 teaspoon ground cinnamon
- 1 tablespoon cold butter
- ⅓ cup chopped walnuts
- 1 tablespoon coarse sugar

**1.** In a large bowl, cream butter and sugar until light and fluffy. Add eggs, one at a time, beating well after each addition. Beat in extracts. Combine flour, baking powder and salt; add to the creamed mixture alternately with heavy whipping cream. Fold in plums. Fill greased or paper-lined muffin cups three-fourths full.

**2.** For the topping, in a small bowl, combine the brown sugar, flour and cinnamon; cut in butter until crumbly. Stir in walnuts. Sprinkle over batter; sprinkle with coarse sugar.

**3.** Bake at 350° for 20-25 minutes or until a toothpick inserted near center comes out clean. Cool for 5 minutes before removing from the pans to wire racks. Serve warm.

**PER SERVING** *255 cal., 12 g fat (6 g sat. fat), 57 mg chol., 194 mg sodium, 33 g carb., 1 g fiber, 4 g pro.*

## Great Garlic Bread

Here's an ever-popular side for so many different entrees. And it's a cinch to fix with just a handful of ingredients.
—*TASTE OF HOME* **TEST KITCHEN**

**START TO FINISH:** 15 MIN.
**MAKES:** 8 SERVINGS

- ½ cup butter, melted
- ¼ cup grated Romano cheese
- 4 garlic cloves, minced
- 1 loaf (1 pound) French bread, halved lengthwise
- 2 tablespoons minced fresh parsley

**1.** Preheat oven to 350°. In a small bowl, mix the butter, cheese and garlic; brush over the cut sides of bread. Place on a baking sheet, cut side up. Sprinkle with parsley.

**2.** Bake 7-9 minutes or until light golden brown. Cut bread into slices; serve warm.

**PER SERVING** *283 cal., 14 g fat (8 g sat. fat), 34 mg chol., 457 mg sodium, 33 g carb., 1 g fiber, 8 g pro.*

## Pumpkin Swirl Bread

This spiced loaf dotted with nuts, raisins and dates has a luscious surprise—a rich, creamy filling. It's like a layer of cheesecake inside each slice of pumpkin bread! Invite friends or neighbors over during fall for a yummy slice and a cup of coffee.

—**CINDY MAY** TROY, MI

**PREP:** 15 MIN. • **BAKE:** 65 MIN. + COOLING
**MAKES:** 3 LOAVES (16 SLICES EACH)

**FILLING**

- 2 packages (8 ounces each) cream cheese, softened
- ¼ cup sugar
- 1 egg
- 1 tablespoon milk

**BREAD**

- 3 cups sugar
- 1 can (15 ounces) solid-pack pumpkin
- 4 eggs
- 1 cup canola oil
- 1 cup water
- 4 cups all-purpose flour
- 4 teaspoons pumpkin pie spice
- 2 teaspoons baking soda
- 1½ teaspoons ground cinnamon
- 1 teaspoon salt
- 1 teaspoon baking powder
- 1 teaspoon ground nutmeg
- ½ teaspoon ground cloves
- 1 cup chopped walnuts
- 1 cup raisins
- ½ cup chopped dates

**OPTIONAL TOPPINGS**

- 1 cup confectioners' sugar
- ¼ teaspoon vanilla extract
- 2 to 3 tablespoons 2% milk
  Additional chopped walnuts

**1.** Preheat oven to 350°. Grease and flour three 8x4-in. loaf pans. In a small bowl, beat the filling ingredients until smooth.

**2.** In a large bowl, beat the sugar, pumpkin, eggs, oil and water until well blended. In another bowl, whisk flour, pie spice, baking soda, cinnamon, salt, baking powder, nutmeg and cloves; gradually beat into pumpkin mixture. Stir in walnuts, raisins and dates.

**3.** Pour half of the batter into the prepared pans, dividing evenly. Spoon the filling over the batter. Cover filling completely with remaining batter.

**4.** Bake 65-70 minutes or until a toothpick inserted in bread portion comes out clean. Cool 10 minutes before removing from pans to wire racks to cool completely. Wrap in foil; refrigerate until serving.

**5.** Just before serving, if desired, in a small bowl, mix confectioners' sugar, vanilla and enough milk to reach a drizzling consistency. Drizzle over bread; sprinkle with walnuts.

**PER SERVING** *189 cal., 8 g fat (2 g sat. fat), 27 mg chol., 132 mg sodium, 27 g carb., 1 g fiber, 3 g pro.*

PUMPKIN SWIRL BREAD

CANDY CANE
CHOCOLATE LOAVES

## Candy Cane Chocolate Loaves

Having a bunch of leftover candy canes after the holidays inspired me to use them for a chocolaty bread. Peppermint extract and a splash of coffee intensify the flavor.
—**SHELLY PLATTEN** AMHERST, WI

**PREP:** 25 MIN. • **BAKE:** 50 MIN. + COOLING
**MAKES:** 3 LOAVES (12 SLICES EACH)

- ¼ cup butter, softened
- 1⅔ cups packed brown sugar
- 4 egg whites
- 2 eggs
- ¾ cup strong brewed coffee
- ½ cup vanilla yogurt
- ¼ cup canola oil
- 1 tablespoon vanilla extract
- ¼ teaspoon peppermint extract
- 3½ cups all-purpose flour
- ¾ cup baking cocoa
- 1½ teaspoons baking soda
- ½ teaspoon salt
- 1½ cups buttermilk
- 1 cup (6 ounces) miniature semisweet chocolate chips

**TOPPING**
- 2 ounces white baking chocolate, melted
- 3 tablespoons crushed candy canes

**1.** Preheat oven to 350°. Coat three 8x4-in. loaf pans with cooking spray. In a large bowl, beat butter and brown sugar until crumbly, about 2 minutes. Add egg whites, eggs, coffee, yogurt, oil and extracts until blended.

**2.** In another bowl, whisk the flour, cocoa, baking soda and salt; add to the brown sugar mixture alternately with buttermilk, beating well after each addition. Fold in chocolate chips.

**3.** Transfer to prepared pans. Bake 50-55 minutes or until a toothpick inserted in center comes out clean. Cool 10 minutes before removing from pans to wire racks to cool completely.

**4.** Drizzle the melted white baking chocolate over the loaves. Sprinkle with crushed candies.

**PER SERVING** *162 cal., 5 g fat (2 g sat. fat), 16 mg chol., 124 mg sodium, 26 g carb., 1 g fiber, 3 g pro.* **Diabetic Exchanges:** *1½ starch, 1 fat.*

## Pumpkin Oat Muffins

It just doesn't seem like Thanksgiving or Christmas in our house until everyone's favorite pumpkin muffins are on the table.
—**CAROL HALE** SARVER, PA

**PREP:** 15 MIN. • **BAKE:** 20 MIN.
**MAKES:** 1 DOZEN

- 1 cup all-purpose flour
- ½ cup packed brown sugar
- 2 teaspoons baking powder
- 1 teaspoon pumpkin pie spice
- ½ teaspoon salt
- ¼ teaspoon baking soda
- 1 egg, lightly beaten
- ¾ cup canned pumpkin
- ¼ cup milk
- ¼ cup canola oil
- 1 cup old-fashioned oats
- ½ cup raisins

**TOPPING**
- ⅓ cup packed brown sugar
- 1 tablespoon all-purpose flour
- ¾ teaspoon pumpkin pie spice
- 1 tablespoon cold butter

**1.** In a large bowl, combine the first six ingredients. Combine egg, pumpkin, milk and oil; add to the dry ingredients just until moistened. Stir in the oats and raisins.

**2.** Fill greased or paper-lined muffin cups two-thirds full. In a small bowl, combine the brown sugar, flour and pumpkin pie spice; cut in the butter until crumbly. Sprinkle 1 rounded teaspoonful over each muffin. Bake at 375° for 15-20 minutes or until a toothpick comes out clean.

**3.** Cool muffins for 5 minutes before removing from the pan to a wire rack. Serve warm.

**PER SERVING** *204 cal., 7 g fat (2 g sat. fat), 21 mg chol., 214 mg sodium, 34 g carb., 2 g fiber, 3 g pro.*

(5)INGREDIENTS FAST FIX ▶

## Hazelnut Crescent Rolls

Yum! These tender crescents are stuffed with Nutella and toffee bits, then dusted with confectioners' sugar. It's a quick and easy way to treat family and friends.
—**PHYLLIS ADKINS** SOUTH CHARLESTON, WV

**START TO FINISH:** 25 MIN.
**MAKES:** 8 SERVINGS

- 1 tube (8 ounces) refrigerated crescent rolls
- ½ cup Nutella, warmed
- ⅓ cup chocolate-covered English toffee bits
- Confectioners' sugar

**1.** Unroll the crescent roll dough; separate into triangles. Spread each with 1 tablespoon Nutella; sprinkle with toffee bits. Roll up from the wide end and place pointed side down 2 in. apart on greased baking sheets. Curve ends to form crescents.

**2.** Bake at 375° for 11-13 minutes or until lightly browned. Dust rolls with confectioners' sugar.

**PER SERVING** *250 cal., 14 g fat (4 g sat. fat), 7 mg chol., 270 mg sodium, 27 g carb., 1 g fiber, 3 g pro.*

HAZELNUT CRESCENT ROLLS

CRANBERRY SWIRL LOAF

## Cranberry Swirl Loaf

My mother has made this loaf for years, but she uses date filling. I came up with my own using cranberries for a slightly tart contrast to the sweet streusel topping. Each slice reveals a bright red swirl that proves impossible to resist.

—**DARLENE BRENDEN** SALEM, OR

**PREP:** 30 MIN. + RISING
**BAKE:** 40 MIN. + COOLING
**MAKES:** 1 LOAF (16 SLICES)

- ⅓ cup sugar
- 1 package (¼ ounce) quick-rise yeast
- ½ teaspoon salt
- 3 to 3½ cups all-purpose flour
- ½ cup water
- ½ cup milk
- ⅓ cup butter, cubed

**FILLING**
- 1 cup chopped fresh or frozen cranberries
- ¼ cup packed brown sugar
- ¼ cup water
- 1 tablespoon butter
- 1 tablespoon lemon juice
- ½ cup chopped walnuts, optional

**TOPPING**
- 2 tablespoons all-purpose flour
- 2 tablespoons sugar
- 2 tablespoons cold butter, divided

**1.** In a large bowl, mix the sugar, yeast, salt and 1 cup flour. In a small saucepan, heat water, milk and butter to 120°-130°. Add to dry ingredients; beat on medium speed 2 minutes. Stir in enough remaining flour to form a soft dough.

**2.** Turn the dough onto a floured surface; knead until smooth and elastic, about 6-8 minutes. Place in a greased bowl, turning once to grease the top. Cover with plastic wrap and let rise in a warm place until doubled, about 1 hour.

**3.** Meanwhile, in a small saucepan, combine the cranberries, brown sugar and water. Cook over medium heat until the cranberries are soft, about 15 minutes. Remove from heat; stir in the butter, lemon juice and, if desired, walnuts. Cool.

**4.** Punch the down dough. Turn onto a lightly floured surface; roll into a 20x10-in. rectangle. Spread the filling to within ½ in. of the edges. Roll up jelly-roll style, starting with a long side; pinch the seam to seal. Transfer to a greased 9x5-in. loaf pan, arranging in a slight zigzag fashion to fit.

**5.** For the topping, in a small bowl, combine the flour and sugar; cut in 1 tablespoon butter until crumbly. Melt remaining butter; brush over dough. Sprinkle with crumb mixture. Cover with a towel; let rise in a warm place until doubled, about 40 minutes. Preheat oven to 350°.

**6.** Bake 40-45 minutes or until golden brown. Carefully remove from pan to a wire rack to cool.

**CONFECTIONERS' SUGAR ICING**
*Mix ¾ cup confectioners' sugar and 1 tablespoon milk. Drizzle over the cooled bread.*

**CRANBERRY-CARAMEL ICING**
*Combine 1½ cups cranberry juice and a cinnamon stick in a small saucepan; bring to a boil. Cook until the liquid is reduced to ½ cup. Reduce heat; remove cinnamon stick. Whisk in 1 cup Kraft caramel bits, ½ cup at a time, until melted. Remove from heat and stir in 1 tablespoon heavy whipping cream; cool. Drizzle over cooled bread.*

**PER SERVING** *210 cal., 9 g fat (4 g sat. fat), 17 mg chol., 140 mg sodium, 30 g carb., 1 g fiber, 4 g pro.*

FAST FIX ▶
## Parmesan Onion Wedges
I serve my cheesy wedges with spaghetti. They're good with soup and salad, too.

—**DIANE HIXON** NICEVILLE, FL

**START TO FINISH:** 30 MIN.
**MAKES:** 8 SERVINGS

- 2 cups biscuit/baking mix
- ⅔ cup milk
- ½ cup grated Parmesan cheese
- 1 small onion, chopped
- ½ cup mayonnaise
- 1 teaspoon Italian seasoning

**1.** In a small bowl, stir the biscuit mix and milk just until moistened. Turn onto a floured surface; gently knead 6-8 times. Roll out to an 11-in. circle; transfer to a greased 12-in. pizza pan. Build up edges slightly.

**2.** Combine the Parmesan cheese, onion and mayonnaise; spread over dough. Sprinkle with Italian seasoning.

**3.** Bake at 400° for 15-20 minutes or until golden brown. Cut into wedges; serve warm. Refrigerate leftovers.

**PER SERVING** *1 slice equals 259 cal., 17 g fat (4 g sat. fat), 11 mg chol., 532 mg sodium, 22 g carb., 1 g fiber, 5 g pro.*

PARMESAN ONION WEDGES

**LIME & GIN COCONUT MACAROONS**
*PAGE 91*

# Cookies, Bars & Candies

Fill your cookie jar, holiday tray or gift tin with the **delightful bites** in this chapter. After trying just one of these sweet-as-can-be treats, your family and friends will **find them irresistible!**

**AUTUMN LEAF CUTOUTS**
*PAGE 92*

**GLAZED APPLE-MAPLE BLONDIES** *PAGE 97*

**CARDAMOM-BLACKBERRY LINZER COOKIES** *PAGE 99*

# Pecan Pie Thumbprints

If you like traditional pecan pie, you're sure to love these buttery thumbprints!

**—PEGGY KEY** GRANT, AL

**PREP:** 30 MIN. + CHILLING
**BAKE:** 10 MIN./BATCH • **MAKES:** 4½ DOZEN

- **1 cup butter, softened**
- **½ cup sugar**
- **2 eggs, separated**
- **½ cup dark corn syrup**
- **2½ cups all-purpose flour**

**FILLING**
- **¼ cup plus 2 tablespoons confectioners' sugar**
- **3 tablespoons butter**
- **2 tablespoons dark corn syrup**
- **¼ cup plus 2 tablespoons finely chopped pecans**

**1.** In a large bowl, cream butter and sugar until light and fluffy. Beat in egg yolks and dark corn syrup. Gradually beat in the flour. Refrigerate, covered, 30 minutes or until firm enough to roll.

**2.** For the pecan filling, in a small saucepan, combine the confectioners' sugar, butter and dark corn syrup. Bring to a boil over medium heat, stirring occasionally. Remove from the heat; stir in the pecans. Remove from the pan; refrigerate 30 minutes or until cold.

**3.** Preheat oven to 375°. Shape the dough into 1-in. balls; place 2 in. apart on parchment paper-lined baking sheets. In a small bowl, whisk the egg whites; brush over tops.

**4.** Bake 5 minutes. Remove from the oven. Gently press an indentation into the center of each cookie using the end of a wooden spoon handle. Fill each indentation with a scant ½ teaspoon pecan filling. Bake 4-5 minutes longer or until edges are light brown.

**5.** Cool on pans 5 minutes. Remove to wire racks to cool.

**PER SERVING** *86 cal., 5 g fat (3 g sat. fat), 18 mg chol., 37 mg sodium, 10 g carb., trace fiber, 1 g pro.*

COCONUT CREME
CHOCOLATES

**⑤INGREDIENTS**

# Coconut Creme Chocolates

My marshmallow-filled chocolate candy is a fun way to treat our kids and grandkids.

**—DOLORES WILDER** TEXAS CITY, TX

**PREP:** 15 MIN. + CHILLING
**MAKES:** 2½ DOZEN

- **1 jar (7 ounces) marshmallow creme**
- **2⅔ cups flaked coconut, toasted**
- **1 teaspoon vanilla extract**
- **Dash salt**
- **1 milk chocolate candy bar (5 ounces), chopped**
- **1½ teaspoons shortening**

**1.** In a large bowl, mix marshmallow creme, coconut, vanilla and salt until blended. Refrigerate, covered, at least 1 hour.

**2.** Shape coconut mixture into 1-in. balls. Place on a waxed paper-lined baking sheet. Refrigerate, covered, at least 3 hours.

**3.** In a microwave, melt the chocolate candy bar and shortening; stir until smooth. Dip the coconut balls in the melted chocolate; allow excess to drip off. Place on waxed paper; let stand until set.

**NOTE** *To toast coconut, spread in a 15x10x1-in. baking pan. Bake at 350° for 5-10 minutes or until golden brown, stirring frequently.*

**PER SERVING** *91 cal., 5 g fat (3 g sat. fat), 1 mg chol., 36 mg sodium, 12 g carb., 1 g fiber, 1 g pro.*

PECAN PIE THUMBPRINTS

## Lime & Gin Coconut Macaroons

**PREP:** 20 MIN.
**BAKE:** 15 MIN./BATCH + COOLING
**MAKES:** 2½ DOZEN

- 4 **egg whites**
- ⅔ **cup sugar**
- 3 **tablespoons gin**
- 1½ **teaspoons grated lime peel**
- ¼ **teaspoon salt**
- ¼ **teaspoon almond extract**
- 1 **package (14 ounces) flaked coconut**
- ½ **cup all-purpose flour**
- 8 **ounces white baking chocolate, melted**

**1.** Preheat oven to 350°. In a small bowl, whisk the first six ingredients until blended. In a large bowl, toss the coconut with the flour; stir in the egg white mixture.

**2.** Drop by tablespoonfuls 2 in. apart onto greased baking sheets. Bake 15-18 minutes or until tops are light brown. Remove from pans to wire racks to cool completely.

**3.** Dip bottoms of cookies into melted chocolate, allowing excess to drip off. Place on waxed paper; let stand until set. Store in an airtight container.

**PER SERVING** *140 cal., 7 g fat (6 g sat. fat), 2 mg chol., 70 mg sodium, 17 g carb., 1 g fiber, 2 g pro.*

I brought Lime & Gin Coconut Macaroons to an annual cookie exchange, where we always name a queen. I won the crown!
—**MILISSA KIRKPATRICK** ANGEL FIRE, NM

LIME & GIN COCONUT MACAROONS

MACADAMIA LEMON BARS

## Macadamia Lemon Bars

These nutty bars are so popular, I bake them for almost all of our get-togethers.
—**EDIE DESPAIN** LOGAN, UT

**PREP:** 25 MIN. • **BAKE:** 10 MIN. + COOLING
**MAKES:** 1 DOZEN

- 1 **cup all-purpose flour**
- ¼ **cup confectioners' sugar**
- ½ **cup butter, melted**
- ¼ **cup chopped macadamia nuts**

**FILLING**

- 1 **cup sugar**
- 2 **tablespoons all-purpose flour**
- ½ **teaspoon baking powder**
- ¼ **teaspoon salt**
- 2 **eggs**
- 2 **tablespoons lemon juice**
- 2 **teaspoons grated lemon peel**
- 2 **tablespoons chopped macadamia nuts**
   **Confectioners' sugar**

**1.** Preheat oven to 350°. In a large bowl, mix flour, confectioners' sugar and melted butter until crumbly; stir in the macadamia nuts. Press onto the bottom and ½ in. up the sides of a greased 8-in.-square baking dish. Bake 15-20 minutes or until light brown.

**2.** Meanwhile, in a small bowl, whisk sugar, flour, baking powder and salt. Beat in eggs, lemon juice and lemon peel until blended.

**3.** Pour the filling over the hot crust. Sprinkle with macadamia nuts. Bake 10-15 minutes or until lightly browned. Cool completely on a wire rack. Cut into bars. Sprinkle with confectioners' sugar. Refrigerate leftovers.

**PER SERVING** *226 cal., 12 g fat (6 g sat. fat), 55 mg chol., 143 mg sodium, 29 g carb., 1 g fiber, 3 g pro.*

AUTUMN LEAF CUTOUTS

## Autumn Leaf Cutouts

Why wait for Christmas to make festive cutouts? Try this fun recipe for fall.
—**DARLENE BRENDEN** SALEM, OR

**PREP:** 25 MIN. + CHILLING
**BAKE:** 15 MIN./BATCH + COOLING
**MAKES:** 4 DOZEN

- 2 **cups butter, softened**
- 1½ **cups sugar**
- 2 **eggs**
- 2 **teaspoons vanilla extract**
- 5½ **cups all-purpose flour**
- ½ **teaspoon baking soda**
- ½ **teaspoon salt**
  **Red, green, orange and yellow paste food coloring**
- 1⅓ **cups confectioners' sugar**
- 5 **to 7 teaspoons warm water**
- 1 **tablespoon meringue powder**
- ¼ **teaspoon almond extract**
- 2 **tablespoons coarse sugar**

**1.** In a large bowl, cream butter and sugar until light and fluffy. Beat in eggs and vanilla. In another bowl, whisk flour, baking soda and salt; gradually beat into creamed mixture.
**2.** Divide dough into four portions; tint one red, one green, one orange and one yellow. Shape each into a disk; wrap in plastic wrap. Refrigerate 30 minutes or until firm enough to roll.

**3.** Preheat oven to 350°. On a lightly floured surface, roll each portion of dough to ¼-in. thickness. Cut with a floured 3-in. leaf-shaped cookie cutter.
**4.** Bake 14-17 minutes or until edges are golden brown. Remove from pans to wire racks to cool completely.
**5.** Meanwhile, in a large bowl, combine the confectioners' sugar, warm water, meringue powder and almond extract; beat on low speed just until blended. Pipe or drizzle on cookies as desired. Sprinkle with coarse sugar. Let stand until set. Store in an airtight container.
**PER SERVING** *162 cal., 8 g fat (5 g sat. fat), 29 mg chol., 96 mg sodium, 21 g carb., trace fiber, 2 g pro.*

⑤ INGREDIENTS

## 5-Ingredient Fudge

You're just a few easy steps and a handful of ingredients away from luscious fudge.
—**SUE TUCKER** EDGEMOOR, SC

**PREP:** 20 MIN. + CHILLING
**MAKES:** ABOUT 2½ POUNDS

- 1½ **teaspoons plus 1 tablespoon butter, divided**
- 2 **cups (12 ounces) semisweet chocolate chips**
- 1 **package (11½ ounces) milk chocolate chips**
- 1 **can (14 ounces) sweetened condensed milk**
- 1 **teaspoon vanilla extract**

**1.** Line a 9-in.-square pan with foil; grease foil with 1½ teaspoons butter.
**2.** In a large microwave-safe bowl, melt chocolate chips and remaining butter; stir until smooth. Stir in milk and vanilla. Spread into prepared pan. Refrigerate until firm.
**3.** Using the foil, lift the fudge out of pan. Remove foil; cut fudge into 1-in. squares. Store in an airtight container in the refrigerator.
**TO MAKE PIE-SPICE SUGAR** *Mix 1½ teaspoons confectioners' sugar, ¼ teaspoon pumpkin pie spice and ¼ teaspoon baking cocoa. Dust fudge with sugar mixture just before serving.*
**PER SERVING** *59 cal., 3 g fat (2 g sat. fat), 3 mg chol., 12 mg sodium, 8 g carb., trace fiber, 1 g pro.*

### ❓ Did you know?

Lining your fudge pan with foil allows you to easily lift the fudge out of the pan in one piece and to cut uniform pieces without scratching the pan. Place the fudge on a cutting board, remove the foil and cut.

## Chocolate-Dipped Spumoni Cookies

Pairing up my favorite cookie and ice cream resulted in one really yummy treat!

—ERICA INGRAM
LAKEWOOD, OH

**PREP:** 20 MIN.
**BAKE:** 10 MIN./BATCH + COOLING
**MAKES:** ABOUT 6 DOZEN

- 1 cup butter, softened
- ¾ cup sugar
- ¾ cup packed brown sugar
- 2 eggs
- 1 tablespoon vanilla extract
- 2½ cups all-purpose flour
- ½ cup Dutch-processed cocoa
- 1 teaspoon baking soda
- ½ teaspoon salt
- 1⅓ cups finely chopped pistachios, divided
- 1⅓ cups finely chopped dried cherries, divided
- 1¾ cups semisweet chocolate chips
- 1 tablespoon shortening

**1.** Preheat oven to 350°. In a large bowl, cream butter and sugars until light and fluffy. Beat in eggs and vanilla. In another bowl, whisk flour, cocoa, baking soda and salt; gradually beat into creamed mixture. Stir in 1 cup each pistachios and cherries.

**2.** Drop by tablespoonfuls 2 in. apart onto ungreased baking sheets. Bake 10-12 minutes or until set. Cool on pans 2 minutes. Remove to wire racks to cool completely.

**3.** In a microwave, melt chocolate chips and shortening; stir until smooth. Dip each cookie halfway into chocolate, allowing excess to drip off; sprinkle with remaining pistachios and cherries. Place on waxed paper; let stand until set.

**PER SERVING** *105 cal., 6 g fat (3 g sat. fat), 13 mg chol., 65 mg sodium, 14 g carb., 1 g fiber, 2 g pro.*

WARREN'S OATMEAL JAM SQUARES

## Warren's Oatmeal Jam Squares

My jam of choice for these bars is usually raspberry. Feel free to use any flavor.

—WARREN PATRICK
TOWNSHEND, VT

**PREP:** 20 MIN. • **BAKE:** 25 MIN. + COOLING
**MAKES:** 16 SQUARES

- 1¼ cups quick-cooking oats
- 1¼ cups all-purpose flour
- ½ cup sugar
- ½ teaspoon baking soda
- ¼ teaspoon salt
- ¾ cup butter, melted
- 2 teaspoons vanilla extract
- 1 jar (10 ounces) seedless raspberry jam or jam of your choice
- 4 whole graham crackers, crushed

**1.** Preheat oven to 350°. In a large bowl, mix the first five ingredients. In a small bowl, mix the melted butter and vanilla; add to the oat mixture, stirring until crumbly. Reserve 1 cup oat mixture for topping.

**2.** Press remaining oat mixture onto the bottom of a greased 9-in.-square baking pan. Spread the raspberry jam over the top to within ½ in. of the edges. Add the crushed graham crackers to the reserved topping; sprinkle over the jam.

**3.** Bake 25-30 minutes or until edges are golden brown. Cool in pan on a wire rack. Cut into squares.

**PER SERVING** *220 cal., 9 g fat (6 g sat. fat), 23 mg chol., 161 mg sodium, 33 g carb., 1 g fiber, 2 g pro.*

CHOCOLATE-DIPPED SPUMONI COOKIES

# Potato Chip Cookies

Here's a fun, sweet-salty treat that appeals to both the young and young-at-heart.
—MONNA LU BAUER LEXINGTON, KY

**PREP:** 15 MIN. • **BAKE:** 10 MIN./BATCH
**MAKES:** 4 DOZEN

- 1 cup butter-flavored shortening
- ¾ cup sugar
- ¾ cup packed brown sugar
- 2 eggs
- 2 cups all-purpose flour
- 1 teaspoon baking soda
- 2 cups crushed potato chips
- 1 cup butterscotch chips

1. Preheat oven to 375°. In a large bowl, cream shortening and sugars until light and fluffy. Beat in eggs. In another bowl, whisk flour and baking soda; gradually beat into creamed mixture. Stir in potato chips and butterscotch chips.
2. Drop by tablespoonfuls 2 in. apart onto ungreased baking sheets. Bake 10-12 minutes or until golden brown. Cool on pans 1 minute. Remove to wire racks to cool.
**PER SERVING** *123 cal., 6 g fat (3 g sat. fat), 9 mg chol., 48 mg sodium, 15 g carb., trace fiber, 1 g pro.*

# Chocolaty Nanaimo Bars

At the Iowa State Fair, this version of the Nanaimo Bar won "Cookie of the Fair."
—KELLY WONG MCCULLEY DES MOINES, IA

**PREP:** 55 MIN. + CHILLING • **COOK:** 10 MIN.
**MAKES:** 16 SERVINGS

- ½ cup butter, cubed
- ¼ cup sugar
- ¼ cup baking cocoa
- 1 egg, lightly beaten
- 1½ cups graham cracker crumbs
- 1 cup flaked coconut, toasted
- ½ cup chopped pecans, toasted
**FILLING**
- ½ cup butter, softened
- 2 tablespoons Bird's custard powder or instant vanilla pudding mix
- 2 cups confectioners' sugar
- 3 tablespoons half-and-half cream
**TOPPING**
- 1 ounce white baking chocolate, melted
- 1 cup (6 ounces) semisweet chocolate chips
- 1 tablespoon shortening

1. Line the bottom of a 9-in.-square baking pan with parchment paper. In a small heavy saucepan, cook and stir the butter, sugar and baking cocoa over medium-low heat until butter is melted. Remove from heat.
2. In a small bowl, whisk a small amount of the hot mixture into egg; return all to pan, whisking constantly. Cook 2-3 minutes or until the mixture is just thick enough to coat a metal spoon and a thermometer reads at least 160°, stirring constantly. Remove from heat.
3. Stir in the graham cracker crumbs, coconut and pecans. Press into the prepared pan. Refrigerate 30 minutes or until cold.
4. For the filling, in a large bowl, beat the butter and custard powder until blended. Beat in the confectioners' sugar and half-and-half cream until smooth. Spread over the graham cracker crust. Refrigerate, covered, 1 hour or until firm.
5. For the topping, fill a small resealable bag with melted white chocolate; set aside, keeping warm. In a microwave, melt the chocolate chips and shortening; stir until smooth. Spread chocolate mixture evenly over filling.
6. Cut a small corner in the bag with white chocolate. Working quickly, pipe parallel lines over the chocolate layer, spacing lines ¼ to ½ in. apart. Working at right angles to the white chocolate lines, pull a toothpick back and forth across the pan, cutting through the piped lines to create a feather design.
7. Refrigerate 10 minutes or until topping is just set (do not allow the chocolate to harden completely). Cut into bars. Store in an airtight container in the refrigerator.
**NOTES** *Bird's custard powder can be found in some Cost Plus World Market stores or at worldmarket.com and amazon.com. To toast coconut and pecans, spread each in a 15x10x1-in. baking pan. Bake at 350° for 5-10 minutes or until lightly browned, stirring occasionally.*
**PER SERVING** *343 cal., 22 g fat (12 g sat. fat), 45 mg chol., 168 mg sodium, 37 g carb., 2 g fiber, 2 g pro.*

# Peanut Butter & Bacon Blondies

**PREP:** 20 MIN. • **BAKE:** 25 MIN. + COOLING
**MAKES:** 2 DOZEN

- 2 cups packed brown sugar
- 1 cup butter, melted
- 2 eggs
- 2 teaspoons vanilla extract
- 2 cups all-purpose flour
- 1 teaspoon baking powder
- ¼ teaspoon baking soda
  Dash salt
- 8 bacon strips, cooked and crumbled
**FROSTING**
- 1 cup creamy peanut butter
- ½ cup butter, softened
- 2 cups confectioners' sugar
- 1 teaspoon vanilla extract
- 3 to 4 tablespoons 2% milk
- 6 bacon strips, cooked and crumbled

1. Preheat oven to 350°. Line a 13x9-in. pan with parchment paper, letting the ends extend up the sides; grease paper.
2. In a large bowl, beat brown sugar and butter until blended. Beat in eggs and vanilla. In another bowl, whisk the flour, baking powder, baking soda and salt; gradually beat into sugar mixture. Fold in bacon.
3. Spread into prepared pan. Bake 25-30 minutes or until a toothpick inserted in the center comes out clean (do not overbake). Cool completely in the pan on a wire rack. Lifting with the parchment paper, remove from pan.
4. For frosting, in a large bowl, beat peanut butter and butter until blended. Gradually beat in the confectioners' sugar, vanilla and enough milk to reach the desired consistency. Frost blondies; sprinkle with bacon. Cut into bars. Refrigerate leftovers.
**PER SERVING** *342 cal., 19 g fat (9 g sat. fat), 53 mg chol., 265 mg sodium, 38 g carb., 1 g fiber, 6 g pro.*

**top tip**

# Parchment Pointers

There is no right or wrong side to parchment paper. For the best baking results, use a fresh sheet for each pan of cookies or bars.

One of the most unusual recipes I have is Peanut Butter & Bacon Blondies. It's also one of the best! Everyone likes the unexpected mix of ingredients.

—JANIE COLLE HUTCHINSON, KS

PEANUT BUTTER & BACON BLONDIES

## Bite-Size Cinnamon Roll Cookies

What do you get when you combine a cinnamon roll and a spiced cookie? The doubly delightful treats here!

**—JASMINE SHETH** NEW YORK, NY

**PREP:** 1 HOUR + CHILLING • **BAKE:** 10 MIN./BATCH
**MAKES:** 6 DOZEN

- ½ cup packed brown sugar
- 4 teaspoons ground cinnamon
- 1¼ cups butter, softened
- 4 ounces cream cheese, softened
- 1½ cups sugar
- 2 eggs
- 2 teaspoons vanilla extract
- 2 teaspoons grated orange peel
- 4¼ cups all-purpose flour
- 1 teaspoon baking powder
- 1 teaspoon active dry yeast
- ½ teaspoon salt

**GLAZE**
- 1 cup confectioners' sugar
- 2 tablespoons 2% milk
- 1 teaspoon vanilla extract

**1.** In a small bowl, mix brown sugar and cinnamon until blended. In a large bowl, cream butter, cream cheese and sugar until light and fluffy. Beat in eggs, vanilla and orange peel. In another bowl, whisk flour, baking powder, yeast and salt; gradually beat into creamed mixture.

**2.** Divide dough into four portions. On a lightly floured surface, roll each into an 8x6-in. rectangle; sprinkle with about 2 tablespoons brown sugar mixture. Roll up tightly jelly-roll style, starting with a long side. Wrap in plastic wrap. Refrigerate 1 hour or until firm.

**3.** Preheat oven to 350°. Cut dough crosswise into ⅜-in. slices. Place 1 in. apart on greased baking sheets. Bake 8-10 minutes or until bottoms are light brown. Remove from pans to wire racks to cool completely.

**4.** In a small bowl, whisk glaze ingredients. Dip cookie tops in glaze. Let stand until set. Store in an airtight container.

**PER SERVING** *92 cal., 4 g fat (2 g sat. fat), 16 mg chol., 52 mg sodium, 13 g carb., trace fiber, 1 g pro.*

BITE-SIZE CINNAMON ROLL COOKIES

CARAMEL SNICKERDOODLE BARS

## Caramel Snickerdoodle Bars

These three-layer goodies showcase some of my favorite dessert ingredients. Cinnamon-sugar makes the perfect topping.

**—NIKI PLOURDE** GARDNER, MA

**PREP:** 30 MIN. • **BAKE:** 25 MIN. + CHILLING • **MAKES:** 4 DOZEN

- 1 cup butter, softened
- 2 cups packed brown sugar
- 2 eggs
- 2 teaspoons vanilla extract
- 2½ cups all-purpose flour
- 2 teaspoons baking powder
- 1 teaspoon salt
- ¼ cup sugar
- 3 teaspoons ground cinnamon
- 2 cans (13.4 ounces each) dulce de leche
- 12 ounces white baking chocolate, chopped
- ⅓ cup heavy whipping cream
- 1 tablespoon light corn syrup

**1.** Preheat oven to 350°. Line a 13x9-in. baking pan with parchment paper, letting ends extend over sides by 1 in.

**2.** In a large bowl, cream butter and brown sugar until light and fluffy. Beat in eggs and vanilla. In another bowl, whisk flour, baking powder and salt; gradually beat into creamed mixture. Spread onto bottom of prepared pan.

**3.** In a small bowl, mix the sugar and cinnamon; sprinkle 2 tablespoons mixture over the batter. Bake 25-30 minutes or until edges are light brown. Cool completely in pan on a wire rack.

**4.** Spread dulce de leche over the crust. In a small saucepan, combine baking chocolate, cream and corn syrup; cook and stir over low heat until smooth. Cool slightly. Spread over dulce de leche. Sprinkle with remaining cinnamon-sugar. Refrigerate, covered, at least 1 hour.

**5.** Lifting with the parchment paper, remove from the pan. Cut into bars. Refrigerate leftovers.

**NOTE** *This recipe was tested with Nestle La Lechera dulce de leche; look for it in the international foods section. If using Eagle Brand dulce de leche (caramel-flavored sauce), thicken according to package directions before using.*

**PER SERVING** *197 cal., 8 g fat (5 g sat. fat), 27 mg chol., 137 mg sodium, 28 g carb., trace fiber, 2 g pro.*

## Glazed Apple-Maple Blondies

My 6-year-old son and I came up with this recipe to use the last of the apples we picked from the local orchard. The blondies are even yummier with a dollop of sweetened whipped cream.
—**HEATHER BATES** ATHENS, ME

**PREP:** 25 MIN. • **BAKE:** 25 MIN. + COOLING • **MAKES:** 2 DOZEN

- 1⅓ cups packed brown sugar
- ½ cup butter, melted and cooled
- ½ cup maple syrup
- 2 teaspoons vanilla extract
- 2 eggs
- 2 cups all-purpose flour
- ¾ teaspoon salt
- ¼ teaspoon baking soda
- 3 cups chopped peeled apples (about 3 medium)

**GLAZE**

- ¼ cup butter, cubed
- ½ cup maple syrup
- ¼ cup packed brown sugar

**1.** Preheat oven to 350°. Line a 13x9-in. baking pan with parchment paper, letting ends extend up sides.
**2.** In a large bowl, beat the brown sugar, melted butter, syrup and vanilla until blended. Beat in eggs. In another bowl, whisk flour, salt and baking soda; gradually beat into brown sugar mixture. Stir in apples (batter will be thick).
**3.** Transfer to prepared pan. Bake 25-30 minutes or until golden brown and a toothpick inserted into center comes out with moist crumbs.
**4.** Meanwhile, in a small saucepan, melt the butter over medium-low heat; stir in syrup and brown sugar. Bring to a boil over medium heat; cook and stir 2-3 minutes or until slightly thickened. Remove from heat; cool slightly.
**5.** Pour glaze over warm blondies. Cool completely in pan on a wire rack. Cut into bars.
**PER SERVING** *192 cal., 6 g fat (4 g sat. fat), 31 mg chol., 149 mg sodium, 33 g carb., trace fiber, 2 g pro.*

GLAZED APPLE-MAPLE BLONDIES

> For extra fun, mix some crushed candy canes into the filling for Peppermint Patty Sandwich Cookies.
> —**AMY MARTIN** VANCOUVER, WA

PEPPERMINT PATTY SANDWICH COOKIES

## Peppermint Patty Sandwich Cookies

**PREP:** 30 MIN. • **BAKE:** 10 MIN./BATCH + COOLING
**MAKES:** 3 DOZEN

- 2 packages devil's food cake mix (regular size)
- 4 eggs
- ⅔ cup canola oil
  Granulated sugar
- 1 package (8 ounces) cream cheese, softened
- ½ cup butter, softened
- 1 teaspoon peppermint extract
- 4 cups confectioners' sugar

**1.** Preheat oven to 350°. In a large bowl, combine the cake mixes, eggs and oil; beat until well blended. Shape into 1-in. balls; place 2 in. apart on greased baking sheets. Flatten with the bottom of a glass dipped in granulated sugar.
**2.** Bake 7-9 minutes or until the tops are cracked. Cool 2 minutes before removing to wire racks to cool completely.
**3.** In a large bowl, beat the cream cheese, butter and extract until blended. Gradually beat in the confectioners' sugar until smooth.
**4.** Spread the filling on the bottoms of half of the cookies; cover with remaining cookies. Refrigerate leftovers in an airtight container.
**PER SERVING** *231 cal., 10 g fat (4 g sat. fat), 37 mg chol., 245 mg sodium, 33 g carb., 1 g fiber, 2 g pro.*

DARK CHOCOLATE RASPBERRY FUDGE

# Dark Chocolate Raspberry Fudge

The pairing of chocolate and raspberry can be addictive. See for yourself!

—**BARBARA LENTO** HOUSTON, PA

**PREP:** 15 MIN. + FREEZING
**COOK:** 5 MIN. + CHILLING
**MAKES:** 3 POUNDS (81 PIECES)

- 1 **package (10 to 12 ounces) white baking chips**
- 1 **teaspoon butter, softened**
- 3 **cups dark chocolate chips**
- 1 **can (14 ounces) sweetened condensed milk**
- ¼ **cup raspberry liqueur**
- ⅛ **teaspoon salt**

**1.** Place white baking chips in a single layer on a small baking sheet. Freeze 30 minutes. Line a 9-in.-square pan with foil; grease foil with butter.
**2.** In a large microwave-safe bowl, combine chocolate chips and milk. Microwave, uncovered, on high for 2 minutes; stir. Microwave in additional 30-second intervals, stirring until smooth. Stir in liqueur and salt. Add the white baking chips; stir just until partially melted. Spread into prepared pan. Refrigerate 1 hour or until firm.
**3.** Using the foil, lift the fudge out of pan. Remove foil; cut fudge into 1-in. squares. Store in an airtight container in the refrigerator.
**NOTE** *This recipe was tested in a 1,100-watt microwave.*
**PER SERVING** *85 cal., 5 g fat (3 g sat. fat), 2 mg chol., 13 mg sodium, 10 g carb., 0 fiber, 1 g pro.*

# Folded Hazelnut Cookies

I have sweet memories of making these treats with my sons when they were small. The boys were wearing aprons, with flour all over them and Nutella on their faces.

—**PAULA MARCHESI** LENHARTSVILLE, PA

**PREP:** 30 MIN. • **BAKE:** 10 MIN./BATCH
**MAKES:** ABOUT 2 DOZEN

- 1 **tablespoon finely chopped hazelnuts**
- 1 **tablespoon sugar**
- 1½ **cups all-purpose flour**
- ½ **cup confectioners' sugar**
- ¼ **cup cornstarch**
- ¾ **cup cold butter, cubed**
- 2 **tablespoons Nutella**
- 1 **egg, lightly beaten**

**1.** Preheat oven to 350°. In a small bowl, mix hazelnuts and sugar. In a large bowl, whisk flour, confectioners' sugar and cornstarch. Cut in butter until crumbly. Transfer to a clean work surface. Knead gently until the mixture forms a smooth dough, about 2 minutes (dough will be crumbly but will come together).
**2.** Divide dough in half. On a lightly floured surface, roll each portion to ⅛-in. thickness. Cut with a floured 2-in. round cookie cutter. Place ¼ teaspoon Nutella in the center. Fold the dough partially in half, just enough to cover filling.
**3.** Place 1 in. apart on greased baking sheets. Brush with the beaten egg; sprinkle with hazelnut mixture. Bake 10-12 minutes or until the bottoms are light brown. Remove from the pans to wire racks to cool.
**PER SERVING** *108 cal., 7 g fat (4 g sat. fat), 24 mg chol., 44 mg sodium, 11 g carb., trace fiber, 1 g pro.*

# Turtle Cookie Cups

For an easy twist on my turtle cups, use white chips instead of semisweet ones.

—**HEATHER KING** FROSTBURG, MD

**PREP:** 35 MIN. + STANDING
**BAKE:** 10 MIN./BATCH + COOLING
**MAKES:** 4 DOZEN

- 1 **cup butter, softened**
- 1 **cup packed brown sugar**
- ½ **cup sugar**
- 2 **eggs**
- 1 **teaspoon vanilla extract**
- 2½ **cups all-purpose flour**
- 1 **teaspoon baking soda**
- ½ **teaspoon salt**
- 1¼ **cups semisweet chocolate chips, divided**
- ½ **cup chopped pecans**
- 1 **cup Kraft caramel bits**
- 3 **tablespoons heavy whipping cream**
- 48 **pecan halves (about ¾ cup)**

**1.** Preheat oven to 375°. In a large bowl, cream butter and sugars until light and fluffy. Beat in eggs and vanilla. In another bowl, whisk flour, baking soda and salt; gradually beat into the creamed mixture.
**2.** Shape dough into 1-in. balls; place in greased mini-muffin cups. Press evenly onto bottoms and up sides of cups. Bake 9-11 minutes or until the edges are golden brown. With the back of a measuring teaspoon, make an indentation in each cup. Immediately sprinkle with ¾ cup chips and chopped pecans. Cool in the pans 10 minutes. Remove to wire racks to cool.
**3.** Meanwhile, in a small saucepan, melt the caramel bits with cream; stir until smooth. Spoon into the cups. Top each with a pecan half. In a microwave, melt the remaining chips; stir until smooth. Drizzle over pecans.
**PER SERVING** *145 cal., 8 g fat (4 g sat. fat), 20 mg chol., 95 mg sodium, 18 g carb., 1 g fiber, 1 g pro.*

TURTLE COOKIE CUPS

RUSTIC NUT BARS

## Rustic Nut Bars

These chewy, gooey bars are guaranteed to please anyone who likes nuts. Four different varieties go into the caramel layer that tops the shortbread-like crust.
—**BARBARA DRISCOLL** WEST ALLIS, WI

**PREP:** 20 MIN. • **BAKE:** 35 MIN. + COOLING
**MAKES:** ABOUT 3 DOZEN

- 1 tablespoon plus ¾ cup cold butter, divided
- 2⅓ cups all-purpose flour
- ½ cup sugar
- ½ teaspoon baking powder
- ½ teaspoon salt
- 1 egg, lightly beaten

**TOPPING**
- ⅔ cup honey
- ½ cup packed brown sugar
- ¼ teaspoon salt
- 6 tablespoons butter, cubed
- 2 tablespoons heavy whipping cream
- 1 cup chopped hazelnuts, toasted
- 1 cup salted cashews
- 1 cup pistachios
- 1 cup salted roasted almonds

**1.** Preheat oven to 375°. Line a 13x9-in. baking pan with foil, letting ends extend over sides by 1 in. Grease foil with 1 tablespoon butter.
**2.** In a large bowl, whisk the flour, sugar, baking powder and salt. Cut in the remaining butter until mixture resembles coarse crumbs. Stir in the egg until blended (mixture will be dry). Press firmly onto the bottom of the prepared pan.
**3.** Bake 18-20 minutes or until edges are golden brown. Cool on a wire rack.
**4.** In a large heavy saucepan, combine the honey, brown sugar and salt; bring to a boil over medium heat, stirring frequently to dissolve sugar. Boil 2 minutes, without stirring. Stir in butter and cream; return to a boil. Cook and stir 1 minute or until smooth. Remove from heat; stir in nuts. Spread over crust.
**5.** Bake 15-20 minutes or until topping is bubbly. Cool completely in pan on a wire rack. Lifting with foil, remove from pan. Discard foil; cut into bars.
**NOTE** *To toast nuts, spread in a 15x10x1-in. baking pan. Bake at 350° for 5-10 minutes or until lightly browned, stirring occasionally. Or, spread in a dry nonstick skillet and heat over low heat until lightly browned, stirring occasionally.*
**PER SERVING** *199 cal., 13 g fat (4 g sat. fat), 21 mg chol., 157 mg sodium, 18 g carb., 1 g fiber, 4 g pro.*

## Cardamom-Blackberry Linzer Cookies

Here's a favorite in our family. The deeply spiced cardamom is the perfect match for the blackberry spreadable fruit.
—**CHRISTIANNA GOZZI** ASTORIA, NY

**PREP:** 50 MIN. + CHILLING
**BAKE:** 10 MIN./BATCH + COOLING
**MAKES:** ABOUT 2 DOZEN

- 2 cups all-purpose flour
- 1 cup salted roasted almonds
- 2 to 3 teaspoons ground cardamom
- ¼ teaspoon salt
- 1 cup unsalted butter, softened
- ½ cup plus 1 teaspoon sugar, divided
- 1 egg
- 1 jar (10 ounces) seedless blackberry spreadable fruit
- 1 tablespoon lemon juice
- 3 tablespoons confectioners' sugar

**1.** In a food processor, combine ½ cup flour and the almonds; pulse until the almonds are finely ground. Add the cardamom, salt and remaining flour; pulse until combined.
**2.** In a large bowl, cream butter and ½ cup sugar until light and fluffy. Beat in egg. Gradually beat in flour mixture. Divide dough in half. Shape each into a disk; wrap in plastic wrap. Refrigerate 1 hour or until firm enough to roll.
**3.** Preheat oven to 350°. On a lightly floured surface, roll each portion to ⅛-in. thickness. Cut with a floured 2-in. round cookie cutter. Using a floured 1-in. round cookie cutter, cut out the centers of half of the cookies. Place solid and window cookies 1 in. apart on greased baking sheets.
**4.** Bake 10-12 minutes or until light brown. Remove from pans to wire racks to cool completely.
**5.** In a small bowl, mix the spreadable fruit, lemon juice and remaining sugar. Spread filling on bottoms of solid cookies; top with window cookies. Dust with confectioners' sugar.
**PER SERVING** *188 cal., 11 g fat (5 g sat. fat), 29 mg chol., 48 mg sodium, 21 g carb., 1 g fiber, 3 g pro.*

CARDAMOM-BLACKBERRY LINZER COOKIES

**MOCHA-HAZELNUT
GLAZED ANGEL FOOD
CAKE** *PAGE 105*

# Cakes & Pies

Surprise loved ones with **a little slice of heaven!** From frosted layer cakes for parties to fresh-from-the-oven pies filled with fruit, these **home-style delights** will make any meal unforgettable.

**CREAMY LIME PIE WITH FRESH BERRIES** *PAGE 107*

**CONFETTI CAKE WITH BROWN SUGAR BUTTERCREAM** *PAGE 110*

**PINEAPPLE MARZIPAN CUPCAKES** *PAGE 108*

MARVELOUS MARBLE CAKE

## Marvelous Marble Cake

Here's a real showstopper thanks to its marbled look and rich chocolate flavor.
—ELLEN RILEY BIRMINGHAM, AL

**PREP:** 45 MIN. • **BAKE:** 20 MIN. + COOLING
**MAKES:** 16 SERVINGS

- 4 ounces bittersweet chocolate, chopped
- 3 tablespoons plus 1¼ cups butter, softened, divided
- 2 cups sugar
- 5 eggs
- 3 teaspoons vanilla extract
- 2¼ cups all-purpose flour
- 2 teaspoons baking powder
- ½ teaspoon salt
- ½ cup sour cream
- ½ cup miniature semisweet chocolate chips, optional

FROSTING
- ¾ cup butter, softened
- 6¾ cups confectioners' sugar
- 2 teaspoons vanilla extract
- ½ to ⅔ cup 2% milk
- 2 tablespoons miniature semisweet chocolate chips

**1.** In top of a double boiler or a metal bowl over barely simmering water, melt the chocolate and 3 tablespoons of butter; stir until smooth. Cool to room temperature.

**2.** Preheat the oven to 375°. Line the bottoms of three greased 8-in. round baking pans with parchment paper; grease the paper.

**3.** In a large bowl, cream remaining butter and sugar until light and fluffy.

Add eggs, one at a time, beating well after each addition. Beat in the vanilla. In another bowl, whisk flour, baking powder and salt; add to the creamed mixture alternately with sour cream, beating well after each addition.

**4.** Remove 2 cups batter to a small bowl; stir in cooled chocolate mixture and, if desired, chips until blended. Drop plain and chocolate batters by tablespoonfuls into prepared pans, dividing batters evenly among pans. To make batter level in pans, bang pans several times on counter.

**5.** Bake 20-25 minutes or until a toothpick inserted in center comes out clean. Cool in pans 10 minutes before removing to wire racks; remove paper. Cool completely.

**6.** For frosting, in a large bowl, cream the butter until smooth. Gradually beat in confectioners' sugar, vanilla and enough milk to reach the desired consistency.

**7.** If cake layers have rounded tops, trim them with a serrated knife to make them level. In a microwave, melt chips; stir until smooth. Cool slightly.

**8.** Place one cake layer on a serving plate; spread with ½ cup frosting. Repeat layers. Top with remaining cake layer. Frost top and sides of cake.

**9.** Drop the cooled chocolate by ½ teaspoonfuls over frosting. Using a large offset spatula, smear chocolate to create a marble design in frosting.
**PER SERVING** *683 cal., 33 g fat (20 g sat. fat), 138 mg chol., 330 mg sodium, 97 g carb., 1 g fiber, 5 g pro.*

## Sweet Potato Ice Cream Pie

My guests never know that canned sweet potatoes are the secret to this cool treat.
—SUSAN BAZAN SEQUIM, WA

**PREP:** 25 MIN. + FREEZING
**MAKES:** 8 SERVINGS

- 2 cups graham cracker crumbs (about 14 whole crackers)
- 3 tablespoons sugar
- ½ cup butter, melted
- 1 can (15 ounces) sweet potatoes, drained
- ½ cup packed brown sugar
- 2 teaspoons pumpkin pie spice
- 1 teaspoon grated orange peel
- ¼ teaspoon salt
- 4 cups vanilla ice cream, softened
- 1 cup heavy whipping cream
- 3 tablespoons confectioners' sugar
- 1 teaspoon vanilla extract

**1.** In a small bowl, mix crumbs and sugar; stir in butter. Press onto bottom and up sides of a greased 9-in. deep-dish pie plate. Refrigerate 30 minutes.

**2.** Place the sweet potatoes, brown sugar, pie spice, orange peel and salt in a food processor; process until smooth. Add ice cream; process until blended. Spread evenly into the crust. Freeze, covered, 8 hours or overnight.

**3.** Remove from the freezer about 10 minutes before serving. Meanwhile, in a small bowl, beat the cream until it begins to thicken. Add confectioners' sugar and vanilla; beat until soft peaks form. Spread over pie.
**PER SERVING** *542 cal., 32 g fat (19 g sat. fat), 100 mg chol., 368 mg sodium, 62 g carb., 2 g fiber, 5 g pro.*

SWEET POTATO ICE CREAM PIE

COCONUT-PECAN
GERMAN CHOCOLATE PIE

## Coconut-Pecan German Chocolate Pie

Love traditional German chocolate cake? Try those ingredients in a pastry-crust pie. You won't be able to put your fork down!
—**ANNA JONES** COPPELL, TX

**PREP:** 50 MIN. + CHILLING
**BAKE:** 35 MIN. + CHILLING
**MAKES:** 8 SERVINGS

- 1¼ cups all-purpose flour
- ¼ teaspoon salt
- 6 tablespoons cold lard
- 3 to 4 tablespoons ice water
**FILLING**
- 4 ounces German sweet chocolate, chopped
- 2 ounces unsweetened chocolate, chopped
- 1 can (14 ounces) sweetened condensed milk
- 4 egg yolks
- 1 teaspoon vanilla extract
- 1 cup chopped pecans
**TOPPING**
- ½ cup packed brown sugar
- ½ cup heavy whipping cream
- ¼ cup butter, cubed
- 2 egg yolks
- 1 cup flaked coconut
- 1 teaspoon vanilla extract
- ¼ cup chopped pecans

**1.** In a small bowl, mix flour and salt; cut in lard until crumbly. Gradually add ice water, tossing with a fork until dough holds together when pressed. Shape into a disk; wrap in plastic wrap. Refrigerate 30 minutes or overnight.

**2.** Preheat oven to 400°. On a lightly floured surface, roll the dough to form a ⅛-in.-thick circle; transfer to a 9-in. pie plate. Trim pastry to ½ in. beyond rim of plate; flute edge. Line unpricked pastry with a double thickness of foil. Fill with pie weights, dried beans or uncooked rice.

**3.** Bake 11-13 minutes or until bottom is lightly browned. Remove the foil and weights; bake 6-8 minutes longer or until light brown. Cool on a wire rack. Reduce oven setting to 350°.

**4.** In a microwave, melt chocolates in a large bowl; stir until smooth. Cool slightly. Whisk in milk, egg yolks and vanilla; stir in pecans. Pour into crust. Bake 16-19 minutes or until set. Cool for 1 hour on a wire rack.

**5.** Meanwhile, in a small heavy saucepan, combine the brown sugar, cream and butter. Bring to a boil over medium heat, stirring to dissolve the sugar. Remove from heat.

**6.** In a small bowl, whisk a small amount of hot mixture into egg yolks; return all to pan, whisking constantly. Cook 2-3 minutes or until the mixture thickens and a thermometer reads 160°, stirring constantly. Remove from heat. Stir in coconut and vanilla; cool for 10 minutes.

**7.** Pour over filling; sprinkle with nuts. Refrigerate 4 hours or until cold.

**PER SERVING** *801 cal., 54 g fat (24 g sat. fat), 215 mg chol., 227 mg sodium, 75 g carb., 5 g fiber, 12 g pro.*

## Kahlua Fudge Sheet Cake

Spiked with coffee liqueur or coffee, this yummy dessert is a crowd-pleaser.
—**NANCY HEISHMAN** LAS VEGAS, NV

**PREP:** 35 MIN. • **BAKE:** 20 MIN. + COOLING
**MAKES:** 24 SERVINGS

- 2 cups all-purpose flour
- 1¾ cups sugar
- 2 teaspoons ground cinnamon
- 1 teaspoon baking soda
- 1 cup Kahlua (coffee liqueur) or strong brewed coffee
- ½ cup butter, cubed
- ½ cup marshmallow creme
- ⅓ cup baking cocoa
- 2 eggs
- ½ cup buttermilk
- ½ cup chopped pecans
**FROSTING**
- ½ cup butter, cubed
- ⅓ cup baking cocoa
- ¼ cup marshmallow creme
- 3¾ cups confectioners' sugar
- ½ to ⅔ cup Kahlua (coffee liqueur) or strong brewed coffee
- ¼ cup chopped pecans

**1.** Preheat oven to 350°. Grease a 15x10x1-in. baking pan. In a large bowl, whisk flour, sugar, cinnamon and baking soda. In a small saucepan, combine Kahlua, butter, marshmallow creme and cocoa; bring just to a boil, stirring occasionally. Add to the flour mixture, stirring just until moistened.

**2.** In a small bowl, whisk the eggs and buttermilk until blended; add to the Kahlua mixture, whisking constantly. Fold in the pecans. Transfer to the prepared pan, spreading evenly. Bake 18-22 minutes or until a toothpick inserted in center comes out clean.

**3.** Meanwhile, for frosting, combine the butter, cocoa and marshmallow creme in a small saucepan; stir over medium heat until smooth. Transfer to a bowl. Beat in the confectioners' sugar and enough Kahlua to reach a spreading consistency.

**4.** Remove cake from oven; place on a wire rack. Spread frosting evenly over warm cake; sprinkle with pecans. Cool completely.

**PER SERVING** *315 cal., 11 g fat (5 g sat. fat), 38 mg chol., 121 mg sodium, 50 g carb., 1 g fiber, 3 g pro.*

KAHLUA FUDGE SHEET CAKE

## Molly's Sweet & Spicy Tzimmes Cake

**PREP:** 35 MIN. • **BAKE:** 45 MIN. + COOLING
**MAKES:** 12 SERVINGS

- 1 cup sugar
- ½ cup canola oil
- 2 eggs
- 1 cup mashed sweet potatoes
- ¼ cup white wine or orange juice
- 1 tablespoon lemon juice
- 1 teaspoon vanilla extract
- 1⅔ cups all-purpose flour
- 3 teaspoons grated orange peel
- 1 teaspoon baking soda
- ½ teaspoon baking powder
- ½ teaspoon salt
- ½ teaspoon ground ginger
- ½ teaspoon ground cinnamon
- ¼ teaspoon ground cloves
- 1 large tart apple, peeled and chopped
- 1 cup dried cranberries
- 1 cup shredded carrots
- ½ cup golden raisins

**1.** Preheat oven to 350°. Grease and flour a 10-in. fluted tube pan.

**2.** In a large bowl, beat sugar and oil until blended. Add eggs, one at a time, beating well after each addition. Beat in sweet potatoes, wine, lemon juice and vanilla.

**3.** In another bowl, whisk the flour, the orange peel, baking soda, baking powder, salt and spices; gradually beat into the sweet potato mixture. Gently fold in the apple, cranberries, carrots and raisins.

**4.** Transfer the cake batter to the prepared pan. Bake 45-55 minutes or until a toothpick inserted in the center comes out clean. Cool in pan 10 minutes before removing to a wire rack to cool.

**NOTE** *To remove cakes easily, use solid shortening to grease plain and fluted tube pans.*

**PER SERVING** *309 cal., 10 g fat (1 g sat. fat), 35 mg chol., 247 mg sodium, 51 g carb., 2 g fiber, 4 g pro.*

We're always on the lookout for new ways to incorporate Jewish traditions into our interfaith home. Try my tzimmes cake for Rosh Hashana or any autumn holiday.
—**MOLLY HAENDLER** PHILADELPHIA, PA

MOLLY'S SWEET & SPICY TZIMMES CAKE

## Jam-Packed Pecan Pie

This chocolaty version of a pecan classic is a must on our Thanksgiving dinner table. We make sure to save room!
—**GRACE MANNON** ABINGDON, VA

**PREP:** 25 MIN. • **BAKE:** 45 MIN. + COOLING
**MAKES:** 8 SERVINGS

- **Pastry for single-crust pie (9 inches)**
- 3 eggs
- ¾ cup sugar
- ¾ cup dark corn syrup
- 2 tablespoons butter, melted
- 1 tablespoon bourbon
- 2 cups (12 ounces) semisweet chocolate chips
- 1 cup plus 3 tablespoons flaked coconut, divided
- 1 cup chopped pecans

**1.** Preheat oven to 350°. On a lightly floured surface, roll the pastry dough to a ⅛-in.-thick circle; transfer to a 9-in. pie plate. Trim the pastry to ½ in. beyond the rim of the pie plate; flute the edge.

**2.** In a large bowl, beat the eggs, sugar, dark corn syrup, butter and bourbon until blended. Stir in the chocolate chips, 1 cup coconut and pecans. Pour into the pastry shell; sprinkle with the remaining coconut.

**3.** Bake for 45-50 minutes or until the filling is set and the coconut is golden brown. Cool on a wire rack; serve or refrigerate within 2 hours.

**PASTRY FOR SINGLE-CRUST PIE (9 INCHES)** *Combine 1¼ cups all-purpose flour and ¼ teaspoon salt; cut in ½ cup cold butter until crumbly. Gradually add 3-5 tablespoons ice water, tossing with a fork until dough holds together when pressed. Wrap in plastic wrap and refrigerate 1 hour.*

**PER SERVING** *608 cal., 35 g fat (17 g sat. fat), 78 mg chol., 225 mg sodium, 74 g carb., 4 g fiber, 6 g pro.*

## ? Did you know?

Traditional tzimmes is a Jewish sweet stew or casserole. It typically contains carrots, other root vegetables like sweet potatoes and dried fruits such as raisins.

BUTTERNUT-SWEET POTATO PIE

# Butternut-Sweet Potato Pie

Mashed butternut squash gives sweet potato pie twice the fall appeal.

—**MARY ANN DELL** PHOENIXVILLE, PA

**PREP:** 15 MIN. • **BAKE:** 50 MIN. + COOLING
**MAKES:** 8 SERVINGS

    Pastry for single-crust pie
      (9 inches)
  4 eggs
  1⅓ cups half-and-half cream
  1 cup mashed cooked butternut
      squash
  1 cup mashed cooked sweet potato
      (about 1 medium)
  ½ cup honey
  1 tablespoon all-purpose flour
  ½ teaspoon salt
  1 teaspoon ground cinnamon
  ½ teaspoon ground ginger
  ¼ teaspoon ground nutmeg
    Dash ground cloves
    Whipped cream, optional

**1.** Preheat oven to 375°. On a lightly floured surface, roll pastry dough to a ⅛-in.-thick circle; transfer to a 9-in. deep-dish pie plate. Trim pastry to ½ in. beyond rim of plate; flute edge.
**2.** In a large bowl, whisk eggs, cream, squash, sweet potato, honey, flour, salt and spices. Pour into pastry shell.
**3.** Bake 50-60 minutes or until a knife inserted near the center comes out clean. Cover the edge loosely with foil during the last 15 minutes if needed to prevent overbrowning. Remove the foil. Cool on a wire rack; serve within 2 hours or refrigerate and serve cold. If desired, top with whipped cream.

**PASTRY FOR SINGLE-CRUST PIE (9 INCHES)** *Combine 1¼ cups all-purpose flour and ¼ teaspoon salt; cut in ½ cup cold butter until crumbly. Gradually add 3-5 tablespoons ice water, tossing with a fork until dough holds together when pressed. Wrap in plastic wrap and refrigerate 1 hour.*
**PER SERVING** *373 cal., 18 g fat (11 g sat. fat), 156 mg chol., 370 mg sodium, 45 g carb., 3 g fiber, 8 g pro.*

# Mocha-Hazelnut Glazed Angel Food Cake

I dressed up this cake with three of my favorites—coffee, cherries and hazelnuts.

—**JOAN PECSEK** CHESAPEAKE, VA

**PREP:** 25 MIN. • **BAKE:** 30 MIN. + COOLING
**MAKES:** 16 SERVINGS

  12 egg whites
  1 cup cake flour
  ¼ teaspoon instant coffee granules
  1 teaspoon cream of tartar
  1 teaspoon almond extract
  ½ teaspoon salt
  1¼ cups sugar
**GLAZE**
  1 cup Nutella
  ½ cup confectioners' sugar
  ⅓ cup brewed coffee
  ¼ cup chopped hazelnuts
  16 maraschino cherries with stems

**1.** Place egg whites in a large bowl; let stand at room temperature 30 minutes.
**2.** Meanwhile, preheat oven to 350°. In a small bowl, mix flour and coffee granules until blended.
**3.** Add cream of tartar, extract and salt to egg whites; beat on medium speed until soft peaks form. Gradually add sugar, 1 tablespoon at a time, beating on high after each addition until sugar is dissolved. Continue beating until soft glossy peaks form. Gradually fold in flour mixture, about ½ cup at a time.
**4.** Gently transfer the cake batter to an ungreased 10-in. tube pan. Cut through the batter with a knife to remove air pockets. Bake on lowest oven rack 30-40 minutes or until the top springs back when lightly touched. Immediately invert pan; cool cake in pan, about 1½ hours.
**5.** Run a knife around sides and center tube of pan. Remove cake to a serving plate. In a small bowl, whisk Nutella, confectioners' sugar and coffee until smooth. Drizzle over cake; sprinkle with hazelnuts. Serve with cherries.
**PER SERVING** *234 cal., 7 g fat (1 g sat. fat), trace chol., 123 mg sodium, 41 g carb., 1 g fiber, 5 g pro.*

MOCHA-HAZELNUT GLAZED
ANGEL FOOD CAKE

CRANBERRY PINEAPPLE UPSIDE-DOWN CAKE

## Cranberry Pineapple Upside-Down Cake

Here's a colorful dessert that both children and adults enjoy. It'll keep for a few days—I think it's even better the second day!

**—SHERRY CONLEY** NOEL HANTS COUNTY, NS

**PREP:** 20 MIN. • **BAKE:** 50 MIN. + COOLING • **MAKES:** 15 SERVINGS

- 1 cup packed brown sugar
- ½ cup butter, melted
- 1 can (20 ounces) sliced pineapple, drained
- 1 cup fresh or frozen cranberries

**CAKE**
- 1 cup butter, softened
- 1¼ cups sugar
- 2 eggs
- 1 teaspoon vanilla extract
- 2 cups all-purpose flour
- 2 teaspoons baking powder
- 1 teaspoon salt
- 1 teaspoon ground cinnamon
- ½ teaspoon ground allspice
- ¾ cup sour cream
- 1 cup fresh or frozen cranberries, halved
  Sweetened whipped cream, optional

**1.** Preheat oven to 350°. In a small bowl, mix brown sugar and butter; spread onto bottom of a greased 13x9-in. baking pan. Top with pineapple slices. Place a whole berry in center of each slice; sprinkle remaining berries around pineapple.
**2.** For cake, in a large bowl, cream butter and sugar until light and fluffy. Add eggs, one at a time, beating well after each addition. Beat in vanilla. In another bowl, whisk flour, baking powder, salt, cinnamon and allspice; add to creamed mixture alternately with sour cream, beating well after each addition. Fold in cranberries; spoon over pineapple.
**3.** Bake 50-60 minutes or until a toothpick inserted in the center comes out clean. Cool 10 minutes; invert onto serving plate. Serve warm; if desired, top with whipped cream.
**PER SERVING** *402 cal., 21 g fat (13 g sat. fat), 84 mg chol., 363 mg sodium, 51 g carb., 1 g fiber, 3 g pro.*

## Little Amaretto Loaf Cakes

Baked in small pans and covered with a glaze, these treats are so moist. The recipe makes four cakes, so you'll have plenty to share.

**—DONNA LAMANO** OLATHE, KS

**PREP:** 25 MIN. • **BAKE:** 35 MIN. + STANDING
**MAKES:** 4 MINI LOAVES (6 SLICES EACH)

- 4 eggs
- 1 cup sugar
- ½ cup water
- ½ cup amaretto
- ½ cup canola oil
- ¼ cup butter, melted
- 2 cups all-purpose flour
- 3 teaspoons baking powder
- 1 teaspoon salt
- ¾ cup sliced almonds

**GLAZE**
- ½ cup sugar
- ½ cup water
- ¼ cup butter, cubed
- ¼ cup amaretto

**1.** Preheat oven to 325°. Grease and flour four 5¾x3x2-in. loaf pans.
**2.** In a large bowl, beat eggs, sugar, water, amaretto, oil and melted butter until well blended. In another bowl, whisk the flour, baking powder and salt; gradually beat into egg mixture. Stir in the almonds.
**3.** Transfer to prepared pans. Bake 35-40 minutes or until a toothpick inserted in center comes out clean.
**4.** Meanwhile, for glaze, combine sugar, water and butter in a small saucepan; bring to a boil. Cook and stir 3 minutes. Remove from heat; stir in amaretto.
**5.** Remove the cakes from oven; cool in pans on a wire rack 5 minutes. Pour the glaze over cakes while in pans; let stand until the glaze is absorbed, about 30 minutes. Remove cakes from pans. Store cooled cakes, covered, in refrigerator.
**PER SERVING** *217 cal., 11 g fat (3 g sat. fat), 45 mg chol., 188 mg sodium, 24 g carb., 1 g fiber, 3 g pro.*

LITTLE AMARETTO LOAF CAKES

FROZEN GRASSHOPPER PIE

# Frozen Grasshopper Pie

With creme de menthe and creme de cacao, this frosty favorite is a great choice for grown-up guests at a holiday party.

—LORRAINE CALAND SHUNIAH, ON

**PREP:** 20 MIN. + CHILLING • **COOK:** 15 MIN. + FREEZING
**MAKES:** 8 SERVINGS

- 1¼ cups chocolate wafer crumbs (about 22 wafers)
- ¼ cup sugar
- ¼ cup butter, melted

**FILLING**
- 1 package (10 ounces) miniature marshmallows
- ⅓ cup 2% milk
- ¼ cup creme de menthe
- 2 tablespoons creme de cacao
- ¼ teaspoon peppermint extract, optional
- 2 cups heavy whipping cream
  Maraschino cherries and additional whipped cream, optional

**1.** In a small bowl, mix the wafer crumbs and sugar; stir in butter. Press onto bottom and up sides of a greased 9-in. pie plate. Refrigerate 30 minutes.

**2.** Meanwhile, in a large saucepan, combine the miniature marshmallows and milk; cook and stir over medium-low heat 12-14 minutes or until smooth. Remove from the heat. Cool to room temperature, stirring occasionally. Stir in liqueurs and, if desired, extract.

**3.** In a large bowl, beat the cream until soft peaks form; fold in marshmallow mixture. Transfer to crust. Freeze 6 hours or until firm. If desired, top with cherries and additional whipped cream just before serving.

**PER SERVING** *520 cal., 30 g fat (18 g sat. fat), 98 mg chol., 187 mg sodium, 55 g carb., 1 g fiber, 3 g pro.*

# Creamy Lime Pie with Fresh Berries

As soon as berry season arrives, I head out to the patch to pick a bunch of juicy little gems for pie. Fresh cilantro and a splash of lime add flavor to the filling, and gingersnap cookies form a sweet-spicy crust.

—ANNELIESE BARZ FORT MILL, SC

**PREP:** 30 MIN. + CHILLING • **BAKE:** 10 MIN. + COOLING
**MAKES:** 8 SERVINGS

- 1¾ cups finely crushed gingersnap cookies (about 30 cookies)
- ¼ cup sugar
- 2 tablespoons all-purpose flour
- ⅓ cup butter, melted

**FILLING**
- 1 package (8 ounces) cream cheese, softened
- 4 teaspoons grated lime peel
- 2 tablespoons lime juice
- 1 cup confectioners' sugar
- 1 teaspoon vanilla extract
- ½ cup coarsely chopped fresh cilantro

**TOPPING**
- 2 cups fresh strawberries, sliced
- 2 cups fresh blueberries
- 2 tablespoons apricot preserves

**1.** Preheat oven to 375°. In a small bowl, mix the crushed cookies, sugar and flour; stir in butter. Press onto bottom and up sides of a greased 9-in. pie plate. Bake 8-10 minutes or until set. Cool completely on a wire rack.

**2.** In a small bowl, beat cream cheese, lime peel and lime juice until blended. Beat in confectioners' sugar and vanilla. Stir in cilantro. Transfer to the crust. Refrigerate, covered, at least 4 hours or until filling is firm.

**3.** Just before serving, arrange berries over pie. In microwave, warm preserves just until melted. Brush over berries.

**PER SERVING** *441 cal., 21 g fat (12 g sat. fat), 51 mg chol., 370 mg sodium, 61 g carb., 3 g fiber, 5 g pro.*

CREAMY LIME PIE WITH FRESH BERRIES

# Crazy for Cupcakes

Stuffed with marshmallow creme, topped with a chocolate glaze...the sweet delights here will make your family and friends beg for more!

Pineapple Marzipan Cupcakes are unusual but yummy. Sometimes I bake the batter in a loaf pan.
—**JOHNNA JOHNSON** SCOTTSDALE, AZ

## Orange Dream Mini Cupcakes

These little favorites have a citrusy, creamy taste that reminds everyone of orange-and-vanilla frozen treats.
—**JEN SHEPHERD** ST. PETERS, MO

**PREP:** 1 HOUR • **BAKE:** 15 MIN. + COOLING • **MAKES:** 4 DOZEN

- ½ cup butter, softened
- 1 cup sugar
- 2 eggs
- 1 tablespoon grated orange peel
- 1 tablespoon orange juice
- ½ teaspoon vanilla extract
- 1½ cups all-purpose flour
- 1½ teaspoons baking powder
- ¼ teaspoon salt
- ½ cup buttermilk

**BUTTERCREAM**
- ½ cup butter, softened
- ¼ teaspoon salt
- 2 cups confectioners' sugar
- 2 tablespoons 2% milk
- 1½ teaspoons vanilla extract
- ½ cup orange marmalade

**1.** Preheat oven to 325°. Line 48 mini-muffin cups with paper liners. In a large bowl, cream butter and sugar until light and fluffy. Add eggs, one at a time, beating well after each addition. Beat in orange peel, orange juice and vanilla. In another bowl, whisk flour, baking powder and salt; add to creamed mixture alternately with buttermilk, beating well after each addition.

**2.** Fill lined cups two-thirds full. Bake for 11-13 minutes or until a toothpick inserted in center comes out clean. Cool in the pans 5 minutes before removing to wire racks to cool completely.

**3.** For the buttercream, in a large bowl, beat butter and salt until creamy. Gradually beat in confectioners' sugar, milk and vanilla until smooth.

**4.** Using a paring knife, cut a 1-in.-wide cone-shaped piece from the top of each cupcake; discard the removed portion. Fill the cavity with orange marmalade. Pipe or spread the buttercream over the tops.

**PER SERVING** *96 cal., 4 g fat (2 g sat. fat), 19 mg chol., 72 mg sodium, 15 g carb., trace fiber, 1 g pro.*

PINEAPPLE MARZIPAN CUPCAKES

## Pineapple Marzipan Cupcakes

**PREP:** 30 MIN. • **BAKE:** 20 MIN. + COOLING • **MAKES:** 16 CUPCAKES

- ¾ cup butter, softened
- 1 package (7 ounces) marzipan, crumbled
- ½ cup sugar
- ¼ cup packed brown sugar
- 3 eggs
- 1 teaspoon vanilla extract
- 2 cups all-purpose flour
- 2 teaspoons baking powder
- 1 can (8 ounces) crushed pineapple, drained

**TOPPING**
- 8 ounces semisweet chocolate, chopped
- 2 tablespoons butter
  Pineapple tidbits, patted dry

**1.** Preheat oven to 350°. Line 16 muffin cups with paper or foil liners.

**2.** In a large bowl, beat butter, marzipan and sugars until blended. Add eggs, one at a time, beating well after each addition. Beat in vanilla. In another bowl, whisk flour and baking powder; gradually beat into butter mixture. Fold in crushed pineapple.

**3.** Fill lined cups two-thirds full. Bake 20-25 minutes or until a toothpick inserted in center comes out clean. Cool in pans 10 minutes before removing to wire racks to cool completely.

**4.** In a small heavy saucepan, melt the chocolate and butter over very low heat; stir until smooth. Cool slightly until the mixture thickens to a spreading consistency. Spread over cupcakes. Top with pineapple.

**PER SERVING** *326 cal., 17 g fat (9 g sat. fat), 66 mg chol., 136 mg sodium, 40 g carb., 2 g fiber, 5 g pro.*

## Marshmallow-Filled Banana Cupcakes

When I moved to my neighborhood 40 years ago, a friend shared her recipe for filled cupcakes. I've been enjoying them ever since!
—**MONIQUE CARON** BUXTON, ME

**PREP:** 40 MIN. • **BAKE:** 20 MIN. + COOLING • **MAKES:** 1½ DOZEN

- ¾ cup shortening
- 1½ cups sugar
- 2 eggs
- 1 cup mashed ripe bananas (about 2 medium)
- 1 teaspoon vanilla extract
- 2 cups all-purpose flour
- 1 teaspoon baking soda
- ¼ teaspoon salt
- ¼ cup buttermilk

**FILLING**
- 1 cup butter, softened
- 2 cups marshmallow creme
- 1½ cups confectioners' sugar
  Additional confectioners' sugar

**1.** Preheat oven to 375°. Line 18 muffin cups with paper or foil liners.

**2.** In a large bowl, cream shortening and sugar until light and fluffy. Add eggs, one at a time, beating well after each addition. Beat in the bananas and vanilla. In another bowl, whisk flour, baking soda and salt; add to creamed mixture alternately with buttermilk, beating well after each addition.

**3.** Fill lined cups two-thirds full. Bake 18-22 minutes or until a toothpick inserted in center comes out clean. Cool in pans 10 minutes before removing to wire racks to cool completely.

**4.** For filling, in a large bowl, beat the butter, marshmallow creme and confectioners' sugar until smooth. Using a sharp knife, cut a 1-in. circle, 1 in. deep, in the top of each cupcake. Carefully remove the cut portion and set aside. Fill cavity with about 1 teaspoon filling. Replace the tops, pressing down lightly. Dollop or pipe remaining filling over tops. Dust with confectioners' sugar.

**PER SERVING** *373 cal., 19 g fat (9 g sat. fat), 50 mg chol., 195 mg sodium, 49 g carb., 1 g fiber, 2 g pro.*

MARSHMALLOW-FILLED BANANA CUPCAKES

KEY LIME PIE CUPCAKES

## Key Lime Pie Cupcakes

I bake over 200 of these goodies for our church suppers. If you can't find Key lime juice, use lime juice and add a tad more sugar.
—**JULIE LEMLER** ROCHESTER, MN

**PREP:** 45 MIN. • **BAKE:** 20 MIN. + COOLING • **MAKES:** 32 CUPCAKES

- 2 packages (14.1 ounces each) refrigerated pie pastry
- 1 cup butter, softened
- 2½ cups sugar
- 4 eggs
- ½ cup Key lime juice
- 2 cups all-purpose flour
- 1½ cups self-rising flour
- 1½ cups buttermilk

**FROSTING**
- 12 ounces cream cheese, softened
- 1½ cups butter, softened
- 1½ teaspoons vanilla extract
- 2¾ to 3 cups confectioners' sugar
- 6 tablespoons Key lime juice
  Fresh raspberries

**1.** Preheat the oven to 350°. Line 32 muffin cups with foil liners. On a lightly floured work surface, unroll the pastry sheets. Cut 32 circles with a floured 2¼-in. round cookie cutter (discard remaining pastry or save for another use). Press one pastry circle into each liner. Bake 10-12 minutes or until lightly browned. Cool on a wire rack.

**2.** In a large bowl, beat butter and sugar until crumbly. Add eggs, one at a time, beating well after each addition. Beat in juice. In another bowl, whisk flours; add to butter mixture alternately with buttermilk, beating well after each addition.

**3.** Pour batter into lined cups. Bake 20-22 minutes or until a toothpick inserted in center comes out clean. Cool in pans 10 minutes before removing to wire racks to cool completely.

**4.** In a large bowl, beat the cream cheese, the butter and vanilla until blended. Beat in enough confectioners' sugar, alternately with juice, to reach desired consistency. Frost cupcakes; top with raspberries. Refrigerate leftovers.

**NOTE** *To substitute 1½ cups self-rising flour, increase all-purpose flour to 3 cups and add 2¼ teaspoons baking powder and ¾ teaspoon salt; whisk flour, baking powder and salt until blended before adding to butter mixture.*

**PER SERVING** *368 cal., 21 g fat (13 g sat. fat), 78 mg chol., 256 mg sodium, 42 g carb., trace fiber, 4 g pro.*

# nfetti Cake
## th Brown Sugar
## Buttercream

Rainbow jimmies, confetti sprinkles, bright yellow frosting—it all adds up to party fun!

—**KAREN BERNER** GREENDALE, WI

**PREP:** 40 MIN. • **BAKE:** 20 MIN. + COOLING
**MAKES:** 16 SERVINGS

- 2¼ cups cake flour
- 1½ cups sugar
- 3½ teaspoons baking powder
- ½ teaspoon salt
- ½ cup unsalted butter, softened
- 4 egg whites
- ¾ cup whole milk
- 1 teaspoon clear vanilla extract
- ½ teaspoon almond extract
- ⅓ cup rainbow jimmies

**BUTTERCREAM**
- 4 egg whites
- 1 cup packed light brown sugar
- ¼ teaspoon salt
- 1½ cups unsalted butter, softened
- 1½ teaspoons clear vanilla extract
- ½ to ¾ teaspoon yellow food coloring
  Confetti sprinkles

**1.** Preheat oven to 350°. Line bottoms of two greased 9-in. round baking pans with parchment paper; grease paper.
**2.** In a large bowl, whisk the flour, sugar, baking powder and salt. Beat in the butter. Add the egg whites, one at a time, beating well after each addition. Gradually beat in milk and extracts. Gently fold in jimmies.

CONFETTI CAKE WITH
BROWN SUGAR BUTTERCREAM

**3.** Transfer the batter to the prepared pans. Bake for 20-25 minutes or until a toothpick inserted in center comes out clean. Cool in pans for 10 minutes before removing to wire racks; remove paper. Cool completely.
**4.** For buttercream, in a heatproof bowl of a stand mixer, whisk the egg whites, brown sugar and salt until blended. Place over simmering water in a large saucepan over medium heat. Whisking constantly, heat the mixture until a thermometer reads 160°, about 2-3 minutes.
**5.** Remove from heat. With whisk attachment of stand mixer, beat on high speed until stiff glossy peaks form, about 7 minutes.
**6.** Gradually beat in butter, a few tablespoons at a time, on medium speed until smooth. Beat in the vanilla and enough food coloring to achieve desired color. Immediately spread frosting between the layers and over the top and sides of cake. Decorate with sprinkles. Store in refrigerator.

**NOTE** *The cake shown was prepared with Eillien's Rainbow Decorettes in the batter. If this product is not available in your area, look for other non-chocolate rainbow jimmies.*

**PER SERVING** *436 cal., 24 g fat (15 g sat. fat), 62 mg chol., 239 mg sodium, 51 g carb., trace fiber, 4 g pro.*

# Mango Pie with Coconut Crust

I love mangoes, so I tried them in a pie. Coconut and rum boost the tropical taste.

—**JENNIFER WORRELL** NILES, IL

**PREP:** 50 MIN. + CHILLING
**BAKE:** 45 MIN. + COOLING
**MAKES:** 8 SERVINGS

- 2½ cups all-purpose flour
- ½ teaspoon salt
- ⅔ cup cold butter, cubed
- ⅔ to ¾ cup ice water
- 5 cups sliced peeled mangoes (about 4 large)
- 2 tablespoons dark rum or orange juice
- ⅓ cup sugar
- 2 tablespoons quick-cooking tapioca
- ¾ teaspoon ground ginger
- ¼ teaspoon ground cardamom
  Dash white pepper

MANGO PIE WITH COCONUT CRUST

- ⅛ teaspoon salt
- ⅓ cup flaked coconut, toasted

**1.** In a large bowl, mix flour and salt; cut in butter until crumbly. Gradually add the ice water, tossing with a fork until the dough holds together when pressed. Divide dough in half. Shape each into a disk; wrap in plastic wrap. Refrigerate 30 minutes or overnight.
**2.** Preheat oven to 400°. In a large bowl, toss the mangoes with the rum. In a small bowl, mix the sugar, tapioca, spices and salt. Gently stir into fruit mixture; let stand 15 minutes.
**3.** Sprinkle the coconut on a lightly floured surface. Place one half of the dough on the coconut; roll dough to a ⅛-in.-thick circle. Transfer to a 9-in. pie plate, coconut side down. Trim pastry even with rim. Add filling.
**4.** Roll the remaining dough to a ⅛-in.-thick circle; cut into ½-in.-wide strips. Arrange over filling in a lattice pattern. Trim and seal strips to edge of bottom pastry; flute edge.
**5.** Bake 45-50 minutes or until the crust is golden brown and the filling is bubbly. Cover edge loosely with foil during the last 15 minutes if needed to prevent overbrowning. Remove foil. Cool on a wire rack.

**NOTE** *To toast coconut, spread in a 15x10x1-in. baking pan. Bake at 350° for 5-10 minutes or until golden brown, stirring frequently.*

**PER SERVING** *414 cal., 17 g fat (11 g sat. fat), 40 mg chol., 305 mg sodium, 60 g carb., 3 g fiber, 5 g pro.*

## Double-Crust Strawberry Pie

Fresh strawberries and a sprinkling of cinnamon make a scrumptious pair. You'll want to pull out this recipe in spring when berry patches are bursting with ripe fruit.

—**PATRICIA KUTCHINS** LAKE ZURICH, IL

**PREP:** 25 MIN. • **BAKE:** 35 MIN. + COOLING
**MAKES:** 8 SERVINGS

- ½ cup plus 1 tablespoon sugar, divided
- ¼ cup all-purpose flour
- ½ teaspoon ground cinnamon
- 4 cups fresh strawberries (about 1¼ pounds), sliced
  Pastry for double-crust pie (9 inches)
- 2 tablespoons 2% milk

**1.** Preheat oven to 425°. In a large bowl, mix ½ cup sugar, flour and cinnamon; add the strawberries and toss to coat.

**2.** On a lightly floured surface, roll one half of pastry dough to a ⅛-in.-thick circle; transfer to a 9-in. pie plate. Trim pastry even with rim. Add filling.

**3.** Roll the remaining dough to form a ⅛-in.-thick circle. Place over filling. Trim, seal and flute edge. Cut slits in top. Brush with milk; sprinkle with remaining sugar.

**4.** Bake 35-40 minutes or until crust is golden brown and filling is bubbly. Cover edge loosely with foil during the last 20 minutes if needed to prevent overbrowning.

**5.** Remove foil. Cool on a wire rack 1 hour before serving.

**PASTRY FOR DOUBLE-CRUST PIE (9 INCHES)** *Combine 2½ cups all-purpose flour and ½ tsp. salt; cut in 1 cup cold butter until crumbly. Gradually add ⅓ to ⅔ cup ice water, tossing with a fork until dough holds together when pressed. Divide dough in half. Shape each into a disk; wrap in plastic wrap. Refrigerate for 1 hour or overnight.*

**PER SERVING** *334 cal., 14 g fat (6 g sat. fat), 10 mg chol., 203 mg sodium, 49 g carb., 2 g fiber, 3 g pro.*

## Blueberry Upside-Down Skillet Cake

Living in Maine, I'm fortunate to have an endless supply of wild blueberries close at hand. I like to use them in a dessert that's similar to pineapple upside-down cake. Cranberries also work well.

—**NETTIE MOORE** BELFAST, ME

**PREP:** 25 MIN. • **BAKE:** 20 MIN.
**MAKES:** 8 SERVINGS

- ¼ cup butter, cubed
- 1 cup packed brown sugar
- ¼ cup orange juice
- 1 cup fresh or frozen blueberries
- 1½ cups all-purpose flour
- ½ cup sugar
- 2 teaspoons baking powder
- ½ teaspoon salt
- 1 egg
- ½ cup 2% milk
- ½ cup butter, melted
- ½ teaspoon almond extract
  Optional toppings: vanilla ice cream, whipped cream and toasted almonds

**1.** Preheat oven to 400°. In a 10-in. ovenproof skillet, melt the cubed butter over medium-low heat; stir in brown sugar until dissolved. Remove from the heat. Stir in the orange juice; sprinkle with blueberries.

**2.** In a large bowl, whisk flour, sugar, baking powder and salt. In another bowl, whisk egg, milk, melted butter and extract until blended. Add to the flour mixture; stir just until moistened. Pour over blueberries.

**3.** Bake for 18-22 minutes or until a toothpick inserted in center comes out clean. Cool 10 minutes before inverting onto a serving plate. Top as desired.

**NOTE** *To toast nuts, spread them in a 15x10x1-in. baking pan. Bake at 350° for 5-10 minutes or until lightly browned, stirring occasionally. Or, spread in a dry nonstick skillet and heat over low heat until lightly browned, stirring occasionally.*

**PER SERVING** *454 cal., 21 g fat (11 g sat. fat), 73 mg chol., 396 mg sodium, 63 g carb., 2 g fiber, 5 g pro.*

BLUEBERRY UPSIDE-DOWN SKILLET CAKE

## Maple Peanut Butter Pie

Maple nut candies have been a favorite of mine since I was a child. Those goodies inspired a whole new dessert my family and I can enjoy by the slice.

—CRYSTAL SCHLUETER NORTHGLENN, CO

**PREP:** 25 MIN. + CHILLING
**MAKES:** 8 SERVINGS

- 1½ cups crushed cream-filled maple sandwich cookies (about 12 cookies)
- 3 tablespoons butter, melted
- ⅓ cup hot fudge ice cream topping
- 1 package (8 ounces) cream cheese, softened
- 1 cup creamy peanut butter
- 1 teaspoon maple flavoring
- 1¼ cups confectioners' sugar
- 1 carton (8 ounces) frozen whipped topping, thawed
- 1 cup heavy whipping cream
- 2 tablespoons maple syrup
- ¼ cup chocolate-covered peanuts, coarsely chopped

**1.** In a small bowl, mix the crushed sandwich cookies and butter. Press onto the bottom and up the sides of an ungreased 9-in. pie plate. Freeze for 5 minutes.

**2.** In a microwave, warm the fudge ice cream topping 5-10 seconds or until spreadable; spread over the bottom and up the sides of the crust. In a large bowl, beat the cream cheese, peanut butter and flavoring until blended.

Gradually beat in confectioners' sugar; fold in whipped topping. Spoon into crust, spreading evenly. Refrigerate 4 hours or until set.

**3.** In a small bowl, beat the heavy whipping cream until it begins to thicken. Add the maple syrup; beat until stiff peaks form. Serve with pie; top with peanuts.

**PER SERVING** *773 cal., 53 g fat (25 g sat. fat), 84 mg chol., 373 mg sodium, 63 g carb., 3 g fiber, 13 g pro.*

## Hazelnut Pear Cake

From the bits of pear to the hazelnuts, this recipe takes pound cake to another level.

—ELISABETH LARSEN PLEASANT GROVE, UT

**PREP:** 30 MIN. • **BAKE:** 55 MIN. + COOLING
**MAKES:** 16 SERVINGS

- 1½ cups whole hazelnuts, toasted and skins removed
- 1 cup unsalted butter, softened
- 2 cups sugar
- 4 eggs
- 2 teaspoons vanilla extract
- 1 teaspoon almond extract
- 2½ cups all-purpose flour
- ½ teaspoon salt
- ½ teaspoon baking soda
- 1 cup ricotta cheese
- 3 ripe medium pears, peeled and chopped (about 2 cups)

**BROWNED BUTTER GLAZE**
- ½ cup butter, cubed
- 3 tablespoons 2% milk
- 1 teaspoon vanilla extract
- 1¾ to 2 cups confectioners' sugar

**1.** Preheat oven to 350°. Grease and flour a 10-in. fluted tube pan. Chop 1 cup hazelnuts. Place the remaining hazelnuts in a food processor; pulse until finely ground.

**2.** In a large bowl, cream butter and sugar until light and fluffy. Add eggs, one at a time, beating well after each addition. Beat in extracts.

**3.** In another bowl, whisk flour, salt, baking soda and ground hazelnuts; add to creamed mixture alternately with ricotta cheese, beating after each addition just until combined. Fold in pears and chopped hazelnuts.

**HAZELNUT PEAR CAKE**

**4.** Transfer the batter to the prepared pan. Bake for 55-65 minutes or until a toothpick inserted in the center comes out clean. Cool in the pan 10 minutes before removing to a wire rack to cool completely.

**5.** For glaze, in a small heavy saucepan, melt butter over medium heat. Heat for 5-7 minutes or until golden brown, stirring constantly. Transfer to a bowl. Stir in the milk, vanilla and enough confectioners' sugar to reach desired consistency. Drizzle over cooled cake.

**NOTE** *To remove cakes easily, use solid shortening to grease plain and fluted tube pans. To toast whole hazelnuts, spread them in a 15x10x1-in. baking pan. Bake in a 350° oven 7-10 minutes or until fragrant and lightly browned, stirring occasionally. To remove skins, wrap hazelnuts in a tea towel; rub with towel to loosen skins.*

**PER SERVING** *533 cal., 30 g fat (13 g sat. fat), 104 mg chol., 193 mg sodium, 62 g carb., 3 g fiber, 8 g pro.*

**MAPLE PEANUT BUTTER PIE**

### top tip · Quick and Easy Glaze

When I need a cake glaze but am short on time, I use convenient canned white frosting. I just put a small amount in a bowl, warm it a bit in the microwave and then thin it with milk or water.

—ELAINE ANDERSON ALIQUIPPA, PA

## Chocolate Chunk Pecan Pie

Our family invites friends to an annual barn party, which is complete with a pie cook-off. Here's one of the delectable entries that won first prize.

—**JANICE SCHNEIDER** KANSAS CITY, MO

**PREP:** 35 MIN. + CHILLING
**BAKE:** 55 MIN. + CHILLING
**MAKES:** 10 SERVINGS

- 1¼ **cups all-purpose flour**
- ⅛ **teaspoon salt**
- 1 **package (3 ounces) cold cream cheese, cubed**
- ¼ **cup cold butter, cubed**
- 2 **to 3 tablespoons ice water**

**FILLING**
- ⅓ **cup sugar**
- 3 **tablespoons butter**
- 2 **cups coarsely chopped semisweet chocolate, divided**
- 4 **eggs**
- 1 **cup dark corn syrup**
- 2 **teaspoons vanilla extract**
  **Dash salt**
- 2½ **cups pecan halves, toasted**

**1.** In a small bowl, mix flour and salt; cut in cream cheese and butter until crumbly. Gradually add the ice water, tossing with a fork until dough holds together when pressed. Shape into a disk; wrap in plastic wrap. Refrigerate 30 minutes or overnight.

**2.** Preheat oven to 350°. On a lightly floured surface, roll the dough to a ⅛-in.-thick circle; transfer to a 9-in. pie plate. Trim pastry to ½ in. beyond rim of plate; flute edge. Refrigerate while making filling.

**3.** In a small saucepan, combine the sugar, the butter and 2 cups chopped chocolate; stir over low heat until smooth. Cool slightly.

**4.** In a large bowl, whisk the eggs, dark corn syrup, vanilla and salt until blended. Stir in the chocolate mixture. Layer the pecans and the remaining chopped chocolate in the pastry shell; pour chocolate mixture over top.

**5.** Bake 55-60 minutes or until set. Cool 1 hour on a wire rack. Refrigerate 2 hours or until cold.

**NOTE** *To toast nuts, spread them in a 15x10x1-in. baking pan. Bake at 350° for 5-10 minutes or until lightly browned, stirring occasionally. Or, spread them in a dry nonstick skillet and heat over low heat until lightly browned, stirring occasionally.*

**PER SERVING** *650 cal., 42 g fat (15 g sat. fat), 115 mg chol., 209 mg sodium, 69 g carb., 5 g fiber, 9 g pro.*

## Glazed Gingerbread Cake

This spiced delight always goes over well during the holiday season. I keep the glaze simple so it doesn't compete with the wonderful blend of flavors in each bite.

—**EDITH EKSTEDT** PASO ROBLES, CA

**PREP:** 25 MIN. • **BAKE:** 40 MIN. + COOLING
**MAKES:** 12 SERVINGS

**CAKE**
- 1 **cup raisins**
- 1 **cup molasses**
- ½ **cup packed brown sugar**
- ½ **cup canola oil**
- ⅓ **cup each strong brewed coffee and orange juice**
- 2 **tablespoons water**
- 3 **eggs**
- 3 **cups all-purpose flour**
- ¼ **cup nonfat dry milk powder**
- 1 **tablespoon ground ginger**
- 1 **tablespoon grated orange peel**
- 1 **teaspoon cream of tartar**
- 1 **teaspoon baking soda**
- ½ **teaspoon each ground cinnamon, mace and nutmeg**

GLAZED GINGERBREAD CAKE

**GLAZE**
- 2½ **cups confectioners' sugar**
- ¼ **cup 2% milk**
- 2 **tablespoons butter, melted**
- ¼ **teaspoon vanilla extract**

**1.** Preheat oven to 350°. Grease and flour a 10-in. fluted tube pan. Place the raisins in a small bowl; add boiling water to cover raisins and let stand 5 minutes. Drain.

**2.** In a large bowl, whisk molasses, brown sugar, oil, coffee, juice and water until blended. In a small bowl, beat eggs on high speed 3-4 minutes or until thick and lemon-colored. In another bowl, whisk remaining cake ingredients. Add to molasses mixture alternately with eggs, mixing just until combined. Fold in raisins.

**3.** Transfer to prepared pan. Bake 40-45 minutes or until a toothpick inserted in the center comes out with moist crumbs (do not overbake). Cool 10 minutes before removing from pan to a wire rack to cool completely.

**4.** In a small bowl, mix the glaze ingredients until smooth. Pour over the cake.

**NOTE** *To remove cakes easily, use solid shortening to grease plain and fluted tube pans.*

**PER SERVING** *452 cal., 10 g fat (2 g sat. fat), 59 mg chol., 163 mg sodium, 88 g carb., 4 g fiber, 7 g pro.*

CHOCOLATE CHUNK PECAN PIE

LAYERED ORANGE SPONGE CAKE

# Layered Orange Sponge Cake

This family recipe, which has been passed down for decades, originally came from a relative who was a French baker. It's light, delicate and delicious.

—JOYCE SPEERBRECHER GRAFTON, WI

**PREP:** 30 MIN. • **BAKE:** 45 MIN. + COOLING
**MAKES:** 12 SERVINGS

- 8 eggs, separated
- 1 cup plus 2 tablespoons all-purpose flour
- ⅔ cup plus ⅔ cup sugar, divided
- ½ cup orange juice
- 3 tablespoons grated orange peel
- ½ teaspoon salt
- ¼ teaspoon cream of tartar

**FROSTING**
- 1½ cups sugar
- 6 tablespoons all-purpose flour
- ⅔ cup orange juice
- 3 tablespoons grated orange peel
- 2 eggs
- 2 cups heavy whipping cream
- 1 cup chopped pecans

**1.** Place the egg whites in a large bowl; let stand at room temperature 30 minutes. Meanwhile, preheat the oven to 325°. Sift flour twice.
**2.** In another large bowl, beat yolks until slightly thickened. Gradually add ⅔ cup sugar, beating on high speed until thick and lemon-colored. Beat in the orange juice and orange peel. Fold in the flour.
**3.** Add the salt and cream of tartar to the egg whites; with clean beaters, beat on medium until soft peaks form. Gradually add the remaining sugar,

1 tablespoon at a time, beating on high after each addition until the sugar is dissolved. Continue beating until soft glossy peaks form. Fold a fourth of the egg whites into the batter, then fold in the remaining whites.
**4.** Gently transfer to an ungreased 10-in. tube pan. Bake on lowest oven rack 45-55 minutes or until the top springs back when lightly touched. Immediately invert pan; cool cake in pan, about 1½ hours.
**5.** Meanwhile, in a large and heavy saucepan, mix sugar and flour. Whisk in the orange juice and orange peel. Cook and stir over medium heat until thickened and bubbly. Reduce heat to low; cook and stir 2 minutes longer. Remove from heat.
**6.** In a small bowl, whisk a small amount of the hot mixture into eggs; return all to pan, whisking constantly. Bring to a gentle boil; cook and stir 2 minutes. Immediately transfer to a clean bowl. Cool 30 minutes. Press plastic wrap onto surface of orange mixture; refrigerate until cold.
**7.** In a large bowl, beat the heavy whipping cream until soft peaks form; fold into the orange mixture. Run a knife around the sides and center tube of pan. Remove cake to a serving plate. Using a long serrated knife, cut cake horizontally into three layers. Spread frosting between layers and over top and sides of cake. Sprinkle with pecans. Refrigerate until serving.
**PER SERVING** *518 cal., 26 g fat (11 g sat. fat), 231 mg chol., 172 mg sodium, 65 g carb., 2 g fiber, 9 g pro.*

# Billie's Southern Sweet Potato Cake

When I first prepared my sweet potato cake years ago, I had never made one from scratch before. Needless to say, I was thrilled when my kids tasted it and said, "Mommy, you're the best baker!"

—BILLIE WILLIAMS-HENDERSON CROFTON, MD

**PREP:** 25 MIN. • **BAKE:** 40 MIN. + COOLING
**MAKES:** 20 SERVINGS

- 4 eggs
- 2 cups sugar
- 2 cups canola oil
- 2 teaspoons vanilla extract

- 2 cups all-purpose flour
- 2 teaspoons baking soda
- 2 teaspoons ground cinnamon
- ½ teaspoon ground ginger
- ½ teaspoon ground allspice
- ½ teaspoon salt
- 3 cups shredded peeled sweet potatoes (about 2 medium)
- 1 cup finely chopped walnuts

**FROSTING**
- 1 package (8 ounces) cream cheese, softened
- ½ cup butter, softened
- 1 teaspoon vanilla extract
- 2 cups confectioners' sugar

**1.** Preheat oven to 350°. Grease a 13x9-in. baking pan.
**2.** In a large bowl, beat the eggs, sugar, oil and vanilla until well blended. In another bowl, whisk the flour, baking soda, spices and salt; gradually beat into the egg mixture. Stir in the sweet potatoes and walnuts.
**3.** Transfer to the prepared pan. Bake for 40-45 minutes or until a toothpick inserted in center comes out clean. Cool completely in pan on a wire rack.
**4.** In a small bowl, beat cream cheese, the butter and vanilla until blended. Gradually beat in confectioners' sugar until smooth. Spread over cooled cake. Refrigerate leftovers.
**PER SERVING** *519 cal., 36 g fat (8 g sat. fat), 67 mg chol., 276 mg sodium, 47 g carb., 1 g fiber, 5 g pro.*

BILLIE'S SOUTHERN SWEET POTATO CAKE

Winter holidays just aren't the same without Cranberry Double-Nut Pie on the table. The tart berries contrast wonderfully with the rich filling.
—**LILY JULOW** LAWRENCEVILLE, GA

**CRANBERRY DOUBLE-NUT PIE**

## Raspberry Swirl Pound Cake

Serve this rich, beautifully swirled dessert whenever you want to surprise guests with something extra-special.
—**CARLY CURTIN** ELLICOTT CITY, MD

**PREP:** 25 MIN. • **BAKE:** 1 HOUR + COOLING
**MAKES:** 12 SERVINGS

- 1 cup unsalted butter, softened
- 2½ cups sugar
- 5 eggs
- 2 teaspoons vanilla extract
- 3 cups all-purpose flour
- ½ teaspoon salt
- ½ teaspoon baking powder
- 1 cup 2% milk
- ½ cup seedless raspberry preserves
  Confectioners' sugar
  Fresh raspberries and mint leaves, optional

**1.** Preheat oven to 325°. Grease and flour a 10-in. fluted tube pan.
**2.** In a large bowl, cream butter and sugar until light and fluffy. Add eggs, one at a time, beating well after each addition. Beat in vanilla. In another bowl, whisk flour, salt and baking powder; add to creamed mixture alternately with milk, beating after each addition just until combined.
**3.** Remove 2⅓ cups batter to a small bowl; stir in the raspberry preserves until blended. Pour half of the plain batter into prepared pan, spreading evenly. Top with the raspberry batter, then the remaining plain batter. Cut through batter with a knife to swirl.
**4.** Bake for 1 to 1¼ hours or until a toothpick inserted in the center comes out clean. Cool in the pan 10 minutes before removing to a wire rack to cool completely. Dust with confectioners' sugar. If desired, serve with berries and mint.
**NOTE** *To remove cakes easily, use solid shortening to grease plain and fluted tube pans.*
**PER SERVING** *484 cal., 18 g fat (11 g sat. fat), 130 mg chol., 157 mg sodium, 75 g carb., 1 g fiber, 7 g pro.*

## Cranberry Double-Nut Pie

**PREP:** 20 MIN. • **BAKE:** 45 MIN. + COOLING
**MAKES:** 8 SERVINGS

  Pastry for single-crust pie (9 inches)
- 3 eggs
- ¾ cup packed brown sugar
- ½ cup light corn syrup
- ⅓ cup butter, melted
- 2 tablespoons molasses
- ¼ teaspoon salt
- 1½ cups fresh or frozen cranberries, thawed
- ¾ cup coarsely chopped walnuts, toasted
- ¾ cup coarsely chopped pecans, toasted

**1.** Preheat oven to 350°. On a lightly floured surface, roll pastry dough to a ⅛-in.-thick circle; transfer to a 9-in. pie plate. Trim pastry to ½ in. beyond the rim of plate; flute the edge.
**2.** In a large bowl, whisk eggs, brown sugar, corn syrup, butter, molasses and salt; stir in the cranberries, walnuts and pecans. Pour into pastry shell.
**3.** Bake for 45-50 minutes or until set. Cool on a wire rack.
**PASTRY FOR SINGLE-CRUST PIE (9 INCHES)** *Combine 1¼ cups all-purpose flour and ¼ teaspoon salt; cut in ½ cup cold butter until crumbly. Gradually add 3-5 tablespoons ice water, tossing with a fork until the dough holds together when pressed. Wrap dough in plastic wrap and refrigerate 1 hour.*
**NOTE** *To toast nuts, spread them in a 15x10x1-in. baking pan. Bake at 350° for 5-10 minutes or until lightly browned, stirring occasionally. Or, spread in a dry nonstick skillet and heat over low heat until lightly browned, stirring occasionally.*
**PER SERVING** *573 cal., 36 g fat (14 g sat. fat), 129 mg chol., 332 mg sodium, 60 g carb., 3 g fiber, 7 g pro.*

# Blue-Ribbon Apple Pie

This recipe is special to me because I won a blue ribbon for it at the local fair.

—**COLLETTE GAUGLER** FOGELSVILLE, PA

**PREP:** 45 MIN. • **BAKE:** 55 MIN. + COOLING
**MAKES:** 8 SERVINGS

**Pastry for double-crust pie (9 inches)**

**WALNUT LAYER**
- ¾ cup ground walnuts
- 2 tablespoons brown sugar
- 2 tablespoons lightly beaten egg
- 1 tablespoon butter, melted
- 1 tablespoon 2% milk
- ¼ teaspoon lemon juice
- ¼ teaspoon vanilla extract

**FILLING**
- 6 cups sliced peeled tart apples (4-5 medium)
- 2 teaspoons lemon juice
- ½ teaspoon vanilla extract
- ¾ cup sugar
- 3 tablespoons all-purpose flour
- 1¼ teaspoons ground cinnamon
- ¼ teaspoon ground nutmeg
- ⅛ teaspoon salt
- 3 tablespoons butter, cubed

**TOPPING**
- 1 teaspoon 2% milk
- 2 teaspoons sugar

**1.** Preheat oven to 375°. On a lightly floured surface, roll one half of pastry to a ⅛-in.-thick circle; transfer to a 9-in. pie plate. Trim pastry even with rim.
**2.** In a small bowl, mix walnut layer ingredients until blended. Spread onto bottom of pastry shell. Refrigerate while preparing filling.
**3.** For the filling, in a large bowl, toss the apples with the lemon juice and vanilla. In a small bowl, mix the sugar, flour, cinnamon, nutmeg and salt; add to apple mixture and toss to coat.
**4.** Pour filling over walnut layer; dot with butter. Roll remaining pastry to a ⅛-in.-thick circle. Place over filling. Trim, seal and flute edge. Brush top with milk; sprinkle with sugar. Cut slits in pastry.
**5.** Place on a baking sheet. Bake 55-65 minutes or until crust is golden brown and filling is bubbly. Cover edge loosely with foil during the last 10 minutes if needed to prevent overbrowning. Remove foil. Cool on a wire rack.

**PASTRY FOR DOUBLE-CRUST PIE (9 INCHES)** *Combine 2½ cups all-purpose flour and ½ teaspoon salt; cut in 1 cup shortening until crumbly. Gradually add 4 to 5 tablespoons ice water, tossing with a fork until the dough holds together when pressed. Divide dough in half and shape into disks; wrap in plastic wrap and refrigerate 1 hour.*
**PER SERVING** *611 cal., 36 g fat (10 g sat. fat), 31 mg chol., 234 mg sodium, 67 g carb., 3 g fiber, 6 g pro.*

# Truffle Torte

A small slice of rich, fudgy torte goes a long way to satisfy a sweet tooth. I like to add a white-chocolate pattern on top for an extra-fancy presentation.

—**MARY CHOATE** SPRING HILL, FL

**PREP:** 35 MIN. • **BAKE:** 30 MIN. + CHILLING
**MAKES:** 16 SERVINGS

- 8 ounces semisweet chocolate, chopped
- ¾ cup butter, cubed
- ¾ cup ground pecans
- ¼ cup all-purpose flour
- 6 eggs
- ¾ cup sugar
- 1 teaspoon vanilla extract

**GANACHE**
- 4 ounces semisweet chocolate, chopped
- ½ cup heavy whipping cream
- 2 tablespoons butter

**DECORATION**
- 2 ounces white baking chocolate, melted

**1.** Preheat oven to 350°. Line bottom of a greased 9-in. springform pan with parchment paper; grease paper.
**2.** In a microwave, melt chocolate and butter; stir until smooth. Cool slightly. In a small bowl, mix pecans and flour.
**3.** In a large bowl, beat the eggs until frothy; gradually add sugar, beating 4-5 minutes or until mixture triples in volume. Gradually beat in chocolate mixture and vanilla. Fold in pecan mixture. Transfer to prepared pan.
**4.** Bake 30-35 minutes or until cake springs back when lightly touched. Cool on a wire rack 15 minutes. Run a knife around sides of pan; remove rim from pan. Invert cake onto a wire rack; carefully remove pan bottom and paper. Cool completely.
**5.** For the ganache, place chocolate in a small bowl. In a small saucepan, bring cream just to a boil. Pour over the chocolate; stir with a whisk until smooth. Stir in the butter. Refrigerate until mixture thickens slightly, about 15 minutes.
**6.** Place the cake on a serving plate. Pour ganache over cake and quickly spread to edges.
**7.** Fill a food-safe plastic bag with the melted white chocolate; cut a small hole in one corner of bag. Pipe thin horizontal lines 1 in. apart over the ganache. Use a sharp knife to draw right angles across the piped lines. Refrigerate until set, about 30 minutes.
**PER SERVING** *380 cal., 30 g fat (14 g sat. fat), 117 mg chol., 103 mg sodium, 27 g carb., 3 g fiber, 6 g pro.*

TRUFFLE TORTE

## Pink Lemonade Stand Cake

If you love a moist, creamy cake, this is it! Lemon juice and lemonade give the layers a tangy touch, and the subtle pink frosting makes it really beautiful.

—**LAUREN KNOELKE** MILWAUKEE, WI

**PREP:** 50 MIN. • **BAKE:** 20 MIN. + COOLING
**MAKES:** 12 SERVINGS

- 1 **cup buttermilk**
- 2 **tablespoons lemon juice**
- 2 **tablespoons seedless strawberry jam, warmed**
- 2 **tablespoons thawed pink lemonade concentrate**
- 2 **tablespoons grenadine syrup**
- 1 **cup unsalted butter, softened**
- 1¼ **cups sugar**
- 3 **tablespoons grated lemon peel**
- 4 **eggs**
- ½ **teaspoon vanilla extract**
- 2½ **cups all-purpose flour**
- 1 **teaspoon baking powder**
- ½ **teaspoon baking soda**
- ½ **teaspoon salt**

**FROSTING**

- 1 **cup unsalted butter, softened**
- 1 **package (8 ounces) cream cheese, softened**
- 1 **tablespoon grated lemon peel**
- 4 **cups confectioners' sugar**
- ⅓ **cup plus 3 tablespoons thawed pink lemonade concentrate, divided**
  **Pink sprinkles**

**1.** Preheat oven to 350°. Line bottoms of three greased 8-in. round baking pans with parchment paper; grease the paper.
**2.** In a small bowl, whisk the first five ingredients until blended. In a large bowl, cream the butter, sugar and lemon peel until light and fluffy. Add the eggs, one at a time, beating well after each addition. Beat in vanilla. In another bowl, whisk the flour, baking powder, baking soda and salt; add to the creamed mixture alternately with the buttermilk mixture, beating well after each addition.
**3.** Transfer the batter to prepared pans. Bake 20-24 minutes or until a toothpick inserted in center comes out clean. Cool in pans 10 minutes before removing to wire racks; remove paper. Cool completely.
**4.** For the frosting, in a large bowl, beat the butter, cream cheese and lemon peel until smooth. Gradually beat in the confectioners' sugar and ⅓ cup pink lemonade concentrate. If necessary, refrigerate until spreadable, up to 1 hour.
**5.** Place one cake layer on a serving plate. Brush 1 tablespoon lemonade concentrate over the cake; spread with ½ cup frosting. Repeat the layers. Top with the remaining cake layer; brush the remaining lemonade concentrate over the top.
**6.** Spread the remaining frosting over top and sides of cake. Decorate with sprinkles. Refrigerate until serving.
**FOR CUPCAKES** *Make the cake batter as directed; fill 24 paper-lined muffin cups three-fourths full. Bake in a preheated 350° oven for 16-19 minutes or until a toothpick comes out clean. Cool in the pans for 10 minutes before removing to wire racks to cool them completely. Prepare the frosting as directed, omitting 3 tablespoons of lemonade concentrate for brushing layers; pipe or spread frosting over tops. Makes: 2 dozen cupcakes.*
**PER SERVING** *732 cal., 39 g fat (24 g sat. fat), 172 mg chol., 291 mg sodium, 91 g carb., 1 g fiber, 7 g pro.*

## Deep-Dish Apple Pie

Here's an oversized apple pie that's great for a crowd. The crust is so flaky, and the filling is sure to please everyone.

— **SALEM CROSS INN** WEST BROOKFIELD, MA

**PREP:** 50 MIN. • **BAKE:** 40 MIN. + COOLING
**MAKES:** 15 SERVINGS

- 2 **cups all-purpose flour**
- ½ **cup shortening**
- 1 **egg**
- ¼ **cup cold water**
- 2 **tablespoons white vinegar**

**FILLING**

- 10 **cups sliced peeled tart apples (about 8 medium)**
- 1 **teaspoon lemon juice**
- ¼ **cup sugar**
- ¼ **cup packed brown sugar**
- 3 **tablespoons all-purpose flour**

DEEP-DISH APPLE PIE

- 1 **teaspoon ground cinnamon**
- ½ **teaspoon ground nutmeg**
- 1 **tablespoon butter**
- 1 **egg**
- 1 **tablespoon milk**

**1.** Place the flour in a large bowl; cut in shortening until crumbly. In a small bowl, whisk the egg, water and vinegar; gradually add to the crumb mixture, tossing with a fork until the dough holds together when pressed. Shape into a rectangle; wrap in plastic wrap. Refrigerate 30 minutes or overnight.
**2.** Preheat oven to 375°. For the filling, in a large bowl, toss the apples with lemon juice. In a small bowl, combine sugars, flour, cinnamon and nutmeg; add to apple mixture and toss to coat. Transfer to a 13x9-in. baking dish; dot with butter.
**3.** On a lightly floured surface, roll the dough to fit top of pie. Place over filling. Trim and flute edges. In a small bowl, whisk egg with milk; brush over pastry. Cut slits in top. Bake 40-50 minutes or until crust is golden brown and apples are tender. Cool on a wire rack.
**PER SERVING** *208 cal., 8 g fat (2 g sat. fat), 30 mg chol., 18 mg sodium, 31 g carb., 2 g fiber, 3 g pro.*

**FROZEN KEY LIME
DELIGHT**
*PAGE 120*

# Just Desserts

The special main course and side dish on your menu deserve a **just-as-fabulous finale**. Page through this chapter to find a wide variety of **sweet sensations** everyone will love.

**COCONUT-WHITE
CHOCOLATE CHEESECAKE**
*PAGE 122*

**HEAVENLY MINT
BROWNIE DESSERT**
*PAGE 132*

**GINGERED CRANBERRY
PEAR CRISP**
*PAGE 127*

## SLOW COOKER
# Very Vanilla Slow Cooker Cheesecake

Cheesecake from a slow cooker? Yes! The mini dessert yields six silky, smooth, utterly luscious servings—and frees up your oven for the rest of your menu.

—KRISTA LANPHIER MILWAUKEE, WI

**PREP:** 40 MIN. • **COOK:** 2 HOURS + CHILLING
**MAKES:** 6 SERVINGS

- ¾ cup graham cracker crumbs
- 1 tablespoon sugar plus ⅔ cup sugar, divided
- ¼ teaspoon ground cinnamon
- 2½ tablespoons butter, melted
- 2 packages (8 ounces each) cream cheese, softened
- ½ cup sour cream
- 2 to 3 teaspoons vanilla extract
- 2 eggs, lightly beaten

**TOPPING**
- 2 ounces semisweet chocolate, chopped
- 1 teaspoon shortening
  Toasted sliced almonds

**1.** Place a greased 6-in. springform pan on a double thickness of heavy-duty foil (about 12 in. square). Wrap foil securely around pan.

**2.** Pour 1 in. water into a 6-qt. slow cooker. Layer two 24-in. pieces of aluminum foil. Starting with a long side, roll up foil to make a 1-in.-wide strip; shape into a circle. Place in the bottom of slow cooker to make a rack.

**3.** In a small bowl, mix the graham cracker crumbs, 1 tablespoon sugar and cinnamon; stir in the butter. Press onto bottom and about 1 in. up sides of prepared pan.

**4.** In a large bowl, beat cream cheese and the remaining sugar until smooth. Beat in the sour cream and the vanilla. Add eggs; beat on low speed just until combined. Pour into crust.

**5.** Place springform pan on foil circle without touching slow cooker sides. Cover slow cooker with a double layer of white paper towels; place the lid securely over towels. Cook, covered, on high 2 hours.

**6.** Do not remove the lid; turn off the slow cooker and let cheesecake stand, covered, in slow cooker for 1 hour.

**7.** Remove the springform pan from slow cooker; remove foil around pan. Cool cheesecake on a wire rack 1 hour longer. Loosen sides from pan with a knife. Refrigerate overnight, covering when completely cooled.

**8.** For topping, in microwave, melt chocolate and shortening; stir until smooth. Cool slightly. Remove rim from springform pan. Pour chocolate mixture over cheesecake; sprinkle with almonds.

**NOTE** *The 6-inch springform pan is available from Wilton Industries. Call 800-794-5866 or visit wilton.com.*

**PER SERVING** *565 cal., 41 g fat (24 g sat. fat), 180 mg chol., 351 mg sodium, 41 g carb., 1 g fiber, 10 g pro.*

FROZEN KEY LIME DELIGHT

# Frozen Key Lime Delight

On a warm summer day, nothing hits the spot quite like this sublime lime treat from the freezer. It's so refreshing.

—MELISSA MILLWOOD LYMAN, SC

**PREP:** 50 MIN. • **BAKE:** 25 MIN. + FREEZING
**MAKES:** 8 SERVINGS

- 1 cup all-purpose flour
- ½ cup salted cashews, chopped
- ½ cup flaked coconut
- ¼ cup packed light brown sugar
- ½ cup butter, melted
- 2 cups heavy whipping cream
- 1½ cups sweetened condensed milk
- 1 cup key lime juice
- 3 teaspoons grated key lime peel
- 1 teaspoon vanilla extract
  Whipped cream and key lime slices

**1.** Preheat the oven to 350°. In a small bowl, combine the flour, nuts, coconut and the brown sugar. Stir in the butter. Sprinkle into a greased 15x10x1-in. baking pan. Bake for 20-25 minutes or until golden brown, stirring once. Cool on a wire rack.

**2.** Meanwhile, in a large bowl, combine the cream, milk, lime juice, peel and vanilla. Refrigerate until chilled.

**3.** Fill cylinder of an ice cream freezer two-thirds full; freeze according to the manufacturer's directions.

**4.** Sprinkle half of the nut mixture into an ungreased 11x7-in. dish. Spread ice cream over the top; sprinkle with remaining nut mixture. Cover; freeze 4 hours or until firm. Garnish servings with whipped cream and lime slices.

**PER SERVING** *672 cal., 46 g fat (27 g sat. fat), 131 mg chol., 258 mg sodium, 60 g carb., 1 g fiber, 9 g pro.*

VERY VANILLA SLOW COOKER CHEESECAKE

## Simple Cherry Cobbler

Berries, peaches...just about any fruit can be substituted in this cobbler. But once you taste the wonderful tart cherries, you may not want it any other way!

—**ELEANOR JACOBY** EUREKA, KS

**PREP:** 15 MIN. • **BAKE:** 25 MIN.
**MAKES:** 3 SERVINGS

- 1 cup canned pitted tart cherries
- ⅓ cup plus 3 tablespoons sugar, divided
- ½ cup all-purpose flour
- ½ teaspoon baking powder
- 1 tablespoon cold butter
- ¼ cup 2% milk

**1.** In a small saucepan over medium heat, bring the cherries and ⅓ cup sugar to a boil. Remove from the heat; set aside.

**2.** In a small bowl, combine the flour, baking powder and remaining sugar. Cut in the cold butter until mixture resembles coarse crumbs. Stir in the milk just until moistened. Spread into a greased 3-cup baking dish; pour the cherries over the top.

**3.** Bake at 375° for 25-30 minutes or until bubbly and the edges are golden brown. Serve warm.

**PER SERVING** *319 cal., 5 g fat (3 g sat. fat), 13 mg chol., 122 mg sodium, 68 g carb., 1 g fiber, 3 g pro.*

TRIPLE BERRY NO-BAKE CHEESECAKE

After trying Triple Berry No-Bake Cheesecake, my husband said he liked it even better than the time-consuming baked ones I've made. That's a big plus for me!

—**JOYCE MUMMAU** HARRISONVILLE, PA

SIMPLE CHERRY COBBLER

## Triple Berry No-Bake Cheesecake

**PREP:** 20 MIN. + CHILLING
**MAKES:** 12 SERVINGS (3⅓ CUPS TOPPING)

- 1½ cups graham cracker crumbs
- ⅓ cup packed brown sugar
- ½ teaspoon ground cinnamon
- ⅓ cup butter, melted

**FILLING**
- 2 packages (8 ounces each) cream cheese, softened
- ⅓ cup sugar
- 2 teaspoons lemon juice
- 2 cups heavy whipping cream

**TOPPING**
- 2 cups sliced fresh strawberries
- 1 cup fresh blueberries
- 1 cup fresh raspberries
- 2 tablespoons sugar

**1.** In a small bowl, mix the graham cracker crumbs, brown sugar and cinnamon; stir in the butter. Press onto the bottom and 1 in. up the sides of an ungreased 9-in. springform pan. Refrigerate 30 minutes.

**2.** In a large bowl, beat cream cheese, sugar and lemon juice until smooth. Gradually add cream; beat until stiff peaks form. Transfer to the prepared crust. Refrigerate, covered, overnight.

**3.** In a bowl, gently toss the berries with sugar. Let stand 15-30 minutes or until juices are released from berries.

**4.** With a knife, loosen the sides of the cheesecake from the pan; remove rim. Serve cheesecake with topping.

**PER SERVING** *432 cal., 34 g fat (21 g sat. fat), 109 mg chol., 229 mg sodium, 29 g carb., 2 g fiber, 5 g pro.*

BERRIES 'N' CREAM PIZZA

## Coconut-White Chocolate Cheesecake

Friends always say how much they like this chocolate cheesecake. A sprinkling of toasted coconut is the perfect finishing touch.
—**JAMIE HARRIS** DANVILLE, IL

**PREP:** 40 MIN. • **BAKE:** 1 HOUR + CHILLING • **MAKES:** 16 SERVINGS

1½ **cups graham cracker crumbs**
6 **tablespoons butter, melted**
5 **packages (8 ounces each) cream cheese, softened**
1 **cup sugar**
1½ **cups white baking chips, melted and cooled**
¾ **cup coconut milk**
2 **teaspoons coconut extract**
1 **teaspoon vanilla extract**
4 **eggs, lightly beaten**
¾ **cup flaked coconut, toasted, divided**

**1.** Preheat oven to 325°. Place a greased 9-in. (3-in.-deep) springform pan on a double thickness of heavy-duty foil (about 18 in. square). Wrap foil securely around the pan.
**2.** In a small bowl, mix cracker crumbs and butter. Press onto bottom of prepared pan.
**3.** In a large bowl, beat the cream cheese and sugar until smooth. Beat in cooled chips, coconut milk and extracts. Add the eggs; beat on low speed just until blended. Fold in ½ cup coconut. Pour over the crust. Place springform pan in a larger baking pan; add 1 in. of hot water to larger pan.
**4.** Bake 60-70 minutes or until center is just set and top appears dull. Remove springform pan from water bath. Cool cheesecake on a wire rack 10 minutes. Loosen sides from the pan with a knife; remove foil. Cool 1 hour longer. Refrigerate overnight, covering when completely cooled.
**5.** Remove rim from pan. Serve cheesecake topped with remaining coconut.
**NOTE** *To toast coconut, spread in a 15x10x1-in. baking pan. Bake at 350° for 5-10 minutes or until golden brown, stirring frequently.*
**PER SERVING** *517 cal., 40 g fat (25 g sat. fat), 144 mg chol., 332 mg sodium, 32 g carb., 1 g fiber, 9 g pro.*

**FAST FIX** ▶
## Berries 'n' Cream Pizza

Looking for a great summer dessert? Smother a crescent-roll crust with a sweet cream cheese layer and fresh fruit.
—*TASTE OF HOME* TEST KITCHEN

**START TO FINISH:** 25 MIN. • **MAKES:** 12 SERVINGS

1 **tube (8 ounces) refrigerated crescent roll dough**
1 **package (8 ounces) cream cheese, softened**
1 **cup confectioners' sugar**
2 **tablespoons seedless raspberry jam**
1 **carton (8 ounces) frozen whipped topping, thawed**
3 **to 4 medium kiwifruit, peeled and sliced**
1⅓ **cups sliced fresh strawberries**
1⅓ **cups each fresh raspberries, blueberries and blackberries**
½ **cup flaked coconut**

**1.** Separate dough into eight triangles. Press onto a greased 12-in. pizza pan; seal seams. Bake at 375° for 8-10 minutes or until the edges are golden. Cool on a wire rack.
**2.** Meanwhile, in a small bowl, beat the cream cheese, the confectioners' sugar and jam until smooth. Fold in whipped topping. Spread over crust. Arrange fruit over top. Sprinkle with coconut. Chill until serving.
**PER SERVING** *284 cal., 15 g fat (10 g sat. fat), 21 mg chol., 215 mg sodium, 32 g carb., 2 g fiber, 3 g pro.*

COCONUT-WHITE CHOCOLATE CHEESECAKE

My slow cooker makes it easy to indulge in a special treat—Rhubarb Strawberry Sauce.
—**KIM BANICK** SALEM, OR

RHUBARB STRAWBERRY SAUCE

**SLOW COOKER**
# Rhubarb Strawberry Sauce

**PREP:** 15 MIN. • **COOK:** 4½ HOURS • **MAKES:** 10 SERVINGS

- 4 **cups sliced fresh or frozen rhubarb, thawed (about 10 stalks)**
- 4 **cups fresh strawberries (about 1¼ pounds), halved**
- 1½ **cups sugar**
- ¼ **cup water**
- 3 **tablespoons butter**
- 1 **teaspoon vanilla extract**
- ¼ **cup cornstarch**
- 3 **tablespoons cold water**
  **Vanilla ice cream**

**1.** In a 3-qt. slow cooker, combine the first six ingredients. Cook, covered, on low 4-5 hours or until rhubarb is tender.
**2.** In a small bowl, mix the cornstarch and cold water until smooth; gradually stir into the sauce. Cook, covered, on low 30 minutes longer or until thickened. Serve with ice cream.
**NOTE** *If using frozen rhubarb, measure rhubarb while still frozen, then thaw completely. Drain in a colander, but do not press liquid out.*
**PER SERVING** *188 cal., 4 g fat (2 g sat. fat), 9 mg chol., 27 mg sodium, 40 g carb., 2 g fiber, 1 g pro.*

# Peach-Rosemary Cobbler

For a deliciously different flavor in my peach cobbler, I mix a little minced fresh rosemary into the biscuit topping.
—**MICHAEL COHEN** LOS ANGELES, CA

**PREP:** 20 MIN. • **BAKE:** 35 MIN. • **MAKES:** 8 SERVINGS

- ¼ **cup honey**
- 2 **tablespoons cornstarch**
- ¾ **teaspoon grated lemon peel**
- 1 **tablespoon lemon juice**
- ⅛ **teaspoon salt**
- ⅛ **teaspoon ground cinnamon**
- 4 **cups fresh or frozen sliced peeled peaches, thawed**

**TOPPING**
- 1½ **cups all-purpose flour**
- ½ **cup packed brown sugar**
- 1½ **teaspoons baking powder**
- 1 **teaspoon ground cinnamon**
- 1 **teaspoon minced fresh rosemary**
- ½ **teaspoon salt**
- ½ **cup cold butter, cubed**
- ¼ **cup plus 2 tablespoons water**
- ½ **teaspoon vanilla extract**
- ¼ **teaspoon almond extract**
  **Vanilla ice cream, optional**

**1.** Preheat the oven to 400°. In a large bowl, mix the first six ingredients. Add peaches and toss to combine. Transfer to a greased 1½-qt. or 8-in.-square baking dish. Bake 15 minutes.
**2.** Meanwhile, in a bowl, whisk flour, brown sugar, baking powder, cinnamon, rosemary and salt. Cut in butter until mixture resembles coarse crumbs. Mix water and extracts; add to flour mixture, stirring just until moistened.
**3.** Drop the dough by heaping tablespoonfuls over peach mixture. Bake, uncovered, 20-25 minutes longer or until filling is bubbly and topping is golden brown. Serve warm. If desired, top with ice cream.
**PER SERVING** *314 cal., 12 g fat (7 g sat. fat), 30 mg chol., 347 mg sodium, 50 g carb., 2 g fiber, 3 g pro.*

PEACH-ROSEMARY COBBLER

# Tempting Tarts

Slice into a new taste treat with the tantalizing desserts here. Filled with chocolate, fruit and more, they're easier to make than you might think—and even more scrumptious!

## Chocolate Pear Hazelnut Tart

As a teenage foreign exchange student in the south of France, I became terribly homesick. Then my host family's grandmother arrived and asked if I'd like to help her prepare a hazelnut tart from scratch. When we began working together in the kitchen, she completely transformed a bad trip into a wonderful one. She also inspired my lifelong passion for baking.
—**LEXI MCKEOWN** LOS ANGELES, CA

**PREP:** 45 MIN. + CHILLING • **BAKE:** 30 MIN. + COOLING
**MAKES:** 12 SERVINGS

- 1¼ cups all-purpose flour
- ⅓ cup ground hazelnuts
- ¼ cup packed brown sugar
- Dash salt
- ½ cup cold butter, cubed
- 3 to 5 tablespoons ice water

**FILLING**

- 3 eggs, separated
- ⅓ cup butter, softened
- ⅓ cup packed brown sugar
- 2 tablespoons amaretto or ½ teaspoon almond extract
- 1 cup ground hazelnuts
- 2 tablespoons baking cocoa
- 6 canned pear halves, drained, sliced and patted dry
- 2 tablespoons honey, warmed
- Confectioners' sugar

**1.** In a small bowl, mix the flour, hazelnuts, brown sugar and salt; cut in the butter until crumbly. Gradually add ice water, tossing with a fork until dough holds together when pressed. Shape into a disk; wrap in plastic wrap. Refrigerate 30 minutes or overnight.

**2.** Place the egg whites in a large bowl; let stand at room temperature 30 minutes. Place oven rack in lowest position and preheat oven to 400°. On a lightly floured surface, roll the dough to a ⅛-in.-thick circle; transfer to a 9-in. fluted tart pan with removable bottom. Trim pastry even with the edge. Prick bottom of pastry with a fork. Refrigerate while preparing filling.

**3.** In a large bowl, cream the butter and brown sugar until blended. Beat in the egg yolks and the amaretto. Beat in the hazelnuts and baking cocoa.

**4.** With clean beaters, beat egg whites on medium speed until stiff peaks form. Fold a third of the egg whites into hazelnut mixture, then fold in remaining whites. Spread onto bottom of pastry shell. Arrange the pears over top.

**5.** Bake on a lower oven rack 30-35 minutes or until the crust is golden brown. Brush the pears with warm honey. Cool on a wire rack. If desired, dust with confectioners' sugar before serving.
**PER SERVING** *302 cal., 19 g fat (9 g sat. fat), 86 mg chol., 125 mg sodium, 29 g carb., 2 g fiber, 5 g pro.*

CHOCOLATE PEAR HAZELNUT TART

## ? Did you know?

As desserts, pies and tarts are similar in that they both contain a sweetened filling. The biggest difference between the two is that tarts are more shallow than pies. Full-size tarts typically measure about one inch high.

GINGERED ALMOND
TRUFFLE TART

# Gingered Almond Truffle Tart

Fresh ginger complements the chocolate truffle filling in this rich, decadent dessert. Small servings are best!

—JANICE ELDER CHARLOTTE, NC

**PREP:** 30 MIN. + CHILLING • **BAKE:** 15 MIN. + COOLING
**MAKES:** 16 SERVINGS

- 1 cup heavy whipping cream
- 2 tablespoons minced fresh gingerroot
- 1 cup all-purpose flour
- ½ cup chopped almonds
- ½ cup confectioners' sugar
- ⅓ cup baking cocoa
- 6 tablespoons cold butter, cubed
- ½ cup amaretto, divided
- 8 ounces bittersweet chocolate, chopped
- ½ cup butter, softened

**1.** Preheat oven to 350°. In a small heavy saucepan, heat cream and ginger until bubbles form around sides of pan. Remove from heat.

**2.** Place flour, almonds, confectioners' sugar and cocoa in a food processor; pulse until blended. Add cold butter; pulse until the butter is the size of peas. While pulsing, add ¼ cup amaretto to form moist crumbs. Press onto bottom and up sides of an ungreased 9-in. fluted tart pan with a removable bottom. Bake 13-16 minutes or until set. Cool on a wire rack.

**3.** Place chocolate in a small bowl. Bring gingered cream just to a boil. Strain through a fine-mesh strainer over the chocolate; discard ginger. Stir the chocolate mixture with a whisk until smooth; stir in softened butter and remaining amaretto until blended. Pour into cooled crust. Refrigerate, covered, at least 2 hours or until set.

**PER SERVING** *309 cal., 24 g fat (13 g sat. fat), 47 mg chol., 77 mg sodium, 22 g carb., 2 g fiber, 3 g pro.*

# Cranberry-Orange Crumb Tart

My mom bet me that I couldn't make a pie or tart out of oranges and cranberries. My creation was gone in a flash, so I think I won!

—HEATHER CUNNINGHAM WHITMAN, MA

**PREP:** 35 MIN. + STANDING • **BAKE:** 10 MIN. + COOLING
**MAKES:** 12 SERVINGS

- 2 cups crushed cinnamon graham crackers (about 14 whole crackers), divided
- ½ cup sugar, divided
- 6 tablespoons butter, melted
- ¼ cup all-purpose flour
- ¼ cup packed brown sugar
- ¼ cup cold butter, cubed

**FILLING**

- 1 large navel orange
- 1 cup sugar
- 3 tablespoons quick-cooking tapioca
- ¼ teaspoon baking soda
- ¼ teaspoon ground cinnamon
- ⅛ teaspoon ground allspice
- 4 cups fresh or frozen cranberries, thawed
- 2 tablespoons brandy or cranberry juice

**1.** Preheat the oven to 375°. In a small bowl, mix 1¾ cups crushed crackers and ¼ cup sugar; stir in the melted butter. Press onto bottom and up sides of an ungreased 11-in. fluted tart pan with removable bottom. Bake 7-8 minutes or until edges are lightly browned. Cool on a wire rack.

**2.** For the topping, in a small bowl, mix flour, brown sugar, and remaining crushed crackers and sugar; cut in the cold butter until crumbly. Refrigerate while preparing filling.

**3.** Finely grate enough peel from the orange to measure 1 tablespoon. Cut a thin slice from top and bottom of orange; stand orange upright on a cutting board. Cut off peel and outer membrane, starting from top. Holding orange over a bowl to catch juices, remove the sections by cutting along membrane. Squeeze membrane to reserve additional juice.

**4.** In a large saucepan, mix the sugar, tapioca, baking soda, cinnamon and allspice. Add the cranberries, brandy, grated peel and reserved juice; toss to coat. Let stand 15 minutes. Preheat oven to 425°.

**5.** Bring cranberry mixture to a full boil, stirring constantly. Add orange sections; heat through. Pour into crust; sprinkle with topping. Bake 10-15 minutes or until topping is golden brown. Cool on a wire rack.

**PER SERVING** *332 cal., 11 g fat (6 g sat. fat), 25 mg chol., 207 mg sodium, 56 g carb., 3 g fiber, 2 g pro.*

CRANBERRY-ORANGE CRUMB TART

## Apple Dumpling Rollups

**PREP:** 35 MIN. • **BAKE:** 45 MIN. + STANDING
**MAKES:** 1 DOZEN

- 3 **cups all-purpose flour**
- 2 **teaspoons baking powder**
- 1½ **teaspoons salt**
- 3 **tablespoons cold butter, cubed**
- 1⅓ **cups 2% milk**
- ¾ **to 1 cup packed brown sugar**
- 2 **teaspoons ground cinnamon**
- 4 **cups chopped apples (about 4 medium)**

**SAUCE**
- 1½ **cups sugar**
- 1½ **cups water**
- 2 **tablespoons all-purpose flour**
- 1 **tablespoon butter**
- 1 **teaspoon ground cinnamon**

**1.** Preheat the oven to 350°. In a large bowl, whisk flour, baking powder and salt. Cut in cold butter until mixture resembles coarse crumbs. Add milk; stir just until moistened (dough will be soft and sticky).

**2.** Turn the dough onto a floured work surface. Roll into an 18x12-in. rectangle. Sprinkle brown sugar and cinnamon to within 1 in. of the edges; top with the apples. Roll up jelly-roll style, starting with a long side; pinch the seam to seal. Using a serrated knife, cut into 12 slices. Place in a greased 13x9-in. baking pan, cut side down.

**3.** In a small saucepan, combine all of the sauce ingredients; bring to a boil, whisking to blend. Cook and stir for 3-4 minutes or until thickened. Pour over the top.

**4.** Bake, uncovered, for 45-55 minutes or until golden brown and bubbly. Let stand 10 minutes before serving.

**PER SERVING** *339 cal., 5 g fat (3 g sat. fat), 12 mg chol., 413 mg sodium, 71 g carb., 2 g fiber, 4 g pro.*

BLUEBERRY-RHUBARB CRISP

**FAST FIX**
## Blueberry-Rhubarb Crisp

I think this microwaved fruit crisp is just as good as oven-baked ones. And it's a great way to use up homegrown rhubarb!
**—LORRI CAMPBELL** MANKATO, MN

**START TO FINISH:** 25 MIN.
**MAKES:** 6 SERVINGS

- 2½ **cups diced fresh or frozen rhubarb, thawed**
- ⅓ **cup sugar**
- 2 **tablespoons all-purpose flour**
- 1 **can (21 ounces) blueberry pie filling**

**TOPPING**
- ¾ **cup all-purpose flour**
- ¾ **cup old-fashioned oats**
- ⅓ **cup packed brown sugar**
- ¾ **teaspoon ground cinnamon**
- ½ **cup cold butter, cubed**

**1.** In a 2-qt. microwave-safe dish, combine the rhubarb, sugar and flour. Cover and microwave on high for 3 minutes; stir. Add pie filling.

**2.** In a small bowl, combine the flour, oats, brown sugar and cinnamon. Cut in butter until mixture is crumbly; sprinkle over filling. Cover and cook 4-5 minutes longer or until bubbly and rhubarb is tender. Serve warm.

**NOTE** *This recipe was tested in a 1,100-watt microwave. If using frozen rhubarb, measure rhubarb while still frozen, then thaw completely. Drain in a colander, but do not press liquid out.*

**PER SERVING** *621 cal., 20 g fat (12 g sat. fat), 48 mg chol., 152 mg sodium, 108 g carb., 6 g fiber, 5 g pro.*

A family friend gave me her easy Apple Dumpling Rollups recipe. Everyone loves the sticky topping.
**—JENNY LEIGHTY** WEST SALEM, OH

APPLE DUMPLING ROLLUPS

SWEET & SALTY PEANUT BUTTER CHEESECAKE

## Gingered Cranberry Pear Crisp

With crystallized ginger, fresh pears and cranberries, this comfort-food dessert is perfect for fall and winter.

—**VIRGINIA MIRACLE** MENASHA, WI

**PREP:** 25 MIN. • **BAKE:** 25 MIN.
**MAKES:** 6 SERVINGS

- ½ cup sugar
- 2 tablespoons all-purpose flour
- 2 tablespoons lemon juice
- 4 cups sliced peeled fresh pears
- 1½ cups fresh or frozen cranberries
- 3 tablespoons finely chopped crystallized ginger

**TOPPING**
- ¾ cup packed brown sugar
- ¾ cup old-fashioned oats
- ⅔ cup all-purpose flour
- 6 tablespoons cold butter

**1.** In a large bowl, combine the sugar and flour; stir in lemon juice. Add the pears, cranberries and ginger; toss to coat. Divide among six greased 10-oz. ramekins or custard cups.

**2.** In a small bowl, combine the brown sugar, oats and flour; cut in the butter until the mixture resembles coarse crumbs. Sprinkle over fruit.

**3.** Bake at 400° for 25-30 minutes or until the topping is golden brown. Serve warm.

**PER SERVING** *466 cal., 12 g fat (7 g sat. fat), 30 mg chol., 98 mg sodium, 89 g carb., 6 g fiber, 4 g pro.*

## Sweet & Salty Peanut Butter Cheesecake

After a co-worker introduced me to her terrific bar cookies, I transformed them into a cheesekcake. Give it a try if you like the combination of sweet and salty flavors.

—**JOYCE SCHAMBERGER** AMBOY, IL

**PREP:** 45 MIN. • **BAKE:** 50 MIN. + CHILLING
**MAKES:** 16 SERVINGS

- 32 **Nutter Butter cookies (16 ounces)**
- ½ **cup butter, melted**

**FILLING**
- 3 **packages (8 ounces each) cream cheese, softened**
- 1 **package (10 ounces) peanut butter chips, melted**
- 1 **can (14 ounces) sweetened condensed milk**
- 1 **teaspoon vanilla extract**
- 3 **eggs, lightly beaten**

**TOPPING**
- 2 **cups miniature marshmallows**
- ¾ **cup peanut butter**
- ⅔ **cup light corn syrup**
- 2 **tablespoons butter**
- 1 **teaspoon vanilla extract**
- 1½ **cups dry roasted peanuts, coarsely chopped, divided**

**1.** Preheat the oven to 325°. Place a greased 10-in. springform pan on a double thickness of heavy-duty foil (about 18 in. square). Wrap the foil securely around pan.

**2.** Place cookies in a food processor; pulse until finely crushed. Transfer to a bowl; stir in melted butter. Press onto bottom of prepared pan.

**3.** In a large bowl, beat cream cheese until smooth. Beat in the melted chips, milk and vanilla. Add the eggs; beat on low speed just until blended. Pour into crust. Place springform pan in a larger baking pan; add 1 in. of hot water to larger pan.

**4.** Bake 45-55 minutes or until center is just set and the top appears dull. Top with marshmallows; bake 2-3 minutes longer or until the marshmallows are softened. Remove the springform pan from water bath. Cool cheesecake on a wire rack 10 minutes. Loosen the sides from the pan with a knife; remove foil. Cool 1 hour longer.

**5.** In a small saucepan, combine the peanut butter, corn syrup and butter; cook and stir ingredients over low heat until blended. Remove from the heat; stir in vanilla. Sprinkle 1 cup peanuts over the cheesecake; top with the peanut butter mixture.

**6.** Refrigerate overnight, covering when completely cooled. Remove the rim from the pan. Sprinkle remaining peanuts over top.

**PER SERVING** *743 cal., 49 g fat (21 g sat. fat), 114 mg chol., 547 mg sodium, 62 g carb., 3 g fiber, 18 g pro.*

GINGERED CRANBERRY PEAR CRISP

TIRAMISU

## Tiramisu

This easy version of the popular Italian dessert can be made a day in advance.
—**LINDA FINN** LOUISVILLE, MS

**PREP:** 25 MIN. + CHILLING
**MAKES:** 12 SERVINGS

- ½ **cup strong brewed coffee**
- 2 **tablespoons coffee liqueur**
- 2 **packages (8 ounces each) cream cheese, softened**
- ⅔ **cup sugar**
- 2 **cups (16 ounces) sour cream**
- ¼ **cup 2% milk**
- ½ **teaspoon vanilla extract**
- 2 **packages (3 ounces each) ladyfingers, split**
- 1 **tablespoon baking cocoa**

**1.** In a small bowl, combine coffee and liqueur; set aside.
**2.** In a large bowl, beat cream cheese and sugar until smooth. Beat in sour cream, milk and vanilla until blended.
**3.** Layer one package of ladyfingers in an ungreased 11x7-in. dish; brush with half of coffee mixture. Top with half of cream cheese mixture. Repeat layers (dish will be full).
**4.** Cover and refrigerate 8 hours or overnight. Just before serving, sprinkle with cocoa.

**PER SERVING** *321 cal., 21 g fat (14 g sat. fat), 100 mg chol., 149 mg sodium, 24 g carb., trace fiber, 6 g pro.*

## Spiced Pumpkin-Swirl Cheesecake

My husband always asks me to make this special cheesecake for his birthday, and my young daughter loves to help.
—**MONIKA WALSH** MONTEREY, CA

**PREP:** 55 MIN. • **BAKE:** 1 HOUR + CHILLING
**MAKES:** 12 SERVINGS

- 2 **cups pecan halves, toasted**
- 2 **tablespoons brown sugar**
- 3 **tablespoons butter, melted**

**FILLING**
- 3 **packages (8 ounces each) cream cheese, softened**
- 1 **cup packed brown sugar, divided**
- ¾ **cup sour cream**
- 2 **teaspoons vanilla extract**
- 3 **eggs, lightly beaten**
- 1 **cup canned pumpkin**
- 1 **teaspoon ground cinnamon**
- ½ **teaspoon ground ginger**
- ¼ **teaspoon ground cloves**
- ¼ **teaspoon ground nutmeg**

**1.** Preheat oven to 325°. Place a greased 9-in. springform pan on a double thickness of heavy-duty foil (about 18 in. square). Wrap the foil securely around pan.
**2.** Place the pecans and brown sugar in a food processor; pulse until fine crumbs form. Add the butter; pulse to combine. Press onto the bottom of the prepared pan. Place pan on a baking sheet. Bake 15-20 minutes or until light brown. Cool on a wire rack.
**3.** In a large bowl, beat cream cheese and ¾ cup brown sugar until smooth. Beat in the sour cream and vanilla. Add the eggs; beat on low speed just until blended.
**4.** In another bowl, mix the pumpkin, spices and remaining brown sugar. Stir in 1½ cups of cream cheese mixture.
**5.** To layer, pour 1½ cups plain cream cheese mixture over the crust. Gently spread 1⅓ cups pumpkin mixture over top. Repeat layers. Cut through the layers with a knife to swirl. Place springform pan in a large baking pan; add 1 in. of hot water to larger pan.
**6.** Bake 60-70 minutes or until the center is just set and the top appears dull. Remove springform pan from water bath. Cool cheesecake on a wire rack for 10 minutes. Loosen sides from pan with a knife; remove foil. Cool for 1 hour longer. Refrigerate overnight. Remove rim from pan.

**NOTE** *To toast nuts, spread them in a 15x10x1-in. baking pan. Bake at 350° for 5-10 minutes or until lightly browned, stirring occasionally. Or, spread them in a dry nonstick skillet and heat over low heat until lightly browned, stirring occasionally.*

**PER SERVING** *483 cal., 39 g fat (18 g sat. fat), 133 mg chol., 220 mg sodium, 27 g carb., 3 g fiber, 8 g pro.*

# Apple-Almond Bake

**PREP:** 40 MIN. • **BAKE:** 50 MIN.
**MAKES:** 1 DOZEN

- ¼ cup maple syrup
- ¾ cup sugar
- 2 tablespoons cornstarch
- ⅔ cup cold water
- 2 tablespoons butter
- 1¾ cups quick-cooking oats
- 1¼ cups all-purpose flour
- 1 cup packed brown sugar
- ½ cup almond flour
- 1 teaspoon baking soda
- ¾ cup cold butter, cubed
- 5 cups sliced peeled tart apples (about 5 medium)
- ½ cup coarsely chopped salted roasted almonds

**1.** Preheat oven to 350°. In a small saucepan, bring the maple syrup to a boil; cook for 3-5 minutes or until the liquid is reduced by half.

**2.** In a small bowl, mix the sugar and cornstarch; whisk in the cold water until smooth. Whisk into the reduced syrup. Return to a boil; cook and stir 1-2 minutes or until thickened. Whisk in 2 tablespoons butter until blended. Remove from heat.

**3.** In a large bowl, mix quick-cooking oats, flour, brown sugar, almond flour and baking soda; cut in the cold butter until crumbly. Reserve 1⅓ cups of the mixture for the topping. Press the remaining mixture onto bottom of a greased 13x9-in. baking pan. Arrange the apples over top; drizzle with the syrup mixture.

**4.** Stir the chopped almonds into the reserved crumb mixture; sprinkle over the top. Bake 50-60 minutes or until the apples are tender and the topping is golden brown.

**PER SERVING** *433 cal., 20 g fat (9 g sat. fat), 36 mg chol., 269 mg sodium, 62 g carb., 3 g fiber, 5 g pro.*

CHOCOLATE
RUM FONDUE

## Chocolate Rum Fondue

Who needs a fancy fondue restaurant? Thanks to this recipe, you can whip up a chocolate sensation in just 10 minutes.
—**ANGIE SAMPLES** MAYSVILLE, GA

**START TO FINISH:** 10 MIN.
**MAKES:** 1½ CUPS

- 3 milk chocolate Toblerone candy bars (3.52 ounces each), coarsely chopped
- ⅔ cup heavy whipping cream
- 4 teaspoons rum or ½ teaspoon rum extract
  Pear slices, cubed cake, large marshmallows and/or macaroon cookies

**1.** In a small heavy saucepan, combine candy bars and cream. Cook and stir over medium-low heat until blended. Remove from the heat; stir in rum.

**2.** Transfer to a small fondue pot and keep warm. Serve with the dippers of your choice.

**PER SERVING** *358 cal., 23 g fat (14 g sat. fat), 46 mg chol., 35 mg sodium, 33 g carb., 1 g fiber, 4 g pro.*

Apple-Almond Bake has been one of my children's favorite treats for years. Served warm, it's even harder to resist with a scoop of vanilla ice cream on top.
—**BARBARA ESTABROOK** RHINELANDER, WI

APPLE-ALMOND BAKE

## top tip  Delightful Dipping

With chocolate fondue, you have so many great options for dippers, from slices or chunks of fresh fruit to crispy cookies, marshmallows and pieces of cake. When I want something especially decadent for dunking, I serve small cubes of unfrosted brownies.
—**JUDY A.** CEDAR HILLS, UT

## Pumpkin Tartlets

For a festive touch, top some of these cute miniature tarts with a leaf-shaped pastry cutout after pouring in the pumpkin filling.

**—JESSIE OLESON** SANTA FE, NM

**PREP:** 20 MIN. • **BAKE:** 40 MIN. + COOLING
**MAKES:** 16 TARTLETS

- 1 package (15 ounces) refrigerated pie pastry
- 1 can (15 ounces) solid-pack pumpkin
- 1 can (12 ounces) evaporated milk
- ¾ cup sugar
- 2 eggs
- ½ teaspoon salt
- 1 teaspoon ground cinnamon
- ½ teaspoon ground ginger
- ¼ teaspoon ground cloves
  Miniature marshmallows, optional

**1.** Preheat the oven to 425°. On a work surface, unroll each pastry sheet; roll to ⅛-in. thickness. Using a floured 4-in. round cutter, cut out 16 circles, rerolling scraps if necessary. Press circles into muffin pans coated with cooking spray.
**2.** In a large bowl, whisk the pumpkin, milk, sugar, eggs, salt and spices until blended. Pour into the pastry cups. Bake for 15 minutes. Reduce oven setting to 350°.
**3.** Bake 25-30 minutes or until a knife inserted near center comes out clean. If desired, top with marshmallows and bake 2-3 minutes longer or until marshmallows are lightly browned. Cool 5 minutes.
**4.** Carefully run a knife around sides to loosen tarts. Cool in pans on wire racks before removing. Serve or refrigerate within 2 hours.
**FOR 9-IN. PUMPKIN PIE** *Preheat the oven to 425°. Unroll 1 refrigerated pie pastry sheet into a 9-in. pie plate; flute the edge. Prepare filling as directed; pour into pastry shell. Bake 15 minutes. Reduce oven setting to 350°; bake 35-45 minutes longer, covering the edge loosely with foil during the last 10 minutes if needed to prevent overbrowning.*
**PER SERVING** *200 cal., 9 g fat (4 g sat. fat), 38 mg chol., 203 mg sodium, 27 g carb., 1 g fiber, 3 g pro.*

PUMPKIN TARTLETS

S'MORES CHEESECAKE

## S'mores Cheesecake

Have your cheesecake and your campfire treats, too! I put all of the classic s'mores ingredients—graham crackers, chocolate and toasty marshmallows—into a rich, creamy dessert served by the slice.

**—KURT ANDERSON** WILLMAR, MN

**PREP:** 30 MIN. + CHILLING • **BAKE:** 1¼ HOURS + COOLING
**MAKES:** 16 SERVINGS

- 2 cups graham cracker crumbs
- ¼ cup sugar
- 6 tablespoons butter, melted
- 1 package (11½ ounces) milk chocolate chips
- 1 can (12 ounces) evaporated milk, divided
- 3 packages (8 ounces each) cream cheese, softened
- 1 jar (7 ounces) marshmallow creme
- 2 tablespoons cornstarch
- 1 teaspoon vanilla extract
- 3 eggs, lightly beaten
- 2½ cups miniature marshmallows

**1.** Preheat oven to 325°. In a small bowl, mix the cracker crumbs and sugar; stir in melted butter. Press onto bottom and 1 in. up sides of a greased 9-in. springform pan. Place pan on a baking sheet. Bake 10 minutes. Cool on a wire rack.
**2.** In top of a double boiler or a metal bowl over barely simmering water, melt chocolate chips with ¾ cup milk; stir until smooth. Pour into crust; freeze just until chocolate is set, about 20 minutes.
**3.** In a large bowl, beat cream cheese until smooth. Beat in the marshmallow creme, cornstarch, vanilla and remaining milk. Add eggs; beat on low speed just until blended. Pour over chocolate. Return pan to baking sheet.
**4.** Bake 65-75 minutes or until the center is almost set. Sprinkle with marshmallows. Bake 6-8 minutes longer or until marshmallows are light brown. Cool on a wire rack 10 minutes. Loosen sides from pan with knife. Cool 1 hour longer.
**5.** Refrigerate overnight, covering when completely cooled. Remove rim from pan.
**PER SERVING** *466 cal., 29 g fat (17 g sat. fat), 110 mg chol., 285 mg sodium, 44 g carb., 1 g fiber, 8 g pro.*

## Autumn Apple Torte

Every year during apple season, we take advantage of the fresh crop by making this rich torte. Sliced almonds add a nice crunch.
—**MARGARET WILSON** SUN CITY, CA

**PREP:** 40 MIN. • **BAKE:** 35 MIN. + COOLING • **MAKES:** 12 SERVINGS

- ½ cup butter, softened
- ½ cup sugar, divided
- ½ teaspoon vanilla extract
- 1 cup all-purpose flour
- 1 package (8 ounces) cream cheese, softened
- 1 egg, lightly beaten
- ½ teaspoon almond extract
- 2 cups thinly sliced, peeled Granny Smith apples (about 2 medium)
- 2 cups thinly sliced, peeled Cortland apples (about 2 medium)
- ¼ cup cinnamon-sugar
- ¼ teaspoon ground nutmeg
- ½ cup confectioners' sugar
- 2 tablespoons 2% milk
- 2 tablespoons sliced almonds, toasted

**1.** Preheat oven to 450°. In a small bowl, cream butter and ¼ cup sugar until light and fluffy. Beat in vanilla. Gradually beat in flour. Press onto the bottom and 1 in. up the sides of a greased 9-in. springform pan.

**2.** In a small bowl, beat cream cheese and remaining sugar until smooth. Add the egg and almond extract; beat on low speed just until blended. Pour into crust.

**3.** Place apples in a large bowl. Mix cinnamon-sugar and nutmeg; add to apples and toss to coat. Arrange over cream cheese mixture. Bake 5 minutes.

**4.** Reduce oven setting to 400°. Bake 30-35 minutes longer or until apples are tender. Cool on a wire rack.

**5.** Remove the rim from the pan. In a small bowl, mix the confectioners' sugar and milk until smooth. Drizzle over torte; sprinkle with almonds. Refrigerate leftovers.

**NOTE** *To toast nuts, place in a dry skillet; cook and stir over low heat until lightly browned.*

**PER SERVING** *270 cal., 15 g fat (9 g sat. fat), 57 mg chol., 136 mg sodium, 31 g carb., 1 g fiber, 3 g pro.*

AUTUMN APPLE TORTE

NEW ORLEANS BREAD PUDDING

## New Orleans Bread Pudding

What says Southern comfort food more than a sweet, buttery bread pudding? Enjoy a scoop warm from the oven.
—**LINDA WIESE** PAYETTE, ID

**PREP:** 35 MIN. • **BAKE:** 35 MIN. • **MAKES:** 12 SERVINGS

- ½ cup raisins
- ¼ cup brandy or unsweetened apple juice
- ½ cup butter, melted, divided
- 1 tablespoon sugar
- 4 eggs, lightly beaten
- 2 cups half-and-half cream
- 1 cup packed brown sugar
- 2 teaspoons vanilla extract
- ½ teaspoon salt
- ½ teaspoon freshly ground nutmeg
- 10 slices day-old French bread (1 inch thick), cubed

**SAUCE**
- ½ cup packed brown sugar
- 2 tablespoons cornstarch
- Dash salt
- 1 cup cold water
- 1 tablespoon butter
- 2 teaspoons vanilla extract

**1.** In a small saucepan, combine the raisins and brandy. Bring to a boil. Remove from the heat; cover and set aside. Brush a shallow 2½-qt. baking dish with 1 tablespoon butter; sprinkle with sugar and set aside.

**2.** In a large bowl, combine the eggs, cream, brown sugar, vanilla, salt and nutmeg. Stir in the remaining butter and reserved raisin mixture. Gently stir in the bread; let stand for 15 minutes or until bread is softened.

**3.** Transfer to the prepared dish. Bake, uncovered, at 350° for 35-40 minutes or until a knife inserted near the center comes out clean.

**4.** For sauce, in a small saucepan, combine the brown sugar, cornstarch and salt; gradually add the water. Bring to a boil; cook and stir for 1-2 minutes or until thickened. Remove from the heat; stir in butter and vanilla. Serve with pudding.

**PER SERVING** *350 cal., 15 g fat (9 g sat. fat), 113 mg chol., 341 mg sodium, 45 g carb., 1 g fiber, 5 g pro.*

## Heavenly Mint Brownie Dessert

This dessert really lives up to its name! It features a brownie base, a decadent layer of chopped Andes candies and a smooth, rich chocolate ganache.

—REBEKAH RADEWAHN WAUWATOSA, WI

**PREP:** 30 MIN. + CHILLING
**BAKE:** 20 MIN. + COOLING
**MAKES:** 12 SERVINGS

- 2 ounces unsweetened chocolate, chopped
- ¼ cup butter, cubed
- 2 eggs
- 1 cup sugar
- ⅛ teaspoon salt
- ½ cup plus 2 tablespoons all-purpose flour
- 12 mint Andes candies, chopped

**FILLING**

- 12 ounces cream cheese, softened
- 6 tablespoons butter, softened
- 1 package (10 to 12 ounces) white baking chips
- 1 tablespoon shortening
- ½ teaspoon peppermint extract
- 3 to 4 drops green food coloring, optional
- 12 mint Andes candies, chopped

**GANACHE**

- 9 ounces semisweet chocolate, chopped
- 1 cup heavy whipping cream

**1.** Preheat oven to 350°. In a microwave, melt the unsweetened chocolate and butter; stir until smooth. Cool slightly.

**2.** In a large bowl, beat the eggs, sugar and salt. Stir in the chocolate mixture. Gradually add flour, mixing well. Fold in candies. Spread into a greased 9-in. springform pan. Bake 20-25 minutes or until a toothpick inserted in center comes out clean. Cool completely on a wire rack.

**3.** For the filling, in a large bowl, beat cream cheese and butter until blended. In a microwave, melt baking chips and the shortening; stir until smooth. Cool slightly. Beat into the cream cheese mixture. Add extract and, if desired, food coloring. Fold in candies. Spread over the brownie layer. Refrigerate until firm, about 2 hours.

**4.** For the ganache, place chocolate in a small bowl. In a small saucepan, bring cream just to a boil. Pour over the chocolate; stir with a whisk until smooth. Cool slightly.

**5.** Spread the ganache over the filling. Refrigerate for 30 minutes or until set. Remove rim from pan.

**PER SERVING** *669 cal., 49 g fat (30 g sat. fat), 122 mg chol., 221 mg sodium, 56 g carb., 3 g fiber, 8 g pro.*

---

(5) INGREDIENTS FAST FIX

## Orange Fudge Sauce

Ice cream lovers can't get enough of this rich, fudgy topping. It's great served warm over pound or angel food cake, too.

—ANNIE RUNDLE MUSKEGO, WI

**START TO FINISH:** 15 MIN.
**MAKES:** 3 CUPS

- 24 ounces bittersweet chocolate, chopped
- 1 cup heavy whipping cream
- ¼ cup butter
- ¼ cup thawed orange juice concentrate
- 2 teaspoons grated orange peel
  Vanilla ice cream, optional

**1.** In a heavy saucepan, combine the chocolate, cream, butter and orange juice concentrate. Cook and stir over medium-low heat until smooth.

**2.** Stir in the orange peel. Serve warm with ice cream or transfer to covered jars and refrigerate.

**PER SERVING** *198 cal., 18 g fat (10 g sat. fat), 19 mg chol., 17 mg sodium, 16 g carb., 2 g fiber, 2 g pro.*

---

## Berry & Cream Chocolate Cups

Here's an adorable treat for a wedding shower, luncheon or any special event. Filled with a homemade pastry cream and berries, the yummy cups can be prepared ahead of time and kept in the fridge.

—AMY BLOM MARIETTA, GA

**PREP:** 50 MIN. + CHILLING
**MAKES:** 1 DOZEN

- 1 package (12 ounces) dark chocolate chips
- 2 ounces cream cheese, softened
- ½ cup sour cream
- ⅓ cup sugar
- 2 tablespoons cornstarch
- 1½ cups milk
- 2 egg yolks, lightly beaten
- 1½ teaspoons vanilla extract
- 1½ cups thinly sliced fresh strawberries

**1.** In a microwave, melt chips; stir until smooth. Spread melted chocolate over the bottoms and up the sides of 12 foil muffin cup liners. Refrigerate for 25 minutes or until firm.

**2.** In a small bowl, beat cream cheese until fluffy; beat in sour cream until smooth. Set aside.

**3.** In a small saucepan, combine the sugar and cornstarch. Stir in the milk until smooth. Cook and stir over medium-high heat until thickened and bubbly. Reduce heat to low; cook and stir 2 minutes longer.

**4.** Remove from heat. Stir a small amount of the hot mixture into the egg yolks; return all to the pan, stirring constantly. Bring to a gentle boil; cook and stir for 2 minutes. Remove from the heat; stir in vanilla and reserved sour cream mixture. Cool to room temperature, stirring occasionally. Refrigerate until chilled.

**5.** Carefully remove foil liners from chocolate cups. Fill cups with pastry cream and berries. Chill until serving.

**PER SERVING** *249 cal., 15 g fat (9 g sat. fat), 49 mg chol., 31 mg sodium, 27 g carb., trace fiber, 4 g pro.*

HEAVENLY MINT BROWNIE DESSERT

## Chipotle-Orange Baklava

Cinnamon, chipotle peppers and a splash of citrus make my version of traditional Greek baklava a little different.

—CHRISTINE NEARY PORTLAND, OR

**PREP:** 1½ HOURS
**BAKE:** 35 MIN. + STANDING
**MAKES:** 3 DOZEN

- 1 package (16 ounces) shelled walnuts
- ⅔ cup sugar
- 3 tablespoons grated orange peel
- 1 teaspoon baking cocoa
- ½ teaspoon ground cinnamon
- 1½ cups butter, melted
- 1 package (16 ounces, 14x9-inch sheets) frozen phyllo dough, thawed

**SYRUP**
- 1¾ cups sugar
- ¾ cup orange juice
- ½ cup honey
- ⅓ cup water
- 1 to 2 dried chipotle chilies, split lengthwise in half
- 2 cinnamon sticks (3 inches each)

**1.** Preheat oven to 350°. In a food processor, combine the first five ingredients; pulse until the walnuts are finely chopped. Brush a 13x9-in. baking pan with some of the butter. Unroll phyllo; trim to fit into pan.
**2.** Layer three sheets of phyllo in the prepared pan, brushing each with butter. Keep remaining phyllo covered with plastic wrap and a damp towel to prevent it from drying out. Sprinkle with ⅓ cup nut mixture. Repeat layers 11 times. Top with remaining sheets, brushing each with butter.
**3.** Cut into 36 triangles. Bake 35-40 minutes or until golden brown.
**4.** Meanwhile, in a large saucepan, combine syrup ingredients; bring to a boil. Reduce heat; simmer, uncovered, 10 minutes, stirring occasionally.
**5.** Strain syrup through a fine mesh strainer; discard chilies and cinnamon sticks. Pour over warm baklava. Cool completely on a wire rack. Cover and let stand several hours or overnight.
**PER SERVING** *258 cal., 16 g fat (6 g sat. fat), 20 mg chol., 110 mg sodium, 28 g carb., 1 g fiber, 3 g pro.*

## Blushing Grapefruit Sorbet

This tangy frozen sorbet is wonderful any time of year, but I enjoy it the most as a cool refresher on hot summer days.

—MARY MARLOWE LEVERETTE
COLUMBIA, SC

**PREP:** 35 MIN. + FREEZING
**MAKES:** 1 QUART

- 3 cups water
- 1 cup sugar
- ½ cup honey
- 1 tablespoon grated grapefruit peel
- 1 tablespoon minced fresh gingerroot
- 2 whole star anise
- 2 whole cloves
- 1 bay leaf
- 2 cups ruby red grapefruit juice, chilled
- 3 tablespoons lemon juice

**1.** In a large saucepan, combine the first eight ingredients. Bring to a boil; cook until the liquid is reduced by half, about 20 minutes. Strain and set aside to cool.
**2.** In a large bowl, combine the ruby red grapefruit juice, lemon juice and sugar syrup. Fill the cylinder of an ice cream freezer; freeze according to the manufacturer's directions. Transfer to a freezer container and freeze for 4 hours or until firm.
**PER SERVING** *188 cal., trace fat (0 sat. fat), 0 chol., 1 mg sodium, 49 g carb., trace fiber, trace pro.*

## Whole Wheat Strawberry Shortcakes

What says springtime better than a fresh strawberry shortcake? It's one of the best treats of the season. My mother and I like to use berries we picked ourselves.

—SARAH HATTER BRODHEAD, WI

**PREP:** 45 MIN. + CHILLING
**BAKE:** 15 MIN. + COOLING
**MAKES:** 6 SERVINGS

- 2½ cups fresh strawberries, hulled
- 1 to 2 tablespoons maple syrup

**SHORTCAKES**
- 2 cups whole wheat flour
- 2½ teaspoons baking powder
- ½ teaspoon salt
- ¼ teaspoon baking soda

WHOLE WHEAT STRAWBERRY SHORTCAKES

- ½ cup cold butter, cubed
- 1 egg
- ½ cup 2% milk
- ¼ cup honey
  Whipped cream

**1.** In a bowl, thoroughly mash ¾ cup strawberries; stir in maple syrup. Cut the remaining strawberries into ¼-in. slices; add to the crushed strawberries and toss to coat. Refrigerate, covered, 1 hour.
**2.** Meanwhile, preheat oven to 400°. In a large bowl, whisk flour, baking powder, salt and baking soda. Cut in butter until mixture resembles coarse crumbs. In a small bowl, whisk egg, milk and honey until blended; stir into flour mixture just until moistened.
**3.** Turn onto a lightly floured surface; knead gently 8-10 times. Pat or roll dough to ¾-in. thickness; cut with a floured 2½-in. biscuit cutter. Place 2 in. apart on parchment paper-lined baking sheets. Bake 12-15 minutes or until light brown. Remove to wire racks to cool slightly.
**4.** To serve, split shortcakes in half. Fill with the strawberry mixture and whipped cream. Top with additional whipped cream.
**PER SERVING** *362 cal., 17 g fat (10 g sat. fat), 77 mg chol., 549 mg sodium, 49 g carb., 6 g fiber, 8 g pro.*

## Toffee Truffle Cheesecake

I combined a few cheesecake recipes and added a homemade caramel sauce. Yum!

**—HANNAH HALSTEAD** BLAIR, NE

**PREP:** 40 MIN. • **BAKE:** 45 MIN. + CHILLING
**MAKES:** 12 SERVINGS (¾ CUP SAUCE)

- 1½ cups graham cracker crumbs
- 3 tablespoons sugar
- 1 tablespoon baking cocoa
- ⅓ cup butter, melted

**FILLING**

- 2 packages (8 ounces each) cream cheese, softened
- ⅔ cup sugar
- 8 ounces bittersweet chocolate, melted and cooled
- 1 tablespoon all-purpose flour
- 1 teaspoon vanilla extract
- 3 eggs, lightly beaten
- 1 cup milk chocolate English toffee bits

**SAUCE**

- ¼ cup butter, cubed
- ⅔ cup packed brown sugar
- 1 tablespoon corn syrup
- ¼ cup heavy whipping cream
- 2 tablespoons plus ½ cup milk chocolate English toffee bits, divided

**1.** Preheat oven to 325°. In a small bowl, mix cracker crumbs, sugar and cocoa; stir in butter. Press onto bottom of a greased 9-in. springform pan.

**2.** In a large bowl, beat cream cheese and sugar until smooth. Beat in cooled chocolate, flour and vanilla. Add eggs; beat on low speed just until blended. Fold in toffee bits. Pour over the crust. Place pan on a baking sheet.

**3.** Bake 45-50 minutes or until the center is almost set. Cool on a wire rack 10 minutes. Loosen sides from pan with a knife. Cool 1 hour longer. Refrigerate overnight, covering when completely cooled.

**4.** For sauce, melt the butter in a small saucepan. Stir in the brown sugar and corn syrup; bring to a boil. Reduce heat to medium; cook and stir until sugar is completely dissolved, about 2 minutes. Stir in cream; return to a boil. Remove from heat; stir in 2 tablespoons toffee.

**5.** Remove rim from springform pan. Sprinkle the remaining toffee over top. Serve with warm sauce.

**PER SERVING** *672 cal., 44 g fat (25 g sat. fat), 146 mg chol., 396 mg sodium, 69 g carb., 2 g fiber, 7 g pro.*

## Chocolate Hazelnut Mousse Cups

Three of my favorite ingredients—puff pastry, chocolate and hazelnuts—come together for an impressive dessert.

**—ROXANNE CHAN** ALBANY, CA

**PREP:** 30 MIN. + COOLING
**MAKES:** 6 SERVINGS

- 1 package (10 ounces) frozen puff pastry shells, thawed
- ½ cup heavy whipping cream
- 1 to 2 tablespoons confectioners' sugar
- ¼ teaspoon vanilla extract
- ½ cup mascarpone cheese
- ½ cup Nutella
- ¼ teaspoon ground cinnamon
- 2 tablespoons miniature semisweet chocolate chips
  Additional miniature semisweet chocolate chips, melted, optional
- 2 tablespoons chopped hazelnuts, toasted

**1.** Bake pastry shells according to package directions. Cool completely.

**2.** In a small bowl, beat the heavy whipping cream until it begins to thicken. Add the confectioners' sugar and vanilla; beat until soft peaks form.

**3.** In another bowl, beat mascarpone cheese, Nutella and cinnamon until blended. Fold in whipped cream and chocolate chips. Spoon into pastry shells. If desired, drizzle with melted chocolate. Sprinkle with hazelnuts. Refrigerate until serving.

**NOTE** *To toast nuts, spread them in a 15x10x1-in. baking pan. Bake at 350° for 5-10 minutes or until lightly browned, stirring occasionally. Or, spread in a dry nonstick skillet and heat over low heat until lightly browned, stirring occasionally.*

**PER SERVING** *581 cal., 48 g fat (19 g sat. fat), 74 mg chol., 269 mg sodium, 36 g carb., 2 g fiber, 9 g pro.*

CHOCOLATE HAZELNUT MOUSSE CUPS

TOFFEE TRUFFLE CHEESECAKE

**top tip**

## Cheesecake Doneness

Our Test Kitchen determines doneness by tapping the side of the pan with a wooden spoon to measure the center of the cheesecake's "jiggle." It should be about the size of a walnut, as a general rule of thumb.

**ZUCCHINI FRITTATA**
*PAGE 142*

# Breakfast & Brunch

Whether you're waking up on a busy workday or a special holiday, rely on the **sunrise sensations** here. These scrumptious yet easy-to-fix recipes have **morning meals covered**.

**MARMALADE FRENCH TOAST SANDWICHES**
*PAGE 140*

**SLOW COOKER HONEY GRANOLA**
*PAGE 143*

**SLOW COOKER HAM & EGGS**
*PAGE 139*

## Sweet Potato and Ham Hash

**PREP:** 20 MIN. • **COOK:** 20 MIN.
**MAKES:** 4 SERVINGS

- 2 **cups cubed peeled sweet potatoes**
- 2 **tablespoons butter**
- 1 **tablespoon olive oil**
- 1 **medium onion, chopped**
- 1 **small sweet red pepper, chopped**
- 3 **green onions, chopped**
- 1 **red chili pepper, seeded and finely chopped**
- 3 **garlic cloves, minced**
- 2 **cups cubed fully cooked ham**
- ½ **teaspoon pepper**
- ¼ **teaspoon salt**
- 4 **eggs**
- ¼ **cup shredded white cheddar cheese**

**1.** In a large skillet, saute the sweet potatoes in the butter and oil until crisp-tender. Add the onion, sweet red pepper, green onions and red chili pepper. Saute 4-5 minutes longer or until tender. Add the garlic; cook 1 minute longer. Stir in the ham, pepper and salt.

**2.** With the back of a spoon, make four wells in the sweet potato mixture; add an egg to each well. Sprinkle with the cheddar cheese. Cover and cook for 4-5 minutes or until the egg whites are completely set.

**NOTE** *Wear disposable gloves when cutting hot peppers; the oils can burn skin. Avoid touching your face.*

**PER SERVING** *379 cal., 22 g fat (9 g sat. fat), 271 mg chol., 1,237 mg sodium, 23 g carb., 4 g fiber, 23 g pro.*

SWEET POTATO AND HAM HASH

CRISPY MASHED POTATO & STUFFING PATTIES

Served in the skillet right from the stovetop, Sweet Potato and Ham Hash is an impressive, filling breakfast. For an easy dinner, pair it with a tossed salad.
—**JUDY ARMSTRONG** PRAIRIEVILLE, LA

**FAST FIX**

## Crispy Mashed Potato & Stuffing Patties

Here's a terrific way to use up leftovers from a holiday feast. Mashed potatoes, turkey and stuffing all go into the savory fried patties. My family loves them!
—**KELLI FEREA** CASA GRANDE, AZ

**START TO FINISH:** 30 MIN.
**MAKES:** 12 PATTIES

- 2 **eggs, lightly beaten**
- 2 **tablespoons finely chopped onion**
- ¼ **teaspoon pepper**
- 2 **cups leftover mashed potatoes**
- 2 **cups leftover chopped cooked turkey**
- 2 **cups leftover stuffing**
- 2 **tablespoons butter**
- 2 **tablespoons canola oil**

**1.** In a large bowl, whisk eggs, onion and pepper. Stir in potatoes, turkey and stuffing.

**2.** In a large skillet, heat butter and oil over medium-high heat. Working in batches, drop the potato mixture by ½ cupfuls into the pan; press to flatten slightly. Fry 4-5 minutes on each side or until golden brown and heated through. Drain on paper towels.

**PER SERVING** *364 cal., 19 g fat (6 g sat. fat), 118 mg chol., 628 mg sodium, 28 g carb., 2 g fiber, 20 g pro.*

## Blueberry Waffles

Think making waffles from scratch is too much fuss? You'll change your mind when you taste these tender homemade treats bursting with blueberries in every bite. The recipe includes a topping of berry sauce, so you get twice the fruit flavor. What a way to start the day!

—DEVYN WEAKLEY HOWARD, KS

**PREP:** 20 MIN. • **COOK:** 5 MIN./BATCH
**MAKES:** 12 WAFFLES (1⅓ CUPS SAUCE)

- 2 cups all-purpose flour
- 2¼ teaspoons baking powder
- ½ teaspoon salt
- 1⅔ cups milk
- 3 eggs, separated
- ¼ cup butter, melted
- ⅔ cup fresh or frozen blueberries

**SAUCE**

- 1½ cups fresh or frozen blueberries
- ½ cup orange juice, divided
- 3 tablespoons honey
- 1 tablespoon cornstarch

1. In a large bowl, combine the flour, the baking powder and salt. Whisk the milk, egg yolks and butter; stir into the dry ingredients just until moistened. Fold in blueberries.

2. In a small bowl, beat the egg whites until stiff peaks form; fold into batter.

3. Bake in a preheated waffle iron according to the manufacturer's directions until golden brown.

4. Meanwhile, in a small saucepan, combine the blueberries, ¼ cup of orange juice and honey. Bring to a boil. Combine cornstarch and remaining orange juice until smooth; gradually stir into berry mixture. Bring to a boil; cook and stir for 2 minutes or until thickened. Serve warm with waffles.

**NOTE** *If using frozen blueberries, use without thawing to avoid discoloring the batter.*

**PER SERVING** *371 cal., 13 g fat (7 g sat. fat), 129 mg chol., 461 mg sodium, 55 g carb., 2 g fiber, 10 g pro.*

**SLOW COOKER**
## Slow Cooker Ham & Eggs

Stir together these ingredients, then just pop them into the slow cooker and let it do most of the work for you. You'll lift the lid to find a wonderful morning meal.

—ANDREA SCHAAK JORDAN, MN

**PREP:** 15 MIN. • **COOK:** 3 HOURS
**MAKES:** 6 SERVINGS

- 6 eggs
- 1 cup biscuit/baking mix
- ⅔ cup 2% milk
- ⅓ cup sour cream
- 2 tablespoons minced fresh parsley
- 2 garlic cloves, minced
- ½ teaspoon salt
- ½ teaspoon pepper
- 1 cup cubed fully cooked ham
- 1 cup (4 ounces) shredded Swiss cheese
- 1 small onion, finely chopped
- ⅓ cup shredded Parmesan cheese

1. In a large bowl, whisk the first eight ingredients until blended; stir in the remaining ingredients. Pour into a greased 3- or 4-qt. slow cooker.

2. Cook, covered, on low 3-4 hours or until eggs are set. Cut into wedges.

**PER SERVING** *315 cal., 18 g fat (9 g sat. fat), 256 mg chol., 942 mg sodium, 17 g carb., 1 g fiber, 21 g pro.*

BLUEBERRY WAFFLES

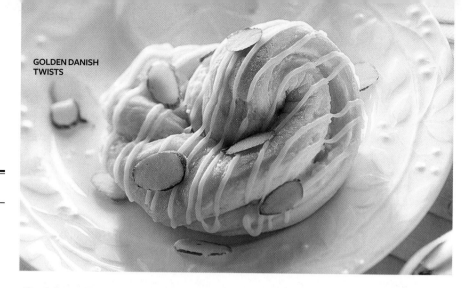

GOLDEN DANISH TWISTS

# Marmalade French Toast Sandwiches

I change up my French toast sandwiches by using different types of jelly. Try a hot pepper variety when you want a little zip.

—DANIELLE LORING LEWISTON, ME

**START TO FINISH:** 25 MIN.
**MAKES:** 6 SERVINGS

- 1 **container (8 ounces) whipped cream cheese**
- 12 **slices sourdough bread**
- ¾ **cup orange marmalade**
- 4 **eggs**
- 2 **tablespoons 2% milk**
  **Maple syrup, optional**

1. Spread cream cheese over six slices of bread; top with the marmalade and remaining bread. In a shallow bowl, whisk eggs and milk.

2. Lightly grease a griddle; heat the griddle over medium heat. Dip both sides of the sandwiches into the egg mixture. Place the sandwiches on the griddle; toast 2-3 minutes on each side or until golden brown. If desired, serve with maple syrup.

**PER SERVING** *447 cal., 16 g fat (9 g sat. fat), 151 mg chol., 628 mg sodium, 65 g carb., 2 g fiber, 13 g pro.*

MARMALADE FRENCH TOAST SANDWICHES

# Golden Danish Twists

These beautiful sweet rolls have a rich filling, crunchy almonds and a lemony icing.

—ANNIE DE LA HOZ
DELTA, CO

**PREP:** 1¼ HOURS + RISING • **BAKE:** 15 MIN.
**MAKES:** 3 DOZEN

- 2 **packages (¼ ounce each) active dry yeast**
- ½ **cup warm water (110° to 115°)**
- 1 **cup canned pumpkin**
- 1 **cup warm 2% milk (110° to 115°)**
- 2 **eggs**
- ¼ **cup sugar**
- ¼ **cup butter, softened**
- 3 **teaspoons salt**
- 6 **to 6½ cups all-purpose flour**

FILLING

- 2 **packages (8 ounces each) cream cheese, softened**
- ⅓ **cup confectioners' sugar**
- ½ **cup heavy whipping cream**
- 2 **teaspoons grated lemon peel**
- 1 **teaspoon vanilla extract**

ICING

- ¼ **cup butter, cubed**
- 2 **tablespoons all-purpose flour**
- ¼ **cup lemon juice**
- 2⅔ **cups confectioners' sugar**
- 1 **tablespoon grated lemon peel**
- ¾ **cup sliced almonds**

1. In a small bowl, dissolve the yeast in the warm water. In a large bowl, combine pumpkin, milk, eggs, sugar, butter, salt, yeast mixture and 3 cups flour; beat on medium speed until smooth. Stir in enough remaining flour to make a soft dough.

2. Turn the dough onto a floured surface; knead until smooth and elastic, about 6-8 minutes. Place in a greased bowl, turning once to grease the top. Cover with plastic wrap and let rise in a warm place until doubled, about 1 hour.

3. For the filling, in a small bowl, beat cream cheese and confectioners' sugar until smooth. Gradually beat in cream, lemon peel and vanilla.

4. Punch the down dough. Turn onto a lightly floured surface. Divide the dough in half. Roll one portion into an 18x12-in. rectangle. Spread half of the filling lengthwise down half of the dough to within ½ in. of the edges. Fold the dough over the filling; seal edges. Cut into eighteen 1-in. strips. Twist and loosely coil each strip. Tuck end under; pinch to seal.

5. Place 2 in. apart on greased baking sheets. Cover with kitchen towels; let rise in a warm place until doubled, about 30 minutes. Repeat with the remaining dough and filling.

6. Preheat oven to 375°. Bake twists 12-15 minutes or until golden brown. Remove to wire racks.

7. For the icing, in a large saucepan, melt the butter. Stir in the flour until smooth. Stir in lemon juice. Bring to a boil; cook and stir 2 minutes or until mixture is thickened. Remove from the heat. Stir in confectioners' sugar and lemon peel until blended. Drizzle icing over the warm twists. Sprinkle with the sliced almonds. Refrigerate the leftovers.

**PER SERVING** *223 cal., 10 g fat (5 g sat. fat), 38 mg chol., 261 mg sodium, 30 g carb., 1 g fiber, 5 g pro.*

## Southwest Tortilla Scramble

**START TO FINISH:** 15 MIN.
**MAKES:** 2 SERVINGS

- 4 **egg whites**
- 2 **eggs**
- ¼ **teaspoon pepper**
- 2 **corn tortillas (6 inches), halved and cut into strips**
- ¼ **cup chopped fresh spinach**
- 2 **tablespoons shredded reduced-fat cheddar cheese**
- ¼ **cup salsa**

**1.** In a large bowl, whisk egg whites, eggs and pepper. Stir in the tortillas, spinach and cheese.

**2.** Heat a large skillet coated with cooking spray over medium heat. Pour in the egg mixture; cook and stir until the eggs are thickened and no liquid egg remains. Stir in salsa.

**PER SERVING** *195 cal., 7 g fat (3 g sat. fat), 217 mg chol., 391 mg sodium, 16 g carb., 2 g fiber, 17 g pro.* **Diabetic Exchanges:** *2 lean meat, 1 starch.*

## Gingerbread Scones

Spiced with ginger and cinnamon, these golden goodies are a wonderful treat during the Christmas season or any time at all. I think they're best served warm from the oven with hot coffee or tea.

—**DAVID BOSTEDT** ZEPHYRHILLS, FL

**PREP:** 20 MIN. • **BAKE:** 15 MIN.
**MAKES:** 1 DOZEN

- 2 **cups all-purpose flour**
- 3 **tablespoons brown sugar**
- 2 **teaspoons baking powder**
- 1 **teaspoon ground ginger**
- ½ **teaspoon salt**
- ½ **teaspoon baking soda**
- ½ **teaspoon ground cinnamon**
- ¼ **cup cold butter, cubed**
- ⅓ **cup molasses**
- ¼ **cup milk**
- 1 **egg, separated**
  **Coarse sugar**

**1.** Preheat the oven to 400°. In a large bowl, whisk the first seven ingredients. Cut in butter until mixture resembles coarse crumbs. In another bowl, whisk the molasses, milk and egg yolk until blended; stir into crumb mixture just until moistened.

**2.** Turn dough onto a lightly floured surface; knead gently 6-8 times. Pat into an 8-in. circle. Cut into 12 wedges. Place wedges 1 in. apart on a greased baking sheet.

**3.** In a small bowl, beat the egg white until frothy; brush over the scones. Sprinkle with the coarse sugar. Bake 12-15 minutes or until golden brown. Serve warm.

**PER SERVING** *157 cal., 5 g fat (3 g sat. fat), 29 mg chol., 269 mg sodium, 26 g carb., 1 g fiber, 3 g pro.*

I describe my Southwest Tortilla Scramble as a deconstructed breakfast burrito. Enjoy!
—**CHRISTINE SCHENHER** EXETER, CA

SOUTHWEST TORTILLA SCRAMBLE

CITRUS MELON MINGLE

⑤ INGREDIENTS FAST FIX

# Zucchini Frittata

Sit down to a hearty frittata that cooks in the microwave in just minutes. A garnish of red pepper adds an extra-special touch.

**—MILDRED FOX** FOSTORIA, OH

**START TO FINISH:** 25 MIN. • **MAKES:** 4 SERVINGS

- 4 cups finely chopped zucchini (3-4 medium)
- 1 small onion, chopped
- 4 eggs
- ¾ teaspoon salt
- ⅛ teaspoon pepper
- 1 cup (4 ounces) shredded cheddar cheese
- 1 cup cubed fully cooked ham

**1.** In a 9-in. microwave-safe pie plate, combine zucchini and onion. Microwave, covered, on high for 3-4 minutes or until tender; drain.

**2.** In a bowl, whisk eggs, salt and pepper; stir in cheese and ham. Carefully pour over zucchini mixture. Microwave at 70% power for 8-9 minutes or until a knife inserted near the center comes out clean.

**NOTE** *This recipe was tested in a 1,100-watt microwave.*
**PER SERVING** *251 cal., 15 g fat (9 g sat. fat), 265 mg chol., 1,134 mg sodium, 7 g carb., 2 g fiber, 22 g pro.*

# Citrus Melon Mingle

The fresh fruits in this colorful salad are great all by themselves, but they're even better tossed with mint, ginger and honey.

**—DORIS HEATH** FRANKLIN, NC

**START TO FINISH:** 20 MIN. • **MAKES:** 8 SERVINGS

- 1½ cups cubed cantaloupe
- 1½ cups cubed honeydew
- 2 medium grapefruit, peeled and sectioned
- 2 medium navel oranges, peeled and sectioned
- 2 firm bananas, sliced
- 1 can (8 ounces) unsweetened pineapple chunks, undrained
- ½ cup orange juice
- 2 tablespoons honey
- 1 tablespoon minced fresh mint or 1 teaspoon dried mint
- 1 teaspoon minced fresh gingerroot

In a large bowl, combine all ingredients, tossing lightly. Refrigerate, covered, until serving.
**PER SERVING** *125 cal., trace fat (trace sat. fat), 0 chol., 10 mg sodium, 31 g carb., 3 g fiber, 2 g pro.* **Diabetic Exchange:** *2 fruit.*

## top tip

## Just Gingerroot

Fresh gingerroot is available in your grocer's produce section. It should have a smooth skin. If it is wrinkled and cracked, the root is dry and past its prime. When stored in a heavy-duty resealable plastic bag, unpeeled gingerroot may be frozen for up to a year. When needed, simply peel and cut or grate.

ZUCCHINI FRITTATA

SLOW COOKER HONEY GRANOLA

## Breakfast Sausage Patties

These homemade patties are nicely seasoned with marjoram, savory, sage, cayenne and more. But the secret ingredient is the buttermilk—it keeps the meat nice and moist.

**—HARVEY KEENEY** MANDAN, ND

**PREP:** 30 MIN. • **COOK:** 10 MIN./BATCH • **MAKES:** 20 PATTIES

- ¾ cup buttermilk
- 2¼ teaspoons kosher salt
- 1½ teaspoons rubbed sage
- 1½ teaspoons brown sugar
- 1½ teaspoons pepper
- ¾ teaspoon dried marjoram
- ¾ teaspoon dried savory
- ¾ teaspoon cayenne pepper
- ¼ teaspoon ground nutmeg
- 2½ pounds ground pork

**1.** In a large bowl, combine the buttermilk and seasonings. Add the pork; mix lightly but thoroughly. Shape into twenty 3-in. patties.

**2.** In a large skillet coated with cooking spray, cook the patties in batches over medium heat 5-6 minutes on each side or until a thermometer reads 160°. Remove to paper towels to drain.

**FREEZE OPTION** *Cool and wrap each patty in plastic wrap; transfer to a resealable plastic freezer bag. May be frozen for up to 3 months. To use, unwrap patties and place on a baking sheet coated with cooking spray. Bake at 350° for 15 minutes on each side or until heated through.*

**PER SERVING** *126 cal., 8 g fat (3 g sat. fat), 38 mg chol., 251 mg sodium, 1 g carb., trace fiber, 11 g pro.*

Why buy cereal from the store? Slow Cooker Honey Granola is so easy to make, and the taste can't be beat.
**—ARISA CUPP** WARREN, OR

**EAT SMART** **SLOW COOKER**
## Slow Cooker Honey Granola

**PREP:** 10 MIN. • **COOK:** 2 HOURS + COOLING
**MAKES:** ABOUT 9 CUPS

- 4 cups old-fashioned oats
- 1 cup sunflower kernels
- 1 cup flaked coconut
- ½ teaspoon salt
- ½ cup canola oil
- ½ cup honey
- 1 cup chopped dried pineapple
- 1 cup chopped dried mangoes

**1.** In a 3-qt. slow cooker, combine oats, sunflower kernels, coconut and salt. In a small bowl, whisk the oil and honey until blended. Stir into oats mixture. Cook, covered, on high for 2 hours, stirring well every 20 minutes.

**2.** Remove the granola to baking sheets, spreading evenly; cool completely. Stir in the dried pineapple and mangoes. Store in airtight containers.

**PER SERVING** *295 cal., 15 g fat (3 g sat. fat), 0 chol., 167 mg sodium, 38 g carb., 4 g fiber, 5 g pro.*

BREAKFAST SAUSAGE PATTIES

CINNAMON-WALNUT STICKY BUNS

## Cinnamon-Walnut Sticky Buns

The sweet honey-walnut topping makes these tender, ooey-gooey rolls a sure hit with everyone who tastes them.
—**DEBBIE BROEKER** ROCKY MOUNT, MO

**PREP:** 1 HOUR + RISING • **BAKE:** 30 MIN.
**MAKES:** 2 DOZEN

- 2 **packages (¼ ounce each) active dry yeast**
- 1½ **cups warm water (110° to 115°)**
- 1 **cup mashed potatoes (without added milk and butter)**
- ½ **cup sugar**
- ½ **cup butter, softened**
- 2 **eggs**
- 2 **teaspoons salt**
- 6 **to 6½ cups all-purpose flour**

**TOPPING**
- ¼ **cup butter**
- 1 **cup packed brown sugar**
- 1 **cup honey**
- 1 **teaspoon ground cinnamon**
- 1 **cup chopped walnuts**

**FILLING**
- ½ **cup sugar**
- 2 **teaspoons ground cinnamon**
- 2 **tablespoons butter, melted**

**1.** In a small bowl, dissolve yeast in warm water. In a large bowl, combine mashed potatoes, sugar, butter, eggs, salt, yeast mixture and 2 cups flour; beat on medium speed until smooth. Stir in enough remaining flour to form a soft dough.
**2.** Turn dough onto a floured surface; knead until smooth and elastic, about 6-8 minutes. Place in a greased bowl, turning once to grease the top. Cover with plastic wrap and let rise in a warm place until doubled, about 1 hour.
**3.** For topping, in a small saucepan, melt the butter. Stir in the brown sugar, honey and cinnamon. Divide mixture among three greased 9-in. round baking pans, spreading evenly. Sprinkle with walnuts.
**4.** For the filling, in a small bowl, mix the sugar and cinnamon. Punch down the dough. Turn onto a lightly floured surface; divide in half. Roll one portion into an 18x12-in. rectangle. Brush with 1 tablespoon melted butter to within ½ in. of edges; sprinkle with ¼ cup sugar mixture.

**5.** Roll up the dough jelly-roll style, starting with a long side; pinch seam to seal. Cut into 12 slices. Repeat with the remaining dough and filling. Place eight slices in each pan, cut side down. Cover with kitchen towels; let rise until doubled, about 30 minutes. Preheat oven to 350°.
**6.** Bake 30-35 minutes or until golden brown. Immediately invert onto serving plates. Serve warm.
**PER SERVING** *328 cal., 10 g fat (5 g sat. fat), 35 mg chol., 257 mg sodium, 55 g carb., 2 g fiber, 5 g pro.*

**FAST FIX ▶**
## Quick Apple Pancakes

Fall is my favorite time to enjoy a stack of apple-filled pancakes, but they're great during any season. I like to use the fruit from our Washington state orchards. Don't forget the yummy spiced syrup!
—**SANDRA GIRARD** OAK HARBOR, WA

**START TO FINISH:** 30 MIN.
**MAKES:** 15 PANCAKES (1¼ CUPS SYRUP)

- 2 **cups biscuit/baking mix**
- 2 **eggs, lightly beaten**
- 1¼ **cups 2% milk**
- 2 **tablespoons canola oil**
- 1 **medium apple, peeled and shredded**
- 1 **tablespoon grated lemon peel**

**APPLE SYRUP**
- 1 **cup packed brown sugar**
- ⅔ **cup unsweetened apple juice**
- 3 **tablespoons butter**
- ⅛ **teaspoon ground cinnamon**
  **Dash ground cloves**

**1.** Place biscuit mix in a large bowl. Combine the eggs, milk and oil; stir into biscuit mix just until moistened. Stir in the apple and lemon peel.
**2.** Pour pancake batter by ¼ cupfuls onto a greased hot griddle; turn when bubbles form on top. Cook until the second side is golden brown.
**3.** In a small saucepan, combine the syrup ingredients over medium heat. Bring to a boil. Reduce heat; simmer, uncovered, for 5 minutes or until it is slightly reduced. Serve the syrup with the pancakes.
**PER SERVING** *560 cal., 23 g fat (8 g sat. fat), 107 mg chol., 730 mg sodium, 83 g carb., 1 g fiber, 8 g pro.*

PESTO EGG WRAPS

**⑤INGREDIENTS FAST FIX ▶**
## Pesto Egg Wraps

When I experimented with some leftover pesto, these 15-minute wraps were the result. They're perfect when I'm in a hurry but want a nutritious, filling breakfast.
—**LISA WATERMAN** LEWISTOWN, MT

**START TO FINISH:** 15 MIN.
**MAKES:** 2 SERVINGS

- ¼ **cup oil-packed sun-dried tomatoes, chopped**
- 4 **eggs, lightly beaten**
- 2 **tablespoons crumbled feta cheese**
- 2 **tablespoons prepared pesto**
- 2 **whole wheat tortillas (8 inches), warmed**

**1.** Heat a large skillet over medium heat. Add the sun-dried tomatoes; cook and stir until heated through. Pour in the eggs; cook and stir until the eggs are thickened and no liquid egg remains. Remove from heat; sprinkle with feta cheese.
**2.** Spread 1 tablespoon of pesto across center of each tortilla; top with the egg mixture. Fold the bottom and sides of tortilla over filling and roll up.
**PER SERVING** *407 cal., 23 g fat (6 g sat. fat), 432 mg chol., 533 mg sodium, 27 g carb., 3 g fiber, 21 g pro.*

## Caramelized Ham & Swiss Buns

My neighbor shared her wonderful recipe for ham-and-cheese buns with me. I like the fact that they can chill overnight and bake in the morning. Plus, they're absolutely delicious!

—IRIS WEIHEMULLER BAXTER, MN

**PREP:** 25 MIN. + CHILLING • **BAKE:** 30 MIN.
**MAKES:** 1 DOZEN

- 1 package (12 ounces) Hawaiian sweet rolls, split
- ½ cup horseradish sauce
- 12 slices deli ham
- 6 slices Swiss cheese, halved
- ½ cup butter, cubed
- 2 tablespoons finely chopped onion
- 2 tablespoons brown sugar
- 1 tablespoon spicy brown mustard
- 2 teaspoons poppy seeds
- 1½ teaspoons Worcestershire sauce
- ¼ teaspoon garlic powder

**1.** Spread the bottoms of rolls with horseradish sauce. Layer with ham and Swiss cheese; replace the tops. Arrange in a single layer in a greased 9-in. square baking pan.

**2.** In a small skillet, heat butter over medium-high heat. Add onion; cook and stir 1-2 minutes or until tender. Stir in the remaining ingredients. Pour over rolls. Refrigerate, covered, several hours or overnight.

**3.** Preheat oven to 350°. Bake, covered, for 25 minutes. Bake, uncovered, 5-10 minutes longer or until golden brown.

**PER SERVING** *288 cal., 17 g fat (9 g sat. fat), 67 mg chol., 447 mg sodium, 21 g carb., 1 g fiber, 11 g pro.*

CARAMELIZED HAM & SWISS BUNS

---

FAST FIX ▶

## Sheepherder's Breakfast

When we went camping, my sister-in-law got everyone going in the morning by serving this wake-up skillet loaded with eggs, bacon, cheddar and hash browns. Add a side of toast and juice, and you have a great kickoff to the day—whether or not you're in a campground!

—PAULETTA BUSHNELL ALBANY, OR

**START TO FINISH:** 30 MIN.
**MAKES:** 8 SERVINGS

- ¾ pound bacon strips, finely chopped
- 1 medium onion, chopped
- 1 package (30 ounces) frozen shredded hash brown potatoes, thawed
- 8 eggs
- ½ teaspoon salt
- ¼ teaspoon pepper
- 1 cup (4 ounces) shredded cheddar cheese

**1.** In a large skillet, cook the bacon and onion over medium heat until the bacon is crisp. Drain, reserving ¼ cup drippings in pan.

**2.** Stir in the hash brown potatoes. Cook, uncovered, over medium heat 10 minutes or until bottom is golden brown; turn the hash browns. With the back of a spoon, make eight evenly spaced wells in hash brown mixture. Break one egg into each well. Sprinkle with salt and pepper.

**3.** Cook, covered, on low 10 minutes or until the eggs are set and the hash browns are tender. Sprinkle with the cheddar cheese; let stand until the cheese is melted.

**PER SERVING** *278 cal., 17 g fat (7 g sat. fat), 198 mg chol., 479 mg sodium, 17 g carb., 1 g fiber, 14 g pro.*

---

BRUNCH BEIGNETS

## Brunch Beignets

Enjoy a New Orleans-style breakfast with beignets. Dusted with confectioners' sugar, the warm and crispy bites are a delight.

—LOIS RUTHERFORD ELKTON, FL

**PREP:** 20 MIN. • **COOK:** 5 MIN./BATCH
**MAKES:** ABOUT 2 DOZEN

- 2 eggs, separated
- 1 cup all-purpose flour
- 1 teaspoon baking powder
- ⅛ teaspoon salt
- ½ cup sugar
- ¼ cup water
- 1 tablespoon butter, melted
- 2 teaspoons grated lemon peel
- 1 teaspoon vanilla extract
- 1 teaspoon brandy, optional
  Oil for deep-fat frying
  Confectioners' sugar

**1.** Place the egg whites in a small bowl; let them stand at room temperature for 30 minutes.

**2.** Meanwhile, in a large bowl, combine the flour, the baking powder and salt. Combine the egg yolks, sugar, water, butter, lemon peel, vanilla and brandy if desired; stir into the dry ingredients just until combined. Beat egg whites on medium speed until soft peaks form; fold into batter.

**3.** In an electric skillet or deep-fat fryer, heat oil to 375°. Drop the batter by teaspoonfuls, a few at a time, into hot oil. Fry until golden brown, about 1½ minutes on each side. Drain on paper towels. Dust with confectioners' sugar. Serve warm.

**PER SERVING** *52 cal., 2 g fat (trace sat. fat), 16 mg chol., 32 mg sodium, 7 g carb., trace fiber, 1 g pro.*

---

## Walnut Streusel Coffee Cake

I love making this coffee cake from my Aunt Suzie. It has a delectable surprise inside each slice—a sweet walnut filling.
—**MICHELLE EDER** GRAND RAPIDS, MI

**PREP:** 20 MIN. • **BAKE:** 45 MIN. + COOLING
**MAKES:** 12 SERVINGS

- 1 **cup chopped walnuts**
- ½ **cup packed brown sugar**
- 2 **tablespoons butter, melted**
- ½ **teaspoon ground cinnamon**

**COFFEE CAKE**
- 4 **eggs, separated**
- 1 **cup butter, softened**
- 1¾ **cups sugar**
- 1 **teaspoon vanilla extract**
- 3 **cups all-purpose flour**
- 2 **teaspoons baking powder**
- ½ **teaspoon baking soda**
- ¼ **teaspoon salt**
- 1 **cup (8 ounces) sour cream**
- 2 **teaspoons confectioners' sugar**

**1.** In a small bowl, mix the walnuts, brown sugar, butter and cinnamon. Place the egg whites in a large bowl; let stand at room temperature 30 minutes. Preheat oven to 350°. Grease and flour a 10-in. fluted tube pan.

**2.** In a large bowl, cream butter and sugar until light and fluffy. Gradually add yolks. Beat in vanilla. In another bowl, whisk the flour, baking powder, baking soda and salt; add to creamed mixture alternately with sour cream, beating well after each addition.

WALNUT STREUSEL COFFEE CAKE

**3.** With clean beaters, beat the egg whites on medium speed until stiff peaks form. Fold into batter.

**4.** Pour half of batter into prepared pan; sprinkle with walnut mixture. Pour in remaining batter. Bake 45-55 minutes or until a toothpick inserted in the center comes out clean. Cool 10 minutes before removing from the pan to a wire rack to cool completely. Dust with confectioners' sugar.

**NOTE** *To remove cakes easily, use solid shortening to grease plain and fluted tube pans.*

**PER SERVING** *540 cal., 29 g fat (14 g sat. fat), 128 mg chol., 323 mg sodium, 65 g carb., 2 g fiber, 8 g pro.*

## Ham, Egg & Cheese Casserole

My saucy casserole is an adaptation of a French classic called *croque madame*, an egg-topped grilled sandwich. Frozen bread dough speeds up the prep.
—**MELISSA MILLWOOD** LYMAN, SC

**PREP:** 35 MIN. • **BAKE:** 40 MIN. + STANDING
**MAKES:** 12 SERVINGS

- 1 **loaf (1 pound) frozen bread dough, thawed**
- ¾ **cup butter, cubed**
- ⅓ **cup all-purpose flour**
- 2½ **cups 2% milk**
- 3 **tablespoons Dijon mustard**
- ¾ **teaspoon pepper**
- ½ **teaspoon salt**
- ½ **teaspoon ground nutmeg**
- ½ **cup grated Parmesan cheese**
- 1 **pound sliced smoked deli ham**
- 2 **cups (8 ounces) shredded Swiss cheese**
- 6 **eggs**
- ¼ **cup minced fresh parsley**

**1.** Preheat oven to 350°. On a lightly floured surface, roll the dough into a 14x10-in. rectangle. Transfer to a greased 13x9-in. baking dish; build up the edges slightly.

**2.** In a large saucepan, melt butter over medium heat. Stir in flour until smooth; gradually whisk in milk. Bring to a boil, stirring constantly; cook and stir for 3-4 minutes or until thickened. Stir in the mustard, pepper, salt and nutmeg. Remove from heat; stir in the Parmesan cheese.

HAM, EGG & CHEESE CASSEROLE

**3.** Place a third of the ham over the dough; top with 1 cup sauce and ⅔ cup Swiss cheese. Repeat the layers twice. Bake, uncovered, 30 minutes or until bubbly and crust is golden brown.

**4.** Using the back of a tablespoon, make six indentations in the top of the casserole to within 2 in. of the edges. Carefully break an egg into each indentation.

**5.** Bake 10-15 minutes longer or until the egg whites are completely set and the yolks begin to thicken but are not hard. (If desired, bake an additional 5 minutes for firmer eggs.) Sprinkle with parsley. Let stand for 10 minutes before cutting.

**PER SERVING** *405 cal., 23 g fat (12 g sat. fat), 176 mg chol., 992 mg sodium, 26 g carb., 2 g fiber, 22 g pro.*

**top tip**

## Coffee Cake Remake

I never worry about ending up with leftover coffee cake. I just cube any extra cake and add it to a trifle for a dinnertime dessert.
—**LOUY CASTONGUAY** WEST FARMINGTON, ME

## Country Sausage & Egg Rolls

**PREP:** 50 MIN. • **BAKE:** 30 MIN.
**MAKES:** 12 SERVINGS

- 1 **pound bulk pork sausage**
- 1 **cup chopped sweet onion**
- 1 **garlic clove, minced**
- ½ **teaspoon pepper, divided**
- 1 **tablespoon butter**
- 8 **eggs**
- 3 **tablespoons whole milk**
- ¼ **teaspoon salt**
- ¾ **cup shredded sharp cheddar cheese**
- 3 **green onions, chopped**
- 15 **sheets phyllo dough, (14 inches x 9 inches)**
- ⅓ **cup butter, melted**

**1.** In a large skillet over medium heat, cook the sausage, sweet onion, garlic and ¼ teaspoon pepper until the meat is no longer pink; drain. Remove and keep warm.

**2.** In the same skillet, melt the butter over medium-high heat. Whisk the eggs, milk, salt and remaining pepper; add to the skillet. Cook and stir until almost set. Stir in the cheese, green onions and sausage mixture. Remove from the heat.

**3.** Place one sheet of phyllo dough on a work surface; brush with melted butter. Layer with four more phyllo sheets, brushing with butter after each layer. (Keep remaining phyllo covered with plastic wrap and a damp towel to prevent it from drying out.) Repeat, making three stacks.

**4.** Cut each stack in half widthwise and in half crosswise, forming a total of four 7x 4½-in. rectangles. Spoon ¼ cup egg mixture along one of the long sides of each rectangle; roll up.

**5.** Place rolls seam side down on an ungreased baking sheet. With a sharp knife, make four shallow slashes across each roll; brush with butter.

**6.** Bake at 350° for 30-35 minutes or until golden brown.

**PER SERVING** *251 cal., 19 g fat (9 g sat. fat), 178 mg chol., 399 mg sodium, 11 g carb., 1 g fiber, 10 g pro.*

> With a homey filling and elegant phyllo wrapping, Country Sausage & Egg Rolls are great for guests.
> —**LISA SPEER** PALM BEACH, FL

COUNTRY SAUSAGE & EGG ROLLS

## Ultimate Bacon-Maple French Toast

This savory update on baked French toast is make-ahead easy. Try it for brunch on a holiday or other special occasion.

—**JOHN WHITEHEAD** GREENVILLE, SC

**PREP:** 30 MIN. + CHILLING
**BAKE:** 40 MIN. + STANDING
**MAKES:** 10 SERVINGS

- 8 **eggs**
- 2 **cups half-and-half cream**
- 1 **cup 2% milk**
- 1 **tablespoon sugar**
- 1 **tablespoon brown sugar**
- 1 **teaspoon vanilla extract**
- ½ **teaspoon ground cinnamon**
- ¼ **teaspoon ground nutmeg**
  **Dash salt**
  **Dash cayenne pepper**
- 1 **loaf (1 pound) French bread, cut into 1-inch slices**

**TOPPING**

- 6 **thick-sliced bacon strips, cooked and crumbled**
- 1 **cup butter, melted**
- 1 **cup packed brown sugar**
- ½ **cup chopped pecans, toasted**
- 2 **tablespoons corn syrup**
- 1 **teaspoon ground cinnamon**
- ½ **teaspoon ground nutmeg**
- ¼ **teaspoon ground cloves**
  **Maple syrup**

**1.** Grease a 13x9-in. baking dish; set it aside.

**2.** In a large shallow bowl, whisk the first 10 ingredients. Dip each slice of bread into the egg mixture. Arrange the slices in the prepared dish. Pour the remaining egg mixture over top. Cover and refrigerate overnight.

**3.** Remove from the refrigerator 30 minutes before baking. Preheat oven to 350°. In a small bowl, combine topping ingredients. Spread over top.

**4.** Bake, uncovered, 40-45 minutes or until a knife inserted near the center comes out clean. Let stand 10 minutes before serving. Drizzle with syrup.

**PER SERVING** *612 cal., 36 g fat (18 g sat. fat), 250 mg chol., 694 mg sodium, 57 g carb., 2 g fiber, 16 g pro.*

EGGS BENEDICT CASSEROLE

## Prosciutto & Cheddar Breakfast Biscuits

I came up with my biscuits as a twist on the traditional breakfast sandwich.
—**KELLY BOE** WHITELAND, IN

**PREP:** 30 MIN. • **BAKE:** 15 MIN.
**MAKES:** 6 SERVINGS

2⅓ cups biscuit/baking mix
½ cup 2% milk
3 tablespoons butter, melted
1 to 2 tablespoons minced fresh chives

**EGGS**

6 eggs
2 tablespoons 2% milk
¼ teaspoon salt
2 ounces thinly sliced prosciutto or deli ham, cut into strips
2 green onions, chopped
1 tablespoon butter
½ cup shredded cheddar cheese

**1.** Preheat oven to 425°. In a bowl, combine biscuit mix, milk, melted butter and chives; mix just until moistened.
**2.** Turn onto a lightly floured surface; knead gently 8-10 times. Pat or roll to ¾-in. thickness; cut with a floured 2½-in. biscuit cutter. Place 2 in. apart on an ungreased baking sheet. Bake 12-14 minutes or until golden brown.
**3.** Meanwhile, in a large bowl, whisk eggs, milk and salt. Place a large skillet over medium heat. Add prosciutto and green onions; cook until prosciutto begins to brown, stirring occasionally. Stir in butter until melted. Add egg mixture; cook and stir until eggs are thickened and no liquid egg remains. Stir in cheese; remove from heat.
**4.** Split warm biscuits in half. Fill with the egg mixture.
**PER SERVING** *397 cal., 24 g fat (11 g sat. fat), 252 mg chol., 1,062 mg sodium, 31 g carb., 1 g fiber, 15 g pro.*

## Eggs Benedict Casserole

Love classic eggs benedict? Combine those ingredients in a baking dish for a delicious crowd-size casserole. I like the convenience of putting it together the day before and popping it into the oven in the morning. Just before serving time, whip up the luscious sauce.
—**SANDIE HEINDEL** LIBERTY, MO

**PREP:** 25 MIN. + CHILLING • **BAKE:** 45 MIN.
**MAKES:** 12 SERVINGS (1⅓ CUPS SAUCE)

12 ounces Canadian bacon, chopped
6 English muffins, split and cut into 1-inch pieces
8 eggs
2 cups 2% milk
1 teaspoon onion powder
¼ teaspoon paprika

**HOLLANDAISE SAUCE**

4 egg yolks
½ cup heavy whipping cream
2 tablespoons lemon juice
1 teaspoon Dijon mustard
½ cup butter, melted

**1.** Place half of the bacon in a greased 3-qt. or 13x9-in. baking dish; top with the muffins and remaining bacon. In a large bowl, whisk eggs, milk and onion powder; pour over top. Refrigerate, covered, overnight.
**2.** Preheat oven to 375°. Remove the casserole from refrigerator while oven heats. Sprinkle top with paprika. Bake, covered, 35 minutes. Uncover; bake 10-15 minutes longer or until a knife inserted near center comes out clean.
**3.** In top of a double boiler or a metal bowl over simmering water, whisk egg yolks, cream, lemon juice and mustard until blended; cook until the mixture is just thick enough to coat a metal spoon and temperature reaches 160°, whisking constantly. Reduce heat to very low. Very slowly drizzle in warm melted butter, whisking constantly. Serve immediately with casserole.
**PER SERVING** *286 cal., 19 g fat (10 g sat. fat), 256 mg chol., 535 mg sodium, 16 g carb., 1 g fiber, 14 g pro.*

**SHRIMP ENCHILADAS
WITH GREEN SAUCE**
PAGE 160

# Potluck Pleasers

**Share your best** at bring-a-dish gatherings with family and friends. In this chapter, you'll find a winning lineup of casseroles, salads, soups and other large-yield recipes to **wow the crowd**.

**MEDITERRANEAN COBB SALAD**
*PAGE 157*

**SHORT RIB COBBLER**
*PAGE 153*

**GRILLED STEAK SALAD WITH TOMATOES & AVOCADO**
*PAGE 161*

## Roasted Autumn Vegetable Soup

I think roasting brings out the best in sweet potatoes, carrots and parsnips. After taking them out of the oven, I blend them into this delicious, wholesome soup.
—STEPHANIE FLAMING WOODLAND, CA

**PREP:** 35 MIN. • **BAKE:** 40 MIN.
**MAKES:** 12 SERVINGS (4 QUARTS)

- 2 pounds sweet potatoes (about 4 medium)
- 2 pounds carrots (about 8 large)
- 1½ pounds parsnips (about 6 medium)
- 2 large onions, quartered
- 6 garlic cloves, peeled
- ¼ cup canola oil
- 3 cartons (32 ounces each) chicken broth
- 1 cup fat-free evaporated milk
- 1 teaspoon salt
- ½ teaspoon pepper
  Minced fresh parsley and sage

**1.** Preheat oven to 400°. Peel and cut sweet potatoes, carrots and parsnips into 1½-in. pieces; place in a large bowl. Add onions and garlic; drizzle with oil and toss to coat. Divide mixture between two greased 15x10x1-in. baking pans. Roast 40-50 minutes or until tender, stirring occasionally.

**2.** Transfer the vegetables to a Dutch oven. Add broth, milk, salt and pepper. Bring to a boil; simmer, uncovered, 10-15 minutes to allow flavors to blend.

**3.** Puree the soup using an immersion blender. Or, cool the soup slightly and puree in batches in a blender; return to the pan and heat through. Sprinkle servings with minced herbs.

**PER SERVING** *240 cal., 6 g fat (trace sat. fat), 6 mg chol., 1,251 mg sodium, 43 g carb., 7 g fiber, 6 g pro.*

## The Most from Roasting

Vegetables roast best when they are arranged in a single layer and not crowded in the pan. They're done roasting when tender and easily pierced with a fork or knife.

Put vegetables from the garden or farmers market to great use in Heirloom Tomato & Zucchini Salad.
—MATTHEW HASS SUSSEX, WI

HEIRLOOM TOMATO & ZUCCHINI SALAD

EAT SMART FAST FIX

## Heirloom Tomato & Zucchini Salad

**START TO FINISH:** 25 MIN.
**MAKES:** 12 SERVINGS (¾ CUP EACH)

- 7 large heirloom tomatoes (about 2½ pounds), cut into wedges
- 3 medium zucchini, halved lengthwise and thinly sliced
- 2 medium sweet yellow peppers, thinly sliced
- ⅓ cup cider vinegar
- 3 tablespoons olive oil
- 1 tablespoon sugar
- 1½ teaspoons salt
- 1 tablespoon each minced fresh basil, parsley and tarragon

**1.** In a large bowl, combine tomatoes, zucchini and peppers. In a small bowl, whisk vinegar, oil, sugar and salt until blended. Stir in herbs.

**2.** Just before serving, drizzle the prepared dressing over the salad; toss gently to coat.

**PER SERVING** *68 cal., 4 g fat (1 g sat. fat), 0 chol., 306 mg sodium, 8 g carb., 2 g fiber, 2 g pro.* **Diabetic Exchanges:** *1 vegetable, ½ fat.*

## Short Rib Cobbler

Two of my family's favorites—beef stew and biscuits—were the inspiration for this comforting, home-style dish. You can be sure no one will leave the table hungry!

—**JANINE TALLEY** ORLANDO, FL

**PREP:** 45 MIN. • **BAKE:** 3 HOURS
**MAKES:** 8 SERVINGS

- ½ cup plus 3 tablespoons all-purpose flour, divided
- 1¼ teaspoons salt, divided
- ½ teaspoon pepper
- 2 pounds well-trimmed boneless beef short ribs, cut into 1½-inch pieces
- 5 tablespoons olive oil, divided
- 1 large onion, chopped
- 1 medium carrot, chopped
- 1 celery rib, chopped
- 1 garlic clove, minced
- 2 tablespoons tomato paste
- 5 cups beef stock
- 1 cup dry red wine or additional beef stock
- 1 teaspoon poultry seasoning
- 1 bay leaf
- 1 package (14 ounces) frozen pearl onions, thawed
- 4 medium carrots, cut into 2-inch pieces

**COBBLER TOPPING**
- 2 cups biscuit/baking mix
- ⅔ cup 2% milk
- Fresh thyme leaves

**1.** Preheat oven to 350°. In a shallow bowl, mix ½ cup flour, ¾ teaspoon salt and pepper. Dip the short ribs in the flour mixture to coat all sides; shake off excess.

**2.** In an ovenproof Dutch oven, heat 3 tablespoons oil over medium heat. Brown the beef in batches. Remove from the pan.

**3.** In same pan, heat the remaining oil over medium heat. Add the onion, chopped carrot and celery; cook and stir 2-3 minutes or until tender. Add garlic; cook 1 minute longer. Stir in tomato paste and remaining flour until blended. Gradually stir in stock and wine until smooth. Return beef to pan; stir in poultry seasoning, bay leaf and remaining salt. Bring to a boil.

**4.** Bake, covered, 1¾ hours. Stir in the pearl onions and carrots. Bake, covered, 30-45 minutes longer or until the beef and onions are tender. Skim fat and remove bay leaf.

**5.** In a small bowl, mix the biscuit mix and milk just until a soft dough forms. Drop by scant ¼ cupfuls over the beef mixture. Bake, uncovered, 40-45 minutes longer or until topping is golden brown. Sprinkle with thyme.

**PER SERVING** *454 cal., 23 g fat (6 g sat. fat), 47 mg chol., 930 mg sodium, 40 g carb., 3 g fiber, 23 g pro.*

## Best Lasagna

For a casual get-together, a rich and meaty lasagna is always a crowd-pleasing choice. My grown sons and daughter-in-law often request it for their birthdays.

—**PAM THOMPSON** GIRARD, IL

**PREP:** 1 HOUR • **BAKE:** 50 MIN. + STANDING
**MAKES:** 12 SERVINGS

- 9 lasagna noodles
- 1¼ pounds bulk Italian sausage
- ¾ pound ground beef
- 1 medium onion, diced
- 3 garlic cloves, minced
- 2 cans (one 28 ounces, one 15 ounces) crushed tomatoes
- 2 cans (6 ounces each) tomato paste
- ⅔ cup water
- 2 to 3 tablespoons sugar
- 3 tablespoons plus ¼ cup minced fresh parsley, divided
- 2 teaspoons dried basil
- ¾ teaspoon fennel seed

BEST LASAGNA

- ¾ teaspoon salt, divided
- ¼ teaspoon coarsely ground pepper
- 1 egg, lightly beaten
- 1 carton (15 ounces) ricotta cheese
- 4 cups (16 ounces) shredded part-skim mozzarella cheese
- ¾ cup grated Parmesan cheese

**1.** Cook noodles according to package directions; drain. Meanwhile, in a Dutch oven, cook sausage, beef and onion over medium heat 8-10 minutes or until the meat is no longer pink, breaking up the meat into crumbles. Add garlic; cook 1 minute longer. Drain.

**2.** Stir in crushed tomatoes, tomato paste, water, sugar, 3 tablespoons parsley, basil, fennel, ½ teaspoon salt and pepper; bring to a boil. Reduce the heat; simmer, uncovered, 30 minutes, stirring occasionally.

**3.** In a small bowl, mix the egg, ricotta cheese, and remaining parsley and salt.

**4.** Preheat oven to 375°. Spread 2 cups meat sauce into an ungreased 13x9-in. baking dish. Layer with three noodles and a third of the ricotta mixture. Sprinkle with 1 cup mozzarella cheese and 2 tablespoons Parmesan cheese. Repeat the layers twice. Top with the remaining meat sauce and cheeses (dish will be full).

**5.** Bake, covered, 25 minutes. Bake, uncovered, 25 minutes longer or until bubbly. Let lasagna stand 15 minutes before serving.

**PER SERVING** *519 cal., 27 g fat (13 g sat. fat), 109 mg chol., 1,013 mg sodium, 35 g carb., 4 g fiber, 35 g pro.*

SHORT RIB COBBLER

## EAT SMART FAST FIX
# Chilled Shrimp Pasta Salad

A refreshing, shrimp-filled pasta salad and a nice ice-cold drink—what more do you need on a warm summer's day?

—MARY PRICE YOUNGSTOWN, OH

**START TO FINISH:** 30 MIN.
**MAKES:** 12 SERVINGS (¾ CUP EACH)

- 3 **cups uncooked small pasta shells**
- ½ **cup sour cream**
- ½ **cup mayonnaise**
- ¼ **cup horseradish sauce**
- 2 **tablespoons grated onion**
- 1½ **teaspoons seasoned salt**
- ¾ **teaspoon pepper**
- 1 **pound peeled and deveined cooked small shrimp**
- 1 **large cucumber, seeded and chopped**
- 3 **celery ribs, thinly sliced Red lettuce leaves, optional**

**1.** Cook the pasta according to the package directions. Drain; rinse with cold water.
**2.** In a large bowl, mix the sour cream, mayonnaise, horseradish sauce, onion, seasoned salt and pepper. Stir in the shrimp, cucumber, celery and pasta. Refrigerate until serving. If desired, serve on lettuce.
**PER SERVING** *239 cal., 12 g fat (2 g sat. fat), 72 mg chol., 344 mg sodium, 20 g carb., 1 g fiber, 11 g pro.* **Diabetic Exchanges:** *2 fat, 1 starch, 1 lean meat.*

CHILLED SHRIMP PASTA SALAD

# Christina's Italian Wedding Soup

When making this chock-full soup, I often double the meatballs and poach them in the broth, then remove half of the meat and freeze it to enjoy another time.

—CHRISTINA HITCHCOCK

MADISON TOWNSHIP, PA

**PREP:** 40 MIN. • **COOK:** 20 MIN.
**MAKES:** 12 SERVINGS (5 QUARTS)

- 2 **eggs, lightly beaten**
- ⅓ **cup grated Parmesan cheese**
- ¼ **cup dry bread crumbs**
- 2 **tablespoons minced fresh parsley**
- 2 **tablespoons 2% milk**
- 4 **garlic cloves, minced**
- 4 **teaspoons grated onion**
- 1 **teaspoon salt**
- 1 **teaspoon pepper**
- ½ **teaspoon grated lemon peel**
- 1½ **pounds ground chicken**

**SOUP**

- 2 **tablespoons olive oil**
- 4 **medium carrots, chopped**
- 4 **celery ribs, chopped**
- 2 **small onions, chopped**
- 6 **garlic cloves, minced**
- 4 **cartons (26 ounces each) chicken stock**
- 1 **teaspoon salt**
- 1 **teaspoon pepper**
- 1½ **cups acini di pepe pasta**
- 2 **packages (10 ounces each) fresh spinach**
  **Additional minced fresh parsley and grated Parmesan cheese**

**1.** In a large bowl, combine the first 10 ingredients. Add chicken; mix lightly but thoroughly. Shape into 1-in. balls.
**2.** For soup, in a stockpot, heat the oil over medium-high heat. Add carrots, celery and onions; cook and stir 6-8 minutes or until onions are tender. Add garlic; cook 1 minute longer.
**3.** Stir in the stock, salt and pepper; bring to a boil. Drop meatballs into soup; cook, uncovered, 10 minutes. Gently stir in pasta; cook 10-12 minutes longer or until meatballs are cooked through and pasta is tender.
**4.** Stir in spinach. Top servings with parsley and cheese.
**PER SERVING** *269 cal., 9 g fat (2 g sat. fat), 71 mg chol., 1,083 mg sodium, 28 g carb., 3 g fiber, 21 g pro.*

# Nikki's Perfect Pastitsio

**PREP:** 45 MIN. • **BAKE:** 50 MIN.
**MAKES:** 12 SERVINGS

- 2½ **cups uncooked penne pasta**
- 2 **tablespoons butter, melted**
- 1 **cup grated Parmesan cheese**
- 1½ **pounds ground sirloin**
- 1 **medium onion, chopped**
- 2 **garlic cloves, minced**
- 1 **can (15 ounces) tomato sauce**
- ½ **teaspoon salt**
- ½ **teaspoon ground cinnamon**
- 1 **cup shredded Parmesan cheese, divided**

**BECHAMEL SAUCE**

- ½ **cup butter, cubed**
- ⅔ **cup all-purpose flour**
- ½ **teaspoon salt**
- ¼ **teaspoon pepper**
- 4 **cups 2% milk**
- 2 **eggs**

**1.** Cook pasta according to package directions; drain. Toss with butter; add grated Parmesan cheese. Transfer to a greased 13x9-in. baking dish.
**2.** Preheat oven to 350°. In a large skillet, cook the beef and onion over medium heat 8-10 minutes or until beef is no longer pink, breaking beef into crumbles; drain. Add the garlic; cook 2 minutes longer. Stir in tomato sauce, salt and cinnamon; heat through. Spoon over pasta. Sprinkle with ½ cup shredded Parmesan cheese.
**3.** In a large saucepan, melt butter. Stir in flour, salt and pepper until smooth; gradually add milk. Bring to a boil; cook and stir 1-2 minutes or until thickened.
**4.** In a small bowl, whisk a small amount of the hot mixture into eggs; return all to pan, whisking constantly. Bring to a gentle boil; cook and stir 2 minutes. Pour over beef mixture. Sprinkle with remaining cheese.
**5.** Bake, covered, 20 minutes. Bake, uncovered, 30-40 minutes longer or until golden brown.
**PER SERVING** *332 cal., 18 g fat (10 g sat. fat), 98 mg chol., 718 mg sodium, 24 g carb., 1 g fiber, 20 g pro.*

Mom always put so much time and effort into preparing her incredible pastitsio, a traditional Greek dish. My recipe is easier to fix and a bit lighter, too.

—**NIKKI TSANGARIS** WESTFIELD, IN

NIKKI'S PERFECT PASTITSIO

(5) INGREDIENTS FAST FIX

# Browned Butter Red Potatoes

**START TO FINISH:** 30 MIN. • **MAKES:** 12 SERVINGS (¾ CUP EACH)

- 16 **medium red potatoes (about 4 pounds), quartered**
- 1 **cup butter, cubed**
- 8 **garlic cloves, minced**
- 2 **teaspoons salt**
- 1 **teaspoon pepper**

**1.** Place potatoes in a Dutch oven; add water to cover. Bring to a boil. Reduce heat; cook, uncovered, 15-20 minutes or until tender.

**2.** Meanwhile, in a small heavy saucepan, melt butter over medium heat. Heat 5-7 minutes or until light golden brown, stirring constantly. Stir in garlic; cook 30 seconds longer or until butter is golden brown. Remove from heat.

**3.** Drain potatoes; transfer to a bowl. Sprinkle with salt and pepper. Drizzle with browned butter and toss to coat.

**PER SERVING** *246 cal., 15 g fat (10 g sat. fat), 40 mg chol., 510 mg sodium, 25 g carb., 3 g fiber, 3 g pro.*

A variation of my father's recipe, Browned Butter Red Potatoes are terrific with just about any entree.

—**ANNE PAVELAK** ENDICOTT, WA

BROWNED BUTTER RED POTATOES

SPLIT PEA SOUP WITH BACON & CRAB

# Split Pea Soup with Bacon & Crab

Many versions of split pea soup incorporate ham and bacon for good, hearty flavor. I take it a step further by stirring in crab.

—**STEPHEN EXEL** DES MOINES, IA

**PREP:** 30 MIN. • **COOK:** 1½ HOURS
**MAKES:** 12 SERVINGS (4 QUARTS)

- 8 **thick-sliced bacon strips, chopped**
- 2 **medium onions, chopped**
- 2 **medium carrots, chopped**
- 2 **celery ribs, chopped**
- 2 **packages (16 ounces each) dried green split peas, rinsed**
- 2 **smoked ham hocks (about 1 pound)**
- 2 **bay leaves**
- 4 **cartons (26 ounces each) chicken stock**
- 1 **cup heavy whipping cream**
- ½ **teaspoon salt**
- ½ **teaspoon pepper**
- 2 **cups lump crabmeat**

**1.** In a Dutch oven, cook bacon over medium heat until crisp, stirring occasionally. Remove with a slotted spoon; drain on paper towels.

**2.** Add onions, carrots and celery to bacon drippings; cook and stir over medium-high heat 8-10 minutes or until onions are tender. Stir in split peas, ham hocks, bay leaves and stock. Bring to a boil. Reduce heat; simmer, covered, 1 to 1½ hours or until split peas are tender, stirring occasionally.

**3.** Discard bay leaves; remove ham hocks from soup. When cool enough to handle, remove the meat from the bones and cut into small cubes; discard bones.

**4.** Puree soup using an immersion blender. Or, cool soup slightly and puree in batches in a blender; return to pan.

**5.** Stir cream, salt, pepper and ham into soup; heat through. In a small bowl, toss crab with bacon; serve with soup.

**FREEZE OPTION** *Freeze cooled soup without toppings in freezer containers; freeze cooked bacon in a small resealable freezer bag. To use, partially thaw in refrigerator overnight. Heat soup through in a saucepan, stirring occasionally, adding a little chicken stock or broth if necessary. Top servings as directed.*

**PER SERVING** *533 cal., 24 g fat (10 g sat. fat), 71 mg chol., 1,036 mg sodium, 50 g carb., 20 g fiber, 32 g pro.*

CRANBERRY-WALNUT
SWEET POTATOES

# Mediterranean Cobb Salad

I love giving classic dishes a twist. With crunchy falafel instead of the usual chicken, a Cobb salad is just as satisfying.
—**JENN TIDWELL** FAIR OAKS, CA

**PREP:** 1 HOUR • **COOK:** 5 MIN./BATCH • **MAKES:** 10 SERVINGS

- 1 package (6 ounces) falafel mix
- ½ cup sour cream or plain yogurt
- ¼ cup chopped seeded peeled cucumber
- ¼ cup 2% milk
- 1 teaspoon minced fresh parsley
- ¼ teaspoon salt
- 4 cups torn romaine
- 4 cups fresh baby spinach
- 3 hard-cooked eggs, chopped
- 2 medium tomatoes, seeded and finely chopped
- 1 medium ripe avocado, peeled and finely chopped
- ¾ cup crumbled feta cheese
- 8 bacon strips, cooked and crumbled
- ½ cup pitted Greek olives, finely chopped

**1.** Prepare and cook the falafel according to the package directions. When cool enough to handle, crumble or coarsely chop falafel.
**2.** In a small bowl, mix the sour cream, cucumber, milk, parsley and salt. In a large bowl, combine the romaine and spinach; transfer to a platter. Arrange the crumbled falafel and remaining ingredients over the greens. Drizzle with the prepared dressing.
**PER SERVING** *258 cal., 18 g fat (5 g sat. fat), 83 mg chol., 687 mg sodium, 15 g carb., 5 g fiber, 13 g pro.*

MEDITERRANEAN
COBB SALAD

# Cranberry-Walnut Sweet Potatoes

Here's my favorite part of Thanksgiving dinner! Feel free to make the sauce a day ahead—just leave out the nuts until serving time.
—**MARY WILHELM** SPARTA, WI

**PREP:** 25 MIN. • **BAKE:** 1 HOUR • **MAKES:** 8 SERVINGS

- 4 large sweet potatoes
- 1 tablespoon butter
- ¼ cup finely chopped onion
- 1 cup fresh or frozen cranberries
- ⅓ cup maple syrup
- ¼ cup cranberry juice
- ¼ teaspoon salt, divided
- ½ cup chopped walnuts, toasted
- 1 teaspoon Dijon mustard
- ¼ teaspoon pepper
- 2 tablespoons minced fresh chives

**1.** Preheat oven to 400°. Scrub the sweet potatoes; pierce several times with a fork. Bake 1 hour or until tender.
**2.** Meanwhile, in a small saucepan, heat the butter over medium-high heat. Add onion; cook and stir until tender. Stir in the cranberries, maple syrup, cranberry juice and ⅛ teaspoon salt. Bring to a boil. Reduce heat; simmer, covered, 10-15 minutes or until cranberries pop, stirring occasionally. Stir in walnuts and mustard; heat through.
**3.** When cool enough to handle, cut each potato lengthwise in half; sprinkle with pepper and remaining salt. Top with cranberry mixture; sprinkle with chives.
**NOTE** *To toast nuts, spread in a 15x10x1-in. baking pan. Bake at 350° for 5-10 minutes or until lightly browned, stirring occasionally. Or, spread in a dry nonstick skillet and heat over low heat until lightly browned, stirring occasionally.*
**PER SERVING** *249 cal., 6 g fat (1 g sat. fat), 4 mg chol., 120 mg sodium, 46 g carb., 6 g fiber, 5 g pro.*

ROASTED SWEET POTATO
& PROSCIUTTO SALAD

## Roasted Sweet Potato & Prosciutto Salad

To me, it's hard to beat the pairing of sweet potatoes and prosciutto.
—**HELEN CONWELL** PORTLAND, OR

**PREP:** 20 MIN. • **BAKE:** 40 MIN. + COOLING
**MAKES:** 8 SERVINGS (¾ CUP EACH)

- 3 **medium sweet potatoes (about 2½ pounds), peeled and cut into 1-inch pieces**
- 4 **tablespoons olive oil, divided**
- ½ **teaspoon salt, divided**
- ⅛ **teaspoon pepper**
- 3 **ounces thinly sliced prosciutto, julienned**
- ½ **cup sliced radishes**
- ⅓ **cup chopped pecans, toasted**
- ¼ **cup finely chopped sweet red pepper**
- 2 **green onions, sliced, divided**
- 1 **tablespoon lemon juice**
- 1 **teaspoon honey**

**1.** Preheat oven to 400°. Place the sweet potatoes in a greased 15x10x1-in. baking pan. Drizzle with 2 tablespoons oil and sprinkle with ¼ teaspoon salt and pepper; toss to coat. Roast 30 minutes, stirring occasionally.

**2.** Sprinkle prosciutto over sweet potatoes; roast 10-15 minutes longer or until potatoes are tender and prosciutto is crisp. Transfer to a large bowl; cool slightly.

**3.** Add the radishes, pecans, red pepper and half of the green onions. In a small bowl, whisk the lemon juice, honey, and remaining oil and salt until blended. Drizzle over the salad; toss to combine. Sprinkle with the remaining green onion.

**NOTE** *To toast nuts, spread them in a 15x10x1-in. baking pan. Bake at 350° for 5-10 minutes or until lightly browned, stirring occasionally. Or, spread in a dry nonstick skillet and heat over low heat until lightly browned, stirring occasionally.*

**PER SERVING** *167 cal., 12 g fat (2 g sat. fat), 9 mg chol., 360 mg sodium, 13 g carb., 2 g fiber, 4 g pro.* **Diabetic Exchanges:** *2 fat, 1 starch.*

## Yellow Squash & Watermelon Salad

I frequently bring this healthier choice to potluck get-togethers, and people tell me they appreciate having a lighter option. Lemon juice combines with feta cheese to coat the summery watermelon, yellow squash, zucchini and greens.
—**CAMILLE PARKER** CHICAGO, IL

**START TO FINISH:** 20 MIN.
**MAKES:** 12 SERVINGS (¾ CUP EACH)

- 6 **cups cubed seedless watermelon**
- 2 **medium yellow summer squash, chopped**
- 2 **medium zucchini, chopped**
- ½ **cup lemon juice**
- 12 **fresh mint leaves, torn**
- 1 **teaspoon salt**
- 8 **cups fresh arugula or baby spinach**
- 1 **cup (4 ounces) crumbled feta cheese**

In a large bowl, combine the first six ingredients. Just before serving, add the arugula and feta cheese; toss gently to combine.

**PER SERVING** *60 cal., 2 g fat (1 g sat. fat), 5 mg chol., 297 mg sodium, 11 g carb., 2 g fiber, 3 g pro.* **Diabetic Exchanges:** *1 vegetable, ½ fruit.*

## Cheese & Herb Potato Fans

Covered with toppings, spuds cut into fans are delicious—and just plain fun to eat!
—**SUSAN CURRY** WEST HILLS, CA

**PREP:** 15 MIN. • **BAKE:** 55 MIN.
**MAKES:** 8 SERVINGS

- 8 **medium potatoes**
- ½ **cup butter, melted**
- 2 **teaspoons salt**
- ½ **teaspoon pepper**
- ⅔ **cup shredded cheddar cheese**
- ⅓ **cup shredded Parmesan cheese**
- 2 **tablespoons each minced fresh chives, sage and thyme**

**1.** Preheat oven to 425°. With a sharp knife, cut each potato into ⅛-in. slices, leaving slices attached at the bottom; fan the potatoes slightly and place in a greased 13x9-in. baking dish. In a small bowl, mix the butter, salt and pepper; drizzle over potatoes.

**2.** Bake 50-55 minutes or until the potatoes are tender. In a small bowl, toss cheeses with herbs; sprinkle over potatoes. Bake about 5 minutes longer or until cheese is melted.

**PER SERVING** *318 cal., 15 g fat (10 g sat. fat), 43 mg chol., 797 mg sodium, 39 g carb., 4 g fiber, 8 g pro.*

CHEESE & HERB
POTATO FANS

LAYERED GRILLED CORN SALAD

## Layered Grilled Corn Salad

This is a go-to dish I've relied on for years. It's great on the side or as a refreshing lunch in lettuce cups with crusty bread.

**—ANGELA SMITH** BLUFFTON, SC

**PREP:** 15 MIN. + CHILLING • **GRILL:** 10 MIN.
**MAKES:** 10 SERVINGS

- 10 medium ears sweet corn, husks removed
- ¼ cup olive oil
- 1 teaspoon salt
- ¾ teaspoon coarsely ground pepper
- ¾ teaspoon crushed red pepper flakes
- 2 large tomatoes, finely chopped
- 1 medium red onion, thinly sliced
- 12 fresh basil leaves, thinly sliced
- 1 cup zesty Italian salad dressing

**1.** Brush the sweet corn with oil. Grill the corn, covered, over medium heat 10-12 minutes or until lightly browned and tender, turning occasionally. Cool slightly.

**2.** Cut the corn from the cobs; transfer to a small bowl. Stir in the salt, pepper and pepper flakes. In a 2-qt. glass bowl, layer a third of each of the following: corn, tomatoes, red onion and basil. Repeat the layers twice. Pour Italian salad dressing over the top; refrigerate at least 1 hour.

**PER SERVING** *224 cal., 15 g fat (2 g sat. fat), 0 chol., 656 mg sodium, 21 g carb., 3 g fiber, 3 g pro.*

## Au Gratin Potatoes with Squash

**PREP:** 30 MIN. • **BAKE:** 25 MIN. + STANDING
**MAKES:** 10 SERVINGS (¾ CUP EACH)

- 2 tablespoons butter
- 2 tablespoons all-purpose flour
- 1 teaspoon salt
- ¼ teaspoon pepper
- ⅛ teaspoon ground nutmeg
- 2 cans (12 ounces each) evaporated milk
- 1 cup water
- 7 medium potatoes (about 2 pounds), peeled and sliced
- 4 cups sliced peeled butternut squash (about 1 pound)
- ¼ cup minced fresh chives
- 2 cups (8 ounces) shredded Swiss cheese

**1.** Preheat oven to 400°. In a Dutch oven, melt the butter over medium heat. Stir in the flour, salt, pepper and nutmeg until smooth; gradually whisk in the evaporated milk and water. Stir in the potatoes, butternut squash and chives. Bring to a boil. Reduce the heat; simmer, uncovered, 8-10 minutes or until the potatoes and squash are almost tender.

**2.** In a greased 13x9-in. baking dish, layer half of the potato mixture and 1 cup cheese. Repeat layers.

**3.** Bake, uncovered, 25-30 minutes or until golden brown and the potatoes are tender. Let stand 10 minutes before serving.

**PER SERVING** *267 cal., 13 g fat (9 g sat. fat), 47 mg chol., 377 mg sodium, 26 g carb., 2 g fiber, 12 g pro.*

After volunteering to take a casserole to a friend's party, I wanted to try something different and created Au Gratin Potatoes with Squash. Everyone loved it!
**—PATRICIA HARMON** HELOTES, TX

AU GRATIN POTATOES WITH SQUASH

## Chicken & Bean Chili

Whatever the season, chili is a terrific choice to please a hungry crowd. This creamy version is a must at my soup party every year.

—**THERESA BAEHR** TRAVERSE CITY, MI

**PREP:** 25 MIN. • **COOK:** 15 MIN.
**MAKES:** 10 SERVINGS (2¾ QUARTS)

- 1 tablespoon olive oil
- 1 tablespoon butter
- 1 medium onion, finely chopped
- 2 large garlic cloves, minced
- 2 cans (16 ounces each) kidney beans, rinsed and drained
- 2 cans (15 ounces each) pinto beans, rinsed and drained
- 1 can (28 ounces) diced tomatoes, undrained
- 3 cups shredded cooked chicken
- 1⅔ cups whole milk
- 1 cup beer or reduced-sodium chicken broth
- 2 tablespoons chicken bouillon granules
- 1 tablespoon sugar
- 1 bay leaf
- 2 teaspoons ground cumin
- 1 teaspoon each onion powder, garlic powder and chili powder
- ½ teaspoon salt
- ¼ teaspoon crushed red pepper flakes
- ¼ teaspoon ground celery seed
- ¼ teaspoon pepper
- ⅛ teaspoon ground turmeric

**1.** In a Dutch oven, heat oil and butter over medium-high heat. Add onion; cook and stir 5-7 minutes or until tender. Add garlic; cook 1 minute longer.

**2.** Stir in remaining ingredients; bring to a boil, stirring occasionally. Reduce heat; simmer, uncovered, 5 minutes. Remove bay leaf.

**PER SERVING** *317 cal., 7 g fat (3 g sat. fat), 45 mg chol., 1,073 mg sodium, 37 g carb., 9 g fiber, 24 g pro.*

CHICKEN & BEAN CHILI

SHRIMP ENCHILADAS WITH GREEN SAUCE

## Shrimp Enchiladas with Green Sauce

When I took a pan of shrimp enchiladas to work, my co-workers couldn't get enough! Top servings with salsa for extra zip.

—**MARI ACEDO** CHANDLER, AZ

**PREP:** 35 MIN. • **BAKE:** 25 MIN. • **MAKES:** 8 SERVINGS

- ½ cup plus 1 tablespoon olive oil, divided
- 16 corn tortillas (6 inches)
- 2 medium tomatoes, chopped
- 2 medium onions, finely chopped
- 4 garlic cloves, minced
- ½ teaspoon ground cumin
- 1½ pounds uncooked small shrimp, peeled and deveined
- 2 packages (10 ounces each) frozen chopped spinach, thawed and squeezed dry
- 2 cups (8 ounces) shredded part-skim mozzarella cheese, divided
- 2 cans (10 ounces each) green enchilada sauce

**1.** Preheat oven to 350°. In a skillet, heat ½ cup oil over medium-high heat. In batches, fry tortillas 10 seconds on each side or until pliable (do not allow to crisp). Drain on paper towels. Cover with foil to keep warm and softened.

**2.** In a large skillet, heat remaining oil over medium-high heat. Add tomatoes, onions, garlic and cumin; cook and stir 3-4 minutes or until onions are tender. Add shrimp; cook 3-4 minutes or until shrimp turn pink, stirring occasionally. Stir in spinach; heat through.

**3.** Place ¼ cup shrimp mixture off center on each tortilla; top with 1 tablespoon cheese. Roll up and place in a greased 13x9-in. baking dish, seam side down. Top with the sauce; sprinkle with remaining cheese.

**4.** Bake, uncovered, 25-30 minutes or until heated through and cheese is melted.

**PER SERVING** *479 cal., 24 g fat (5 g sat. fat), 120 mg chol., 810 mg sodium, 37 g carb., 5 g fiber, 27 g pro.*

# Mediterranean Mashed Potatoes

These spuds are so popular in our house, it's hard for us to imagine eating mashed potatoes any other way.

**—NIKKI HADDAD** GERMANTOWN, MD

**PREP:** 25 MIN. • **COOK:** 15 MIN.
**MAKES:** 16 SERVINGS (¾ CUP EACH)

- 8 **large potatoes (about 6½ pounds), peeled and cubed**
- 3 **garlic cloves**
- 1 **teaspoon plus ¾ teaspoon salt, divided**
- ½ **cup olive oil**
- ¼ **cup lemon juice**
- ½ **cup pine nuts, toasted**

**1.** Place potatoes in a stockpot; add water to cover. Bring to a boil. Reduce heat; cook, uncovered, 10-15 minutes or until tender.

**2.** Meanwhile, mince garlic; sprinkle with 1 teaspoon salt. Mash garlic with flat side of knife blade, forming a smooth paste. In a small bowl, whisk oil, lemon juice, garlic mixture and remaining salt until blended.

**3.** Drain potatoes; return to pan. Mash potatoes, gradually adding oil mixture. Transfer to a serving dish; sprinkle with pine nuts.

**NOTE** *To toast nuts, spread them in a 15x10x1-in. baking pan. Bake at 350° for 5-10 minutes or until lightly browned, stirring occasionally. Or, spread in a dry nonstick skillet and heat over low heat until lightly browned, stirring occasionally.*

**PER SERVING** *192 cal., 9 g fat (1 g sat. fat), 0 chol., 262 mg sodium, 26 g carb., 2 g fiber, 3 g pro.* **Diabetic Exchanges:** *1½ starch, 1½ fat.*

MEDITERRANEAN MASHED POTATOES

# Grilled Steak Salad with Tomatoes & Avocado

My family loves a good steak dinner, but with our busy schedules, I'm often thinking about ways to simplify. The 30-minute salad entree I came up with quickly became one of my husband's favorite weeknight meals.

**—LYNDSAY WELLS** LADYSMITH, BC

**START TO FINISH:** 30 MIN. • **MAKES:** 12 SERVINGS

- 1 **beef top sirloin steak (1¼ inches thick and 1½ pounds)**
- 1 **tablespoon olive oil**
- 3 **teaspoons Creole seasoning**
- 2 **large tomatoes, chopped**
- 1 **can (15 ounces) white kidney or cannellini beans, rinsed and drained**
- 1 **can (15 ounces) black beans, rinsed and drained**
- 3 **green onions, chopped**
- ¼ **cup minced fresh cilantro**
- 2 **teaspoons grated lemon peel**
- 2 **tablespoons lemon juice**
- ¼ **teaspoon salt**
- 1 **medium ripe avocado, peeled and cubed (½ inch)**

**1.** Rub both sides of the steak with oil; sprinkle with Creole seasoning. Grill, covered, over medium heat or broil 4 in. from heat 5-8 minutes on each side or until meat reaches the desired doneness (for medium-rare, a thermometer should read 145°; medium, 160°; well-done, 170°). Let stand 5 minutes.

**2.** In a large bowl, combine tomatoes, beans, green onions, cilantro, lemon peel, lemon juice and salt; gently stir in avocado. Cut steak into slices; serve with bean mixture.

**NOTE** *The following spices may be substituted for 3 teaspoons Creole seasoning: ¾ teaspoon each salt, garlic powder and paprika; and ⅛ teaspoon each dried thyme, ground cumin and cayenne pepper.*

**PER SERVING** *169 cal., 6 g fat (1 g sat. fat), 23 mg chol., 355 mg sodium, 13 g carb., 4 g fiber, 16 g pro.*

**CHRISTMAS TREE
BROWNIES**
*PAGE 193*

# Holiday & Seasonal Celebrations

When special occasions call for **festive food**, turn to this extra-big chapter. You'll find everything you need for **fun-filled menus** on Christmas, Thanksgiving, Easter, Halloween and more!

**PEANUT BUTTER EASTER EGGS** *PAGE 167*

**CREAMY PASTEL MINTS** *PAGE 164*

**PRETZEL TURKEY TREATS** *PAGE 183*

# February Favorites

Love makes the world go 'round...and there's plenty of love packed into the sweet treats here. Surprise someone special for Valentine's Day.

EASY PEANUT BUTTER TRUFFLES

**(5) INGREDIENTS**

## Creamy Pastel Mints

These simple mints are always fun to share. I bring them to all sorts of get-togethers, from baby showers to birthdays.

—**JANICE BRADY** SEATTLE, WA

**PREP:** 40 MIN. • **MAKES:** ABOUT 5 DOZEN

- 3 **ounces (6 tablespoons) cream cheese**
- ¼ **to ½ teaspoon peppermint extract**
  **Red food coloring**
- 3 **cups confectioners' sugar**

**1.** Place the cream cheese in a bowl; let it stand at room temperature to soften slightly. Stir in extract until blended. Tint mixture pink or red as desired. Gradually mix in half of the confectioners' sugar.

**2.** On a work surface, knead in the remaining confectioners' sugar until smooth. Divide mixture into three portions; roll each to ¼-in. thickness. (Flour or additional confectioners' sugar is not necessary for rolling.)

**3.** Cut candy with a 1-in. heart-shaped cookie cutter. Store between layers of waxed paper in an airtight container in the refrigerator.

**PER SERVING** *28 cal., 1 g fat (trace sat. fat), 2 mg chol., 4 mg sodium, 6 g carb., 0 fiber, trace pro.*

My husband works in the beekeeping industry. So in our house, honey is a staple! That versatile ingredient makes my Easy Peanut Butter Truffles especially soft and sweet.

—**TAMI KUEHL** LOUP CITY, NE

## Easy Peanut Butter Truffles

**PREP:** 20 MIN. • **COOK:** 10 MIN. + CHILLING • **MAKES:** 64 TRUFFLES

- 1 **teaspoon plus ¼ cup butter, divided**
- ¼ **cup honey**
- 2 **cups creamy peanut butter**
- 1¼ **cups confectioners' sugar**
- 1 **teaspoon vanilla extract**
- 1½ **cups finely chopped honey-roasted peanuts or miniature semisweet chocolate chips**

**1.** Line an 8-in.-square pan with foil; grease the foil with 1 teaspoon butter.

**2.** In a small saucepan, combine the honey and remaining butter over medium heat; cook and stir until blended. Stir in peanut butter until smooth. Remove from heat; whisk in confectioners' sugar and vanilla. Spread into prepared pan. Refrigerate, covered, for 2 hours or until firm.

**3.** Place peanuts in a shallow bowl. Using foil, lift candy out of pan. Remove the foil; cut candy into 64 squares. Shape squares into balls; roll in peanuts. Store between layers of waxed paper in an airtight container in the refrigerator.

**NOTE** *Reduced-fat peanut butter is not recommended for this recipe.*

**PER SERVING** *87 cal., 6 g fat (1 g sat. fat), 2 mg chol., 54 mg sodium, 6 g carb., 1 g fiber, 3 g pro.*

CREAMY PASTEL MINTS

## Caramel Pretzel Bites

I wanted to make my own version of a yummy pretzel log dipped in caramel, chocolate and pecans that I saw at a popular candy store. These ooey-gooey little bites were the result.

**—MICHILENE KLAVER** GRAND RAPIDS, MI

**PREP:** 45 MIN. + COOLING • **MAKES:** 6 DOZEN

- 2 **teaspoons butter, softened**
- 4 **cups pretzel sticks**
- 2½ **cups pecan halves, toasted**
- 2¼ **cups packed brown sugar**
- 1 **cup butter, cubed**
- 1 **cup corn syrup**
- 1 **can (14 ounces) sweetened condensed milk**
- ⅛ **teaspoon salt**
- 1 **teaspoon vanilla extract**
- 1 **package (11½ ounces) milk chocolate chips**
- 1 **tablespoon plus 1 teaspoon shortening, divided**
- ⅓ **cup white baking chips**

**1.** Line a 13x9-in. pan with foil; grease foil with softened butter. Spread pretzels and nuts on bottom of prepared pan.
**2.** In a large heavy saucepan, combine brown sugar, cubed butter, corn syrup, milk and salt; cook and stir over medium heat until a candy thermometer reads 240°(soft-ball stage). Remove from heat. Stir in vanilla. Pour over pretzel mixture.
**3.** In a microwave, melt chocolate chips and 1 tablespoon shortening; stir until smooth. Spread over the caramel layer. In microwave, melt baking chips and remaining shortening; stir until smooth. Drizzle over top. Let stand until set.
**4.** Using the foil, lift the candy out of the pan; remove foil. Using a buttered knife, cut candy into bite-size pieces.
**PER SERVING** *146 cal., 8 g fat (3 g sat. fat), 10 mg chol., 76 mg sodium, 19 g carb., 1 g fiber, 1 g pro.*

> With a classic look and homemade taste, Quick & Easy Gumdrops appeal to people of all ages.
> **—LEAH REKAU** GREENDALE, WI

QUICK & EASY GUMDROPS

**⑤ INGREDIENTS**
## Quick & Easy Gumdrops

**PREP:** 25 MIN. + CHILLING • **MAKES:** 1 POUND (64 PIECES)

- 3 **envelopes unflavored gelatin**
- ½ **cup plus ¾ cup water, divided**
- 1½ **cups sugar**
- ¼ **to ½ teaspoon raspberry extract**
  **Red food coloring**
  **Additional sugar**

**1.** In a small bowl, sprinkle the gelatin over ½ cup water; let stand 5 minutes. In a small saucepan, bring the sugar and remaining water to a boil over medium heat, stirring constantly. Add gelatin; reduce heat. Simmer 5 minutes, stirring frequently. Remove from heat; stir in extract and food coloring as desired.
**2.** Pour into a greased 8-in.-square pan. Refrigerate, covered, 3 hours or until firm.
**3.** Loosen edges of candy from pan with a knife; turn onto a sugared work surface. Cut into 1-in squares; roll in sugar. Let stand, uncovered, at room temperature 3-4 hours or until all sides are dry, turning every hour. Store between layers of waxed paper in an airtight container in refrigerator.
**NOTE** *For lemon gumdrops, use lemon extract and yellow food coloring. For orange gumdrops, use orange extract, yellow food coloring and a drop of red food coloring.*
**PER SERVING** *19 cal., 0 fat (0 sat. fat), 0 chol., 1 mg sodium, 5 g carb., 0 fiber, trace pro.*

CARAMEL PRETZEL BITES

# Easter Pleasers

Get your family hopping straight to the Sunday dinner table with this joyful menu. You'll find both traditional dishes and exciting new recipes to create an unforgettable holiday feast.

TRADITIONAL HOT CROSS BUNS

## (5) INGREDIENTS
## Jelly Bean Bark

Homemade candy doesn't get much easier than this. All you need are three ingredients, a microwave and a pan!
—**MAVIS DEMENT** MARCUS, IA

**PREP:** 15 MIN. + STANDING • **MAKES:** 2 POUNDS

- 1 tablespoon butter
- 1¼ pounds white candy coating, coarsely chopped
- 2 cups small jelly beans

**1.** Line a 15x10x1-in. pan with foil; grease foil with butter. In a microwave, melt white candy coating; stir until smooth. Spread into the prepared pan. Top with jelly beans, pressing to adhere. Let stand until set.

**2.** Cut or break the bark into pieces. Store in an airtight container.

**PER SERVING** *154 cal., 5 g fat (5 g sat. fat), 1 mg chol., 10 mg sodium, 27 g carb., trace fiber, trace pro.*

JELLY BEAN BARK

## Traditional Hot Cross Buns

On Easter morning, our family always sat down to a breakfast of dyed hard-cooked eggs and Mom's hot cross buns.
—**BARBARA JEAN LULL** FULLERTON, CA

**PREP:** 25 MIN. + RISING • **BAKE:** 15 MIN. + COOLING
**MAKES:** 2½ DOZEN

- 2 packages (¼ ounce each) active dry yeast
- 2 cups warm whole milk (110° to 115°)
- 2 eggs
- ⅓ cup butter, softened
- ¼ cup sugar
- 1½ teaspoons salt
- 1 teaspoon ground cinnamon
- ¼ teaspoon ground allspice
- 6 to 7 cups all-purpose flour
- ½ cup dried currants
- ½ cup raisins
- 1 egg yolk
- 2 tablespoons water

**ICING**

- 1½ cups confectioners' sugar
- 4 to 6 teaspoons whole milk

**1.** In a small bowl, dissolve yeast in warm milk. In a large bowl, combine eggs, butter, sugar, salt, spices, yeast mixture and 3 cups flour; beat on medium speed until smooth. Stir in currants, raisins and enough remaining flour to form a soft dough (dough will be sticky).

**2.** Turn dough onto a floured surface; knead until dough is smooth and elastic, about 6-8 minutes. Place in a greased bowl, turning once to grease the top. Cover with plastic wrap; let rise in a warm place until doubled, about 1 hour.

**3.** Punch down dough. Turn onto a lightly floured surface; divide and shape into 30 balls. Place 2 in. apart on greased baking sheets. Cover with kitchen towels; let rise in a warm place until doubled, 30-45 minutes. Preheat oven to 375°.

**4.** Using a sharp knife, cut a cross on top of each bun. In a small bowl, whisk egg yolk and water; brush over tops. Bake 15-20 minutes or until golden brown. Remove from pans to wire racks to cool slightly.

**5.** For icing, mix confectioners' sugar and enough milk to reach desired consistency. Pipe a cross on top of each bun. Serve warm.

**PER SERVING** *171 cal., 3 g fat (2 g sat. fat), 28 mg chol., 145 mg sodium, 31 g carb., 1 g fiber, 4 g pro.*

# Fresh Green Beans & Garlic

**START TO FINISH:** 25 MIN. • **MAKES:** 8 SERVINGS

- 2 tablespoons canola oil
- 2 tablespoons butter
- 4 garlic cloves, sliced
- 2 pounds fresh green beans
- 1 cup reduced-sodium chicken broth
- ½ teaspoon salt
- ¼ teaspoon pepper

**1.** In a Dutch oven, heat oil and butter over medium-high heat. Add the garlic; cook and stir 45-60 seconds or until golden. Using a slotted spoon, remove the garlic from pan; reserve. Add green beans to pan; cook and stir 4-5 minutes or until crisp-tender.

**2.** Stir in the chicken broth, salt and pepper. Bring to a boil. Reduce heat; simmer, uncovered, 8-10 minutes or just until beans are tender and broth is almost evaporated, stirring occasionally. Stir in reserved garlic.

**PER SERVING** *91 cal., 6 g fat (2 g sat. fat), 8 mg chol., 245 mg sodium, 8 g carb., 3 g fiber, 2 g pro.* **Diabetic Exchanges:** *1½ fat, 1 vegetable.*

I like Fresh Green Beans & Garlic not only when we have veggies in the garden, but any time of year.
—**CAROL MAYER** SPARTA, IL

FRESH GREEN BEANS & GARLIC

PEANUT BUTTER EASTER EGGS

# Peanut Butter Easter Eggs

Get the kids involved in making these chocolaty, peanut buttery confections. They're well worth the sticky fingers!
—**MARY JOYCE JOHNSON** UPPER DARBY, PA

**PREP:** 35 MIN. + CHILLING • **COOK:** 5 MIN. • **MAKES:** 16 EGGS

- ¾ cup creamy peanut butter
- ½ cup butter, softened
- ½ teaspoon vanilla extract
- 2⅔ cups confectioners' sugar
- 1 cup graham cracker crumbs
- 1½ cups dark chocolate chips
- 2 tablespoons shortening
- Confectioners' sugar icing, optional

**1.** In a large bowl, beat the peanut butter, butter and vanilla until blended. Gradually beat in confectioners' sugar and graham cracker crumbs. Shape mixture into 16 eggs; place on waxed paper-lined baking sheets. Refrigerate 30 minutes or until firm.

**2.** In a microwave, melt the chocolate chips and shortening; stir until smooth. Dip the eggs in chocolate mixture; allow excess to drip off. Return eggs to baking sheets. Refrigerate 30 minutes.

**3.** If desired, decorate eggs with icing. Let them stand until set. Store in airtight containers in refrigerator.

**CONFECTIONERS' SUGAR ICING** *In a bowl, mix 2 cups confectioners' sugar, 4 teaspoons corn syrup, 1 teaspoon almond extract and 1-2 tablespoons milk until smooth. Tint with paste food coloring if desired. Makes: ⅔ cup.*

**TO DECORATE EGGS WITH BUNNY EARS** *Cut decorative paper into bunny ears. Tape each ear to a toothpick; insert into top of eggs. Remove ears before eating.*

**PER SERVING** *346 cal., 21 g fat (10 g sat. fat), 15 mg chol., 128 mg sodium, 37 g carb., 1 g fiber, 5 g pro.*

MAPLE-PEACH GLAZED HAM

## Smoked Salmon Deviled Eggs

Want to break away from the usual deviled eggs? Flaky smoked salmon adds terrific flavor to the filling. Drizzle the creamy sauce on top or serve it on the side.
—**MARINELA DRAGAN** PORTLAND, OR

**PREP:** 40 MIN. • **MAKES:** 32 APPETIZERS

- 16 **hard-cooked eggs**
- 4 **ounces cream cheese, softened**
- ⅓ **cup mayonnaise**
- 2 **tablespoons snipped fresh dill**
- 1 **tablespoon capers, drained and finely chopped**
- 1 **tablespoon lemon juice**
- 1 **teaspoon horseradish sauce**
- 1 **teaspoon prepared mustard**
- ½ **teaspoon freshly ground pepper**
- ¾ **cup flaked smoked salmon fillet**

**SAUCE**

- 1 **cup mayonnaise**
- ¼ **cup plus 2 tablespoons ketchup**
- 1 **tablespoon horseradish sauce**
- 1 **tablespoon prepared mustard**
- ¼ **cup smoked salmon fillets, optional**

**1.** Cut the eggs lengthwise in half. Remove the egg yolks, reserving the egg whites. In a small bowl, mash the yolks. Mix in the cream cheese, mayonnaise, dill, capers, lemon juice, horseradish sauce, mustard and pepper. Fold in the salmon. Spoon into the egg whites. Refrigerate, covered, until serving.
**2.** For the sauce, in a small bowl, mix the mayonnaise, ketchup, horseradish sauce and mustard. If desired, top eggs with salmon; serve with sauce.
**PER SERVING** *129 cal., 12 g fat (3 g sat. fat), 115 mg chol., 180 mg sodium, 1 g carb., trace fiber, 4 g pro.*

## Deviled Eggs On the Go

Don't have an egg plate? Put your deviled eggs in miniature cupcake liners to keep them in place when you're transporting them to a potluck or other event. I like to use the foil cupcake liners.
—**SHEILA WIRTH** STOCKTON, CA

---

**⑤INGREDIENTS**
## Maple-Peach Glazed Ham

My husband makes this ham regularly on weekends because it's so delicious.
—**BONNIE HAWKINS**
ELKHORN, WI

**PREP:** 5 MIN. • **BAKE:** 2 HOURS
**MAKES:** 16 SERVINGS
(ABOUT 2 CUPS SAUCE)

- 1 **fully cooked bone-in ham (7 to 9 pounds)**
- 2 **cups peach preserves or orange marmalade**
- ½ **cup maple syrup**
- ⅓ **cup orange juice**
- 2 **tablespoons ground ancho chili pepper, optional**

**1.** Preheat oven to 325°. Place ham on a rack in a shallow roasting pan. Cover and bake 1¾ to 2¼ hours or until a thermometer reaches 130°.
**2.** Meanwhile, in a small saucepan, mix preserves, syrup, orange juice and, if desired, chili pepper until blended. Remove ¾ cup mixture for glaze.
**3.** Remove ham from oven; brush with some of the glaze. Bake, uncovered, for 15-20 minutes longer or until a thermometer reads 140°, brushing occasionally with remaining glaze.
**4.** Bring the preserves mixture in the saucepan to a boil over medium heat, stirring occasionally. Cook and stir 1-2 minutes or until slightly thickened. Serve ham with sauce.
**PER SERVING** *294 cal., 5 g fat (2 g sat. fat), 87 mg chol., 1,040 mg sodium, 34 g carb., 0 fiber, 29 g pro.*

## Roasted Chicken & Red Potatoes

This home-style dinner is ready for the oven in just 15 minutes. I love it!

**—SHERRI MELOTIK** OAK CREEK, WI

**PREP:** 15 MIN. • **BAKE:** 55 MIN.
**MAKES:** 6 SERVINGS

- 2 pounds red potatoes, cut into 1-inch pieces
- 1 package (9 ounces) fresh spinach
- 1 large onion, cut into 1-inch pieces
- 2 tablespoons olive oil
- 4 garlic cloves, minced
- 1 teaspoon salt, divided
- 1 teaspoon dried thyme
- ¾ teaspoon pepper, divided
- 6 chicken leg quarters
- ¾ teaspoon paprika

**1.** Preheat the oven to 375°. Place the potatoes, the spinach and onion in a greased shallow roasting pan. Add the oil, garlic, ¾ teaspoon salt, thyme and ½ teaspoon pepper; toss to combine.
**2.** Arrange chicken over vegetables; sprinkle with paprika and remaining salt and pepper. Roast 55-60 minutes or until a thermometer inserted in the chicken reads 180° and the potatoes are tender.
**PER SERVING** *449 cal., 21 g fat (5 g sat. fat), 105 mg chol., 529 mg sodium, 29 g carb., 4 g fiber, 35 g pro.*

**ROASTED CHICKEN & RED POTATOES**

**EASTER BASKET CUPCAKES**

## Easter Basket Cupcakes

When I was a child, my mom and I would make cute basket cupcakes for Easter.

**—KATHY KITTELL** LENEXA, KS

**PREP:** 35 MIN. • **BAKE:** 20 MIN. + COOLING
**MAKES:** 2½ DOZEN

- 4 eggs
- 1 cup sugar
- 1 cup packed brown sugar
- 1 cup canola oil
- 3 teaspoons vanilla extract
- 3 cups all-purpose flour
- 2 teaspoons baking powder
- 2 teaspoons ground cinnamon
- 1 teaspoon salt
- 1 teaspoon baking soda
- ½ teaspoon ground ginger
- ¼ teaspoon ground nutmeg
- ¾ cup buttermilk
- 1 pound carrots, grated
- 2 cups chopped walnuts, toasted
- 1 can (8 ounces) crushed pineapple, drained
- 1 cup flaked coconut

**FROSTING/DECORATIONS**
- 1 package (8 ounces) cream cheese, softened
- ½ cup butter, softened
- 1 teaspoon grated orange peel
- 1 teaspoon vanilla extract
- 4 cups confectioners' sugar
- 1 teaspoon water
- 6 drops green food coloring
- 3 cups flaked coconut
  Optional candies: jelly beans, bunny Peeps candy and Sour Punch straws

**1.** Preheat the oven to 350°. Line 30 muffin cups with paper liners. In a large bowl, beat the eggs, sugars, oil and vanilla until well blended. In another bowl, whisk the flour, baking powder, cinnamon, salt, baking soda, ginger and nutmeg; add to egg mixture alternately with buttermilk, beating well after each addition. Stir in carrots, walnuts, pineapple and coconut.
**2.** Fill prepared cups three-fourths full. Bake for 20-25 minutes or until a toothpick inserted in the center comes out clean. Cool in the pans 10 minutes before removing to wire racks to cool completely.
**3.** In a large bowl, beat cream cheese and butter until blended. Beat in the orange peel and the vanilla. Gradually beat in the confectioners' sugar until smooth. Frost cupcakes.
**4.** In a large resealable plastic bag, mix water and green food coloring; add coconut. Seal the bag and shake it until the coconut is evenly tinted. Sprinkle over the cupcakes. Decorate with candies, as desired. Refrigerate until serving.
**NOTE** *To toast the nuts, spread them in a 15x10x1-in. baking pan. Bake at 350° for 5-10 minutes or until lightly browned, stirring occasionally. Or, spread in a dry nonstick skillet and heat them over low heat until lightly browned, stirring occasionally.*
**PER SERVING** *420 cal., 24 g fat (9 g sat. fat), 45 mg chol., 253 mg sodium, 50 g carb., 2 g fiber, 5 g pro.*

# Patriotic Picnic

Fired up for July Fourth? Independence Day celebrations are sure to sparkle when you fix the summer sensations here, from All-American grilled burgers to homemade ice cream.

## Skillet Blueberry Slump

Our family has enjoyed this home-style dessert for many years. My mother-in-law used to make a slump of wild blueberries with dumplings, served with a pitcher of farm cream.

**—ELEANORE EBELING** BREWSTER, MN

**PREP:** 25 MIN. • **BAKE:** 20 MIN. • **MAKES:** 6 SERVINGS

- 4 **cups fresh or frozen blueberries**
- ½ **cup sugar**
- ½ **cup water**
- 1 **teaspoon grated lemon peel**
- 1 **tablespoon lemon juice**
- 1 **cup all-purpose flour**
- 2 **tablespoons sugar**
- 2 **teaspoons baking powder**
- ½ **teaspoon salt**
- 1 **tablespoon butter**
- ½ **cup 2% milk**
  **Vanilla ice cream**

**1.** Preheat the oven to 400°. In a 10-in. ovenproof skillet, combine the first five ingredients; bring to a boil. Reduce heat; simmer, uncovered, for 9-11 minutes or until slightly thickened, stirring occasionally.

**2.** Meanwhile, in a small bowl, whisk flour, sugar, baking powder and salt. Cut in the butter until mixture resembles coarse crumbs. Add milk; stir just until moistened.

**3.** Drop the batter in six portions on top of the simmering blueberry mixture. Transfer to the oven. Bake, uncovered, 17-20 minutes or until dumplings are golden brown. Serve warm with ice cream.

**PER SERVING** *239 cal., 3 g fat (2 g sat. fat), 7 mg chol., 355 mg sodium, 52 g carb., 3 g fiber, 4 g pro.*

## Did you know?

You should resist the urge to flatten burgers with a spatula as they cook on the grill. You'll press out the juices that make them moist. Also, avoid overhandling the meat before cooking. First combine the filling ingredients, then add the meat and mix just until combined.

GOOD OL' BURGER

## Good Ol' Burger

Light the spark at your summertime party with these juicy grilled burgers. A splash of chili sauce gives the beef patties some zip.

**—RON TREADAWAY** ACWORTH, GA

**START TO FINISH:** 30 MIN. • **MAKES:** 4 SERVINGS

- 1 **egg, lightly beaten**
- ¼ **cup dry red wine or beef broth**
- 1 **tablespoon chili sauce**
- ¼ **teaspoon Italian seasoning**
- ¼ **teaspoon pepper**
- 1 **pound ground beef**
- 4 **hamburger buns, split**
- 4 **lettuce leaves**
- 4 **slices tomato**
- 4 **slices onion**

**1.** In a large bowl, combine the first five ingredients. Add ground beef; mix lightly but thoroughly. Shape into four ½-in.-thick patties.

**2.** Grill burgers, covered, over medium heat 5-7 minutes on each side or until a thermometer reads 160°.

**3.** Grill hamburger buns over medium heat, cut side down, 30-60 seconds or until toasted. Serve burgers on buns with lettuce, tomato and onion.

**PER SERVING** *364 cal., 16 g fat (6 g sat. fat), 123 mg chol., 349 mg sodium, 25 g carb., 2 g fiber, 26 g pro.*

## Fourth of July Baked Beans

**PREP:** 10 MIN. • **BAKE:** 55 MIN. • **MAKES:** 8 SERVINGS

- ½ **pound ground beef**
- 1 **large onion, finely chopped**
- ½ **cup sugar**
- ½ **cup packed brown sugar**
- ½ **cup ketchup**
- ½ **cup barbecue sauce**
- 2 **tablespoons yellow mustard**
- 2 **tablespoons molasses**
- ½ **teaspoon chili powder**
- 2 **cans (13.7 ounces each) beans with tomato sauce**
- ½ **pound bacon strips, cooked and crumbled**

**1.** Preheat the oven to 350°. In a large skillet, cook beef and onion over medium heat for 6-8 minutes or until beef is no longer pink, breaking up beef into crumbles; drain. Stir in sugars, ketchup, barbecue sauce, mustard, molasses and chili powder. Add beans and bacon.

**2.** Transfer to a greased 13x9-in. baking dish. Bake, covered, 45 minutes. Bake, uncovered, 10-15 minutes longer or until heated through.

**PER SERVING** *323 cal., 8 g fat (3 g sat. fat), 28 mg chol., 970 mg sodium, 51 g carb., 4 g fiber, 14 g pro.*

> We love Fourth of July Baked Beans because they have a meaty twist and a nice sweetness.
> —**WENDY HODOROWSKI** BELLAIRE, OH

FOURTH OF JULY BAKED BEANS

RED, WHITE & BLUE POTATO SALAD

## Red, White & Blue Potato Salad

I toss my cooked, drained potatoes with stock and white wine. The liquid absorbs like magic, infusing the spuds with flavor.
—**GEORGE LEVINTHAL** GOLETA, CA

**PREP:** 40 MIN. • **COOK:** 10 MIN.
**MAKES:** 12 SERVINGS (1 CUP EACH)

- 1¼ **pounds small purple potatoes (about 11), quartered**
- 1 **pound small Yukon Gold potatoes (about 9), quartered**
- 1 **pound small red potatoes (about 9), quartered**
- ½ **cup chicken stock**
- ¼ **cup white wine or additional chicken stock**
- 2 **tablespoons sherry vinegar**
- 2 **tablespoons white wine vinegar**
- 1½ **teaspoons Dijon mustard**
- 1½ **teaspoons stone-ground mustard**
- ¾ **teaspoon salt**
- ½ **teaspoon coarsely ground pepper**
- 6 **tablespoons olive oil**
- 3 **celery ribs, chopped**
- 1 **small sweet red pepper, chopped**
- 8 **green onions, chopped**
- ¾ **pound bacon strips, cooked and crumbled**
- 3 **tablespoons each minced fresh basil, dill and parsley**
- 2 **tablespoons toasted sesame seeds**

**1.** Place all the potatoes in a Dutch oven; add water to cover. Bring to a boil. Reduce heat; cook, uncovered, 10-15 minutes or until tender. Drain; transfer to a large bowl. Drizzle the potatoes with stock and wine; toss gently, allowing liquids to absorb.

**2.** In a small bowl, whisk the vinegars, mustards, salt and pepper. Gradually whisk in the oil until blended. Add the vinaigrette, vegetables, bacon and herbs to potato mixture; toss to combine. Sprinkle with sesame seeds. Serve warm.

**PER SERVING** *221 cal., 12 g fat (2 g sat. fat), 10 mg chol., 405 mg sodium, 22 g carb., 3 g fiber, 7 g pro.* **Diabetic Exchanges:** *2 fat, 1-1½ starch.*

## Roasted Green Bean Salad

Here's how I make homegrown green beans extra-special. A tangy dill and Dijon mustard vinaigrette coats them without being overpowering, letting the wonderful fresh-picked flavor come through.
—**KATHY SHELL** SAN DIEGO, CA

**PREP:** 10 MIN. • **BAKE:** 30 MIN.
**MAKES:** 6 SERVINGS

- 2 **pounds fresh green beans, trimmed**
- 3 **tablespoons olive oil, divided**
- ¾ **teaspoon salt, divided**
- 2 **tablespoons white wine vinegar**
- 2 **tablespoons snipped fresh dill or 2 teaspoons dill weed**
- 1½ **teaspoons Dijon mustard**
- 1½ **teaspoons sugar**
- ¼ **teaspoon pepper**

**1.** Preheat the oven to 400°. In a large bowl, toss beans with 1 tablespoon oil and ½ teaspoon salt. Transfer to two ungreased 15x10x1-in. baking pans.
**2.** Roast 30-35 minutes or until the beans are tender and lightly browned, stirring occasionally.
**3.** In a small bowl, whisk the white wine vinegar, the dill, mustard, sugar, pepper and the remaining oil and salt until blended. Transfer the beans to a large bowl. Drizzle with the vinaigrette and toss to coat.
**PER SERVING** *108 cal., 7 g fat (1 g sat. fat), 0 chol., 335 mg sodium, 11 g carb., 5 g fiber, 3 g pro.* ***Diabetic Exchanges:*** *1½ fat, 1 vegetable.*

SOUTHERN-STYLE OVEN-FRIED CHICKEN

The secret to Southern-Style Oven-Fried Chicken is in the breading. The buttery crackers result in a golden brown crunch, and the meat stays nice and moist.
—**ELAINA MORGAN** RICKMAN, TN

## Southern-Style Oven-Fried Chicken

**PREP:** 15 MIN. • **BAKE:** 35 MIN.
**MAKES:** 6 SERVINGS

- 2 **cups Ritz crackers (about 50)**
- 1 **tablespoon minced fresh parsley**
- 1 **teaspoon garlic salt**
- 1 **teaspoon paprika**
- ½ **teaspoon pepper**
- ¼ **teaspoon ground cumin**
- ¼ **teaspoon rubbed sage**
- 2 **eggs**
- 1 **broiler/fryer chicken (3 to 4 pounds), cut up**

**1.** Preheat oven to 400°. Place a rack in a 15x10x1-in. baking pan; coat the rack with cooking spray.
**2.** In a shallow bowl, mix first seven ingredients. In a separate shallow bowl, whisk eggs. Dip chicken in eggs, then cracker mixture, patting to help coating adhere. Place on prepared rack.
**3.** Bake for 20 minutes. Turn chicken; bake for 15-25 minutes longer or until the chicken is golden brown and juices run clear.
**PER SERVING** *418 cal., 22 g fat (5 g sat. fat), 123 mg chol., 638 mg sodium, 21 g carb., 1 g fiber, 31 g pro.*

ROASTED GREEN BEAN SALAD

**LEMONY SHRIMP & TOMATOES**

## Lemony Shrimp & Tomatoes

My family loves grilled shrimp, so I created marinated kabobs and added tomatoes for bright color and nutrition.

—**LISA SPEER** PALM BEACH, FL

**PREP:** 20 MIN. + MARINATING • **GRILL:** 5 MIN.
**MAKES:** 4 KABOBS (½ CUP SAUCE)

- ⅓ **cup lemon juice**
- 2 **tablespoons olive oil**
- 2 **garlic cloves, minced**
- ½ **teaspoon grated lemon peel**
- 1 **pound uncooked jumbo shrimp, peeled and deveined**
- ⅔ **cup fresh arugula**
- 2 **green onions, sliced**
- ¼ **cup plain yogurt**
- 2 **teaspoons 2% milk**
- 1 **teaspoon cider vinegar**
- 1 **teaspoon Dijon mustard**
- ½ **teaspoon sugar**
- ½ **teaspoon salt, divided**
- 12 **cherry tomatoes**
- ¼ **teaspoon pepper**

**1.** In a large bowl, whisk the lemon juice, oil, garlic and lemon peel until blended. Add the shrimp; toss to coat. Let stand 10 minutes.

**2.** Place the arugula, green onions, yogurt, milk, cider vinegar, mustard, sugar and ¼ teaspoon salt in a food processor; process until smooth.

**3.** On four metal or soaked wooden skewers, alternately thread shrimp and tomatoes. Sprinkle with pepper and remaining salt.

**4.** Grill, covered, over medium-high heat or broil 3-4 in. from heat for 2-3 minutes on each side or until shrimp are no longer pink. Serve with sauce.

**PER SERVING** *147 cal., 5 g fat (1 g sat. fat), 140 mg chol., 475 mg sodium, 6 g carb., 1 g fiber, 20 g pro.* **Diabetic Exchanges:** *3 lean meat, ½ starch, ½ fat.*

## Crab Cakes with Peanut Sauce

These sensational cakes are always on my party food list. You won't want to skip the peanut sauce—it really finishes the dish.

—**AMBER MASSEY** ARGYLE, TX

**PREP:** 25 MIN. + CHILLING
**COOK:** 5 MIN./BATCH
**MAKES:** 1 DOZEN (⅓ CUP SAUCE)

- ¼ **cup rice vinegar**
- 2 **tablespoons creamy peanut butter**
- 1 **garlic clove, minced**
- 1 **teaspoon brown sugar**
- 1 **teaspoon olive oil**
- ¼ **teaspoon ground mustard**
  **Dash cayenne pepper**

**CRAB CAKES**
- 1 **cup plain Greek yogurt**
- ⅔ **cup crushed saltines (about 15 crackers)**
- ¼ **cup finely chopped celery**
- ¼ **cup finely chopped roasted sweet red pepper**
- ¼ **cup minced fresh parsley**
- 2 **tablespoons finely chopped onion**
- 1 **egg white, lightly beaten**
- 1 **tablespoon fresh lemon juice**
- 2 **teaspoons prepared horseradish**
- ½ **teaspoon paprika**
- ¼ **teaspoon salt**
- 1 **pound lump crabmeat, drained**
- 1 **tablespoon olive oil**

**1.** In a small bowl, whisk the first seven ingredients until blended. Set aside.

**2.** In a large bowl, mix the first 11 crab cake ingredients until blended. Fold in the crab. Shape into twelve ½-in.-thick patties. Refrigerate, covered, for 30 minutes.

**3.** In a large skillet, heat 1 tablespoon oil over medium-high heat. Add crab cakes in batches; cook 2-3 minutes on each side or until golden brown. Serve with the sauce.

**PER SERVING** *114 cal., 6 g fat (2 g sat. fat), 49 mg chol., 270 mg sodium, 6 g carb., trace fiber, 10 g pro.*

⑤INGREDIENTS
## Rhubarb Ice Cream

Have lots of rhubarb? Put it to wonderful use in a rich and tangy ice cream.

—**RACHEL GARCIA**

FORT KNOX, KY

**PREP:** 25 MIN. + FREEZING
**BAKE:** 30 MIN. + COOLING
**MAKES:** ABOUT 2¾ CUPS

- 3 **cups sliced fresh rhubarb**
- 2 **cups sugar**
- 1 **teaspoon lemon juice**
- 1 **cup heavy whipping cream**

**1.** Preheat the oven to 375°. In an ungreased 13x9-in. baking dish, combine the rhubarb and sugar; toss to combine. Bake, covered, for 30-40 minutes or until tender, stirring occasionally. Cool slightly.

**2.** Place the rhubarb mixture in a blender; cover and process it until pureed. Transfer to a bowl; refrigerate, covered, until cold.

**3.** Stir lemon juice into rhubarb. In a small bowl, beat the cream until stiff peaks form; fold into rhubarb mixture. Transfer to a shallow 1-qt. freezer container. Freeze 1 hour, stirring every 15 minutes. Freeze, covered, overnight or until firm.

**PER SERVING** *489 cal., 18 g fat (11 g sat. fat), 65 mg chol., 22 mg sodium, 85 g carb., 1 g fiber, 2 g pro.*

RHUBARB ICE CREAM

# Best of Oktoberfest

Strike up the oompah band and get in on these German specialties—from schnitzel to strudel!

## Potato Dumplings

Potato dumplings (called *kartoffel kloesse* in Germany) are a great addition to a German feast—and just about any other one!

**—ARLINE HOFLAND** DEER LODGE, MT

**PREP:** 40 MIN. • **COOK:** 10 MIN. • **MAKES:** 8 SERVINGS

- 3 **pounds medium potatoes (about 10), peeled and quartered**
- 1 **cup all-purpose flour**
- 3 **eggs, lightly beaten**
- ⅔ **cup dry bread crumbs**
- 1 **teaspoon salt**
- ½ **teaspoon ground nutmeg**
- 12 **cups water**

**BROWNED BUTTER SAUCE**

- ½ **cup butter, cubed**
- 1 **tablespoon chopped onion**
- ¼ **cup dry bread crumbs**

**1.** Place potatoes in a Dutch oven; add water to cover. Bring to a boil. Reduce the heat; cook, uncovered, 15-20 minutes or until tender. Drain; transfer to a large bowl.

**2.** Mash potatoes. Stir in flour, eggs, bread crumbs, salt and nutmeg. Shape into sixteen (2-in.) balls.

**3.** In a Dutch oven, bring the water to a boil. Carefully add dumplings. Reduce heat; simmer, uncovered, 7-9 minutes or until a toothpick inserted in center comes out clean.

**4.** Meanwhile, in a small heavy saucepan, heat butter and onion over medium heat. Heat 5-7 minutes or until butter is golden brown, stirring constantly. Remove from heat; stir in bread crumbs. Serve with dumplings.

**PER SERVING** *367 cal., 14 g fat (8 g sat. fat), 100 mg chol., 524 mg sodium, 51 g carb., 5 g fiber, 9 g pro.*

## German Apple Strudel

This gorgeous, melt-in-your-mouth strudel has just what you crave in fall—thin layers of flaky crust and lots of juicy apples.

**—DARLENE BRENDEN** SALEM, OR

**PREP:** 1 HOUR + STANDING • **BAKE:** 45 MIN.
**MAKES:** 2 STRUDELS (8 SLICES EACH)

- 3 **cups all-purpose flour**
- ½ **cup canola oil, divided**
- ¾ **cup warm water (120°)**
- 1 **egg, lightly beaten**

**FILLING**

- 1½ **cups fresh bread crumbs**
- 6 **cups chopped peeled apples (about 5 medium)**
- ½ **cup raisins**
- 1 **cup sugar**
- 1½ **teaspoons ground cinnamon**
- ⅓ **cup butter, melted**
- 3 **tablespoons sour cream**

**1.** Place flour in a mixer bowl; beat in ¼ cup oil (mixture will be slightly crumbly). In a small bowl, slowly whisk the warm water into the beaten egg; add to the flour mixture, mixing well. Beat in remaining oil until smooth. Transfer to a greased bowl, turning once to grease the top. Cover with plastic wrap and let rest in a warm place, about 30 minutes.

**2.** Preheat the oven to 350°. Spread bread crumbs into an ungreased 15x10x1-in. baking pan. Bake 10-15 minutes or until golden brown, stirring occasionally. Cool completely.

**3.** Tape a 30x15-in. sheet of parchment paper onto a work surface; dust lightly with flour. Divide dough in half; place one half on sheet and roll to a very thin 24x15-in. rectangle. (Keep remaining dough covered.) Remove tape from sheet.

**4.** Sprinkle ¾ cup bread crumbs over rectangle to within 1 in. of edges. Starting 3 inches from a short side, sprinkle 3 cups apples and ¼ cup raisins across dough covering a 3-in.-wide section. Mix sugar and cinnamon; sprinkle half of the mixture over fruit. Drizzle with half of melted butter.

**5.** Roll up jelly-roll style, starting at fruit end and lifting with parchment sheet; fold in sides of dough as you roll to contain filling. Trim sheet to fit a 15x10x1-in. baking pan; lifting with sheet, carefully transfer strudel to prepared pan.

**6.** Bake on lowest oven rack 45-55 minutes or until golden brown, brushing the top with sour cream two times while baking. Cool on a wire rack. Repeat with remaining dough and filling. Serve warm or at room temperature.

**NOTE** *To make fresh bread crumbs, tear bread into pieces and place in a food processor; pulse until fine crumbs form. Two to three bread slices will yield 1½ cups crumbs.*

**PER SERVING** *285 cal., 12 g fat (3 g sat. fat), 24 mg chol., 61 mg sodium, 42 g carb., 2 g fiber, 4 g pro.*

GERMAN APPLE STRUDEL

OKTOBERFEST
RED CABBAGE

PORK SCHNITZEL WITH DILL SAUCE

## Pork Schnitzel with Dill Sauce

My husband is of German descent, and schnitzel is one of his favorites because the taste takes him back to the old country.

**—JOYCE FOLKER** PARAOWAN, UT

**PREP:** 20 MIN. • **COOK:** 20 MIN. • **MAKES:** 6 SERVINGS

- ½ cup all-purpose flour
- 2 teaspoons seasoned salt
- ½ teaspoon pepper
- 2 eggs
- ¼ cup 2% milk
- 1½ cups dry bread crumbs
- 2 teaspoons paprika
- 6 pork sirloin cutlets (4 ounces each)
- 6 tablespoons canola oil

**DILL SAUCE**

- 2 tablespoons all-purpose flour
- 1½ cups chicken broth, divided
- 1 cup (8 ounces) sour cream
- ½ teaspoon dill weed

**1.** In a shallow bowl, mix flour, seasoned salt and pepper. In a second shallow bowl, whisk eggs and milk until blended. In a third bowl, mix bread crumbs and paprika.

**2.** Pound pork with a meat mallet to ¼-in. thickness. Dip in flour mixture to coat both sides; shake off excess. Dip in egg mixture, then crumb mixture, patting to help coating adhere.

**3.** In a large skillet, heat oil over medium heat. Add pork in batches; cook 2-3 minutes on each side or until golden brown. Remove to a plate; keep warm. Wipe skillet clean if necessary.

**4.** In a small bowl, whisk flour and broth until smooth; stir into same skillet. Bring to a boil, stirring constantly; cook and stir 2 minutes or until thickened.

**5.** Reduce heat to low. Stir in sour cream and dill; heat through (do not boil). Spoon over pork.

**PER SERVING** *412 cal., 25 g fat (8 g sat. fat), 107 mg chol., 1,025 mg sodium, 32 g carb., 1 g fiber, 11 g pro.*

## Oktoberfest Red Cabbage

Four generations of our family celebrate Oktoberfest. We love the tart and sweet flavors in this dish, also known as *rotkohl*.

**—DIANA LIKES** CHANDLER, AZ

**PREP:** 20 MIN. • **COOK:** 50 MIN. • **MAKES:** 6 SERVINGS

- 3 tablespoons bacon drippings or canola oil
- 1 small head red cabbage (about 1½ pounds), shredded
- 2 medium tart apples, peeled and chopped
- 1 cup water
- ¼ cup sugar
- ¾ teaspoon salt
- ¼ teaspoon pepper
- ⅛ teaspoon ground cloves
- ¼ cup white vinegar

**1.** In a Dutch oven, heat the bacon drippings over medium heat. Add cabbage and apples; cook and stir for 2-3 minutes. Stir in the water, sugar, salt, pepper and cloves.

**2.** Bring to a boil. Reduce the heat; simmer, covered, for 40-45 minutes or until the cabbage is tender, stirring it occasionally. Stir in vinegar.

**PER SERVING** *146 cal., 7 g fat (3 g sat. fat), 6 mg chol., 331 mg sodium, 22 g carb., 3 g fiber, 1 g pro.*

# Halloween Hijinks

Boo! These tricks and treats with funny faces will bring eye-popping fun to any October bash. Plus, each frightfully festive recipe can be made easily with ordinary ingredients.

## Devil's Food Cupcakes with Chocolaty Frosting

This devilishly rich cake is on my husband's short list of favorite desserts—and he's a pie guy through and through! Made into a batch of candy-trimmed cupcakes, the recipe is great for parties of all kinds.
—**DAWN KOESTNER** ST. LOUIS PARK, MN

**PREP:** 40 MIN. + CHILLING • **BAKE:** 15 MIN. + COOLING
**MAKES:** 2 DOZEN

- 1 **ounce unsweetened chocolate, chopped**
- 1 **cup hot strong brewed coffee**
- 1¾ **cups sugar**
- ⅔ **cup canola oil**
- 1 **egg**
- 2 **cups all-purpose flour**
- ½ **cup baking cocoa**
- 3 **teaspoons baking soda**
- ½ **teaspoon salt**
- 1 **cup buttermilk**

DEVIL'S FOOD CUPCAKES
WITH CHOCOLATY FROSTING

### FROSTING

- 2 **cups (12 ounces) semisweet chocolate chips**
- 1½ **cups heavy whipping cream**
- ½ **cup light corn syrup**
- 1 **teaspoon vanilla extract**
  Optional decorations: gumdrops, regular or Dum Dums lollipops and semisweet or mini chocolate chips

**1.** Preheat oven to 350°. Line 24 muffin cups with paper liners. Place the chocolate in a small bowl. Pour hot coffee over the chocolate; whisk until smooth. Cool to lukewarm.
**2.** In a large bowl, beat the sugar, oil, egg and coffee mixture until well blended. In another bowl, whisk the flour, cocoa, baking soda and salt; add to coffee mixture alternately with buttermilk, beating well after each addition.
**3.** Fill prepared cups two-thirds full. Bake 15-20 minutes or until a toothpick inserted in the center comes out clean. Cool in the pans 10 minutes before removing to wire racks to cool completely.
**4.** For frosting, place chocolate chips in a large bowl. In a small saucepan, bring cream and corn syrup just to a boil. Pour over chocolate; stir with a whisk until smooth. Stir in vanilla. Cool to room temperature, stirring occasionally. Refrigerate, covered, until completely cold.
**5.** Beat the chocolate mixture on medium speed just until fluffy (do not overbeat). Immediately spread over cupcakes. Decorate cupcakes as desired. For gumdrops, trim ends to attach to lollipops and for attaching regular-size chocolate chips. Refrigerate until serving.
**PER SERVING** *308 cal., 17 g fat (7 g sat. fat), 29 mg chol., 233 mg sodium, 40 g carb., 2 g fiber, 3 g pro.*

## Owl Cookies

I came up with owl-shaped cookies as a classroom treat for my children. Kids think they're a hoot and yummy, too.
—**STARRLETTE HOWARD** OGDEN, UT

**PREP:** 35 MIN. + CHILLING • **BAKE:** 15 MIN.
**MAKES:** 1 DOZEN

- ⅔ **cup butter, softened**
- 1 **cup creamy peanut butter**
- 1 **cup packed brown sugar**
- 1 **egg**
- 1 **teaspoon vanilla extract**
- 1⅓ **cups all-purpose flour**
- 1 **cup quick-cooking oats**
- 1 **teaspoon baking powder**
- ½ **teaspoon salt**
- 1 **ounce unsweetened chocolate, melted**
- 12 **whole cashews**
- 24 **striped chocolate kisses, unwrapped**
- 24 **semisweet chocolate chips**

**1.** In a large bowl, beat the butter, peanut butter and brown sugar until blended. Beat in the egg and vanilla. In another bowl, mix the flour, oats, baking powder and salt; gradually beat into the creamed mixture.

OWL COOKIES

**2.** If necessary, cover and refrigerate the dough 1 hour or until firm enough to shape. Divide dough in half; shape one portion into an 8-in.-long roll. Mix the melted chocolate into the remaining dough. Roll chocolate dough between two sheets of waxed paper into an 8-in. square. Place plain roll on chocolate dough. Wrap chocolate dough around plain dough, pinching together at the seam to seal. Wrap in plastic wrap; refrigerate 3 hours or until firm.

**3.** Preheat oven to 350°. Unwrap and cut dough crosswise into 24 slices (⅜ inch). To make owls, place two slices side by side on an ungreased baking sheet; pinch the top of each slice for ears. Place a cashew between the slices for a beak. Repeat with remaining dough.

**4.** Bake 12-15 minutes or until set. Cool on pans 5 minutes before removing to wire racks. While cookies are warm, place two kisses on each cookie, pointed side down, for eyes. (Kisses will melt slightly.) Top each kiss with a chocolate chip. Cool completely.

**PER SERVING** *380 cal., 23 g fat (10 g sat. fat), 43 mg chol., 332 mg sodium, 38 g carb., 3 g fiber, 9 g pro.*

## Frosted Pistachio Bars

Bar cookies are my go-to goodies because they're so quick and easy. Have a blast decorating them to suit the occasion.
**—SHANNON SHEEHY** CHESTERFIELD, VA

**PREP:** 20 MIN. • **BAKE:** 20 MIN. + COOLING • **MAKES:** 2 DOZEN

- **2 cups all-purpose flour**
- **2 packages (3.4 ounces each) instant pistachio pudding mix**
- **½ cup sugar**
- **1 teaspoon baking powder**
- **½ teaspoon salt**
- **1 egg**
- **½ cup butter, melted**
- **½ cup canola oil**
- **¼ cup water**
- **1 teaspoon vanilla extract**
- **½ cup chopped pistachios, optional**

**FROSTING**
- **3 ounces cream cheese, softened**
- **¼ cup butter, softened**
- **1 teaspoon vanilla extract**
- **⅛ teaspoon salt**
- **3 cups confectioners' sugar**
  Optional decorations: candy eyeballs, M&M's minis, milk chocolate M&M's, Life Savers hard candies and gummies, regular and mini peanut butter cups, licorice twists, shoestring licorice, Starburst fruit chews, mega and regular Smarties, Nerds, Runts, Snaps chewy candies, candy corn, tiny-size Chiclets gum, butterscotch hard candies, Rolo candies, Caramel Creams and PayDay candy bar

**1.** Preheat the oven to 350°. In a large bowl, whisk the flour, pudding mix, sugar, baking powder and the salt. In another bowl, whisk egg, melted butter, oil, water and vanilla until blended; stir into flour mixture. If desired, stir in pistachios. (Dough will be stiff.)

**2.** Press the dough into a greased 13x9-in. baking pan. Bake for 20-25 minutes or until the edges begin to brown. Cool completely in pan on a wire rack.

**3.** In a large bowl, beat cream cheese, butter, vanilla and salt until blended. Gradually beat in confectioners' sugar. Spread over top. Decorate as desired.

**4.** Cut into bars before serving. Store in the refrigerator.

**PER SERVING** *253 cal., 12 g fat (5 g sat. fat), 27 mg chol., 259 mg sodium, 35 g carb., trace fiber, 2 g pro.*

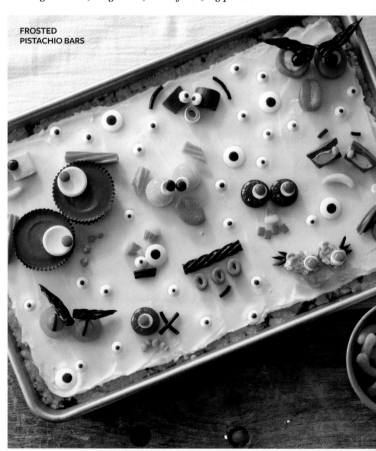

FROSTED PISTACHIO BARS

# Giving Thanks

Take it easy this Thanksgiving with the holiday menu here. From slow-cooked sensations to make-ahead favorites, these special recipes offer built-in convenience for busy cooks.

## Creamy Cranberry Salad

One of my piano students shared her overnight cranberry salad recipe with me. The tart berries blend so well with the crunchy nuts, fluffy marshmallows and bits of apple and pineapple.
—**ALEXANDRA LYPECKY** DEARBORN, MI

**PREP:** 15 MIN. + CHILLING • **MAKES:** 16 SERVINGS (½ CUP EACH)

- 3 cups fresh or frozen cranberries (thawed), chopped
- 1 can (20 ounces) unsweetened crushed pineapple, drained
- 2 cups miniature marshmallows
- 1 medium apple, chopped
- ⅔ cup sugar
- ⅛ teaspoon salt
- 2 cups heavy whipping cream
- ¼ cup chopped walnuts

**1.** In a large bowl, mix the first six ingredients until blended. Refrigerate, covered, overnight.

**2.** In a large bowl, beat the heavy whipping cream until stiff peaks form. Just before serving, fold the cream and walnuts into the cranberry mixture.

**PER SERVING** *200 cal., 12 g fat (7 g sat. fat), 41 mg chol., 33 mg sodium, 23 g carb., 1 g fiber, 1 g pro.*

CREAMY CRANBERRY SALAD

SWEET POTATO STUFFING

**SLOW COOKER**

## Sweet Potato Stuffing

For holiday feasts, my mother slow cooks a large batch of her wonderful sweet potato stuffing to ensure there's plenty for the whole family. Everyone clamors for a scoop!
—**KELLY POLLOCK** LONDON, ON

**PREP:** 15 MIN. • **COOK:** 4 HOURS • **MAKES:** 10 SERVINGS

- ¼ cup butter, cubed
- ½ cup chopped celery
- ½ cup chopped onion
- ½ cup chicken broth
- ½ teaspoon salt, optional
- ½ teaspoon rubbed sage
- ½ teaspoon poultry seasoning
- ½ teaspoon pepper
- 6 cups dry bread cubes
- 1 large sweet potato, cooked, peeled and finely chopped
- ¼ cup chopped pecans

**1.** In a Dutch oven, heat the butter over medium-high heat. Add the celery and onion; cook and stir until tender. Stir in the broth and seasonings. Add the remaining ingredients; toss to combine.

**2.** Transfer to a greased 3-qt. slow cooker. Cook, covered, on low 4 hours or until heated through.

**PER SERVING** *200 cal., 8 g fat (3 g sat. fat), 12 mg chol., 337 mg sodium, 30 g carb., 3 g fiber, 5 g pro.*

# Braised & Creamy Vidalia Onions

Here in Georgia, sweet Vidalia onions are king. I like to use them in this creamy side dish, which goes well with poultry and beef.

**—ELAINE OPITZ** MARIETTA, GA

**PREP:** 10 MIN. • **COOK:** 40 MIN. • **MAKES:** 6 SERVINGS

- 2 **tablespoons butter**
- 3 **tablespoons honey**
- 10 **cups sliced Vidalia or other sweet onions (about 5 onions)**
- ¼ **cup chicken broth**
- ½ **teaspoon salt**
- ⅛ **teaspoon white pepper**
- ⅛ **teaspoon ground mace**
- ½ **cup heavy whipping cream**

**1.** In a Dutch oven, melt the butter over medium heat; stir in the honey until blended. Add onions, chicken broth and seasonings. Bring to a boil. Reduce heat; simmer, covered, 15-18 minutes or until onions are tender.

**2.** Cook, uncovered, over medium-high heat 15-20 minutes or until liquid is almost evaporated, stirring occasionally. Stir in heavy whipping cream; cook 3-5 minutes longer or until sauce is thickened.

**PER SERVING** *242 cal., 11 g fat (7 g sat. fat), 37 mg chol., 283 mg sodium, 34 g carb., 5 g fiber, 3 g pro.*

BRAISED & CREAMY VIDALIA ONIONS

# Maple Walnut Cake

This wonderful dessert with candied walnuts honors my grandpa, who made maple syrup. If you want to get baking ahead of time, wrap each cake layer tightly in plastic wrap and then foil, and store them in the freezer. Thaw them in the fridge overnight.

**—LORI FEE** MIDDLESEX, NY

**PREP:** 45 MIN. • **BAKE:** 15 MIN. + COOLING
**MAKES:** 16 SERVINGS

- ½ **cup unsalted butter, softened**
- 1½ **cups packed light brown sugar**
- 3 **eggs**
- 1 **teaspoon maple flavoring or maple syrup**
- 2 **cups all-purpose flour**
- 1 **teaspoon baking powder**
- 1 **teaspoon baking soda**
- ¼ **teaspoon salt**
- 1 **cup buttermilk**

**CANDIED WALNUTS**
- 1 **tablespoon unsalted butter**
- 1½ **cups coarsely chopped walnuts**
- 1 **tablespoon maple syrup**
- ¼ **teaspoon salt**

**FROSTING**
- 2 **cups unsalted butter, softened**
- 5 **cups confectioners' sugar**
- 1 **teaspoon maple flavoring or maple syrup**
- ¼ **teaspoon salt**
- ¼ **to ½ cup half-and-half cream**
- 3 **tablespoons maple syrup, divided**

**1.** Preheat oven to 350°. Line bottoms of three greased 9-in. round baking pans with parchment paper; grease paper.

**2.** In a large bowl, cream the butter and brown sugar until blended. Add the eggs, one at a time, beating well after each addition. Beat in maple flavoring. In another bowl, whisk the flour, baking powder, baking soda and salt; add to the creamed mixture alternately with the buttermilk, beating well after each addition.

**3.** Transfer the batter to prepared pans. Bake 11-13 minutes or until a toothpick inserted in the center comes out clean. Cool in the pans 10 minutes before removing to wire racks. Cool completely.

**4.** For the candied walnuts, in a large skillet, melt butter. Add walnuts; cook and stir over medium heat until nuts are toasted, about 5 minutes. Stir in maple syrup and salt; cook and stir 1 minute longer. Spread on foil to cool completely.

**5.** For the frosting, in a large bowl, beat butter until creamy. Beat in the confectioners' sugar, maple flavoring, salt and enough cream to reach desired consistency.

**6.** Place one cake layer on a serving plate; spread with 1 cup frosting. Sprinkle with ½ cup candied walnuts and drizzle with 1 tablespoon maple syrup. Repeat layers.

**7.** Top with the remaining layer. Frost top and sides of cake. Top with remaining walnuts and syrup.

**PER SERVING** *650 cal., 38 g fat (20 g sat. fat), 119 mg chol., 259 mg sodium, 75 g carb., 1 g fiber, 5 g pro.*

CRISPY POTATO PUFFS

# Mandarin Orange & Romaine Salad

A light blend of romaine, oranges and celery makes a refreshing companion for turkey. I top my salad with a homemade dressing that gets a kick from hot sauce.
—CATHY PAWLOWSKI NAPERVILLE, IL

**START TO FINISH:** 20 MIN.
**MAKES:** 10 SERVINGS (1 CUP EACH)

- ¼ cup canola oil
- 2 tablespoons sugar
- 2 tablespoons tarragon vinegar
- ½ teaspoon salt
- ¼ teaspoon hot pepper sauce
- ⅛ teaspoon pepper
- 10 cups torn romaine
- 1 cup (15 ounces) mandarin oranges, drained
- 2 celery ribs, chopped
- 2 green onions, sliced
- 2 tablespoons minced fresh parsley

In a small bowl, whisk the first six ingredients until blended. In a large bowl, combine remaining ingredients. Drizzle with the dressing; toss lightly to coat.

**PER SERVING** *84 cal., 6 g fat (trace sat. fat), 0 chol., 132 mg sodium, 8 g carb., 2 g fiber, 1 g pro.* **Diabetic Exchanges:** *1 fat, ½ starch.*

## Crispy Potato Puffs
**EAT SMART**

Cornflakes and sesame seeds surround a velvety potato filling in these adorable puffs, which offer freezer convenience.
—EVA TOMLINSON BRYAN, OH

**PREP:** 35 MIN. • **BAKE:** 15 MIN.
**MAKES:** 12 SERVINGS (2 PUFFS EACH)

- 4 pounds cubed peeled potatoes (about 11 cups)
- ½ cup 2% milk
- ¼ cup butter, cubed
- 1½ teaspoons salt
- ½ cup shredded cheddar cheese
- 1½ cups crushed cornflakes
- 6 tablespoons sesame seeds, toasted

**1.** Place potatoes in a saucepan; add water to cover. Bring to a boil. Reduce the heat; cook, uncovered, 10-15 minutes or until tender. Drain; return to the pan.

**2.** Mash potatoes, gradually adding milk, butter and salt; stir in cheese. Transfer to a large bowl; refrigerate, covered, 2 hours or until firm enough to shape.

**3.** In a shallow dish, combine the cornflakes and sesame seeds. Shape the potato mixture into 1½-in. balls; roll in cornflake mixture.

**4.** Place potato balls on baking sheets; cover and freeze until firm. Transfer to resealable plastic freezer bags. Freeze up to 3 months.

**5.** To serve, preheat oven to 400°. Place frozen puffs on greased baking sheets. Bake 15-20 minutes or until golden brown and heated through.

**PER SERVING** *248 cal., 7 g fat (4 g sat. fat), 16 mg chol., 466 mg sodium, 42 g carb., 3 g fiber, 5 g pro.*

MANDARIN ORANGE & ROMAINE SALAD

GINGER-MAPLE ROASTED PECANS

> Tide over guests on holidays or anytime by serving my Ginger-Maple Roasted Pecans. They're addictive!
>
> —ANGIE THANOPOULOS
> ARLINGTON HEIGHTS, IL

## Ginger-Maple Roasted Pecans

**PREP:** 15 MIN. • **BAKE:** 20 MIN.
**MAKES:** 3 CUPS

- ⅓ cup maple syrup
- ¼ cup butter, cubed
- 6 slices fresh gingerroot (cut from a 1½-inch piece)
- 1 tablespoon water
- 2 teaspoons hot pepper sauce
- 1½ teaspoons salt
- 1½ teaspoons ground ginger
- ¾ pound pecan halves (about 3 cups)

**1.** Preheat oven to 325°. Grease a foil-lined 15x10x1-in. baking pan. In a small saucepan, combine the first seven ingredients; bring to a boil. Reduce heat; simmer 2-3 minutes or until syrupy, stirring occasionally. Strain and discard ginger slices.

**2.** Place the pecans in a large bowl; drizzle with the syrup mixture and toss to coat. Transfer to the prepared pan. Roast 20-25 minutes or until toasted, stirring occasionally. Cool completely in the pan on a wire rack. Store in an airtight container.

**PER SERVING** *339 cal., 32 g fat (6 g sat. fat), 13 mg chol., 437 mg sodium, 14 g carb., 4 g fiber, 4 g pro.*

**EAT SMART**
## Roasted Green Vegetable Medley

I've prepared vegetables many different ways. But the first time I tried roasting, it became my favorite method of cooking them. Prep the veggies the day before your feast to prevent last-minute fuss.

—**SUZAN CROUCH** GRAND PRAIRIE, TX

**PREP:** 15 MIN. • **BAKE:** 20 MIN.
**MAKES:** 12 SERVINGS (¾ CUP EACH)

- 2 cups fresh broccoli florets
- 1 pound thin fresh green beans, trimmed and cut into 2-inch pieces
- 10 small fresh mushrooms, halved
- 8 fresh Brussels sprouts, halved
- 2 medium carrots, cut into ¼-inch slices
- 1 medium onion, sliced
- 3 to 5 garlic cloves, thinly sliced
- 4 tablespoons olive oil, divided
- ½ cup grated Parmesan cheese
- 3 tablespoons julienned fresh basil leaves, optional
- 2 tablespoons minced fresh parsley
- 2 tablespoons lemon juice
- 1 tablespoon grated lemon peel
- ¼ teaspoon salt
- ¼ teaspoon pepper

**1.** Preheat oven to 425°. Place the first seven ingredients in a large bowl; drizzle with 2 tablespoons oil and toss to coat. Divide between two 15x10x1-in. baking pans coated with cooking spray. Roast 20-25 minutes or until tender, stirring occasionally.

**2.** Transfer to a large serving bowl. In a small bowl, mix the remaining oil with the remaining ingredients; add to the vegetables and toss to combine.

**PER SERVING** *80 cal., 5 g fat (1 g sat. fat), 3 mg chol., 63 mg sodium, 7 g carb., 2 g fiber, 3 g pro.* **Diabetic Exchanges:** *1 vegetable, 1 fat.*

ROASTED GREEN VEGETABLE MEDLEY

MAKE-AHEAD TURKEY AND GRAVY

# Spiced Ambrosia Punch

Spicy chai tea inspired my slow-cooked twist on a basic cider punch.

**—AYSHA SCHURMAN** AMMON, ID

**PREP:** 15 MIN. • **COOK:** 3 HOURS
**MAKES:** 10 SERVINGS (¾ CUP EACH)

- 3½ **cups apple cider or juice**
- 3 **cups apricot nectar**
- 1 **cup peach nectar or additional apricot nectar**
- ¼ **cup water**
- 3 **tablespoons lemon juice**
- ½ **teaspoon ground cardamom**
- ½ **teaspoon ground nutmeg**
- 2 **cinnamon sticks (3 inches)**
- 1 **teaspoon finely chopped fresh gingerroot**
- 1 **teaspoon grated orange peel**
- 8 **whole cloves**
  **Lemon or orange slices, optional**

**1.** In a 3- or 4-qt. slow cooker, combine the first seven ingredients. Place cinnamon sticks, ginger, orange peel and cloves on a double thickness of cheesecloth. Gather corners of cloth to enclose the seasonings; tie securely with string. Place bag in slow cooker.

**2.** Cook, covered, on low 3-4 hours or until heated through. Remove and discard spice bag. Serve warm, with lemon slices, if desired.

**PER SERVING** *115 cal., trace fat (trace sat. fat), 0 chol., 14 mg sodium, 29 g carb., 1 g fiber, trace pro.*

SPICED AMBROSIA PUNCH

# Make-Ahead Turkey and Gravy

This sensational bird is cooked, sliced and ready to serve any time you want. It's also a great option for a potluck.

**—MARIE PARKER** MILWAUKEE, WI

**PREP:** 4¼ HOURS + FREEZING
**BAKE:** 50 MIN.
**MAKES:** 16 SERVINGS (2½ CUPS GRAVY)

**TURKEY**
- 1 **turkey (14 to 16 pounds)**
- 2 **teaspoons poultry seasoning**
- 1 **teaspoon pepper**
- 3 **cups reduced-sodium chicken broth**
- ½ **cup minced fresh parsley**
- ¼ **cup lemon juice**
- 1 **tablespoon minced fresh thyme or 1 teaspoon dried thyme**
- 1 **tablespoon minced fresh rosemary or 1 teaspoon dried rosemary, crushed**
- 2 **teaspoons grated lemon peel**
- 2 **garlic cloves, minced**

**FOR SERVING**
- 1½ **cups reduced-sodium chicken broth**
- 1 **tablespoon butter**
- 1 **tablespoon all-purpose flour**

**1.** Preheat oven to 325°. Sprinkle turkey with poultry seasoning and pepper. Tuck wings under turkey; tie drumsticks together. Place on a rack in a shallow roasting pan, breast side up.

**2.** Roast, uncovered, 30 minutes. In a 4-cup measuring cup, mix remaining turkey ingredients; carefully pour over the turkey. Roast, uncovered, 3 to 3½ hours longer or until a thermometer inserted in thigh reads 180°, basting occasionally with the broth mixture. Cover loosely with foil if the turkey browns too quickly.

**3.** Remove the turkey from the pan; let stand for at least 20 minutes before carving. Skim fat from cooking juices.

**4.** Carve the turkey; place in shallow freezer containers. Pour the strained juices over turkey; cool completely. Freeze, covered, up to 3 months.

**5.** To serve, partially thaw the turkey in the refrigerator overnight. Preheat oven to 350°. Transfer the turkey and cooking juices to a baking dish; pour the chicken broth over turkey. Bake, covered, 50-60 minutes or until a thermometer reads 165°.

**6.** Remove turkey from baking dish, reserving cooking liquid; keep warm. In a small saucepan, melt butter; stir in flour until smooth. Gradually whisk in the reserved cooking liquid. Bring to a boil, stirring constantly; cook and stir 2 minutes or until thickened. Serve with turkey.

**NOTE** *It is best not to use a prebasted turkey for this recipe.*

**PER SERVING** *479 cal., 22 g fat (7 g sat. fat), 216 mg chol., 318 mg sodium, 2 g carb., trace fiber, 64 g pro.*

## Pretzel Turkey Treats

**PREP:** 2 HOURS + STANDING
**MAKES:** 1 DOZEN

- 6 **Fruit by the Foot fruit rolls**
- 9 **circus peanut candies**
- 1 **cup butterscotch chips, divided**
- 24 **candy eyeballs**
- 6 **chocolate-covered thin mints**
- 12 **large sourdough pretzels**
- 36 **milk chocolate kisses, unwrapped**
- 12 **vanilla wafers**

**1.** Using kitchen scissors, cut feathers and 12 wattles from the fruit rolls. Cut three circus peanuts crosswise in half. Cut 24 turkey feet from remaining circus peanuts.

**2.** Reserve 12 butterscotch chips for beaks. In a microwave, melt ½ cup of the remaining chips; stir until smooth. Using melted chips, attach two candy eyeballs, a wattle and a beak to each halved circus peanut. Repeat, using thin mints for heads.

**3.** Place a pretzel on a waxed paper-lined microwave-safe plate. Place a chocolate kiss in each of the three holes. Microwave on high for 15-20 seconds or until melted. While still warm, arrange feathers in a fan shape over the pretzel, pressing gently into melted chocolate to adhere. Repeat with the remaining pretzels and chocolate kisses.

**4.** Melt remaining butterscotch chips. Using melted chips, attach a vanilla wafer to each pretzel for body; attach heads. Attach circus peanut pieces for feet. Let stand until set.

**PER SERVING** *283 cal., 12 g fat (8 g sat. fat), 4 mg chol., 170 mg sodium, 45 g carb., 1 g fiber, 2 g pro.*

Get your kids in a festive mood! Let them help you make cute Pretzel Turkey Treats as edible favors.
—LORRI REINHARDT BIG BEND, WI

PRETZEL TURKEY TREATS

# Kiddie Table Treats

Gather the little ones in your life to help assemble these Thanksgiving goodies.
They're a cinch to make using doughnuts, chocolates, cookies and even clementines.

**1** **Cornucopia Snacks** are irresistible to guests of any age. First, whip up a sweet snack mix of your choice—I like to use honey-roasted peanuts, Cinnamon Burst Cheerios and dried fruit. Roll waffle cones in melted semisweet chocolate, then in gold sanding sugar. Rest them on waxed paper to let the chocolate set. When they're ready, pour in the snack mix and nibble away.
—**MANDY HEASTON** GREELEY, CO

**2** I make **Pilgrim Doughnut Ships.** Cut a sail out of paper. Bend it vertically and make two small slits. Thread a pretzel stick "mast" through the slits and push the pretzel into the inner edge of a mini doughnut. Cut a triangle flag out of strawberry Fruit by the Foot and wrap it around the pretzel. Then eat it all up, except the paper!
—**NORENE COX** EDMONDS, WA

**3** You need only three ingredients to make **Acorn Treats.** Use melted chocolate to attach a Nutter Butter Bite to the flat side of a Hershey's Kiss. Pipe the remaining melted chocolate onto the opposite side of the cookie to make a stem. Refrigerate the little acorns on waxed paper-lined baking sheets until set. How cute is that?
—**JANE STASIK** GREENDALE, WI

**4** For **Candy Corn Rice Krispies Cupcakes,** prepare a batch of Rice Krispies Treats with 3-4 drops of yellow food coloring. When slightly cooled, press enough of the mixture into each cup of a muffin pan to fill halfway. Prepare more Rice Krispies Treats with orange food coloring and layer the orange mixture on top of the yellow one. When set, pop the treat out of the pan and pipe on canned vanilla frosting mixed with a little confectioners' sugar. Top each creation with a candy corn—a real one!
—**HOLLY LOFTHOUSE** WASHINGTON, UT

**5** **Pumpkin Clementines** are a healthy fall snack. Peel a clementine, then poke a short piece of green Twizzler or Tootsie Roll into the hole for the pumpkin stem.
—**TABITHA PHILEN** MOBILE, AL

**6** We dreamed up these **Pilgrim Hat Cookies** for a yummy treat to take to school. Dip the top of a miniature peanut butter cup into yellow frosting and place the cup over the hole of an upside-down fudge-striped cookie, letting the edges of the frosting squish out into a "hatband." Add a red mini Chiclets gum for the buckle.
—**MEGAN & MITCHELL VOGEL** JEFFERSON, WI

**7** Sweeten snack time with **Calico Corn Cakes.** Cut three 8-in.-long pieces of yellow Fruit Roll-Ups, making a point at one end of each. Fan out the strips on a plate, points facing out. Place a snack-size Twinkie on the Roll-Ups and cover it with a thick layer of frosting. Twist the bottoms of the Roll-Ups to make a husk around the cake, then poke rows of classic and harvest-colored candy corn into the frosting.
—**KELLI RINTA** VANCOUVER, WA

**8** Use your favorite roll-out cookie dough to make **Handprint Turkey Cookies.** Cut it with a hand-shaped cookie cutter or use a cardboard cutout of a child's hand. Bake and cool. Paint the palm and thumb of each cookie with a glaze tinted light brown, and paint the fingers with glazes of assorted colors. Pipe on a beak, eye, wattle and wing.
—**PAT THOMPSON** SUN PRAIRIE, WI

**9** Delight kids with **Caramel Corn Treats.** Mix 5 cups caramel corn, 2 cups mini pretzels and 1 cup each Goldfish Baby cheddar crackers and Reese's Pieces. Melt 1 package miniature marshmallows and ¼ cup butter; stir in ¼ teaspoon vanilla and pour over the caramel corn mixture. Press the mixture into a greased pan and top with Reese's Pieces. Once set, cut into bars.
—**CATHY TANG** REDMOND, WA

**10** To make **Turkey Cupcakes,** bake your best cupcake recipe and spread on white frosting. Form the turkey's body with chocolate frosting. Use candy corn for the tail feathers, an M&M for the face, an edible pen to draw the eyes, an orange rainbow chip sprinkle for the beak and red heart confetti for the wattle.
—**MICHELE CHOCK** SAN LEANDRO, CA

1

2

3

4

6

7

5

Joey

Sarah

9

8

10

# Feast for Christmas

Home cooking for the holidays just got easier! These special dishes are on the simpler side, so you can spend less time in the kitchen.

## Gingerbread People

What treat says "Christmas" more than gingerbread cutouts? These soft, chewy little characters always get smiles from my grandchildren, who love to help with the decorating. The recipe includes directions for preparing royal icing you can tint and use to dress up the cookies. Or, save time by spreading them with canned frosting and sprinkling on colored sugar.

—**JOAN TRUAX** PITTSBORO, IN

**PREP:** 45 MIN. + CHILLING • **BAKE:** 10 MIN./BATCH + COOLING
**MAKES:** 2½ DOZEN

- 6  **tablespoons butter, softened**
- ¾  **cup packed dark brown sugar**
- ½  **cup molasses**
- 1  **egg**
- 2  **teaspoons vanilla extract**
- 1  **teaspoon grated lemon peel**
- 3  **cups all-purpose flour**
- 3  **teaspoons ground ginger**
- 1½  **teaspoons baking powder**
- 1¼  **teaspoons ground cinnamon**
- ¾  **teaspoon baking soda**
- ¼  **teaspoon salt**
- ¼  **teaspoon ground cloves**
  **Decorating icing and assorted candies**

**1.** In a large bowl, cream the butter and brown sugar until light and fluffy. Beat in the molasses, egg, vanilla and lemon peel. In another bowl, whisk flour, ginger, baking powder, cinnamon, baking soda, salt and cloves; gradually beat into creamed mixture. Divide dough in half. Shape each into a disk; wrap in plastic wrap. Refrigerate 30 minutes or until easy to handle.

**2.** Preheat oven to 350°. On a lightly floured surface, roll each portion to ¼-in. thickness. Cut with a floured 4-in. gingerbread man cookie cutter.

**3.** Place cutouts 2 in. apart on greased baking sheets. Bake 7-9 minutes or until edges are firm. Remove from pans to wire racks to cool completely. Decorate as desired.

**TO DECORATE WITH ROYAL ICING** *In a bowl, combine 2 cups confectioners' sugar, 2 tablespoons plus 2 teaspoons water, 4½ teaspoons meringue powder and ¼ teaspoon cream of tartar; beat on low speed just until combined. Beat on high 4-5 minutes or until stiff peaks form. If desired, tint the icing with food coloring and pipe with a pastry bag and small pastry tips. Keep unused icing covered at all times; beat again on high to restore the texture as necessary. Yield: 1 cup icing.*

**PER SERVING** *99 cal., 2 g fat (1 g sat. fat), 12 mg chol., 88 mg sodium, 18 g carb., trace fiber, 1 g pro.*

GINGERBREAD PEOPLE

GARLIC MASHED
RUTABAGAS & POTATOES

⑤INGREDIENTS EAT SMART FAST FIX

## Garlic Mashed Rutabagas & Potatoes

My family can't get enough of garlic mashed potatoes. I decided to blend in a few healthy rutabagas to cut down the calories a bit and to sneak in some extra nutrition. If you prefer, boil the spuds in chicken broth to add even more flavor.

**—ROSEMARY TATUM** STERLINGTON, LA

**START TO FINISH:** 30 MIN. • **MAKES:** 8 SERVINGS

- 4 medium potatoes, peeled and cubed (about 4 cups)
- 2 medium rutabagas, peeled and cubed (about 5 cups)
- 2 garlic cloves, peeled
- 2 tablespoons butter
- 1 teaspoon salt
- ¼ teaspoon pepper
- ¼ to ⅓ cup warm buttermilk

**1.** Place the potatoes, rutabagas and garlic in a Dutch oven; add water to cover. Bring to a boil. Reduce the heat; cook, uncovered, 15-20 minutes or until tender.

**2.** Drain; return to pan. Mash potatoes, gradually adding butter, salt, pepper and enough buttermilk to reach desired consistency.

**PER SERVING** *220 cal., 4 g fat (3 g sat. fat), 10 mg chol., 478 mg sodium, 42 g carb., 7 g fiber, 6 g pro.*

## ❓ Did you know?

Carving a beef rib roast is easy. Put the meat, large side down, on a cutting board with the bones to one side. To separate the meat from the bone, make a 1- to 2-in. cut along the curve of the bone. Slice the meat horizontally into ¼-in. to ½-in. slices from the top edge to the bones. Repeat slicing, loosening the meat from the bones as necessary.

⑤INGREDIENTS

## Salt-Encrusted Prime Rib

The prime rib entrees at fancy restaurants have nothing on this sensational recipe. For meat lovers, it's a dream come true!

**—ROGER BOWLDS** BAKERSFIELD, CA

**PREP:** 15 MIN. • **BAKE:** 2¼ HOURS + STANDING
**MAKES:** 10 SERVINGS

- 1 box (3 pounds) kosher salt (about 6 cups), divided
- 1 bone-in beef rib roast (6 to 8 pounds)
- 3 tablespoons Worcestershire sauce
- 2 tablespoons cracked black pepper
- 2 teaspoons garlic powder
- ½ cup water

**1.** Preheat oven to 450°. Line a shallow roasting pan with heavy-duty foil. Place 3 cups salt on foil, spreading evenly to form a ½-in. layer.

**2.** Brush roast with Worcestershire sauce; sprinkle with pepper and garlic powder. Place roast on layer of salt, fat side up. In a small bowl, mix the water and remaining salt (mixture should be just moist enough to pack). Beginning at base of roast, press salt mixture onto sides and top of roast.

**3.** Roast 15 minutes. Reduce oven setting to 325°. Roast 2 to 2¼ hours or until a thermometer reaches 130° for medium-rare; 145° for medium. (Temperature of roast will continue to rise about 15° upon standing.) Let stand 20 minutes.

**4.** Remove and discard the salt crust; brush away any remaining salt. Carve roast into slices.

**PER SERVING** *325 cal., 18 g fat (7 g sat. fat), 107 mg chol., 900 mg sodium, 2 g carb., trace fiber, 37 g pro.*

SALT-ENCRUSTED PRIME RIB

CAESAR SALAD IN PEPPERED
PARMESAN BOWLS

## Caesar Salad in Peppered Parmesan Bowls

Here's an impressive salad for holidays.
The simple cheese bowls are always a hit.
—**MELISSA WILKES** ST. AUGUSTINE, FL

**PREP:** 20 MIN. • **COOK:** 15 MIN.
**MAKES:** 8 SERVINGS

- **2 cups shredded Parmesan cheese**
- **½ teaspoon coarsely ground pepper**
- **2 romaine hearts, cut into bite-size pieces (about 6 cups)**
- **1 cup grape tomatoes, halved**
- **¾ cup Caesar salad croutons, slightly crushed**
- **¼ cup creamy Caesar salad dressing**

**1.** In a small bowl, toss the cheese with pepper. Heat a small nonstick skillet over medium heat. Evenly sprinkle ¼ cup cheese mixture into the pan to form a 6-in. circle; cook, uncovered, 1-2 minutes or until bubbly and edges are golden brown. Remove pan from heat; let stand 15 seconds.
**2.** Using a spatula, carefully remove the cheese and immediately drape over an inverted 4-oz. ramekin; press gently to form a bowl. Cool completely. Repeat with the remaining cheese, making eight bowls.
**3.** In a large bowl, combine romaine, tomatoes and croutons. Just before serving, drizzle with dressing and toss to coat. Serve in cheese bowls.
**PER SERVING** *138 cal., 9 g fat (4 g sat. fat), 17 mg chol., 463 mg sodium, 5 g carb., 1 g fiber, 9 g pro.*

⑤**INGREDIENTS** **EAT SMART**
## Roasted Garlic Green Beans with Cashews

When my mother got a garlic roaster, my kitchen was soon overflowing with sweet, gooey roasted bulbs. This recipe, one of my experiments, has become a popular addition to my dinner menus.
—**VIRGINIA STURM** SAN FRANCISCO, CA

**PREP:** 40 MIN. • **COOK:** 15 MIN.
**MAKES:** 8 SERVINGS

- **10 garlic cloves, unpeeled**
- **2 teaspoons plus ¼ cup olive oil, divided**
- **2 pounds fresh green beans, trimmed**
- **1 cup water**
- **1 cup lightly salted cashews, coarsely chopped**
- **½ teaspoon salt**
- **¼ teaspoon pepper**

**1.** Preheat oven to 375°. Cut the stem ends off unpeeled garlic cloves. Place the cloves on a piece of foil. Drizzle with 2 teaspoons oil; wrap in foil. Bake 25-30 minutes or until cloves are soft. Unwrap and cool slightly. Squeeze the garlic from skins; mash with a fork to form a paste.
**2.** In a Dutch oven, heat the remaining oil over medium-high heat. Add the green beans and garlic; cook and stir 2-3 minutes. Add the water; bring to a boil. Reduce heat; simmer, uncovered, 7-10 minutes or until the beans are crisp-tender and the water is almost evaporated, stirring occasionally. Add nuts, salt and pepper; toss to combine.
**PER SERVING** *208 cal., 16 g fat (3 g sat. fat), 0 chol., 187 mg sodium, 13 g carb., 4 g fiber, 6 g pro.*

# Thyme-Roasted Carrots

These tender carrots are a snap to prepare but special enough to serve as a side dish for your Christmas meal. And they go with just about anything! I typically slice them lengthwise for a fancy presentation. For an extra touch, add sprigs of fresh thyme or parsley as a garnish.

**—DEIRDRE COX** KANSAS CITY, MO

**START TO FINISH:** 30 MIN.
**MAKES:** ABOUT 12 SERVINGS (2 CARROT HALVES EACH)

- 3 **pounds medium carrots, halved lengthwise**
- 2 **tablespoons minced fresh thyme or 2 teaspoons dried thyme**
- 2 **tablespoons canola oil**
- 1 **tablespoon honey**
- 1 **teaspoon salt**

Preheat oven to 400°. Divide carrots between two greased 15x10x1-in. baking pans. In a small bowl, mix the thyme, oil, honey and salt; brush over carrots. Roast 20-25 minutes or until carrots are tender.

**PER SERVING** *73 cal., 3 g fat (trace sat. fat), 0 chol., 275 mg sodium, 12 g carb., 3 g fiber, 1 g pro.* **Diabetic Exchanges:** *1 vegetable, ½ starch, ½ fat.*

RASPBERRY SWIRLED CHEESECAKE PIE

THYME-ROASTED CARROTS

# Raspberry Swirled Cheesecake Pie

My dad's favorite dessert was cheesecake pie with a red raspberry swirl. Though he is now gone, I remember his smile every time I make it. Feel free to use a different fruit pie filling to suit your family's tastes.

**—PEGGY GRIFFIN** ELBA, NE

**PREP:** 15 MIN. • **BAKE:** 35 MIN. + CHILLING
**MAKES:** 8 SERVINGS

- 1 **package (8 ounces) cream cheese, softened**
- ½ **cup sugar**
- 2 **eggs, lightly beaten**
- 1 **graham cracker crust (9 inches)**
- 1 **can (21 ounces) raspberry pie filling, divided**

**1.** Preheat the oven to 350°. In a large bowl, beat the cream cheese and sugar until smooth. Add the eggs; beat on low speed just until blended. Pour into the graham cracker crust. Drop ½ cup raspberry pie filling by tablespoonfuls over batter. Cut through batter with a knife to swirl.

**2.** Bake for 35-45 minutes or until the filling is set. Transfer the remaining raspberry filling to a covered container; refrigerate until serving.

**3.** Cool the pie 1 hour on a wire rack. Refrigerate at least 2 hours, covering when completely cooled. Serve with reserved filling.

**PER SERVING** *337 cal., 16 g fat (8 g sat. fat), 84 mg chol., 253 mg sodium, 44 g carb., 2 g fiber, 5 g pro.*

# Yuletide Goodies

The merriest time of year calls for extra-special treats. Spread plenty of Christmas cheer with the festively decorated cookies, rich brownies, luscious cupcakes and more here.

BLACK FOREST WAFFLES

**⑤ INGREDIENTS | FAST FIX**

## Ornament Popcorn Balls

These ooey-gooey snowmen are great for kids to help with and fun to hang on the tree—not to mention yummy!

—**DEIRDRE COX** KANSAS CITY, MO

**START TO FINISH:** 30 MIN. • **MAKES:** 1 DOZEN

- 10 **cups popped popcorn**
- 1 **package (10 ounces) large marshmallows**
- ¼ **cup butter, cubed**
- ¼ **teaspoon salt**
  **Optional decorations: candy canes, candy spearmint leaves and assorted gumdrops**

**1.** Place the popcorn in a large bowl. In a large saucepan, combine the marshmallows, butter and salt. Cook and stir over medium-low heat until melted. Pour over popcorn; mix well. Cool slightly.

**2.** With greased hands, shape the popcorn mixture into 12 balls, about ¾ cup each. Place on waxed paper. Decorate as desired; let stand until set.

**PER SERVING** *162 cal., 8 g fat (3 g sat. fat), 10 mg chol., 184 mg sodium, 23 g carb., 1 g fiber, 1 g pro.*

ORNAMENT POPCORN BALLS

**FAST FIX**

## Black Forest Waffles

Inspired by traditional German Black Forest cake, I mixed dark chocolate into plain waffle batter and spooned on cherry pie filling and whipped cream before serving.

—**EDITH JOHNSON** FRUITA, CO

**START TO FINISH:** 30 MIN. • **MAKES:** 5 WAFFLES

- 1 **cup heavy whipping cream**
- 3 **tablespoons confectioners' sugar**
- 2 **ounces unsweetened chocolate, chopped**
- 3 **tablespoons shortening**
- 1¾ **cups cake flour**
- 6 **tablespoons sugar**
- 1 **tablespoon baking powder**
- ½ **teaspoon salt**
- 2 **eggs, separated**
- 1 **cup milk**
- 1 **can (21 ounces) cherry pie filling**
  **Chocolate sprinkles or fresh mint, optional**

**1.** In a small bowl, beat the cream until it begins to thicken. Add the confectioners' sugar; beat until soft peaks form. Refrigerate until serving.

**2.** In a microwave, melt chocolate and shortening; stir until smooth. Cool slightly. In a large bowl, whisk the flour, sugar, baking powder and salt. In another bowl, whisk egg yolks and milk until blended. Stir in chocolate mixture. Add to dry ingredients; stir just until moistened.

**3.** In a clean bowl, beat the egg whites until stiff but not dry. Fold into batter. Bake in a preheated waffle iron according to manufacturer's directions until set.

**4.** Serve with whipped cream and pie filling. If desired, top with sprinkles.

**PER SERVING** *706 cal., 32 g fat (16 g sat. fat), 157 mg chol., 567 mg sodium, 96 g carb., 2 g fiber, 10 g pro.*

# Peppermint Crunch Christmas Cookies

Transform basic shortbread into these Christmastime delights. It's easy with food coloring, candy coating and peppermints.
—**HEATHER CARTER** WASILLA, AK

**PREP:** 25 MIN. + CHILLING • **BAKE:** 10 MIN./BATCH + COOLING
**MAKES:** 3½ DOZEN

- 1 **cup butter, softened**
- ½ **cup sugar**
- 1 **teaspoon peppermint extract**
- 1 **teaspoon vanilla extract**
- 2¼ **cups all-purpose flour**
  **Red and green paste food coloring**
- 8 **ounces dark chocolate candy coating, melted**
- ¾ **cup crushed peppermint candies**

**1.** In a large bowl, cream butter and sugar until light and fluffy. Beat in extracts. Gradually beat in flour. Divide dough in half; tint one portion red and the other green. Wrap each in plastic wrap; refrigerate 2 hours or until easy to handle.
**2.** Preheat the oven to 350°. On a lightly floured surface, roll each portion of dough to ¼-in. thickness. Cut with a floured 1½-in. round cookie cutter. Place 1 in. apart on ungreased baking sheets. Bake 8-10 minutes or until firm. Remove from pans to wire racks to cool completely.
**3.** Dip half of each cookie into melted candy coating; allow excess to drip off. Sprinkle with crushed candies. Place on waxed paper; let stand until set.
**PER SERVING** *107 cal., 6 g fat (4 g sat. fat), 11 mg chol., 32 mg sodium, 13 g carb., trace fiber, 1 g pro.*

CALLAHAN CHRISTMAS WREATHS

# Callahan Christmas Wreaths

When my family asked for good old Norwegian wreath cookies, I studied a few recipes for ideas, then added my own touches.
—**CASSIDY CALLAHAN** FITCHBURG, MA

**PREP:** 30 MIN. • **BAKE:** 10 MIN./BATCH • **MAKES:** 2½ DOZEN

- ½ **cup butter, softened**
- ½ **cup shortening**
- 1 **cup sugar**
- 2 **eggs**
- 2 **teaspoons grated orange peel**
- ½ **teaspoon almond extract**
- 2½ **cups all-purpose flour**
  **Green food coloring**
  **Red and green candied cherries**

**1.** Preheat oven to 400°. In a large bowl, cream the butter, shortening and sugar until light and fluffy. Beat in the eggs, orange peel and almond extract. Gradually beat in the flour. Divide the cookie dough in half; tint one portion green with food coloring.
**2.** For each cookie wreath, shape two 6-inch ropes using 2 teaspoons plain dough for one and 2 teaspoons green dough for the other. Place the two ropes side by side; press together lightly, then twist several times. Shape into a circle, pinching ends to seal. Place 2 in. apart on ungreased baking sheets. Repeat with remaining dough.
**3.** Cut the candied cherries into small pieces and place on the wreaths to decorate as desired, pressing lightly to adhere. Bake the cookies 6-8 minutes or until set and the bottoms are light brown.
**4.** Remove from the pans to wire racks to cool. Store in an airtight container.
**PER SERVING** *125 cal., 7 g fat (3 g sat. fat), 22 mg chol., 26 mg sodium, 15 g carb., trace fiber, 2 g pro.*

PEPPERMINT CRUNCH CHRISTMAS COOKIES

YULETIDE EGGNOG CUPCAKES

# Yuletide Eggnog Cupcakes

If I want a creamier frosting on my little cakes, I just add more eggnog. The nog lovers in my life never complain!

—**SALINA MOORE** WOODWARD, OK

**PREP:** 30 MIN. • **BAKE:** 20 MIN. + COOLING
**MAKES:** 2 DOZEN

- 4 **eggs, separated**
- ⅔ **cup butter, softened**
- 1½ **cups sugar, divided**
- 2⅓ **cups all-purpose flour**
- 3 **teaspoons baking powder**
- ½ **teaspoon ground nutmeg**
- ¼ **teaspoon salt**
- 1 **cup eggnog**

**FROSTING**
- 1 **package (8 ounces) cream cheese, softened**
- ¼ **cup butter, softened**
- 3¾ **cups confectioners' sugar**
- 2 **tablespoons eggnog**
  **Freshly grated or additional ground nutmeg**

**1.** Place the egg whites in a large bowl; let stand at room temperature for 30 minutes. Preheat oven to 350°. Line muffin cups with paper liners.
**2.** In a large bowl, cream butter and 1¼ cups sugar until light and fluffy. Add yolks, one at a time, beating well after each addition. In another bowl, whisk flour, baking powder, nutmeg and salt; add to the creamed mixture alternately with eggnog, beating well after each addition.

**3.** With clean beaters, beat the egg whites on medium speed until soft peaks form. Gradually add remaining sugar, 1 tablespoon at a time, beating on high after each addition until sugar is dissolved. Continue beating until stiff glossy peaks form. Fold into batter.
**4.** Fill lined cups three-fourths full. Bake 18-22 minutes or until a toothpick inserted in center comes out clean. Cool in pans 10 minutes before removing to wire racks to cool completely.
**5.** For frosting, in a large bowl, beat cream cheese and butter until blended. Gradually beat in the confectioners' sugar and eggnog until smooth. Frost the cupcakes. Sprinkle with nutmeg. Refrigerate leftovers.
**PER SERVING** *296 cal., 12 g fat (7 g sat. fat), 71 mg chol., 170 mg sodium, 44 g carb., trace fiber, 4 g pro.*

# Christmas Graham Houses

Children will love helping you build these cute holiday homes. They can be enjoyed as a treat or used as decorations.
—***TASTE OF HOME*** TEST KITCHEN

**PREP:** 40 MIN. + STANDING
**MAKES:** 4 HOUSES (2 TALL AND 2 SHORT)

- 19 **whole graham crackers, divided**
- 1 **can (16 ounces) vanilla frosting**
- 2 **cups confectioners' sugar**
  **Assorted candies and cookies**

**1.** Using a serrated knife, cut 10 graham crackers in half to make 20 squares. Cut four of the squares diagonally in half to make eight triangles.
**2.** Empty frosting into a large bowl; gradually beat in confectioners' sugar. Cut a small hole in the tip of a pastry bag or in a corner of a food-safe plastic bag; insert #4 round pastry tip. Fill bag two-thirds full with frosting mixture.
**3.** For each roof (make four), pipe a strip of frosting along three edges of two of the squares. Pipe a strip of frosting along the short edges of two of the triangles. Hold triangles upright with unfrosted edges at bottom. Place the squares on top of the triangles, lining up edges to make a sloped roof (unfrosted edges should be at bottom). Let stand 1 hour to set.
**4.** For each short house (make two), pipe frosting on two opposite edges of four of the squares. Join frosted edges to form walls. For each tall house (make two), pipe frosting on long edges of four rectangles; join to form walls.
**5.** Cut remaining graham cracker to make four doors; attach to houses with frosting. Pipe a thin strip of frosting along the bottoms of the roofs; place on the walls. Decorate as desired. Let stand 2 hours or until set.
**PER SERVING** *273 cal., 6 g fat (1 g sat. fat), 0 chol., 185 mg sodium, 53 g carb., 1 g fiber, 1 g pro.*

CHRISTMAS GRAHAM HOUSES

CHRISTMAS TREE BROWNIES

# Christmas Tree Brownies

My grown son acts like a kid when he sees these brownies! Shape them into a merry tree or follow the directions at the end of the recipe to make wreaths or reindeer.

—**JEANNINE SCHNEIDER** FREMONT, CA

**PREP:** 30 MIN. • **BAKE:** 25 MIN. + COOLING
**MAKES:** 1 TREE, 2 WREATHS OR
24 REINDEER BROWNIES

- ¾ **cup butter, cubed**
- 4 **oz. unsweetened chocolate, chopped**
- 3 **eggs**
- 2 **cups sugar**
- ¼ **teaspoon salt**
- 1 **teaspoon vanilla extract**
- 1 **cup all-purpose flour**
- 1 **can (16 ounces) vanilla frosting**
  **Green paste food coloring, optional**
  **Assorted nonpareils**

**1.** Preheat the oven to 350°. Line a 13x9-in. baking pan with foil, letting the ends extend up the sides; grease foil. In a microwave, melt the butter and chocolate; stir until smooth. Cool slightly. In a large bowl, beat the eggs, sugar and salt. Stir in vanilla extract and chocolate mixture. Gradually add flour, mixing well.

**2.** Spread into the prepared pan. Bake 25-30 minutes or until the brownie begins to pull away from the sides of the pan. Cool completely in pan on a wire rack.

**3.** Lifting with foil, remove brownie from pan. Cut brownie to form a tree. If desired, tint frosting green. Frost tree; decorate as desired.

**FOR HOLIDAY WREATH BROWNIES**
*Prepare the Christmas Tree Brownies through Step 2, but use two parchment paper-lined 9-in. round baking pans in place of the 13x9-in. pan; cool in pans for 10 minutes before removing to wire racks. Using a 3-in. round cookie cutter, cut out center of each brownie to form a wreath. Tint the frosting green. Frost wreaths. Use AirHeads Xtremes Sour Belt candies to make bows. Decorate with white M&M's as desired.*

**FOR REINDEER BROWNIES**
*Prepare Christmas Tree Brownies through Step 2. Lifting with the foil, remove brownie from pan. Spread 1 can (16 oz.) chocolate frosting over top. Cut brownie into 12 squares; cut squares into triangles. Attach candies and pretzels to make reindeer faces.*

**DAD'S FAMOUS
STUFFIES**
*PAGE 199*

# Family Best

It's hard to beat home-cooked dishes from **Mom and Dad**. In this chapter, cooks from across the country share their heartwarming family stories—and plenty of **best-loved recipes**, too!

**MY MOM'S BEST MEAT LOAF**

*PAGE 202*

**HAM & CHEESE GRITS CASSEROLE**

*PAGE 197*

**RED & GREEN SALAD WITH TOASTED ALMONDS**

*PAGE 201*

# Southern Comforts

Learning fabulous **Alabama-style cooking** at her grandparents' sides taught this Texas mother that **Southern food is love**. It can be good for you, too!

RECIPES & STORY BY **DEBI MITCHELL** | FLOWER MOUND, TX

BAKED COCONUT SHRIMP &
APRICOT SAUCE

At my grandparents' farm near Cedar Bluff, Alabama, breakfast was almost always fried chicken and homemade biscuits dripping in gravy. They made it with love—and lard. When I started cooking on my own, I fried everything. I even kept a can of bacon grease within easy reach on my kitchen counter.

I've been a working mom now for many years. With my family's health in mind, I've gradually come up with better-for-you versions of some of the Southern dishes I was raised with. They're what I call "un-fried."

I studied nutrition, cookbooks and TV cooking shows for ways to lighten up our menus. I began adding flavor-boosting ingredients like garlic and lots of fresh herbs from my garden.

My kids—Andrea, Lance and Ashton—live on their own now. Andrea's a terrific cook who brings many of my recipes to life. And her daughters love to stay with me and my husband to play, help and learn in my kitchen.

I wish I had my grandma's fried chicken recipe, but she never wrote it down. My own family has inspired me to write a cookbook so they can pass along their favorites someday, too.

## Baked Coconut Shrimp & Apricot Sauce

**PREP:** 25 MIN. • **BAKE:** 10 MIN. • **MAKES:** 6 SERVINGS

- 1½ **pounds uncooked large shrimp**
- 1½ **cups flaked coconut**
- ½ **cup panko (Japanese) bread crumbs**
- 4 **egg whites**
- 3 **dashes Louisiana-style hot sauce**
- ¼ **teaspoon salt**
- ¼ **teaspoon pepper**
- ½ **cup all-purpose flour**

**SAUCE**
- 1 **cup apricot preserves**
- 1 **teaspoon cider vinegar**
- ¼ **teaspoon crushed red pepper flakes**

**1.** Preheat oven to 425°. Place a wire rack on each of two baking sheets; coat the racks with cooking spray. Peel and devein shrimp, leaving tails on.

**2.** In a shallow bowl, toss the coconut with bread crumbs; remove half of the mixture and reserve. In another shallow bowl, whisk egg whites, hot sauce, salt and pepper. Place the flour in a third shallow bowl.

**3.** Dip shrimp in flour to coat lightly; shake off excess. Dip in egg white mixture, then in coconut mixture, patting to help coating adhere. Refresh coconut mixture in bowl with reserved mixture as needed.

**4.** Place the shrimp on the racks of the prepared pans. Bake 5-6 minutes on each side or until coconut is lightly browned and shrimp turn pink.

**5.** Meanwhile, combine the sauce ingredients in a small saucepan; cook and stir over medium-low heat until the preserves are melted. Serve shrimp with sauce.

**PER SERVING** *367 cal., 9 g fat (7 g sat. fat), 138 mg chol., 290 mg sodium, 51 g carb., 1 g fiber, 22 g pro.*

# Jalapeno Buttermilk Corn Bread

**PREP:** 15 MIN. • **BAKE:** 20 MIN. • **MAKES:** 8 SERVINGS

- 1 cup self-rising flour
- 1 cup yellow cornmeal
- 1 cup buttermilk
- ¼ cup egg substitute
- 3 tablespoons canola oil, divided
- 2 tablespoons honey
- 1 tablespoon reduced-fat mayonnaise
- ¼ cup fresh or frozen corn, thawed
- 3 tablespoons shredded reduced-fat cheddar cheese
- 3 tablespoons finely chopped sweet red pepper
- ½ to 1 jalapeno pepper, seeded and finely chopped

**1.** Preheat oven to 425°. In a large bowl, whisk flour and cornmeal. In another bowl, whisk the buttermilk, egg substitute, 2 tablespoons oil, honey and mayonnaise. Pour remaining oil into an 8-in. ovenproof skillet; place skillet in oven 4 minutes.

**2.** Meanwhile, add buttermilk mixture to flour mixture; stir just until moistened. Fold in corn, cheese and peppers.

**3.** Carefully tilt and rotate skillet to coat bottom with oil; add the batter. Bake 20-25 minutes or until a toothpick inserted in center comes out clean. Serve warm.

**NOTE** *As a substitute for 1 cup of self-rising flour, place 1½ teaspoons baking powder and ½ teaspoon salt in a measuring cup. Add all-purpose flour to measure 1 cup. Wear disposable gloves when cutting hot peppers; the oils can burn skin. Avoid touching your face.*

**PER SERVING** *180 cal., 4 g fat (1 g sat. fat), 4 mg chol., 261 mg sodium, 32 g carb., 2 g fiber, 6 g pro.* **Diabetic Exchanges:** *2 starch, 1 fat.*

# Baked Parmesan Breaded Squash

**PREP:** 20 MIN. • **BAKE:** 20 MIN. • **MAKES:** 6 SERVINGS

- 4 cups thinly sliced yellow summer squash (3 medium)
- 3 tablespoons olive oil
- ½ teaspoon salt
- ½ teaspoon pepper
- ⅛ teaspoon cayenne pepper
- ¾ cup panko (Japanese) bread crumbs
- ¾ cup grated Parmesan cheese

**1.** Preheat oven to 450°. Place the squash in a large bowl. Add oil and seasonings; toss to coat.

**2.** In a shallow bowl, mix panko bread crumbs and cheese. Dip squash in the crumb mixture to coat both sides, patting to help coating adhere. Place on parchment paper-lined baking sheets. Bake 20-25 minutes or until golden brown, rotating pans halfway through baking.

**PER SERVING** *137 cal., 10 g fat (2 g sat. fat), 7 mg chol., 346 mg sodium, 8 g carb., 2 g fiber, 5 g pro.* **Diabetic Exchanges:** *2 fat, 1 vegetable.*

# Ham & Cheese Grits Casserole

**PREP:** 30 MIN. • **BAKE:** 35 MIN. + STANDING
**MAKES:** 6 SERVINGS

- 3 cups chicken stock
- 1 cup quick-cooking grits
- ½ cup Southwestern-style egg substitute
- 5 ounces reduced-fat process cheese (Velveeta), cubed
- ¼ cup 2% milk
- 2 tablespoons butter
- 1¼ cups cubed fully cooked ham
- 3 green onions, chopped
- ¼ teaspoon salt
- ¼ teaspoon garlic powder
- ¼ teaspoon pepper
- ⅛ to ¼ teaspoon crushed red pepper flakes
- ¾ cup shredded cheddar cheese

**1.** Preheat the oven to 350°. In a large saucepan, bring the chicken stock to a boil. Slowly stir in the grits. Reduce heat to medium-low; cook, covered, for about 5 minutes or until thickened, stirring occasionally. Remove from the heat. In a small bowl, stir a small amount of the hot grits into egg substitute; return all to pan, mixing well.

**2.** Add the process cheese, milk and butter; stir until the cheese is melted. Stir in ham, green onions and seasonings. Transfer to a greased 11x7-in. baking dish. Sprinkle with cheddar cheese.

**3.** Bake, uncovered, 35-40 minutes or until the edges are golden brown and cheese is melted. Let stand 10 minutes before serving.

**PER SERVING** *284 cal., 12 g fat (7 g sat. fat), 51 mg chol., 1,212 mg sodium, 26 g carb., 1 g fiber, 20 g pro.*

HAM & CHEESE GRITS CASSEROLE

# Happy as Clams

You've got to love **recipes that become events**. In this Rhode Island family, Dad's famous "stuffies" are the all-stars of the summer season. Throw in a few more **Ocean State specialties**—hot wieners and Coffee Milk—and it's a party!

RECIPES & STORY BY **KAREN BARROS** | BRISTOL, RI

S
ince I was a child, our Fourth of July celebrations have always started a day early. The family gathers in the garage to make Dad's famous stuffed quahogs, also known as "stuffies." Out come the tools, including a worktable, propane burner, huge pot and food processor. Then it's all hands on deck.

Dad, whose nickname is Big Bob, presides over the entire process from his lawn chair. He makes sure someone thoroughly washes and scrubs the clams—all 100 of them—before they go into the pot, and he inspects the onions to confirm that they've been finely chopped.

The first time my husband was summoned for quahog duty, he nearly tossed the reserved clam broth—big mistake! We've been married 14 years now, and he's still hearing about it.

The process continues until Big Bob tells us they're perfect, and that's when the holiday can officially begin. Making stuffies has provided me with some of my warmest family memories.

## Rhode Island Hot Wieners

**PREP:** 15 MIN. • **COOK:** 50 MIN. • **MAKES:** 8 SERVINGS

- ¼ **cup butter, cubed**
- 1 **medium onion, finely chopped**
- 2 **tablespoons Worcestershire sauce**
- 2 **tablespoons paprika**
- 2 **tablespoons chili powder**
- 3 **teaspoons ground cumin**
- 1 **teaspoon ground mustard**
- ¾ **teaspoon ground cinnamon**
- ½ **teaspoon ground allspice**
- 1 **pound ground beef**
- ¼ **cup water**
- 8 **hot dogs**
- 8 **hot dog buns, split and warmed**
  **Toppings: yellow mustard, finely chopped onion and celery salt**

RHODE ISLAND HOT WIENERS

**1.** In a large skillet, heat the butter over medium heat. Add the onion; cook and stir 3-4 minutes or until tender. Stir in the Worcestershire sauce and seasonings. Add the beef; cook 6-8 minutes or until no longer pink, breaking into crumbles. Stir in the water; bring to a boil. Reduce heat; simmer, uncovered, 30 minutes.

**2.** In a large skillet, cook the hot dogs over medium heat for 8-10 minutes or until lightly browned, turning occasionally. Serve in buns with meat sauce and toppings as desired.

**PER SERVING** *447 cal., 29 g fat (12 g sat. fat), 75 mg chol., 803 mg sodium, 28 g carb., 3 g fiber, 20 g pro.*

DAD'S FAMOUS STUFFIES

## Dad's Famous Stuffies

**PREP:** 1¼ HOURS • **BAKE:** 20 MIN.
**MAKES:** 10 SERVINGS (3 CLAMS EACH)

- 20 fresh large quahog clams (about 10 pounds)
- 1 pound hot chourico or linguica (smoked Portuguese sausage) or fully cooked Spanish chorizo
- 1 large onion, chopped (about 2 cups)
- 3 teaspoons seafood seasoning
- 1 package (14 ounces) herb stuffing cubes
- 1 cup water
  - Lemon wedges, optional
  - Hot pepper sauce, optional

**1.** Add 2 in. of water to a stockpot. Add clams and chourico; bring to a boil. Cover and steam 15-20 minutes or until the clams open.

**2.** Remove clams and sausage from pot, reserving 2 cups cooking liquid; cool slightly. Discard any unopened clams.

**3.** Preheat oven to 350°. Remove the clam meat from the shells. Separate shells; reserve 30 half shells for stuffing. Place clam meat in a food processor; process until finely chopped. Transfer to a large bowl.

**4.** Remove the casings from the sausage; cut sausage into 1½-in. pieces. Place in a food processor; process until finely chopped. Add sausage, onion and seafood seasoning to the chopped clams. Stir in the stuffing cubes. Add the reserved cooking liquid and enough water to reach the desired moistness, about 1 cup.

**5.** Spoon the clam mixture into the reserved shells. Place in 15x10x1-in. baking pans. Bake 15-20 minutes or until heated through. Preheat broiler.

**6.** Broil clams 4-6 in. from heat 4-5 minutes or until golden brown. If desired, serve with lemon wedges and hot sauce.

**NOTE** *Hot chourico can be found at michaelsprovision.com and gasparssausage.com.*

**FREEZE OPTION** *Cover and freeze unbaked stuffed clams in a 15x10x1-in. baking pan until firm. Transfer to resealable freezer bags; return to the freezer. To use, place two stuffed clams on a microwave-safe plate. Cover with a paper towel; microwave on high 2½ to 3 minutes or until heated through. Serve as directed.*

**PER SERVING** *296 cal., 11 g fat (3 g sat. fat), 71 mg chol., 1,188 mg sodium, 34 g carb., 2 g fiber, 18 g pro.*

⑤ INGREDIENTS FAST FIX
## Coffee Milk

**START TO FINISH:** 5 MIN.
**MAKES:** 8 SERVINGS (ABOUT 1 CUP EACH)

- 2 quarts cold 2% or whole milk
- 1 cup Eclipse coffee syrup

In a large pitcher, mix milk and coffee syrup until blended.
**TO MAKE YOUR OWN COFFEE MILK SYRUP** *Brew ½ cup finely ground coffee with 2 cups cold water in a coffeemaker. Combine the brewed coffee and 1 cup sugar in a saucepan; simmer until reduced by half, about 30 minutes. Refrigerate until cold or up to 2 weeks. Use as directed. Yield: 1 cup syrup.*

**PER SERVING** *135 cal., 5 g fat (3 g sat. fat), 18 mg chol., 122 mg sodium, 15 g carb., 0 fiber, 8 g pro.*

COFFEE MILK

# Sides to Celebrate

**The world always needs more hugs**—and bowls brimming with vegetables. This Illinois mom has plenty of both to **share with family and friends.**

RECIPES & STORY BY **JASMINE ROSE** | CRYSTAL LAKE, IL

I have a large family to celebrate with on holidays: my husband, four children, eight grandchildren, nieces and nephews, three brothers—and friends, too, if they're in town. So, our get-togethers are always eclectic. No matter who's there, everyone can count on lots of fun and plenty of belly laughs.

I used to make the whole meal, but I taught my kids how to prepare the holiday dishes that they loved. Now they're really great cooks, too.

I'm all about fresh, clean eating. My children were raised picking berries on farms, and I've always tried to choose recipes that use seasonal ingredients—even in the dead of winter. Root vegetables, squash, mushrooms and home-dried herbs are so satisfying, we don't mind the long wait for spring as much.

The bottom line is, food is truly a gift. In our family, we try to eat at least one meal together each day. We give thanks and share with as many people as possible, even if it's just my husband and me, now that our kids are grown. And while we eat, we really talk with each other. It's a value I learned from my grandmothers, Elsie and Hattie, and something I'm teaching my own grandchildren today.

I believe we can build communities by bringing people together at the table. Gather with kindness, and there will be abundance for all.

BUTTERNUT SQUASH & POTATO MASH

**EAT SMART**
## Butternut Squash & Potato Mash

**PREP:** 15 MIN. • **COOK:** 20 MIN.
**MAKES:** 10 SERVINGS (¾ CUP EACH)

- 8 **cups cubed peeled butternut squash (about 4 pounds)**
- 4 **cups cubed peeled potatoes (about 4 medium)**
- 16 **garlic cloves, peeled**
- 2 **tablespoons sesame seeds**
- 1 **teaspoon ground cumin**
- 1 **cup (4 ounces) shredded Colby-Monterey Jack cheese**
- 2 **tablespoons butter**
- 1½ **teaspoons salt**
- ½ **teaspoon pepper**

**1.** Place the squash, potatoes and garlic in a Dutch oven; add water to cover. Bring to a boil. Reduce the heat; cook, uncovered, 10-15 minutes or until tender.

**2.** Meanwhile, in a dry small skillet, toast the sesame seeds and cumin over medium-low heat 3-4 minutes or until aromatic, stirring frequently. Remove from heat.

**3.** Drain squash mixture. Mash vegetables, adding cheese, butter, salt and pepper. Sprinkle with sesame seed mixture.

**PER SERVING** *190 cal., 7 g fat (4 g sat. fat), 16 mg chol., 448 mg sodium, 31 g carb., 4 g fiber, 6 g pro.* **Diabetic Exchanges:** *2 starch, 1½ fat.*

## EAT SMART
# Thyme-Roasted Vegetables

**PREP:** 25 MIN. • **BAKE:** 45 MIN.
**MAKES:** 10 SERVINGS (¾ CUP EACH)

- 2 pounds red potatoes, cubed (about 9 cups)
- 3 cups sliced sweet onions (about 1½ large)
- 3 medium carrots, sliced
- ½ pound medium fresh mushrooms, halved
- 1 large sweet red pepper, cut into 1½-inch pieces
- 1 large sweet yellow pepper, cut into 1½-inch pieces
- 2 tablespoons butter, melted
- 2 tablespoons olive oil
- 1 tablespoon minced fresh thyme or 1 teaspoon dried thyme
- 1 teaspoon salt
- ¼ teaspoon pepper

**1.** Preheat oven to 400°. In a large bowl, combine the vegetables. Add remaining ingredients; toss to coat.
**2.** Transfer to a 15x10x1-in. baking pan. Roast 45-50 minutes or until tender, stirring occasionally.
**PER SERVING** *151 cal., 5 g fat (2 g sat. fat), 6 mg chol., 274 mg sodium, 24 g carb., 4 g fiber, 3 g pro.* **Diabetic Exchanges:** *1 starch, 1 vegetable, 1 fat.*

THYME-ROASTED VEGETABLES

RED & GREEN SALAD
WITH TOASTED ALMONDS

## EAT SMART  FAST FIX ▷
# Red & Green Salad with Toasted Almonds

**START TO FINISH:** 25 MIN. • **MAKES:** 12 SERVINGS (1⅓ CUPS EACH)

- ¼ cup red wine vinegar
- 1 tablespoon reduced-sodium soy sauce
- 2 garlic cloves, minced
- 2 teaspoons sesame oil
- 2 teaspoons honey
- 1 teaspoon minced fresh gingerroot or ½ teaspoon ground ginger
- ⅛ teaspoon Louisiana-style hot sauce
- ½ cup grapeseed or canola oil

**SALAD**
- 2 heads Boston or Bibb lettuce, torn
- 1 head red leaf lettuce
- 1 medium sweet red pepper, julienned
- 2 celery ribs, sliced
- 1 cup sliced English cucumber
- 1 cup frozen peas, thawed
- 1 cup grape tomatoes, halved
- 1 cup sliced almonds, toasted

**1.** In a small bowl, whisk the first seven ingredients. Gradually whisk in grapeseed oil until blended.
**2.** In a large bowl, combine lettuces, red pepper, celery, cucumber, peas and tomatoes. Just before serving, pour dressing over salad and toss to coat. Sprinkle with almonds.
**NOTE** *To toast nuts, spread them in a 15x10x1-in. baking pan. Bake at 350° for 5-10 minutes or until lightly browned, stirring occasionally. Or, spread the nuts in a dry nonstick skillet and heat over low heat until lightly browned, stirring them occasionally.*
**PER SERVING** *168 cal., 14 g fat (1 g sat. fat), 0 chol., 90 mg sodium, 8 g carb., 3 g fiber, 4 g pro.* **Diabetic Exchanges:** *3 fat, 1 vegetable.*

# Mom's Specialties

Give it up for Mom! Five family cooks share a **favorite childhood recipe** from the women who taught them that **cooking is love**.

When I was a newlywed living in another state, I would call my mom, Maxine Haynes, and she'd help me with recipes like Sunday Pork Roast over the phone. Now I'm back in my hometown of Memphis and, though my cooking style has changed, being in the kitchen still reminds me of Mom and her home cooking.

—**SANDI PICHON** MEMPHIS, TN

**EAT SMART**
## Sunday Pork Roast

**PREP:** 20 MIN. • **BAKE:** 1 HOUR 10 MIN. + STANDING
**MAKES:** 12 SERVINGS

- 2  medium onions, chopped
- 2  medium carrots, chopped
- 1  celery rib, chopped
- 4  tablespoons all-purpose flour, divided
- 1  bay leaf, finely crushed
- ½  teaspoon dried thyme
- 1¼  teaspoons salt, divided
- 1¼  teaspoons pepper, divided
- 1  boneless pork loin roast (3 to 4 pounds)
- ⅓  cup packed brown sugar

**1.** Preheat oven to 350°. Place the vegetables on bottom of a shallow roasting pan. Mix 2 tablespoons flour, bay leaf, thyme, and 1 teaspoon each salt and pepper; rub over roast. Place roast on top of the vegetables, fat side up. Add 1 cup water to pan.

**2.** Roast 1 hour, basting once with the pan juices if desired. Sprinkle brown sugar over the roast. Roast 10-15 minutes longer or until a thermometer reads 140°. (Temperature of roast will continue to rise about 5-10° upon standing.)

**3.** Remove the roast to a platter. Tent with foil; let stand 15 minutes before slicing.

**4.** Strain the drippings from roasting pan into a measuring cup; discard vegetables. Skim fat. Add enough water to the drippings to measure 1½ cups.

**5.** In a small saucepan, whisk remaining flour and ⅓ cup water until smooth. Gradually whisk in drippings mixture and remaining salt and pepper. Bring to a boil, stirring constantly; cook and stir 2 minutes or until thickened. Serve roast with gravy.

**FREEZE OPTION** *Freeze cooled sliced pork and gravy in freezer containers. To use, partially thaw in refrigerator overnight. Heat through in a covered saucepan, gently stirring and adding a little broth or water if necessary.*

**PER SERVING** *148 cal., 5 g fat (2 g sat. fat), 46 mg chol., 287 mg sodium, 8 g carb., trace fiber, 16 g pro.* **Diabetic Exchanges:** *2 lean meat, ½ starch.*

I used to help my mother, Vicki Pinner, make dinner dishes like My Mom's Best Meat Loaf. Eventually, the job would get too messy for little hands, and she would have to take over. When I prepare this meat loaf now, I always think of her. My stepson even asked to have it on his birthday—just like I used to do on mine.

—**KELLY SIMMONS** HOPKINSVILLE, KY

## My Mom's Best Meat Loaf

**PREP:** 10 MIN. • **BAKE:** 1 HOUR + STANDING
**MAKES:** 8 SERVINGS

- ½  cup chili sauce
- ¼  cup ketchup
- 2  cups Rice Krispies
- 1  medium onion, finely chopped
- 1  small green or sweet red pepper, finely chopped
- ¾  cup shredded part-skim mozzarella cheese
- 1  egg, lightly beaten
- ½  teaspoon salt

SUNDAY PORK ROAST

MY MOM'S BEST MEAT LOAF

## Swedish Creme

**PREP:** 20 MIN. + CHILLING • **MAKES:** 8 SERVINGS

- 2 cups heavy whipping cream
- 1 cup plus 2 teaspoons sugar, divided
- 1 envelope unflavored gelatin
- 1 teaspoon vanilla extract
- 1 teaspoon almond extract
- 2 cups (16 ounces) sour cream
- 1 cup fresh or frozen red raspberries

**1.** In a large saucepan, combine heavy whipping cream and 1 cup sugar; cook and stir over low heat until a thermometer reads 160°(do not allow to boil). Stir in the gelatin until completely dissolved.
**2.** Remove from heat; stir in the extracts. Cool 10 minutes. Whisk in the sour cream. Pour into eight dessert dishes. Refrigerate at least 1 hour.
**3.** Just before serving, lightly crush raspberries; gently stir in remaining sugar. Spoon over tops.
**PER SERVING** *440 cal., 32 g fat (21 g sat. fat), 122 mg chol., 55 mg sodium, 32 g carb., 1 g fiber, 4 g pro.*

SWEDISH CREME

¼ teaspoon pepper
2 pounds ground beef

**1.** Preheat oven to 350°. In a small bowl, mix the chili sauce and ketchup. In a large bowl, combine Rice Krispies, onion, green pepper, cheese, egg, salt and pepper; stir in half of the chili sauce mixture. Add beef; mix lightly but thoroughly.
**2.** Transfer the beef mixture to an ungreased 9x5-in. loaf pan. Make a shallow indentation down the center of loaf. Spread remaining chili sauce mixture over loaf, being sure to fill indentation.
**3.** Bake 60-70 minutes or until a thermometer reads 160°; use a turkey baster to remove drippings every 20 minutes. Let stand 10 minutes before slicing.
**PER SERVING** *299 cal., 16 g fat (6 g sat. fat), 103 mg chol., 657 mg sodium, 14 g carb., 1 g fiber, 24 g pro.*

My mother, Clara Martha Victoria Bergstrom (shown at right), was a teacher when my younger brother and I were kids. Our family lived in California, but my mother was from a Swedish Minnesota farm family. Whenever she was feeling homesick, she'd whip up comforting Midwestern foods like her Swedish Creme dessert. These dishes helped bring her back to her roots.
—**LINDA NILSEN** ANOKA, MN

P.S. I LOVE YOU CAKE

1. Grease a 13x9-in. baking pan. Prepare cake mix batter according to the package directions, adding pudding mix, poppy seeds and extract before mixing batter. Transfer to prepared pan. Bake and cool as package directs.

2. Using a fork, poke holes in top of cake. In a small bowl, whisk milk and pudding mix 2 minutes. Pour over cake. Refrigerate until pudding is set, about 20 minutes.

3. For topping, in a large bowl, gently mix whipped topping, pudding mix and milk until blended. Spread over the cake; sprinkle with poppy seeds. Refrigerate until serving.

**PER SERVING** *318 cal., 15 g fat (5 g sat. fat), 45 mg chol., 420 mg sodium, 43 g carb., 1 g fiber, 4 g pro.*

Born in Toledo, my mom, Barbara Barocsi (shown below), learned her cooking skills from her own mother. Mom worked full time when we were kids, but she still made from-scratch dishes such as Sour Cream Cucumbers. She planned meals on Sundays to prepare for the week ahead, and now I do, too.
—**PAMELA EATON** MONCLOVA, OH

**⑤INGREDIENTS EAT SMART**

## Sour Cream Cucumbers

**PREP:** 15 MIN. + CHILLING • **MAKES:** 8 SERVINGS

½ cup sour cream
3 tablespoons white vinegar
1 tablespoon sugar
   Pepper to taste
4 medium cucumbers, peeled if desired and thinly sliced
1 small sweet onion, thinly sliced and separated into rings

In a large bowl, whisk the sour cream, vinegar, sugar and pepper until blended. Add the cucumbers and sweet onion; toss to coat. Refrigerate, covered, at least 4 hours. Serve with a slotted spoon.

**PER SERVING** *62 cal., 3 g fat (2 g sat. fat), 10 mg chol., 5 mg sodium, 7 g carb., 2 g fiber, 2 g pro. **Diabetic Exchanges:** 1 vegetable, ½ fat.*

Now that I have my own family, my mother, Marion Pahs, and I like to pool our recipe ideas. She even sleeps with a notepad and pen next to her bed in case she gets inspired during the night! Mom cooks and bakes all kinds of dishes that she dreams up in her cozy cabin nestled in the woods of Hatfield, Wisconsin. Our family is always happy to taste creations like P.S. I Love You Cake.
—**SUE GROETSCH** LACROSSE, WI

## P.S. I Love You Cake

**PREP:** 25 MIN. + CHILLING • **BAKE:** 30 MIN. + COOLING
**MAKES:** 15 SERVINGS

1 yellow cake mix (regular size)
1 package (3.4 ounces) instant coconut cream pudding mix
¼ cup poppy seeds
½ teaspoon coconut extract
**FILLING**
2 cups 2% milk
1 package (3.4 ounces) instant vanilla pudding mix
**TOPPING**
1 carton (8 ounces) frozen whipped topping, thawed
¼ cup instant coconut cream pudding mix
3 tablespoons 2% milk
½ teaspoon poppy seeds

SOUR CREAM CUCUMBERS

# Home Away From Home

**Stir things up** and break away from your dinnertime routine with this mom's **sensational Thai recipe**.

RECIPE & STORY BY **MONNIE NORASING** | MANSFIELD, TX

My family fled from Thailand to Woodstock, Minnesota, to escape the Communists when I was 11. Minnesota in January was a world away from our tropical monsoon climate. We had never seen snow—or the oatmeal, pancakes and scrambled eggs the church ladies made us for breakfast.

Because we barely spoke English, we couldn't ask what we were eating. But one day we saw rice at a store when our sponsors from the First American Reformed Church took us there. Eventually, we found fish sauce and soy sauce, too—just enough Asian ingredients to overcome our homesickness. I remember the eggs my mom made. They were fried with fish sauce and served with rice.

Now, Mom tends a backyard of Thai ingredients at her home in Texas: bamboo shoots, kaffir lime and banana trees, lemongrass, bitter melon and mustard greens among them. When my family—now scattered from Hawaii to Germany—gets together, the meal is like a homecoming. But even when it's just my sons, Roman and Raden, my husband, Max Rattanakone, and me, I love to make Thai dishes.

Being a family means coming together in the kitchen, where good things happen. That's a lesson I'm proud to have learned from my mom.

COCONUT CURRY CHICKEN SOUP

## Coconut Curry Chicken Soup

**PREP:** 20 MIN. • **COOK:** 35 MIN. • **MAKES:** 6 SERVINGS

- 2 **cans (13.66 ounces each) coconut milk**
- ⅓ to ½ **cup red curry paste**
- 1 **package (8.8 ounces) thin rice noodles**
- 2 **cans (14½ ounces each) chicken broth**
- ¼ **cup packed brown sugar**
- 2 **tablespoons fish sauce or soy sauce**
- ¾ **teaspoon garlic salt**
- 3 **cups shredded rotisserie chicken**
- 1½ **cups shredded cabbage**
- 1½ **cups shredded carrots**
- ¾ **cup bean sprouts**
  **Fresh basil and cilantro leaves**

**1.** In a Dutch oven, bring the coconut milk to a boil. Cook, uncovered, 10-12 minutes or until the liquid is reduced to 3 cups. Stir in the curry paste until completely dissolved.

**2.** Meanwhile, prepare the rice noodles according to the package directions.

**3.** Add the chicken broth, brown sugar, fish sauce and garlic salt to the curry mixture; return to a boil. Reduce the heat; simmer, uncovered, 10 minutes, stirring occasionally. Stir in chicken; heat through.

**4.** Drain the noodles; divide among six large soup bowls. Ladle the soup over noodles; top servings with vegetables, basil and cilantro.

**NOTE** *The soup recipe was tested with Thai Kitchen Red Curry Paste.*

**PER SERVING** *601 cal., 34 g fat (26 g sat. fat), 65 mg chol., 1,722 mg sodium, 50 g carb., 4 g fiber, 27 g pro.*

**RAINBOW CAKE
WITH CLOUDS**
PAGE 209

# Field Editor Favorites

*Taste of Home* Field Editors—cooks like you from around the country—**love to share** their best-loved recipes. Enjoy this chapter of favorites that are sure to please **your own family**.

**APPLE & CHEDDAR
MINI SCONES**
*PAGE 214*

**NO-BAKE FUDGY
COCONUT COOKIES**
*PAGE 213*

**SWEET POTATO
CINNAMON BREAD**
*PAGE 217*

# Shamrock Sweets

Our Field Editors know a St. Patrick's Day party isn't complete unless there's a little something for guests at the end of the rainbow.

## Shamrock Cutout Pound Cake

**PREP:** 1 HOUR • **BAKE:** 50 MIN. + COOLING
**MAKES:** 1 LOAF (16 SLICES)

2   **packages (16 ounces each) pound cake mix**
10  **drops green food coloring**
½   **teaspoon peppermint extract**
**GLAZE**
1   **cup confectioners' sugar**
⅛   **teaspoon peppermint extract**
3   **to 5 teaspoons 2% milk**

**1.** Preheat oven according to package directions. Grease a 9x5-in. loaf pan. Prepare one package cake mix according to package directions, adding food coloring and extract before mixing batter. Transfer to prepared pan. Bake and cool as package directs.

**2.** Cut cooled cake into 1-in. thick slices. Cut slices with a 2½-in. shamrock-shaped cookie cutter (save remaining cake for another use). Stand the shamrock slices at an angle in a greased 9x5-in. loaf pan.

**3.** Prepare the remaining cake mix according to package directions. Pour batter around and over shamrock slices. Bake and cool as package directs.

**4.** For the glaze, in a small bowl, mix confectioners' sugar, extract and enough milk to reach desired consistency. Pour glaze over cake, allowing some to flow over sides.

**NOTE** *Remaining pound cake may be cubed and served in dessert dishes, layered with warm fudge sauce. Top with chopped mint Andes candies.*

**PER SERVING** *462 cal., 23 g fat (8 g sat. fat), 91 mg chol., 339 mg sodium, 60 g carb., 0 fiber, 6 g pro.*

My son Gabriel gets a kick out of the surprise inside Shamrock Cutout Pound Cake. And guests always want to know the secret to creating it!
—**ANGELA LIVELY** SPRING, TX

SHAMROCK CUTOUT POUND CAKE

RAINBOW CAKE
WITH CLOUDS

## Rainbow Cake with Clouds

This spectacular dessert stands on its own—no frosting needed!
Use a little whipped cream to make fluffy clouds.
**—JANET TIGCHELAAR** JERSEYVILLE, ON

**PREP:** 30 MIN. • **BAKE:** 40 MIN. + COOLING • **MAKES:** 16 SERVINGS

- 1  **package white cake mix (regular size)**
   **Purple, blue, green, yellow, orange and red paste food coloring**
- 1  **cup heavy whipping cream**
- 3  **tablespoons confectioners' sugar**
- ½  **teaspoon vanilla extract**

**1.** Preheat oven to 325°. Grease and flour a 10-in. fluted tube pan. Prepare the cake mix according to the package directions. Transfer 1⅓ cups batter to the prepared pan; spread evenly. Remove an additional 2 tablespoons batter to a small bowl; reserve.

**2.** Divide remaining batter into six separate bowls, tinting each with food coloring to make the following: 2 tablespoons purple batter, ¼ cup blue batter, ⅓ cup green batter, ½ cup yellow batter, ⅔ cup orange batter, and remaining batter red.

**3.** Fill six small food-safe plastic bags with a different color batter. Cut a small hole in a corner of red batter bag; pipe a wide ring onto white batter to within ½ in. of pan edges. Pipe a ring of orange in the middle of red ring, leaving some red visible on each side. Repeat by piping remaining colors in the middle of the previous layer, in rainbow color order. (Each ring will be narrower than the previous layer.) Fill a bag with reserved white batter; pipe over purple ring only.

**4.** Bake for 40-45 minutes or until a toothpick inserted in center comes out clean. Cool completely in pan on wire rack.

**5.** Remove the cake from the pan; place on a serving plate. In a bowl, beat the heavy whipping cream until it begins to thicken. Add confectioners' sugar and vanilla; beat until soft peaks form. Serve cake with whipped cream clouds.

**NOTE** *To remove cakes easily, use solid shortening to grease plain and fluted tube pans.*

**PER SERVING** *208 cal., 11 g fat (4 g sat. fat), 20 mg chol., 216 mg sodium, 24 g carb., 0 fiber, 2 g pro.*

## Caramelized Baked Custards

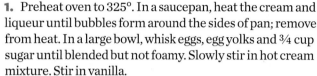

**PREP:** 20 MIN. + CHILLING • **BAKE:** 20 MIN. • **MAK**

- 2  **cups heavy whipping cream**
- ¼  **cup Irish cream liqueur**
- 3  **eggs**
- 2  **egg yolks**
- ¾  **cup plus 2 tablespoons sugar, divided**
- 1  **teaspoon vanilla extract**

**1.** Preheat oven to 325°. In a saucepan, heat the cream and liqueur until bubbles form around the sides of pan; remove from heat. In a large bowl, whisk eggs, egg yolks and ¾ cup sugar until blended but not foamy. Slowly stir in hot cream mixture. Stir in vanilla.

**2.** Place six 6-oz. broiler-safe ramekins in a baking pan large enough to hold them without touching. Pour cream mixture into ramekins. Place pan on oven rack; add very hot water to pan to within ½ in. of top of ramekins.

**3.** Bake 20-25 minutes or until a knife inserted near center comes out clean; centers will still be soft. Immediately remove the ramekins from the water bath to a wire rack; cool 10 minutes. Refrigerate until cold.

**4.** To caramelize the topping with a kitchen torch, sprinkle the custards evenly with remaining sugar. Hold the torch flame about 2 in. above custard surface and rotate it slowly until the sugar is evenly caramelized. Serve immediately or refrigerate up to 1 hour.

**5.** To caramelize the topping in a broiler, place ramekins on a baking sheet; let stand at room temperature 15 minutes. Preheat broiler. Sprinkle custards evenly with remaining sugar. Broil 3-4 in. from heat 5-7 minutes or until sugar is caramelized. Serve immediately or refrigerate up to 1 hour.

**PER SERVING** *481 cal., 35 g fat (20 g sat. fat), 283 mg chol., 68 mg sodium, 34 g carb., 0 fiber, 6 g pro.*

I combined creme brulee and Irish cream liqueur to make my Caramelized Baked Custards.
**—JOYCE MOYNIHAN** LAKEVILLE, MN

CARAMELIZED BAKED CUSTARDS

# Ready for Rhubarb

Head to the garden patch! After a long winter, Field Editors like to share their best sweet-tart rhubarb treats with friends and family.

> I describe Rhubarbecue as a roller-coaster ride for your taste buds! The sauce is a complex blend of flavors and goes with many meats.
> —**RD STENDEL-FREELS** ALBUQUERQUE, NM

## Rhubarbecue

**PREP:** 45 MIN. • **BAKE:** 2½ HOURS • **MAKES:** 8 SERVINGS

- 1½ teaspoons salt
- 1½ teaspoons paprika
- 1 teaspoon coarsely ground pepper
- 3 to 4 pounds boneless country-style pork ribs

**SAUCE**

- 3 cups sliced fresh or frozen rhubarb (about 7 stalks)
- 2 cups fresh strawberries, halved
- 2 to 3 tablespoons olive oil
- 1 medium onion, chopped
- 1 cup packed brown sugar
- ¾ cup ketchup
- ½ cup red wine vinegar
- ½ cup bourbon
- ¼ cup reduced-sodium soy sauce
- ¼ cup honey
- 2 tablespoons Worcestershire sauce
- 2 teaspoons garlic powder
- 1 teaspoon crushed red pepper flakes
- 1 teaspoon coarsely ground pepper

1. Preheat oven to 325°. Mix the salt, paprika and pepper; sprinkle over the pork ribs. Refrigerate, covered, while preparing sauce.
2. In a large saucepan, combine the rhubarb and strawberries; add water to cover. Bring to a boil. Cook, uncovered, 8-10 minutes or until the rhubarb is tender. Drain rhubarb and strawberries; return to the pan. Mash until blended.
3. In an ovenproof Dutch oven, heat 1 tablespoon oil over medium heat. Brown ribs in batches, adding additional oil as needed. Remove from pan.

RHUBARBECUE

4. Add the onion to the same pan; cook and stir 4-6 minutes or until tender. Add the remaining ingredients; stir in the rhubarb mixture. Return the ribs to the pan, turning to coat. Bring to a boil. Cover and bake 2 hours or until the ribs are tender. Bake, uncovered, 30-35 minutes or until the sauce is slightly thickened.

**PER SERVING** *533 cal., 19 g fat (6 g sat. fat), 98 mg chol., 1,158 mg sodium, 52 g carb., 2 g fiber, 31 g pro.*

### (top tip) Fruit from the Freezer

In spring, I clean and chop fresh rhubarb, then place 3-cup portions in freezer bags and pop them in the freezer. In summer, I do the same with just-picked strawberries. With the premeasured ingredients, I can whip up batches of our favorite strawberry-rhubarb jam whenever we want it.
—**HARRIET MILLER** STEWARTVILLE, MN

## Rhubarb Scones

**PREP:** 30 MIN. • **BAKE:** 20 MIN. • **MAKES:** 16 SCONES

- 1¼ cups whole wheat pastry flour
- 1¼ cups all-purpose flour
- ½ cup sugar
- 1 tablespoon baking powder
- 1 teaspoon ground cardamom
- ½ teaspoon salt
- ½ cup unsalted butter, cubed
- 1½ cups finely chopped fresh or frozen rhubarb, thawed (3-4 stalks)
- ½ cup heavy whipping cream
- ¼ cup fat-free milk
- 1 teaspoon vanilla extract
- Coarse sugar

**1.** Preheat oven to 400°. In a large bowl, whisk the first six ingredients. Cut in butter until mixture resembles coarse crumbs. Add rhubarb; toss to coat.

**2.** In another bowl, whisk cream, milk and vanilla; stir into crumb mixture just until moistened.

**3.** Turn the dough onto a floured surface; knead gently 4-5 times. Divide dough in half; pat into two 6-in. circles. Cut each into eight wedges. Place wedges on parchment paper-lined baking sheets; sprinkle with coarse sugar. Bake 18-22 minutes or until golden brown. Serve warm.

**NOTE** *If using frozen rhubarb, measure rhubarb while still frozen, then thaw completely. Drain in a colander, but do not press liquid out.*

**PER SERVING** *166 cal., 9 g fat (5 g sat. fat), 25 mg chol., 155 mg sodium, 20 g carb., 1 g fiber, 2 g pro.*

My grandfather's garden supplies us with a crop we put to good use in yummy Rhubarb Scones.
—**DANIELLE ULAM** HOOKSTOWN, PA

RHUBARB SCONES

ROSY RHUBARB UPSIDE-DOWN CAKE

## Rosy Rhubarb Upside-Down Cake

Looking for a wonderful springtime dessert for guests? Look no further! This delightful, rosy-colored cake is moist on top and light as a feather on the bottom. Cinnamon and nutmeg add a bit of spice.
—**DAWN LOWENSTEIN** HATBORO, PA

**PREP:** 35 MIN. • **BAKE:** 35 MIN. + COOLING • **MAKES:** 9 SERVINGS

- 3 cups cubed fresh or frozen rhubarb (1-inch, about 8 stalks)
- ¾ cup sugar
- ¾ cup water
- 1 tablespoon lemon juice
- ½ teaspoon ground cinnamon
- ¼ teaspoon ground nutmeg

**CAKE**

- 3 tablespoons butter, melted
- ¼ cup packed brown sugar
- 1 cup all-purpose flour
- 1 teaspoon baking powder
- ¼ teaspoon salt
- 2 eggs
- ⅔ cup sugar
- 1 teaspoon lemon extract

**1.** Preheat oven to 350°. In a large saucepan, combine the first six ingredients; bring to a boil. Reduce heat; simmer, uncovered, 6-8 minutes or until rhubarb is crisp-tender, stirring to dissolve sugar. Drain, reserving 6 tablespoons cooking liquid.

**2.** Pour butter into an 8-in.-square baking dish. Sprinkle with the brown sugar; top with drained rhubarb. Sift flour, baking powder and salt together twice.

**3.** In a large bowl, beat the eggs on high speed for 3 minutes. Gradually add sugar, beating until thick and lemon-colored. Beat in the extract and reserved cooking liquid. Fold in flour mixture. Pour over rhubarb. Bake 35-40 minutes or until top springs back when lightly touched.

**4.** Cool for 10 minutes before inverting onto a serving plate. Serve warm.

**PER SERVING** *257 cal., 5 g fat (3 g sat. fat), 57 mg chol., 157 mg sodium, 50 g carb., 1 g fiber, 3 g pro.*

# Summery Sensations

As these Field Editors know, homemade treats and summertime go hand in hand. Serve them up and get ready to see happy faces!

## Soft Blueberry Button Cookies

I look back fondly on picking blueberries and sipping lemonade at my aunt's house. This recipe is my way of combining those flavors and memories. I place the berries on top so they resemble the holes of a button.
—**RENEE MURBY** JOHNSTON, RI

**PREP:** 30 MIN. • **BAKE:** 15 MIN./BATCH • **MAKES:** ABOUT 2½ DOZEN

- ½ cup butter, softened
- ½ cup sugar
- ½ cup packed brown sugar
- 1½ teaspoons grated lemon peel
- 1 egg
- ½ cup fat-free lemon Greek yogurt
- ⅓ cup blueberry juice cocktail
- 1 teaspoon almond extract
- 2 cups all-purpose flour
- 1½ teaspoons ground cinnamon
- 1 teaspoon baking powder
- ¼ teaspoon salt
- ¼ teaspoon baking soda
- 1 to 1½ cups fresh blueberries

**GLAZE**
- 1 cup confectioners' sugar
- 2 tablespoons blueberry juice cocktail
- 1 tablespoon butter, melted

**1.** Preheat oven to 350°. In a large bowl, cream butter, sugars and lemon peel until light and fluffy. Beat in egg. Beat in yogurt, juice and extract until blended. In another bowl, whisk the flour, cinnamon, baking powder, salt and baking soda; gradually beat into creamed mixture.

**2.** Drop dough by rounded tablespoonfuls 2 in. apart onto ungreased baking sheets. Press four blueberries into each cookie to resemble a button.

**3.** Bake 13-15 minutes or until the edges begin to brown. Remove from pans to wire racks to cool slightly.

**4.** In a small bowl, mix the glaze ingredients until smooth. Spoon over the warm cookies. Let stand until set. Store in airtight containers.

**PER SERVING** *114 cal., 4 g fat (2 g sat. fat), 16 mg chol., 74 mg sodium, 19 g carb., trace fiber, 1 g pro.*

SOFT BLUEBERRY BUTTON COOKIES

GIANT LEMON SUGAR COOKIES

## No-Bake Fudgy Coconut Cookies

**PREP:** 30 MIN. + CHILLING • **MAKES:** 3½ DOZEN

1½ cups sugar
⅔ cup 2% milk
½ cup baking cocoa
½ cup butter, cubed
½ teaspoon salt
⅓ cup creamy peanut butter
1 teaspoon vanilla extract
2 cups quick-cooking oats
1 cup flaked coconut
½ cup white baking chips
1 teaspoon shortening

**1.** In a large saucepan, combine the first five ingredients. Bring to a boil, stirring constantly. Cook and stir 3 minutes.
**2.** Remove from heat; stir in the peanut butter and vanilla until blended. Stir in the oats and coconut. Drop mixture by tablespoonfuls onto waxed paper-lined baking sheets.
**3.** In a microwave, melt the baking chips and shortening; stir until smooth. Drizzle over cookies; refrigerate until set. Store in airtight containers.
**PER SERVING** *101 cal., 5 g fat (3 g sat. fat), 6 mg chol., 63 mg sodium, 13 g carb., 1 g fiber, 2 g pro.*

My Giant Lemon Sugar Cookies get their tang from both the fruit juice and zest. Coarse sugar adds sparkle.
—**MICHAEL VYSKOCIL** GLEN ROCK, PA

When my daughter works at summer camp, I send her treats like No-Bake Fudgy Coconut Cookies.
—**SUE KLEMM** RHINELANDER, WI

## Giant Lemon Sugar Cookies

**PREP:** 25 MIN. • **BAKE:** 15 MIN./BATCH • **MAKES:** 14 COOKIES

1 cup unsalted butter, softened
1½ cups sugar
½ cup packed brown sugar
2 eggs
1½ teaspoons grated lemon peel
2 tablespoons lemon juice
3 cups all-purpose flour
1 teaspoon baking soda
¼ teaspoon salt
¼ teaspoon cream of tartar
4 teaspoons coarse sugar

**1.** Preheat oven to 350°. In a large bowl, cream butter and sugars until light and fluffy. Beat in eggs. Beat in lemon peel and juice. In another bowl, whisk the flour, baking soda, salt and cream of tartar; gradually beat into creamed mixture.
**2.** Shape ¼ cupfuls of cookie dough into balls. Place 6 in. apart on greased baking sheets. Flatten to ¾-in. thickness with bottom of a measuring cup. Lightly brush the tops with water; sprinkle with coarse sugar.
**3.** Bake 12-15 minutes or until light brown. Remove from the pans to wire racks to cool completely. Store cookies in airtight containers.
**PER SERVING** *340 cal., 14 g fat (8 g sat. fat), 65 mg chol., 147 mg sodium, 51 g carb., 1 g fiber, 4 g pro.*

NO-BAKE FUDGY COCONUT COOKIES

# Fun Fall Starters

Fondue, fritters and scones are a happy excuse for a neighborhood drop-in. These Field Editors share their best fall bites, ideal for a full house.

*With a sprinkling of sage, Apple & Cheddar Mini Scones will add zip to an autumn brunch, tailgate party or other get-together.*

—SUE GRONHOLZ BEAVER DAM, WI

## Apple & Cheddar Mini Scones

**PREP:** 25 MIN. • **BAKE:** 10 MIN. • **MAKES:** 32 SCONES

- 3 **cups all-purpose flour**
- 3 **teaspoons baking powder**
- ½ **teaspoon salt**
- ½ **teaspoon baking soda**
- 1 **cup cold butter**
- 1 **egg**
- ¾ **cup (6 ounces) vanilla yogurt**
- 3 **tablespoons 2% milk, divided**
- ⅓ **cup shredded peeled apple**
- ⅓ **cup shredded sharp cheddar cheese**
- 1 **tablespoon minced fresh sage**
- 1 **tablespoon sugar**

**1.** Preheat oven to 425°. In a large bowl, whisk flour, baking powder, salt and baking soda. Cut in butter until mixture resembles coarse crumbs. In another bowl, whisk the egg, yogurt and 2 tablespoons milk; stir into crumb mixture just until moistened. Stir in apple, cheese and sage.

**2.** Turn the dough onto a lightly floured surface; knead it gently 10 times. Divide the dough in half; pat each portion into a 6-in. circle. Cut each circle into eight wedges; cut each wedge in half.

**3.** Transfer to parchment paper-lined baking sheets. Brush the tops with the remaining milk; sprinkle with sugar. Bake 10-12 minutes or until golden brown. Serve warm.

**FOR REGULAR-SIZE SCONES** *Do not cut the wedges in half. Bake as directed, increasing baking time to 12-14 minutes. Yield: 16 regular scones*

**PER SERVING** *109 cal., 7 g fat (4 g sat. fat), 23 mg chol., 159 mg sodium, 10 g carb., trace fiber, 2 g pro.*

APPLE & CHEDDAR MINI SCONES

## Spicy Pumpkin Fritters

My husband has disliked vegetables since he was a child. But when he sampled these deep-fried pumpkin fritters, he fell in love! I usually pair them with chipotle mayonnaise or ranch dressing for dipping.
—**TRISHA KRUSE** EAGLE, ID

**PREP:** 10 MIN. • **COOK:** 5 MIN./BATCH • **MAKES:** ABOUT 3 DOZEN

- 1½ cups all-purpose flour
- 2 teaspoons baking powder
- 1¼ teaspoons salt
- ¾ teaspoon chili powder
- ½ teaspoon onion powder
- ¼ teaspoon crushed red pepper flakes
- 2 eggs
- 1 can (15 ounces) solid-pack pumpkin
- ½ cup 2% milk
- 2 tablespoons butter, melted
  Oil for deep-fat frying
  Chipotle mayonnaise, optional

**1.** In a large bowl, whisk the first six ingredients. In another bowl, whisk the eggs, pumpkin, milk and the melted butter until blended. Add to the dry ingredients, stirring just until moistened.

**2.** In an electric skillet or deep fryer, heat the oil to 375°. Drop the batter by tablespoonfuls, a few at a time, into hot oil. Fry 1½ to 2 minutes on each side or until golden brown. Drain on paper towels. Serve warm. If desired, serve with chipotle mayonnaise.

**PER SERVING** *50 cal., 3 g fat (1 g sat. fat), 11 mg chol., 105 mg sodium, 5 g carb., trace fiber, 1 g pro.*

FUN-DO FONDUE

FAST FIX
## Fun-do Fondue

This rich fondue is always a hit when we entertain. The younger crowd likes to dunk bread, while adults prefer fruits or veggies.
—**JUDY BATSON** TAMPA, FL

**START TO FINISH:** 20 MIN. • **MAKES:** 3 CUPS

- 2 cups (8 ounces) shredded Jarlsberg cheese
- ½ cup shredded Swiss cheese
- ¼ cup all-purpose flour
- ½ teaspoon ground mustard
- ½ teaspoon freshly ground pepper
- 1 cup heavy whipping cream
- 1 cup reduced-sodium chicken broth
- 1 tablespoon honey
- 1 teaspoon lemon juice
  Cubed French bread, sliced pears and assorted fresh vegetables

**1.** In a small bowl, combine the first five ingredients; toss to combine. In a saucepan, combine the cream, broth and honey; bring just to a boil, stirring occasionally. Reduce heat to medium-low. Add ½ cup cheese mixture; stir constantly until almost completely melted. Continue adding cheese, ½ cup at a time, allowing cheese to almost melt completely between additions. Continue stirring until thickened and smooth. Stir in lemon juice.

**2.** Transfer the mixture to a heated fondue pot; keep the fondue bubbling gently. Serve with bread cubes, pears and vegetables for dipping. If fondue becomes too thick, stir in a little additional broth.

**PER SERVING** *166 cal., 13 g fat (8 g sat. fat), 43 mg chol., 151 mg sodium, 5 g carb., trace fiber, 7 g pro.*

SPICY PUMPKIN FRITTERS

# Leftovers To Love

Go ahead, check your fridge for ready-made food you can transform today. Turn yesterday's feast into an all-new, deliciously different dish!

## Turkey & Stuffing Eggs Benedict

**PREP:** 20 MIN. • **COOK:** 25 MIN. • **MAKES:** 4 SERVINGS

- 3 **cups leftover cooked stuffing**
- 4 **egg yolks**
- 1 **tablespoon lemon juice**
- ½ **cup butter, melted**
- 1 **tablespoon minced fresh parsley**

**Dash salt**

**Dash ground nutmeg**

- 1 **tablespoon olive oil**
- 4 **eggs**
- ¾ **pound sliced leftover cooked turkey, warmed**

**1.** Shape stuffing into four ½-in.-thick patties; set aside. In top of a double boiler or a metal bowl over simmering water, whisk egg yolks and lemon juice until blended; cook until mixture is just thick enough to coat a metal spoon and temperature reaches 160°, whisking constantly.

**2.** Reduce heat to very low. Very slowly drizzle in the warm melted butter, whisking constantly. Whisk in parsley, salt and nutmeg. Transfer to a small bowl. Place bowl in a larger bowl of warm water. Keep warm, stirring occasionally, until ready to serve, up to 30 minutes.

**3.** In a large nonstick skillet, heat oil over medium heat. Cook the stuffing patties 3-4 minutes on each side or until thermometer reads 165°. Keep warm.

**4.** Meanwhile, place 2-3 in. of water in a large saucepan or skillet with high sides. Bring to a boil; adjust the heat to maintain a gentle simmer. Break cold eggs, one at a time, into a small bowl; holding bowl close to surface of water, slip egg into water.

**5.** Cook, uncovered, 3-5 minutes or until the egg whites are completely set and the egg yolks begin to thicken but are not hard. Using a slotted spoon, lift the eggs out of the water.

**6.** To serve, place the turkey and eggs on stuffing patties. Top with hollandaise sauce.

**PER SERVING** *767 cal., 53 g fat (22 g sat. fat), 541 mg chol., 1,151 mg sodium, 34 g carb., 4 g fiber, 39 g pro.*

Turkey & Stuffing Eggs Benedict may use leftovers, but it looks and tastes special enough to serve with champagne for brunch.
—**BRITTANY ALLYN** NASHVILLE, TN

TURKEY & STUFFING EGGS BENEDICT

**GOBBLE-UP STRATA**

## Sweet Potato Cinnamon Bread

My family enjoys many different kinds of quick bread. This one featuring mashed sweet potatoes is moist and spicy. Don't have mini loaf pans? Follow the directions for a larger size at the end of the recipe.

—**NANCY FOUST** STONEBORO, PA

**PREP:** 20 MIN. • **BAKE:** 35 MIN. + COOLING
**MAKES:** 4 LOAVES (6 SLICES EACH)

- 3½ cups all-purpose flour
- 2⅔ cups sugar
- 2 teaspoons baking soda
- 1 teaspoon salt
- ½ teaspoon baking powder
- 1½ teaspoons ground cinnamon
- 1 teaspoon ground ginger
- ½ teaspoon ground cloves
- 4 eggs
- 2 cups mashed sweet potatoes
- ⅔ cup canola oil
- ⅔ cup 2% milk
- 1½ cups raisins
- 1 cup chopped walnuts

**1.** Preheat oven to 350°. In a large bowl, whisk the first eight ingredients. In another bowl, whisk the eggs, sweet potatoes, oil and milk until blended. Add to flour mixture; stir just until moistened. Fold in raisins and walnuts.
**2.** Transfer to four greased 5¾x3x2-in. loaf pans. Bake for 35-40 minutes or until a toothpick inserted in center comes out clean. Cool in pans 10 minutes before removing to wire racks to cool.
**FOR LARGER LOAVES** *Prepare the recipe as directed, using two greased 9x5-in. loaf pans. Bake in preheated 350° oven 55-60 minutes or until a toothpick inserted near center comes out clean. Yield: 2 loaves (12 slices each).*
**PER SERVING** *299 cal., 10 g fat (1 g sat. fat), 36 mg chol., 236 mg sodium, 49 g carb., 2 g fiber, 4 g pro.*

## Gobble-Up Strata

It's an annual tradition for me to fix my strata after Thanksgiving. We invite our neighbors, and they think it's neat that I create a whole new meal out of the extras from our holiday dinner.

—**BONNIE HAWKINS** ELKHORN, WI

**PREP:** 15 MIN. • **BAKE:** 65 MIN. + STANDING • **MAKES:** 6 SERVINGS

- 3 cups leftover cooked stuffing
- 2 cups cubed leftover cooked turkey
- 4 green onions, thinly sliced
- 1 medium sweet red pepper, finely chopped
- 6 eggs
- 1½ cups 2% milk
- ¼ cup mayonnaise

**1.** Preheat oven to 350°. In a greased 8-in.-square baking dish, layer stuffing, turkey, green onions and pepper. In a large bowl, whisk eggs, milk and mayonnaise until blended. Pour over layers.
**2.** Bake, uncovered, 65-75 minutes or until a knife inserted near the center comes out clean. Let stand for 10 minutes before serving.
**PER SERVING** *433 cal., 24 g fat (6 g sat. fat), 255 mg chol., 728 mg sodium, 27 g carb., 4 g fiber, 26 g pro.*

**SWEET POTATO CINNAMON BREAD**

# December Delights

Take a victory lap in your kitchen—the crown at the Christmas cookie swap is yours! Four Field Editors show you the way to seasonal success.

## Almond Bonbon Cookies

These cookie balls dipped in chocolate and vanilla icing remind me of England—with a touch of America! The center of almond paste makes them extra-special. Have fun adding any kind of sprinkles you like.
—**TERI RASEY** CADILLAC, MI

**PREP:** 20 MIN. • **BAKE:** 10 MIN./BATCH • **MAKES:** 4 DOZEN

- 1 **cup butter, softened**
- ⅔ **cup confectioners' sugar**
- ¼ **cup 2% milk**
- 1 **teaspoon vanilla extract**
- 3 **cups all-purpose flour**
- 1 **package (7 ounces) almond paste**

**VANILLA ICING**
- 1 **cup confectioners' sugar**
- 4½ **teaspoons 2% milk**
- 1 **teaspoon vanilla extract**

**CHOCOLATE ICING**
- 1 **cup confectioners' sugar**
- 1 **ounce unsweetened chocolate, melted and cooled**
- 3 **tablespoons 2% milk**
- 1 **teaspoon vanilla extract**
  **Assorted sprinkles**

**1.** Preheat oven to 375°. In a large bowl, cream butter and confectioners' sugar until light and fluffy. Beat in milk and vanilla. Gradually beat in flour.

**2.** Cut the almond paste into 12 slices (make about ¼ in. thick); cut each slice into quarters. Shape into balls. Wrap tablespoons of prepared cookie dough around the almond paste to cover completely. Place 2 in. apart on ungreased baking sheets.

**3.** Bake 10-12 minutes or until golden brown. Remove to wire racks to cool completely.

**4.** In a small bowl, mix the vanilla icing ingredients until smooth. For chocolate icing, mix the confectioners' sugar, cooled chocolate, milk and vanilla until smooth. Dip the cookies in the icings as desired; allow the excess to drip off. Decorate with sprinkles. Place on waxed paper; let stand until set. Store in airtight containers.

**PER SERVING** *112 cal., 5 g fat (3 g sat. fat), 10 mg chol., 29 mg sodium, 15 g carb., 1 g fiber, 1 g pro.*

## Pistachio Cream Cheese Cookies

My son-in-law is a big fan of pistachios. He looks forward to these buttery, nut-coated goodies every holiday season.
—**LILY JULOW** LAWRENCEVILLE, GA

**PREP:** 30 MIN. + CHILLING • **BAKE:** 10 MIN./BATCH
**MAKES:** 5 DOZEN

- ½ **cup butter, softened**
- 3 **ounces cream cheese, softened**
- 1½ **cups confectioners' sugar**
- 1 **egg**
- 3 **teaspoons grated lemon peel**
- 1½ **teaspoons vanilla extract**
- 1 **to 2 drops green food coloring**
- 2½ **cups all-purpose flour**
- ½ **teaspoon baking powder**
- ½ **teaspoon salt**
- ½ **cup finely chopped pistachios**
- 60 **shelled pistachios (about ⅓ cup)**

**1.** In a large bowl, beat the butter, the cream cheese and confectioners' sugar until blended. Beat in the egg, lemon peel, vanilla and green food coloring. In another bowl, whisk the flour, baking powder and salt; gradually beat into the creamed mixture.

**2.** Divide the dough in half; shape each into a 7½-in.-long roll. Roll in the chopped pistachios. Wrap in plastic wrap. Refrigerate 2 hours or until firm.

**3.** Preheat oven to 375°. Unwrap and cut crosswise into ¼-in. slices. Place 1 in. apart on ungreased baking sheets. Press a whole pistachio into the center of each cookie.

**4.** Bake 7-9 minutes or until edges are lightly browned. Remove from pans to wire racks to cool.

**PER SERVING** *61 cal., 3 g fat (1 g sat. fat), 9 mg chol., 46 mg sodium, 8 g carb., trace fiber, 1 g pro.*

PISTACHIO CREAM CHEESE COOKIES

SANTA CLAUS
SUGAR COOKIES

## Santa Claus Sugar Cookies

At Christmastime, my mother always baked a batch of cutouts shaped like Santa Claus. We'd put the decorated treats into little clear bags tied with ribbon and hang them on the tree. It's a wonderful memory.

—**ANN BUSH** COLORADO CITY, CO

**PREP:** 45 MIN. + CHILLING • **BAKE:** 10 MIN./BATCH
**MAKES:** 4 DOZEN

- 1 cup unsalted butter
- 1½ cups sugar
- 2 eggs
- 1 teaspoon vanilla extract
- 3½ cups all-purpose flour
- 1 teaspoon baking soda
- 1 teaspoon cream of tartar
- ½ teaspoon ground nutmeg
- ¼ teaspoon salt

**FROSTING**

- ¾ cup unsalted butter, softened
- 6 tablespoons 2% milk
- 2¼ teaspoons vanilla extract
- ¼ teaspoon salt
- 6¾ cups confectioners' sugar
  Optional decorations: red colored sugar, miniature semisweet chocolate chips and Red Hots

**1.** In a large bowl, cream butter and sugar until light and fluffy. Beat in eggs and vanilla. In another bowl, whisk flour, baking soda, cream of tartar, nutmeg and salt; gradually beat into creamed mixture.

**2.** Divide the dough in half. Shape each into a disk; wrap in plastic wrap. Refrigerate 1 hour or until firm enough to roll.

**3.** Preheat oven to 375°. On a lightly floured surface, roll each portion of dough to ¼-in. thickness. Cut with a floured 3-in. Santa-shaped cookie cutter. Place 2 in. apart on greased baking sheets.

**4.** Bake 8-10 minutes or until light brown. Remove from pans to wire racks to cool completely.

**5.** For the frosting, in a large bowl, beat the butter until creamy. Beat in the milk, vanilla and salt. Gradually beat in

confectioners' sugar until smooth. Pipe onto the cookies and decorate as desired.

**PER SERVING** *186 cal., 7 g fat (4 g sat. fat), 27 mg chol., 56 mg sodium, 30 g carb., trace fiber, 1 g pro.*

## My Christmas Fudge

After years of searching for just the right fudge, I discovered one that's virtually foolproof and so creamy you won't believe it.

—**BARB MILLER** OAKDALE, MN

**PREP:** 15 MIN. • **COOK:** 10 MIN. + COOLING
**MAKES:** 5¾ POUNDS (96 PIECES)

- 4½ cups sugar
- 1 can (12 ounces) evaporated milk
- ½ cup butter, cubed
- 2 packages (11½ ounces each) milk chocolate chips
- 4½ cups miniature marshmallows
- 2 ounces unsweetened chocolate, chopped
- 3 cups chopped walnuts, toasted
- 2 teaspoons vanilla extract
- 4 ounces white baking chocolate, melted

**1.** Line a 13x9-in. pan with foil; coat with cooking spray.

**2.** In a heavy Dutch oven, combine sugar, milk and butter. Bring to a rapid boil over medium heat, stirring constantly. Cook and stir 5 minutes. Remove from heat.

**3.** Stir in chips, marshmallows and chopped chocolate until melted. Fold in nuts and vanilla. Immediately spread into prepared pan. Drizzle with melted chocolate; cool completely.

**4.** Using the foil, lift the fudge out of the pan. Remove foil; cut fudge into 96 squares. Store between layers of waxed paper in airtight containers.

**NOTE** *To toast the nuts, spread in a 15x10x1-in. baking pan. Bake them at 350° for 5-10 minutes or until lightly browned, stirring occasionally. Or, spread in a dry nonstick skillet and heat over low heat until lightly browned, stirring occasionally.*

**PER SERVING** *127 cal., 6 g fat (2 g sat. fat), 6 mg chol., 18 mg sodium, 17 g carb., 1 g fiber, 2 g pro.*

MY CHRISTMAS FUDGE

**MUSHROOM & SWISS
PITA PIZZAS**
*PAGE 225*

# Quick Fixes

Even the busiest schedules are no match for the **super-fast fare** in this chapter! So skip the trip to the drive-thru and enjoy a meal of home-cooked dishes you can fix in **30 minutes or less**.

**SIRLOIN STIR-FRY WITH RAMEN NOODLES**
*PAGE 222*

**SMOKY GOUDA & CHICKEN SANDWICHES**
*PAGE 229*

**EASY ASIAN CHICKEN SLAW**
*PAGE 234*

# Sirloin Stir-Fry with Ramen Noodles

One day when I was craving Chinese food but didn't want takeout, I stirred together this meal-in-one. Any leftovers taste just as good reheated the next day.

—**ANNETTE HEMSATH** SUTHERLIN, OR

**START TO FINISH:** 30 MIN.
**MAKES:** 4 SERVINGS

- 2 **packages (3 ounces each) beef ramen noodles**
- 2 **tablespoons cornstarch**
- 2 **cups beef broth, divided**
- 1 **pound beef top sirloin steak, cut into thin strips**
- 2 **tablespoons canola oil**
- 2 **tablespoons reduced-sodium soy sauce**
- 2 **cans (14 ounces each) whole baby corn, rinsed and drained**
- 2 **cups fresh broccoli florets**
- 1 **cup diced sweet red pepper**
- 1 **cup shredded carrots**
- 4 **green onions, cut into 1-inch pieces**
- ½ **cup unsalted peanuts**

**1.** Set aside the seasoning packets from the ramen noodles. Cook ramen noodles according to the package directions.

**2.** Meanwhile, in a small bowl, combine the cornstarch and ¼ cup beef broth until smooth; set aside. In a large skillet or wok, stir-fry the beef in oil until no longer pink. Add the soy sauce; cook for 3-4 minutes or until the liquid has evaporated. Remove beef and keep warm.

**3.** Add the corn, broccoli, red pepper, carrots, onions and remaining broth to the pan. Sprinkle with the contents of the seasoning packets. Stir-fry for 5-7 minutes or until the vegetables are crisp-tender.

**4.** Stir the cornstarch mixture and add to skillet. Bring to a boil; cook and stir for 2 minutes or until thickened. Drain the noodles. Add the beef and noodles to pan; heat through. Garnish with peanuts.

**PER SERVING** *593 cal., 28 g fat (8 g sat. fat), 46 mg chol., 2,022 mg sodium, 49 g carb., 8 g fiber, 38 g pro.*

ZESTY CHICKEN SOFT TACOS

> I've made my Zesty Chicken Soft Tacos with the usual tortillas, but naan flatbread is our favorite.
>
> —**JESSIE GREARSON-SAPAT**
> FALMOUTH, ME

# Zesty Chicken Soft Tacos

**START TO FINISH:** 25 MIN.
**MAKES:** 6 SERVINGS

- 1 **cup (8 ounces) reduced-fat sour cream**
- 2 **tablespoons Sriracha Asian hot chili sauce**
- 2 **tablespoons lime juice**
- 1½ **teaspoons grated lime peel**
- ½ **teaspoon salt**
- ⅛ **teaspoon pepper**
- 6 **naan flatbreads, warmed**
- 1 **rotisserie chicken, skin removed, shredded**
  **Minced fresh cilantro, optional**

In a small bowl, mix the first six ingredients. Spread over the naan flatbreads; top with the chicken and, if desired, cilantro.

**PER SERVING** *420 cal., 14 g fat (5 g sat. fat), 111 mg chol., 942 mg sodium, 33 g carb., 1 g fiber, 37 g pro.*

SIRLOIN STIR-FRY WITH RAMEN NOODLES

## Portobello Pizza Burgers

Portobello mushrooms are always a great meatless option, especially tucked inside a bun with tomatoes and melty mozzarella.

—**SALLY LAUF** WEST DEPTFORD, NJ

**START TO FINISH:** 25 MIN.
**MAKES:** 4 SERVINGS

- 4 **large portobello mushrooms (4 to 4½ inches)**
- 4 **teaspoons plus 1 tablespoon olive oil, divided**
- 1½ **cups finely chopped plum tomatoes**
- ¾ **cup shredded part-skim mozzarella cheese**
- 1½ **teaspoons Italian seasoning**
- 4 **hamburger buns, split**

**1.** Preheat the broiler. Remove and discard the stems from mushrooms; with a spoon, scrape and remove the gills. Brush caps with 4 teaspoons oil.

Place in an ungreased 15x10x1-in. baking pan, stem side down. Broil 4 in. from heat 5 minutes.

**2.** In a small bowl, mix the plum tomatoes, mozzarella cheese, Italian seasoning and remaining oil. Remove the mushrooms from the broiler; turn over and fill the caps with the tomato mixture.

**3.** Broil 4-6 minutes longer or until mushrooms are tender and cheese is melted. Serve on buns.

**NOTE** *Mushrooms may also be grilled. Place mushroom caps on grill rack over medium heat, stem side down. Grill, covered, 5 minutes. Remove from grill; fill caps with tomato mixture. Grill, covered, 4-6 minutes longer or until mushrooms are tender and cheese is melted. Serve on buns.*

**PER SERVING** *284 cal., 13 g fat (4 g sat. fat), 12 mg chol., 314 mg sodium, 29 g carb., 3 g fiber, 12 g pro.* **Diabetic Exchanges:** *2 starch, 1½ fat, 1 medium-fat meat, 1 vegetable.*

CHICKEN SALAD WITH DIJON VINAIGRETTE

PORTOBELLO PIZZA BURGERS

## Chicken Salad with Dijon Vinaigrette

With its crunchy almonds, bold blue cheese, shredded rotisserie chicken and from-scratch dressing, this light main course has a wonderful blend of tastes and textures.

—**LYNNE KEAST** MONTE SERENO, CA

**START TO FINISH:** 15 MIN.
**MAKES:** 8 SERVINGS

- 2 **tablespoons champagne vinegar or rice vinegar**
- 4 **teaspoons Dijon mustard**
- ¼ **teaspoon salt**
- ¼ **teaspoon pepper**
- ¼ **cup olive oil**
- 10 **cups torn Bibb or Boston lettuce**
- 1 **rotisserie chicken, skin removed, shredded**
- ⅓ **cup crumbled blue cheese**
- ½ **cup sliced almonds, optional**

**1.** In a small bowl, whisk the vinegar, mustard, salt and pepper. Gradually whisk in oil until blended.

**2.** In a large bowl, combine lettuce, chicken, blue cheese and, if desired, almonds. Drizzle with the vinaigrette; toss to coat.

**PER SERVING** *275 cal., 17 g fat (4 g sat. fat), 74 mg chol., 275 mg sodium, 4 g carb., 1 g fiber, 26 g pro.* **Diabetic Exchanges:** *3 lean meat, 2½ fat.*

5-CHEESE RAVIOLI MARINARA

I appreciate the fact that I can get 5-Cheese Ravioli Marinara on the table in less than half an hour.
—**NANCY SOUSLEY** LAFAYETTE, IN

**⑤INGREDIENTS FAST FIX**

## 5-Cheese Ravioli Marinara

**START TO FINISH:** 25 MIN. • **MAKES:** 4 SERVINGS

- 1 package (25 ounces) frozen five-cheese or chicken ravioli
- 4 small zucchini, thinly sliced (about 4 cups)
- 1 jar (24 ounces) marinara sauce
- ⅓ cup shaved Parmesan cheese

**1.** Cook the ravioli according to the package directions. Meanwhile, in a large skillet, combine the zucchini and marinara sauce; bring to a boil. Reduce the heat; simmer, uncovered. 7-9 minutes or until zucchini is crisp-tender, stirring occasionally.
**2.** Drain ravioli; add to zucchini mixture. Heat through, stirring gently to combine. Top with cheese.
**PER SERVING** *422 cal., 10 g fat (4 g sat. fat), 24 mg chol., 1,188 mg sodium, 64 g carb., 7 g fiber, 18 g pro.*

**FAST FIX ▶**

## Fresh Broccoli Salad with Lemon

The homemade dressing in this salad has a slightly sweet flavor that contrasts wonderfully with the saltiness of the bacon bits. Love cauliflower? Try using it in place of the broccoli.
—**JANET ROTH** TEMPE, AZ

**START TO FINISH:** 30 MIN. • **MAKES:** 12 SERVINGS (1 CUP EACH)

- ¼ cup cider vinegar
- ¼ cup lemon juice
- ½ cup reduced-fat mayonnaise
- ¼ cup sugar
- 2 tablespoons prepared mustard
- 1 teaspoon garlic salt
- ⅛ teaspoon pepper
- 6 ounces cream cheese, softened
- 14 cups fresh small broccoli florets (about 2¼ pounds)
- 12 ounces fresh mushrooms, stems removed, chopped
- 16 bacon strips, cooked and crumbled
- 1 cup raisins
- ⅓ cup chopped red onion
   Lemon wedges, optional

**1.** Place the first eight ingredients in a blender; cover and process until smooth.
**2.** In a large bowl, combine broccoli, mushrooms, bacon, raisins and red onion. Pour the dressing over the salad; toss to coat. Refrigerate until serving. If desired, serve with lemon wedges.
**PER SERVING** *222 cal., 13 g fat (5 g sat. fat), 30 mg chol., 520 mg sodium, 21 g carb., 3 g fiber, 8 g pro.*

FRESH BROCCOLI SALAD WITH LEMON

MUSHROOM & SWISS PITA PIZZAS

# Chicken Pesto with Pasta

Keep a container of pesto in the freezer. The next time you have leftover chicken, you can whip up this simple but yummy pasta.
—*TASTE OF HOME* TEST KITCHEN

**START TO FINISH:** 20 MIN. • **MAKES:** 8 SERVINGS

- 1 **package (16 ounces) cellentani or spiral pasta**
- 2 **cups cubed rotisserie chicken**
- 2 **medium tomatoes, chopped**
- 1 **container (7 ounces) prepared pesto**
- ¼ **cup pine nuts, toasted**

In a Dutch oven, cook the pasta according to the package directions; drain and return to the pan. Stir in the chicken, tomatoes and pesto; heat through. Sprinkle with pine nuts.

**NOTE** *To toast nuts, spread them in a 15x10x1-in. baking pan. Bake at 350° for 5-10 minutes or until lightly browned, stirring occasionally. Or, spread nuts in a dry nonstick skillet and heat over low heat until lightly browned, stirring occasionally.*

**PER SERVING** *433 cal., 18 g fat (5 g sat. fat), 40 mg chol., 239 mg sodium, 45 g carb., 3 g fiber, 24 g pro.*

Mushroom & Swiss Pita Pizzas are quick to fix and delicious—the perfect meal for weeknights!
—**MELISSA REINDL** MANITOWOC, WI

# Mushroom & Swiss Pita Pizzas

**START TO FINISH:** 25 MIN. • **MAKES:** 5 SERVINGS

- 1 **pound bulk Italian sausage**
- 1 **package (12 ounces) whole pocketless pita breads or flatbreads**
- 1¼ **cups tomato basil pasta sauce or Alfredo sauce**
- 5 **slices reduced-fat Swiss cheese**
- 1¼ **cups sliced fresh mushrooms**

**1.** Preheat oven to 350°. In a large skillet, cook the sausage over medium heat for 8-10 minutes or until no longer pink, breaking into crumbles; drain.
**2.** Place the pita breads on baking sheets. Spread with pasta sauce; top with cheese, mushrooms and cooked sausage. Bake 10-15 minutes or until cheese is melted.

**PER SERVING** *579 cal., 29 g fat (12 g sat. fat), 74 mg chol., 1,413 mg sodium, 49 g carb., 3 g fiber, 31 g pro.*

CHICKEN PESTO WITH PASTA

## Polenta Lasagna

Using slices of polenta instead of pasta gives lasagna a deliciously different twist. Round out the meal with a green salad.
—YEVGENIYA FARRER FREMONT, CA

**START TO FINISH:** 25 MIN.
**MAKES:** 4 SERVINGS

- 1½ cups marinara sauce
- 1 teaspoon garlic powder
- 1 teaspoon herbes de Provence
- 1 tube (18 ounces) polenta, cut into 10 slices
- 1½ cups (6 ounces) shredded part-skim mozzarella cheese

1. In a small bowl, mix marinara sauce, garlic powder and herbes de Provence. Arrange half of the polenta slices in a greased 8-in. skillet. Top with half of the sauce; sprinkle with ¾ cup cheese. Repeat layers.
2. Cook, uncovered, over medium heat 12-14 minutes or until bubbly. Cover; cook 2-3 minutes longer or until cheese is melted.
**NOTE** *Look for herbes de Provence in the spice aisle.*
**PER SERVING** *280 cal., 10 g fat (5 g sat. fat), 25 mg chol., 1,120 mg sodium, 32 g carb., 3 g fiber, 14 g pro.*

POLENTA LASAGNA

Love Mexican? Consider Sweet Potato & Bean Quesadillas for a great change-of-pace entree.
—BRITTANY HUBBARD ST. PAUL, MN

SWEET POTATO & BEAN QUESADILLAS

## Sweet Potato & Bean Quesadillas

**START TO FINISH:** 30 MIN.
**MAKES:** 4 SERVINGS

- 2 medium sweet potatoes
- 4 whole wheat tortillas (8 inches)
- ¾ cup canned black beans, rinsed and drained
- ½ cup shredded pepper jack cheese
- ¾ cup salsa

1. Scrub the sweet potatoes; pierce several times with a fork. Place on a microwave-safe plate. Microwave, uncovered, on high 7-9 minutes or until very tender, turning once.
2. When cool enough to handle, cut each potato lengthwise in half. Scoop out pulp. Spread onto one half of each tortilla; top with the beans and cheese. Fold other half of tortilla over filling.
3. Heat a griddle or skillet over medium heat. Cook the quesadillas 2-3 minutes on each side or until golden brown and cheese is melted. Serve with salsa.
**PER SERVING** *306 cal., 8 g fat (3 g sat. fat), 15 mg chol., 531 mg sodium, 46 g carb., 6 g fiber, 11 g pro.*

### top tip Quick Quesadillas

When I have leftover chicken or brisket, I often use it to make a fast meal of quesadillas. Canned refried beans and cheese are the only other items needed for the filling. To easily cut the quesadillas into wedges, I use a pizza cutter.
—KATE B. DUNCANVILLE, TX

# Zesty Veggie Pitas

I spread my pita breads with hummus, then stuff them with plenty of vegetables and pepper Jack cheese. But I think the key is the cilantro—its refreshing, robust flavor comes through in every bite.

**—KRISTA FRANK** RHODODENDRON, OR

**START TO FINISH:** 20 MIN.
**MAKES:** 4 SERVINGS

- ½ **cup hummus**
- 4 **whole pocketless pita breads or flatbreads, warmed**
- 4 **slices pepper jack cheese**
- 1 **cup thinly sliced cucumber**
- 1 **large tomato, cut into wedges**
- ¼ **cup sliced pepperoncini**
- ¼ **cup sliced ripe olives**
- ¼ **cup fresh cilantro leaves**

Spread the hummus over pita breads. Top with the remaining ingredients; fold pitas to serve.
**PER SERVING** *323 cal., 11 g fat (4 g sat. fat), 23 mg chol., 758 mg sodium, 42 g carb., 4 g fiber, 14 g pro.* **Diabetic Exchanges:** *3 starch, 1 medium-fat meat.*

# Bacon-Wrapped Scallops with Pineapple Quinoa

This is the first dish I developed using healthy quinoa as one of the ingredients. My husband really enjoyed helping me taste-test the recipe! With bacon, scallops and bits of pineapple, it's one of our dinnertime favorites.

**—LAURA GREENBERG** LAKE BALBOA, CA

**START TO FINISH:** 30 MIN.
**MAKES:** 4 SERVINGS

- 1 **can (14½ ounces) vegetable broth**
- 1 **cup quinoa, rinsed**
- ¼ **teaspoon salt**
- ⅛ **teaspoon plus ¼ teaspoon pepper, divided**
- 10 **bacon strips**
- 16 **sea scallops (about 2 pounds), side muscles removed**
- 1 **cup drained canned pineapple tidbits**

1. In a small saucepan, bring the vegetable broth to a boil. Add quinoa, salt and ⅛ teaspoon pepper. Reduce heat; simmer, covered, 12-15 minutes or until liquid is absorbed.
2. Meanwhile, place the bacon in a large nonstick skillet. Cook over medium heat, removing eight of the bacon strips when partially cooked but not crisp. Continue cooking the remaining bacon strips until crisp. Remove to paper towels to drain. Finely chop the crisp bacon strips. Cut the remaining bacon strips lengthwise in half.
3. Wrap a halved bacon strip around each scallop; secure with a toothpick. Sprinkle with remaining pepper.
4. Wipe pan clean, if necessary; heat over medium-high heat. Add scallops; cook 3-4 minutes on each side or until scallops are firm and opaque.
5. Remove the quinoa from the heat; fluff with a fork. Stir in pineapple and chopped bacon. Serve with scallops.
**NOTE** *Look for quinoa in the cereal, rice or organic food aisle.*
**PER SERVING** *468 cal., 11 g fat (3 g sat. fat), 89 mg chol., 1,364 mg sodium, 43 g carb., 3 g fiber, 48 g pro.*

BACON-WRAPPED SCALLOPS
WITH PINEAPPLE QUINOA

LASAGNA SOUP

FAST FIX ›
# Lasagna Soup

This delicious soup is easier to prepare than traditional lasagna—and every bit as heartwarming on a cool day.
—**SHERYL OLENICK** DEMAREST, NJ

**START TO FINISH:** 30 MIN.
**MAKES:** 8 SERVINGS (2¾ QUARTS)

- 1 **pound lean ground beef (90% lean)**
- 1 **large green pepper, chopped**
- 1 **medium onion, chopped**
- 2 **garlic cloves, minced**
- 2 **cans (14½ ounces each) diced tomatoes, undrained**
- 2 **cans (14½ ounces each) reduced-sodium beef broth**
- 1 **can (8 ounces) tomato sauce**
- 1 **cup frozen corn**
- ¼ **cup tomato paste**
- 2 **teaspoons Italian seasoning**
- ¼ **teaspoon pepper**
- 2½ **cups uncooked spiral pasta**
- ½ **cup shredded Parmesan cheese**

**1.** In a large saucepan, cook the beef, green pepper and onion over medium heat 6-8 minutes or until the meat is no longer pink, breaking up beef into crumbles. Add garlic; cook 1 minute longer. Drain.

**2.** Stir in the tomatoes, beef broth, tomato sauce, corn, tomato paste, Italian seasoning and pepper. Bring to a boil. Stir in the pasta. Return to a boil. Reduce heat; simmer, covered, 10-12 minutes or until pasta is tender. Sprinkle with cheese.

**PER SERVING** *280 cal., 7 g fat (3 g sat. fat), 41 mg chol., 572 mg sodium, 35 g carb., 4 g fiber, 20 g pro.* **Diabetic Exchanges:** *2 lean meat, 2 vegetable, 1½ starch.*

FAST FIX ›
# Italian-Style Chicken & Peppers

Discovering my mom's well-used recipe card for chicken and peppers brought back so many fond memories. I had forgotten just how good it was!
—**DONNA MILLER** GROSSE POINTE, MI

**START TO FINISH:** 30 MIN.
**MAKES:** 4 SERVINGS

- 2 **cups meatless pasta sauce**
- 2 **teaspoons olive oil**
- 1 **medium green pepper, finely chopped**
- 4 **ounces cream cheese, softened**
- 4 **boneless skinless chicken breast halves (4 ounces each)**
- ¼ **teaspoon salt**
- ⅛ **teaspoon pepper**
- 4 **slices part-skim mozzarella cheese**

**1.** Preheat oven to 425°. Place sauce in a microwave-safe bowl; microwave, covered, on high for 3-4 minutes or until hot, stirring halfway.

**2.** Meanwhile, in a large skillet, heat oil over medium-high heat. Add green pepper; cook and stir 3-4 minutes or until tender. Transfer to a small bowl; stir in cream cheese.

**3.** Arrange the chicken in a greased 13x9-in. baking dish; sprinkle with salt and pepper. Spoon the green pepper mixture onto chicken. Pour warmed sauce over the top. Place cheese over sauce. Bake, covered, 25-30 minutes or until a thermometer inserted in chicken reads 165°.

**PER SERVING** *394 cal., 22 g fat (10 g sat. fat), 112 mg chol., 1,030 mg sodium, 14 g carb., 3 g fiber, 34 g pro.*

## Smoky Gouda & Chicken Sandwiches

**START TO FINISH:** 20 MIN.
**MAKES:** 4 SERVINGS

- ¼ cup garlic-herb mayonnaise, divided
- 8 slices country white bread (½ inch thick), toasted
- 2 cups shredded rotisserie chicken
- ¼ teaspoon salt
- ⅛ teaspoon pepper
- 2 small peaches or medium plums, thinly sliced
- 4 slices smoked Gouda cheese

**1.** Preheat the broiler. Spread 2 tablespoons mayonnaise over four toasts; place on a foil-lined baking sheet. Arrange chicken over the top; sprinkle with salt and pepper. Layer with peaches and cheese.

**2.** Broil 3-4 in. from heat 2-3 minutes or until the cheese is melted. Spread the remaining mayonnaise over the remaining toasts; place over tops.

**PER SERVING** *352 cal., 17 g fat (7 g sat. fat), 100 mg chol., 678 mg sodium, 18 g carb., 1 g fiber, 30 g pro.*

The depth of flavor in Smoky Gouda & Chicken Sandwiches keeps my husband and I coming back for more. Fresh peaches are a surprising but wonderful addition.
—**NANCY MOCK** COLCHESTER, VT

SMOKY GOUDA & CHICKEN SANDWICHES

VEGGIE SALMON CHOWDER

## Veggie Salmon Chowder

I created this as a way to use up the odds and ends in my refrigerator. Loaded with veggies and salmon, the chunky chowder has become a dinnertime mainstay.
—**LIV VORS** PETERBOROUGH, ON

**START TO FINISH:** 30 MIN.
**MAKES:** 2 SERVINGS

- 1 medium sweet potato, peeled and cut into ½-inch cubes
- 1 cup reduced-sodium chicken broth
- ½ cup fresh or frozen corn
- ½ small onion, chopped
- 2 garlic cloves, minced
- 1½ cups fresh spinach, torn
- ½ cup flaked smoked salmon fillet
- 1 teaspoon pickled jalapeno slices, chopped
- 1 tablespoon cornstarch
- ½ cup 2% milk
- 1 tablespoon minced fresh cilantro
  Dash pepper

**1.** In a large saucepan, combine the first five ingredients; bring to a boil. Reduce the heat; simmer, covered, 8-10 minutes or until potato is tender.

**2.** Stir in the spinach, salmon fillet and jalapeno; cook 1-2 minutes or until the spinach is wilted. In a small bowl, mix the cornstarch and the milk until smooth; stir into the soup. Bring to a boil; cook and stir for 2 minutes or until thickened. Stir in the cilantro and pepper.

**PER SERVING** *202 cal., 3 g fat (1 g sat. fat), 12 mg chol., 645 mg sodium, 32 g carb., 4 g fiber, 13 g pro.* **Diabetic Exchanges:** *2 starch, 1 lean meat, 1 vegetable.*

## EAT SMART FAST FIX
# Hearty Vegetable Beef Ragout

My family gobbles up this pasta ragout, and it's ready to eat in only 30 minutes.

**—KIM VAN DUNK** CALDWELL, NJ

**START TO FINISH:** 30 MIN.
**MAKES:** 8 SERVINGS

- 4 **cups uncooked whole wheat spiral pasta**
- 1 **pound lean ground beef (90% lean)**
- 1 **large onion, chopped**
- 3 **garlic cloves, minced**
- 2 **cans (14½ ounces each) Italian diced tomatoes, undrained**
- 1 **jar (24 ounces) meatless spaghetti sauce**
- 2 **cups finely chopped fresh kale**
- 1 **package (9 ounces) frozen peas, thawed**
- ¾ **teaspoon garlic powder**
- ¼ **teaspoon pepper**
  **Grated Parmesan cheese, optional**

**1.** Cook spiral pasta according to the package directions; drain. Meanwhile, in a Dutch oven, cook beef, onion and garlic over medium heat 6-8 minutes or until the beef is no longer pink, breaking up beef into crumbles; drain.

**2.** Stir in the tomatoes, the spaghetti sauce, kale, peas, garlic powder and pepper. Bring to a boil. Reduce heat; simmer, uncovered, 8-10 minutes or until the kale is tender. Stir the spiral pasta into the sauce. If desired, serve with Parmesan cheese.

**PER SERVING** *302 cal., 5 g fat (2 g sat. fat), 35 mg chol., 837 mg sodium, 43 g carb., 7 g fiber, 20 g pro.* **Diabetic Exchanges:** *2 starch, 2 lean meat, 2 vegetable.*

## FAST FIX
# Super Quick Chicken Fried Rice

After my first child was born, I looked for meals that were satisfying but fuss-free. Fried rice with convenient rotisserie chicken has become a menu staple.

**—ALICIA GOWER** AUBURN, NY

**START TO FINISH:** 30 MIN.
**MAKES:** 6 SERVINGS

- 1 **package (12 ounces) frozen mixed vegetables**
- 2 **tablespoons olive oil, divided**
- 2 **eggs, lightly beaten**
- 4 **tablespoons sesame oil, divided**
- 3 **packages (8.8 ounces each) ready-to-serve garden vegetable rice**
- 1 **rotisserie chicken, skin removed, shredded**
- ¼ **teaspoon salt**
- ¼ **teaspoon pepper**

**1.** Prepare mixed vegetables according to the package directions. Meanwhile, in a large skillet, heat 1 tablespoon olive oil over medium-high heat. Pour in the eggs; cook and stir until eggs are thickened and no liquid egg remains. Remove from pan.

**2.** In same skillet, heat 2 tablespoons sesame oil and remaining olive oil over medium-high heat. Add the rice; cook and stir 10-12 minutes or until the rice begins to brown.

**3.** Stir in the chicken, salt and pepper. Add eggs and vegetables; heat through, breaking eggs into small pieces and stirring to combine. Drizzle with the remaining sesame oil.

**PER SERVING** *548 cal., 25 g fat (5 g sat. fat), 163 mg chol., 934 mg sodium, 43 g carb., 3 g fiber, 38 g pro.*

PESTO TURKEY SANDWICHES WITH STRAWBERRY MUSTARD

## (5)INGREDIENTS FAST FIX
# Pesto Turkey Sandwiches with Strawberry Mustard

I've never been a big fan of mustard, and neither have my kids, but we all love the strawberry version in these sandwiches. They're perfect when we want a warm lunch or dinner in a flash.

**—SHANNON HUMPHREY** HAMPTON, VA

**START TO FINISH:** 15 MIN.
**MAKES:** 4 SANDWICHES

- 4 **Asiago cheese bagels, split**
- 2 **tablespoons prepared pesto**
- 3 **tablespoons seedless strawberry jam**
- 2 **teaspoons Dijon mustard**
- 8 **ounces sliced oven roasted turkey breast**

**1.** Preheat oven to 350°. Place the bagels on an ungreased baking sheet, cut side up; spread with pesto. Bake 5-8 minutes or until lightly toasted.

**2.** In a small microwave-safe bowl, combine the strawberry jam and Dijon mustard. Microwave, uncovered, on high for 15-30 seconds or until the jam is melted; stir to blend. Spread over the bagel bottoms. Top with turkey; replace bagel tops.

**PER SERVING** *489 cal., 11 g fat (4 g sat. fat), 32 mg chol., 1,260 mg sodium, 72 g carb., 2 g fiber, 28 g pro.*

HEARTY VEGETABLE BEEF RAGOUT

# Bean Soup with Sausage

Think delicious homemade soup takes too long to fix? This one will change your mind. In half an hour, you'll be savoring a hearty bowlful loaded with sausage and veggies.

—GAIL WILKERSON HOUSE SPRINGS, MO

**START TO FINISH:** 30 MIN.
**MAKES:** 10 SERVINGS (2½ QUARTS)

- 8 **ounces bulk lean turkey breakfast sausage**
- 1 **medium onion, chopped**
- 1 **medium green pepper, chopped**
- 2 **cans (16 ounces each) kidney beans, rinsed and drained**
- 1 **medium potato, peeled and cubed**
- 4 **cups water**
- 1 **bay leaf**
- ½ **teaspoon each garlic salt, seasoned salt and pepper**
- ½ **teaspoon dried thyme**
- 1 **can (28 ounces) diced tomatoes, undrained**

1. In a large saucepan, cook sausage, onion and green pepper over medium heat 4-6 minutes or until vegetables are tender and sausage is no longer pink, breaking up sausage into crumbles; drain.

2. Stir in the kidney beans, potato, water and seasonings; bring to a boil. Reduce the heat; simmer, uncovered, 10-15 minutes or until potato is tender. Stir in tomatoes and heat through. Remove bay leaf.

**PER SERVING** *160 cal., 2 g fat (1 g sat. fat), 24 mg chol., 645 mg sodium, 23 g carb., 6 g fiber, 13 g pro.* **Diabetic Exchanges:** *1 starch, 1 lean meat, 1 vegetable.*

HERB-ROASTED SALMON FILLETS

Whether I need a busy-day entree or a special main course for company, Herb-Roasted Salmon Fillets are my go-to dish.
—LUANNE ASTA NEW YORK, NY

# Herb-Roasted Salmon Fillets

**START TO FINISH:** 30 MIN.
**MAKES:** 4 SERVINGS

- 4 **salmon fillets (6 ounces each)**
- 4 **garlic cloves, minced**
- 1 **tablespoon minced fresh rosemary or 1 teaspoon dried rosemary, crushed**
- 1 **tablespoon olive oil**
- 2 **teaspoons minced fresh thyme or ½ teaspoon dried thyme**
- ¾ **teaspoon salt**
- ½ **teaspoon pepper**

Preheat oven to 425°. Place salmon fillets in a greased 15x10x1-in. baking pan, skin side down. Combine the remaining ingredients; spread over fillets. Roast 15-18 minutes or until desired doneness.

**PER SERVING** *301 cal., 19 g fat (4 g sat. fat), 85 mg chol., 529 mg sodium, 1 g carb., trace fiber, 29 g pro.* **Diabetic Exchanges:** *4 lean meat, 1 fat.*

BEAN SOUP WITH SAUSAGE

CHIPOTLE-RASPBERRY PORK CHOPS

## ⑤ INGREDIENTS | FAST FIX
# Broiled Chicken & Artichokes

**START TO FINISH:** 15 MIN. • **MAKES:** 8 SERVINGS

- **8** boneless skinless chicken thighs (about 2 pounds)
- **2** jars (7½ ounces each) marinated quartered artichoke hearts, drained
- **2** tablespoons olive oil
- **1** teaspoon salt
- **½** teaspoon pepper
- **¼** cup shredded Parmesan cheese
- **2** tablespoons minced fresh parsley

**1.** Preheat boiler. In a large bowl, toss the chicken thighs and artichokes with the oil, salt and pepper. Transfer to a broiler pan.

**2.** Broil the chicken 3 in. from heat 8-10 minutes or until a thermometer inserted in the chicken reads 170°, turning chicken and artichokes halfway through cooking. Sprinkle with Parmesan cheese. Broil 1-2 minutes longer or until cheese is melted. Sprinkle with parsley.

**PER SERVING** *288 cal., 21 g fat (5 g sat. fat), 77 mg chol., 584 mg sodium, 4 g carb., trace fiber, 22 g pro.*

## ⑤ INGREDIENTS EAT SMART FAST FIX
# Chipotle-Raspberry Pork Chops

With only four simple ingredients and a 10-minute prep time, these zippy chops are fast enough to throw together after a long day at work. Fire up the grill and enjoy!

—**JENNIFER RAY** PONCHA SPRING, CO

**START TO FINISH:** 20 MIN. • **MAKES:** 4 SERVINGS (¼ CUP SAUCE)

- **½** cup seedless raspberry preserves
- **1** chipotle pepper in adobo sauce, finely chopped
- **4** bone-in pork loin chops (7 ounces each)
- **½** teaspoon salt

**1.** In a small saucepan, cook and stir the preserves and chipotle pepper over medium heat until heated through. Reserve ¼ cup for serving. Sprinkle the pork chops with salt; brush with remaining raspberry sauce.

**2.** Lightly grease a grill or broiler pan rack. Grill the chops, covered, over medium heat or broil 4 in. from heat for 4-5 minutes on each side or until a thermometer reads 145°. Let stand 5 minutes before serving. Serve with reserved sauce.

**PER SERVING** *308 cal., 9 g fat (3 g sat. fat), 86 mg chol., 395 mg sodium, 27 g carb., trace fiber, 30 g pro.*

## ❓ Did you know?

A chipotle is a smoked and dried jalapeno pepper originating in the area around Mexico City. Often found canned in a chili sauce in the United States, chipotles are medium to hot in heat level and are used in a variety of Mexican and American dishes that require spicy flavor.

BROILED CHICKEN & ARTICHOKES

My wife and I originally tried Broiled Chicken & Artichokes as newlyweds. We've been hooked since!
—**CHRIS KOON** MIDLOTHIAN, VA

ELEGANT PORK MARSALA

## Elegant Pork Marsala

Marsala wine and fresh mushrooms make this Italian-style entree special. I mix the flour and pepper in a large plastic bag and toss in the pork to coat it, so cleanup is really easy.
—**KIM GILLIS** HIGH FALLS, NY

**START TO FINISH:** 30 MIN. • **MAKES:** 6 SERVINGS

- ⅓ **cup whole wheat flour**
- ½ **teaspoon pepper**
- 6 **boneless pork loin chops (4 ounces each)**
- 1 **tablespoon olive oil**
- 2 **cups sliced fresh mushrooms**
- ⅓ **cup chopped onion**
- 2 **turkey bacon strips, chopped**
- ¼ **teaspoon minced garlic**
- 1 **cup Marsala wine or additional reduced-sodium chicken broth**
- 5 **teaspoons cornstarch**
- ⅔ **cup reduced-sodium chicken broth**

**1.** In a shallow bowl, mix flour and pepper. Dip the pork chops in flour mixture to coat both sides; shake off excess.
**2.** In a large nonstick skillet coated with cooking spray, heat oil over medium heat. Add pork chops; cook 4-5 minutes on each side or until a thermometer reads 145°. Remove from pan; keep warm.
**3.** In same skillet, add the mushrooms, onion and bacon to drippings; cook and stir 2-3 minutes or until mushrooms are tender. Add the garlic; cook 1 minute longer. Add wine; increase heat to medium-high. Cook, stirring to loosen the browned bits from pan.
**4.** In a small bowl, mix cornstarch and broth until smooth; add to pan. Bring to a boil; cook and stir 2 minutes or until slightly thickened. Serve with pork.
**PER SERVING** *232 cal., 10 g fat (3 g sat. fat), 60 mg chol., 161 mg sodium, 7 g carb., 1 g fiber, 24 g pro.* **Diabetic Exchanges:** *3 lean meat, ½ starch, ½ fat.*

## Shrimp Pasta Alfredo

Any recipe that features Alfredo sauce goes
When he was still single and starting to cook,
one of the first recipes he prepared. Now his
—**GAIL LUCAS** OLIVE BRANCH, MS

**START TO FINISH:** 25 MIN. • **MAKES:** 4 SERVING

- 3 **cups uncooked bow tie pasta**
- 2 **cups frozen peas**
- 1 **pound peeled and deveined cooked medium shrimp, tails removed**
- 1 **jar (15 ounces) Alfredo sauce**
- ¼ **cup shredded Parmesan cheese**

**1.** In a Dutch oven, cook the pasta according to the package directions, adding peas during the last 3 minutes of cooking; drain and return to pan.
**2.** Stir in the shrimp and sauce; heat through over medium heat, stirring occasionally. Sprinkle with cheese.
**PER SERVING** *545 cal., 16 g fat (9 g sat. fat), 206 mg chol., 750 mg sodium, 60 g carb., 6 g fiber, 41 g pro.*

SHRIMP PASTA ALFREDO

## Easy Asian Chicken Slaw

INGREDIENTS EAT SMART FAST FIX

The first time I served this entree, the bowl was scraped clean. I knew it was a hit!
—**BESS BLANCO**
VAIL, AZ

**START TO FINISH:** 15 MIN.
**MAKES:** 8 SERVINGS

- 1 package (3 ounces) ramen noodles
- 1 rotisserie chicken, skin removed, shredded
- 1 package (16 ounces) coleslaw mix
- 6 green onions, finely chopped
- 1 cup reduced-fat Asian toasted sesame salad dressing

Discard the seasoning packet from the ramen noodles or save seasoning for another use. Break the ramen noodles into small pieces; place in a large bowl. Add the chicken, coleslaw mix and green onions. Drizzle with the salad dressing; toss to coat.
**PER SERVING** *267 cal., 10 g fat (3 g sat. fat), 70 mg chol., 405 mg sodium, 18 g carb., 2 g fiber, 26 g pro.* **Diabetic Exchanges:** *3 lean meat, 1 starch, ½ fat.*

EASY ASIAN CHICKEN SLAW

---

### (5) INGREDIENTS FAST FIX
## Chipotle BLT Wraps

Traditional bacon, lettuce and tomato sandwiches are so good, but the toasted bread can result in a lot of messy crumbs. Flour tortillas bundle everything together in a neat, easy-to-eat wrap.
—**DARLENE BRENDEN** SALEM, OR

**START TO FINISH:** 15 MIN.
**MAKES:** 4 SERVINGS

- 3 cups chopped romaine
- 2 plum tomatoes, finely chopped
- 8 bacon strips, cooked and crumbled
- ⅓ cup reduced-fat chipotle or regular mayonnaise
- 4 flour tortillas (8 inches), warmed

**1.** In a large bowl, combine romaine, tomatoes and bacon. Add mayonnaise; toss to coat.
**2.** Spoon about 1 cup romaine mixture down center of each tortilla. Fold the bottom of tortilla over filling; fold both sides to close. Serve immediately.
**PER SERVING** *294 cal., 15 g fat (3 g sat. fat), 23 mg chol., 705 mg sodium, 31 g carb., 1 g fiber, 11 g pro.*

---

### FAST FIX
## Garlicky Chicken Pizza

When I cook chicken for a different dish, I often make extra to top a quick pizza later in the week. To speed things up even more, I use a refrigerated crust. Be sure to drain the tomatoes well to keep it crispy.
—**TERI OTTE** CANNON FALLS, MN

**START TO FINISH:** 25 MIN.
**MAKES:** 6 SERVINGS

- 1 tube (13.8 ounces) refrigerated pizza crust
- 2 tablespoons olive oil
- 2 garlic cloves, minced
- 1 can (14½ ounces) diced tomatoes, well drained
- 1 large onion, thinly sliced (about 1 cup)
- ⅓ cup pitted kalamata olives, halved
- 2 cups cubed or shredded cooked chicken
- 1⅓ cups crumbled goat cheese
- 1 teaspoon minced fresh rosemary or ¼ teaspoon dried rosemary, crushed
- ½ teaspoon garlic salt
- ½ teaspoon pepper

**1.** Preheat oven to 400°. Unroll and press dough onto bottom and ½-in. up sides of a greased 15x10x1-in. baking pan. Bake 8-10 minutes or until edges are lightly browned.
**2.** Mix oil and garlic; brush over crust. Top with the tomatoes, onion, olives, chicken and goat cheese. Sprinkle with rosemary, garlic salt and pepper. Bake 10-12 minutes or until crust is golden.
**PER SERVING** *418 cal., 19 g fat (6 g sat. fat), 73 mg chol., 957 mg sodium, 39 g carb., 3 g fiber, 25 g pro.*

---

### (5) INGREDIENTS FAST FIX
## Spinach-Artichoke Rigatoni

Our house is full of pasta lovers—who aren't quite as keen on veggies! This baked rigatoni is cheesy comfort food that gets everyone eating spinach and artichokes.
—**YVONNE STARLIN** HERMITAGE, TN

**START TO FINISH:** 30 MIN.
**MAKES:** 4 SERVINGS

- 3 cups uncooked rigatoni or large tube pasta
- 1 package (10 ounces) frozen creamed spinach
- 1 can (14 ounces) water-packed artichoke hearts, rinsed, drained and quartered
- 2 cups (8 ounces) shredded part-skim mozzarella cheese, divided
- ¼ cup grated Parmesan cheese
- ½ teaspoon salt
- ¼ teaspoon pepper

**1.** Preheat broiler. Prepare rigatoni and spinach according to the package directions.
**2.** Drain the pasta, reserving ½ cup pasta water; return to the pan. Add the artichoke hearts, ½ cup mozzarella cheese, Parmesan cheese, salt, pepper and creamed spinach; toss to combine, adding some of the reserved pasta water to thin, if desired.
**3.** Transfer to a greased 2-qt. broiler-safe baking dish; sprinkle with the remaining mozzarella cheese. Broil 4-6 in. from heat 2-3 minutes or until cheese is melted.
**PER SERVING** *448 cal., 14 g fat (8 g sat. fat), 37 mg chol., 1,224 mg sodium, 54 g carb., 3 g fiber, 28 g pro.*

SPINACH-ARTICHOKE RIGATONI

## Zucchini-Parmesan Bake

When your garden is bursting with a crop of homegrown zucchini, put it to terrific use in this skillet recipe. Cut into wedges, the cheesy egg dish is great for breakfast or as a side dish any time of day.
—**SHANNON DAVIS** MASON, MI

**START TO FINISH:** 30 MIN.
**MAKES:** 6 SERVINGS

- 3 **eggs**
- ½ **cup canola oil**
- 3 **cups shredded zucchini (about 1 pound)**
- 1 **cup reduced-fat biscuit/baking mix**
- ½ **cup shredded Parmesan cheese**

**1.** Preheat the oven to 375°. In a large bowl, whisk eggs and oil until blended. Stir in remaining ingredients.
**2.** Transfer mixture to a greased 10-in. ovenproof skillet. Bake 25-30 minutes or until golden brown.
**PER SERVING** *314 cal., 24 g fat (4 g sat. fat), 111 mg chol., 387 mg sodium, 17 g carb., 1 g fiber, 8 g pro.*

## Mint-Cucumber Tomato Sandwiches

I tweaked the teatime classic—cucumber sandwiches—to suit our tastes. When I was pregnant, the refreshing little bites even helped satisfy my cravings.
—**NAMRATA TELUGU** TERRE HAUTE, IN

**START TO FINISH:** 15 MIN.
**MAKES:** 4 SANDWICHES

- 3 **tablespoons butter, softened**
- 8 **slices sourdough bread**
- 1 **large cucumber, thinly sliced**
- 2 **medium tomatoes, thinly sliced**
- ¼ **teaspoon salt**
- ⅛ **teaspoon pepper**
- ¼ **cup fresh mint leaves**

Spread butter over four slices of sourdough bread. Layer with the cucumber and tomatoes; sprinkle with salt, pepper and mint. Top with remaining bread. If desired, cut each sandwich into quarters.
**PER SERVING** *286 cal., 10 g fat (6 g sat. fat), 23 mg chol., 631 mg sodium, 42 g carb., 3 g fiber, 9 g pro.*

## Tenderloin with Horseradish Cream Cheese

**START TO FINISH:** 20 MIN.
**MAKES:** 4 SERVINGS

- 4 **beef tenderloin steaks (4 ounces each)**
- ¼ **teaspoon salt**
- ¼ **teaspoon pepper**
- 1 **teaspoon olive oil**
- 1 **package (8 ounces) cream cheese, softened**
- 2 **tablespoons grated Parmesan cheese**
- 2 **tablespoons prepared horseradish**
- 2 **tablespoons minced fresh parsley**

**1.** Sprinkle the steaks with salt and pepper. In a large skillet, heat the oil over medium heat. Add the steaks; cook 4-6 minutes on each side or until the meat reaches desired doneness (for medium-rare, a thermometer should read 145°; medium, 160°; well-done, 170°).
**2.** Meanwhile, in a small bowl, mix cream cheese, Parmesan cheese and horseradish until blended. Serve with steaks. Sprinkle with parsley.
**PER SERVING** *387 cal., 28 g fat (16 g sat. fat), 114 mg chol., 378 mg sodium, 3 g carb., trace fiber, 30 g pro.*

TENDERLOIN WITH HORSERADISH CREAM CHEESE

> We often have Tenderloin with Horseradish Cream Cheese for dinner. Both my husband and I love it!
> —**MARY LOU COOK** WELCHES, OR

OPEN-FACED GRILLED SALMON SANDWICHES

## Pasta with Roas[ted] Garlic & Tomat[oes]

Dress up up your bow tie [pasta—any] kind you like—with a crea[my] sauce featuring roasted tomatoes and garlic. It's simple but tastes like a treat.

—AYSHA SCHURMAN AMMON, ID

**START TO FINISH:** 20 MIN.
**MAKES:** 4 SERVINGS

- 1½ **pounds cherry tomatoes**
- 12 **garlic cloves, peeled**
- 3 **tablespoons olive oil**
- 3 **cups uncooked bow tie pasta**
- 4 **ounces (½ cup) cream cheese, softened**
- ½ **teaspoon salt**

**1.** Preheat oven to 450°. In a bowl, toss tomatoes and garlic cloves with oil; transfer to a greased 15x10x1-in. baking pan. Roast 14-16 minutes or until very soft. Meanw=hile, cook the pasta according to package directions.
**2.** Cool the tomato mixture slightly. Reserve 12 tomatoes for serving with pasta. Transfer the remaining tomato mixture to a food processor. Add the cream cheese and salt; process until smooth. Transfer to a large bowl.
**3.** Drain the pasta; add to the tomato mixture and toss to coat. Top with reserved tomatoes.
**PER SERVING** *441 cal., 22 g fat (8 g sat. fat), 32 mg chol., 401 mg sodium, 52 g carb., 4 g fiber, 12 g pro.*

In my family, we like to fish. What better reward is there after a day of angling than eating what you just caught? Open-Faced Grilled Salmon Sandwiches are a favorite.
—**STEPHANIE HANISAK** PORT MURRAY, NJ

## Open-Faced Grilled Salmon Sandwiches

**START TO FINISH:** 30 MIN.
**MAKES:** 4 SERVINGS

- 4 **salmon fillets (1 inch thick and 5 ounces each), skin removed**
- ¾ **cup mesquite marinade**
- ¼ **teaspoon pepper**
- 4 **slices sourdough bread (½ inch thick)**
- ¼ **cup tartar sauce**
- 4 **iceberg lettuce leaves**
- 4 **lemon wedges, optional**

**1.** Place fillets in an 8-in.-square dish. Pour marinade over fillets; turn fish to coat. Let stand 15 minutes.

**2.** Drain the salmon fillets, discarding the marinade. Sprinkle the fillets with pepper.
**3.** Moisten a paper towel with cooking oil; using long-handled tongs, rub on the grill rack to coat lightly. Grill the salmon, covered, over medium heat or broil 4 in. from the heat 4-6 minutes on each side or until fish just begins to flake easily with a fork.
**4.** Grill the sourdough bread, covered, over medium heat 1-2 minutes on each side or until lightly toasted. Spread with tartar sauce; top with the lettuce and salmon. If desired, serve with lemon wedges.
**PER SERVING** *436 cal., 17 g fat (3 g sat. fat), 74 mg chol., 1,226 mg sodium, 37 g carb., 1 g fiber, 31 g pro.*

PASTA WITH ROASTED GARLIC & TOMATOES

**FETA SHRIMP SKILLET**
*PAGE 252*

# Cooking Lighter

Whether you cook for a special diet or just a healthier lifestyle, rely on this chapter. You'll find dozens of **trimmed-down dishes** to help you make the **best choices** for you and your family.

**SLOW-ROASTED CHICKEN WITH VEGETABLES**
*PAGE 241*

**BLACK BEAN CHIP & DIP BURGERS**
*PAGE 244*

**HONEY-LEMON CHICKEN ENCHILADAS**
*PAGE 258*

⑤ INGREDIENTS **EAT SMART** FAST FIX

# Chicken & Vegetable Kabobs

We fire up the grill a lot during summer. Kabobs are fun and look great, too!

—**TINA OLES**
NASHWAUK, MN

**START TO FINISH:** 30 MIN.
**MAKES:** 4 SERVINGS

1 **pound boneless skinless chicken breasts, cut into 1½ inch cubes**
1 **medium sweet red pepper, cut into 1½ inch pieces**
1 **medium zucchini, cut into 1½ inch pieces**
1 **medium red onion, cut into thick wedges**
⅔ **cup sun-dried tomato salad dressing, divided**

**1.** In a large bowl, combine chicken and vegetables. Drizzle with ⅓ cup dressing and toss to coat. Alternately thread chicken and vegetables onto four metal or soaked wooden skewers.
**2.** Grill the kabobs, covered, over medium heat or broil 4 in. from heat 8-10 minutes or until chicken is no longer pink, turning occasionally and basting with the remaining dressing during the last 3 minutes.
**PER SERVING** *228 cal., 10 g fat (1 g sat. fat), 63 mg chol., 515 mg sodium, 11 g carb., 2 g fiber, 24 g pro.* **Diabetic Exchanges:** *3 lean meat, 1 vegetable, 1 fat.*

CHICKEN & VEGETABLE KABOBS

GINGER-SESAME STEAMED VEGETABLE SALAD

**EAT SMART**

# Ginger-Sesame Steamed Vegetable Salad

This dish is a tribute to my father's Laotian roots. The warm salad traditionally blends baby bok choy, mustard greens, peapod shoots and snow peas, but you can use any seasonal green veggies you like.
—**MONNIE NORASING** MANSFIELD, TX

**PREP:** 25 MIN. • **COOK:** 10 MIN.
**MAKES:** 6 SERVINGS

2 **tablespoons grated fresh gingerroot**
2 **tablespoons sesame oil**
1 **tablespoon fish sauce or reduced-sodium soy sauce**
1 **teaspoon sugar**
½ **teaspoon reduced-sodium soy sauce**
¼ **teaspoon salt**
1 **cup cut fresh green beans (2-inch pieces)**
4 **cups fresh broccoli florets**
2 **large carrots, julienned**
1 **package (9 ounces) fresh spinach**
½ **cup finely chopped unsalted dry roasted peanuts**
**Coarsely chopped fresh cilantro and julienned fresh gingerroot**

**1.** In a small bowl, mix the first six ingredients.
**2.** In a stockpot, place steamer insert or basket over 2 in. of water. Place the green beans, broccoli and carrots in insert. Bring water to a boil. Reduce the heat to maintain a simmer; steam the vegetables, covered, 5-7 minutes or just until crisp-tender. Add spinach; cook, covered, 1-2 minutes longer or until spinach is wilted.
**3.** Transfer vegetables to a large bowl. Add ginger mixture; toss to combine. Just before serving, sprinkle with peanuts, cilantro and julienned ginger.
**PER SERVING** *156 cal., 11 g fat (2 g sat. fat), 0 chol., 407 mg sodium, 11 g carb., 5 g fiber, 6 g pro.* **Diabetic Exchanges:** *2 vegetable, 2 fat.*

# Cajun Shrimp Skillet

The zesty flavor of this shrimp entree is so good, I always have some bread on the side so I can soak up every drop of sauce!

—**MARK OPPE** NORTH POLE, AK

**START TO FINISH:** 25 MIN.
**MAKES:** 4 SERVINGS

- 3 tablespoons butter
- 2 garlic cloves, minced
- ½ cup amber beer or beef broth
- 1 teaspoon Worcestershire sauce
- 1 teaspoon pepper
- ½ teaspoon salt
- ½ teaspoon dried thyme
- ½ teaspoon dried rosemary, crushed
- ½ teaspoon crushed red pepper flakes
- ¼ teaspoon cayenne pepper
- ⅛ teaspoon dried oregano
- 1 pound uncooked large shrimp, peeled and deveined
  Hot cooked grits, optional

In a large skillet, heat the butter over medium-high heat. Add the garlic; cook and stir 1 minute. Stir in beer, Worcestershire sauce and seasonings; bring to a boil. Add the shrimp; cook 3-4 minutes or until shrimp turn pink, stirring occasionally. If desired, serve over grits.

**PER SERVING** *186 cal., 10 g fat (6 g sat. fat), 160 mg chol., 505 mg sodium, 3 g carb., trace fiber, 19 g pro.* **Diabetic Exchanges:** *3 lean meat, 2 fat.*

CAJUN SHRIMP SKILLET

SLOW-RO
WIT

Do just a little prep, and you'll come home to the comfort of Slow-Roasted Chicken with Vegetables.

—**ANITA BELL** HERMITAGE, TN

# Slow-Roasted Chicken with Vegetables

**PREP:** 15 MIN.
**COOK:** 6 HOURS + STANDING
**MAKES:** 6 SERVINGS

- 2 medium carrots, halved lengthwise and cut into 3-inch pieces
- 2 celery ribs, halved lengthwise and cut into 3-inch pieces
- 8 small red potatoes, quartered
- ¾ teaspoon salt, divided
- ⅛ teaspoon pepper
- 1 medium lemon, halved
- 2 garlic cloves, crushed
- 1 broiler/fryer chicken (3 to 4 pounds)
- 1 tablespoon dried rosemary, crushed
- 1 tablespoon lemon juice
- 1 tablespoon olive oil
- 2 teaspoons paprika

**1.** Place the carrots, celery and red potatoes in a 6-qt. slow cooker; toss with ¼ teaspoon salt and pepper. Place the lemon halves and garlic in the chicken cavity. Tuck the chicken wings under the chicken; tie the drumsticks together.

**2.** Place the chicken over the vegetables in the slow cooker, breast side up. Mix the rosemary, lemon juice, oil, paprika and remaining salt; rub over the chicken.

**3.** Cook, covered, on low 6-8 hours or until a thermometer reads 165° when inserted in center of stuffing and thigh reaches at least 170° and vegetables are tender.

**4.** Remove the chicken to a serving platter; tent with foil. Let stand 15 minutes before carving. Serve with vegetables.

**PER SERVING** *329 cal., 17 g fat (4 g sat. fat), 88 mg chol., 400 mg sodium, 14 g carb., 3 g fiber, 29 g pro.*

THAI CHICKEN
PEANUT NOODLES

Authentic-tasting Thai
Chicken Peanut Noodles
get my husband breaking
out the chopsticks!

—**JENNIFER FISHER** AUSTIN, TX

---

## Thai Chicken
## Peanut Noodles

**START TO FINISH:** 30 MIN.
**MAKES:** 6 SERVINGS

- ¼ cup creamy peanut butter
- ½ cup reduced-sodium chicken broth
- ¼ cup lemon juice
- ¼ cup reduced-sodium soy sauce
- 4 teaspoons Sriracha Asian hot chili sauce
- ¼ teaspoon crushed red pepper flakes
- 12 ounces uncooked multigrain spaghetti
- 1 pound lean ground chicken
- 1½ cups julienned carrots
- 1 medium sweet red pepper, chopped
- 1 garlic clove, minced
- ½ cup finely chopped unsalted peanuts
- 4 green onions, chopped

**1.** In a small bowl, whisk the first six ingredients until blended. Cook the spaghetti according to the package directions; drain.
**2.** Meanwhile, in a large skillet, cook chicken, carrots, pepper and garlic over medium heat 5-6 minutes or until chicken is no longer pink, breaking up chicken into crumbles; drain.
**3.** Stir in the peanut butter mixture; bring to a boil. Reduce heat; simmer, uncovered, 3-5 minutes or until the sauce is slightly thickened. Serve with the spaghetti. Top with the peanuts and green onions.
**PER SERVING** *475 cal., 17 g fat (3 g sat. fat), 54 mg chol., 711 mg sodium, 51 g carb., 7 g fiber, 33 g pro.*

---

# Juicy & Delicious Mixed
# Spice Burgers

We love these
Mediterranean
spiced burgers,
known as *kofta*.

—**ANNE HENRY**
TORONTO, ON

**START TO FINISH:** 30 MIN.
**MAKES:** 6 SERVINGS

- 1 medium onion, finely chopped
- 3 tablespoons minced fresh parsley
- 2 tablespoons minced fresh mint
- 1 garlic clove, minced
- ¾ teaspoon ground allspice
- ¾ teaspoon pepper
- ½ teaspoon ground cinnamon
- ½ teaspoon salt
- ¼ teaspoon ground nutmeg
- 1½ pounds lean ground beef (90% lean)
    Refrigerated tzatziki sauce, optional

**1.** In a large bowl, combine the first nine ingredients. Add beef; mix lightly but thoroughly. Shape into six 4x2-in. oblong patties.
**2.** Grill patties, covered, over medium heat or broil 4 in. from heat 4-6 minutes on each side or until a thermometer reads 160°. If desired, serve with sauce.
**PER SERVING** *192 cal., 9 g fat (4 g sat. fat), 71 mg chol., 259 mg sodium, 3 g carb., 1 g fiber, 22 g pro.* **Diabetic Exchange:** *3 lean meat.*

JUICY & DELICIOUS MIXED SPICE BURGERS

---

BLUEBERRY-STUFFED
FRENCH TOAST

# Garlic Chick

In New Mexico, we ad
ingredients like sun-dri
garlic. I put both in my c
a weeknight dinner that a

—JUDY CRAWFORD DEMING

**START TO FINISH:** 30 MIN.
**MAKES:** 4 SERVINGS

- 8 **ounces uncooked rigatoni or large tube pasta**
- ¼ **cup sun-dried tomatoes (not packed in oil)**
- ½ **cup boiling water**
- ½ **pound boneless skinless chicken breasts, cut into 1-inch cubes**
- ¼ **teaspoon garlic salt**
- 2 **tablespoons all-purpose flour**
- 2 **tablespoons olive oil, divided**
- 1½ **cups sliced fresh mushrooms**
- 3 **garlic cloves, minced**
- ¼ **cup reduced-sodium chicken broth**
- ¼ **cup white wine or additional reduced-sodium chicken broth**
- 2 **tablespoons minced fresh parsley**
- ¼ **teaspoon dried basil**
- ⅛ **teaspoon salt**
- ⅛ **teaspoon pepper**
- ⅛ **teaspoon crushed red pepper flakes**
- ¼ **cup grated Parmesan cheese**

1. Cook the rigatoni according to the package directions. In a small bowl, combine the tomatoes and boiling water; let stand 5 minutes. Drain; chop the tomatoes.

2. Sprinkle the chicken with garlic salt; add the flour and toss to coat. In a large skillet, heat 1 tablespoon oil over medium-high heat. Add chicken; cook and stir 4-5 minutes or until no longer pink. Remove from pan.

3. In same skillet, heat the remaining oil over medium-high heat. Add the mushrooms and garlic; cook and stir until tender. Add the chicken broth, white wine, parsley, seasonings and chopped tomatoes; bring to a boil. Stir in chicken; heat through.

4. Drain the rigatoni; add to chicken mixture. Sprinkle with Parmesan cheese and toss to coat.

**PER SERVING** *398 cal., 11 g fat (2 g sat. fat), 36 mg chol., 290 mg sodium, 50 g carb., 3 g fiber, 23 g pro.*

---

# Blueberry-Stuffed French Toast

Here's a recipe for holiday-special French toast topped with a blueberry-orange sauce. No one will guess it's light!

—MYRNA KOLDENHOVEN SANBORN, IA

**PREP:** 35 MIN. • **BAKE:** 15 MIN.
**MAKES:** 8 SERVINGS

- 1½ **cups fresh or frozen blueberries**
- 3 **tablespoons sugar, divided**
- 8 **slices Italian bread (1¼ inches thick)**
- 4 **eggs**
- ½ **cup orange juice**
- 1 **teaspoon grated orange peel**
  **Dash salt**

**SAUCE**
- ¼ **cup orange juice**
- ¼ **cup water**
- 3 **tablespoons sugar**
- 1 **tablespoon cornstarch**
- ⅛ **teaspoon salt**
- 1½ **cups orange sections**
- 1 **cup fresh or frozen blueberries**
- ⅓ **cup sliced almonds, toasted**

1. Preheat oven to 400°. In a small bowl, toss the blueberries with 2 tablespoons sugar. Cut a pocket horizontally in each slice of bread. Fill with blueberries.

2. In a shallow bowl, whisk eggs, orange juice, orange peel, salt and remaining sugar. Dip both sides of bread in egg mixture, being careful to not squeeze out berries. Place in a greased 15x10x1-in. baking pan. Bake 14-17 minutes or until golden brown, carefully turning once.

3. Meanwhile, in a small saucepan, whisk the first five sauce ingredients until smooth. Bring to a boil, stirring constantly; cook and stir 1-2 minutes or until thickened. Reduce heat; stir in the fruit and heat through. Serve the French toast with the sauce; sprinkle with almonds.

**NOTE** *To toast the nuts, spread them in a 15x10x1-in. baking pan. Bake at 350° for 5-10 minutes or until lightly browned, stirring occasionally. Or, spread in a dry nonstick skillet and heat them over low heat until lightly browned, stirring occasionally.*

**PER SERVING** *167 cal., 5 g fat (1 g sat. fat), 106 mg chol., 118 mg sodium, 27 g carb., 3 g fiber, 5 g pro.* **Diabetic Exchanges:** *1½ starch, 1 fat, ½ fruit.*

## Cilantro Shrimp & Rice

**START TO FINISH:** 30 MIN. • **MAKES:** 8 SERVINGS

- 2 packages (8½ ounces each) ready-to-serve basmati rice
- 2 tablespoons olive oil
- 2 cups frozen corn, thawed
- 2 medium zucchini, quartered and sliced
- 1 large sweet red pepper, chopped
- ½ teaspoon crushed red pepper flakes
- 3 garlic cloves, minced
- 1 pound peeled and deveined cooked large shrimp, tails removed
- ½ cup chopped fresh cilantro
- 1 tablespoon grated lime peel
- 2 tablespoons lime juice
- ¾ teaspoon salt
  Lime wedges, optional

**1.** Prepare the rice according to the package directions.

**2.** Meanwhile, in a large skillet, heat oil over medium-high heat. Add the corn, zucchini, red pepper and pepper flakes; cook and stir 3-5 minutes or until zucchini is crisp-tender. Add garlic; cook 1 minute longer. Add shrimp; cook and stir 3-5 minutes or until heated through.

**3.** Stir in the rice, cilantro, lime peel, lime juice and salt. If desired, serve with lime wedges.

**PER SERVING** *243 cal., 6 g fat (1 g sat. fat), 86 mg chol., 324 mg sodium, 28 g carb., 3 g fiber, 16 g pro.* **Diabetic Exchanges:** *2 lean meat, 1½ starch, ½ fat.*

> Cilantro Shrimp & Rice has an incredible aroma. Even my son—who has a picky palate—can't resist!
> —NIBEDITA DAS FORT WORTH, TX

CILANTRO SHRIMP & RICE

BLACK BEAN CHIP & DIP BURGERS

## Black Bean Chip & Dip Burgers

I wanted to create a veggie burger that didn't have a dry, crumbly texture or bland flavor. I know I've hit on something because my grandkids now request these patties instead of the usual beef!

—KT REHRIG ALLENTOWN, PA

**PREP:** 30 MIN. • **GRILL:** 10 MIN. • **MAKES:** 8 SERVINGS

- ⅔ cup water
- ⅓ cup quinoa, rinsed
- 1 can (15 ounces) black beans, rinsed and drained
- 1 jar (16 ounces) salsa, divided
- 1 cup crushed baked tortilla chip scoops
- 2 tablespoons reduced-sodium taco seasoning
- 8 whole wheat hamburger buns, split
- 8 lettuce leaves
- 8 slices tomato
- 8 slices red onion

**1.** In a small saucepan, bring the water to a boil. Add quinoa. Reduce heat; simmer, covered, 12-15 minutes or until liquid is absorbed. Remove from heat; fluff with a fork.

**2.** In a large bowl, mash black beans. Add 1 cup salsa, tortilla chips, taco seasoning and cooked quinoa; mix well. Shape into eight ¼-in.-thick patties.

**3.** Grill, covered, over medium heat 5-6 minutes on each side or until heated through. Serve on buns with lettuce, tomato, onion and remaining salsa.

**TO BAKE PATTIES** *Preheat oven to 350°. Place patties on a baking sheet coated with cooking spray. Bake 25-30 minutes or until heated through, turning once.*

**PER SERVING** *247 cal., 3 g fat (1 g sat. fat), 0 chol., 700 mg sodium, 47 g carb., 7 g fiber, 8 g pro.*

## Slow-Cooked Coconut Chicken

**PREP:** 10 MIN. • **COOK:** 4 HOURS • **MAKES:** 6 SERVINGS

- ½ cup light coconut milk
- 2 tablespoons brown sugar
- 2 tablespoons reduced-sodium soy sauce
- 2 garlic cloves, minced
- ⅛ teaspoon ground cloves
- 6 boneless skinless chicken thighs (about 1½ pounds)
- 6 tablespoons flaked coconut, toasted
  Minced fresh cilantro

In a large bowl, combine the first five ingredients. Place the chicken in a 3-qt. slow cooker. Pour coconut milk mixture over top. Cook, covered, on low 4-5 hours or until chicken is tender. Serve with coconut and cilantro.

**NOTE** *To toast coconut, spread in a 15x10x1-in. baking pan. Bake at 350° for 5-10 minutes or until golden brown, stirring frequently.*

**PER SERVING** *201 cal., 10 g fat (3 g sat. fat), 76 mg chol., 267 mg sodium, 6 g carb., trace fiber, 21 g pro. Diabetic Exchanges: 3 lean meat, ½ starch, ½ fat.*

Whenever guests sample Slow-Cooked Coconut Chicken for the first time, they ask me for the recipe.
—**ANN SMART** NORTH LOGAN, UT

SLOW-COOKED COCONUT CHICKEN

MAKEOVER CREAMY MAC & CHEESE

## Makeover Creamy Mac & Cheese

Macaroni and cheese just may be the king of all comfort foods. This version has all the creamy goodness but fewer calories.
—**APRIL TAYLOR** HOLCOMB, KS

**PREP:** 30 MIN. • **BAKE:** 25 MIN. • **MAKES:** 10 SERVINGS

- 1 package (16 ounces) elbow macaroni
- ⅓ cup all-purpose flour
- ½ teaspoon garlic powder
- ½ teaspoon pepper
- ¼ teaspoon salt
- 2 cups fat-free half-and-half
- 2 tablespoons butter
- 2 cups fat-free milk
- 3 cups (12 ounces) shredded reduced-fat sharp cheddar cheese

**OPTIONAL TOPPING**
- 2 tablespoons butter
- 1 medium onion, chopped
- 5 cups cubed bread
- ½ cup shredded reduced-fat cheddar cheese

**1.** Preheat oven to 350°. Cook the macaroni according to package directions; drain.

**2.** Meanwhile, in small bowl, whisk flour, seasonings and half-and-half until smooth. In a large saucepan, melt butter over medium heat. Stir in half-and-half mixture. Add milk. Bring to a gentle boil, stirring constantly; remove from heat. Add cheese; stir until melted. Stir in macaroni. Transfer to a 13x9-in. baking dish coated with cooking spray.

**3.** For optional topping, in a large skillet, heat butter over medium-high heat. Add onion; cook and stir until tender. Add cubed bread; cook and stir 2 minutes longer. Sprinkle over macaroni mixture; top with cheese.

**4.** Bake, uncovered, 25-30 minutes or until heated through.

**PER SERVING** *363 cal., 12 g fat (2 g sat. fat), 184 mg chol., 497 mg sodium, 34 g carb., trace fiber, 29 g pro. Diabetic Exchanges: 3 lean meat, 2 starch, 2 fat.*

SAUSAGE SPINACH SALAD

COOKING LIGHTER

## EAT SMART · SLOW COOKER
# Curried Ham & Split Pea Soup

Love split pea soup? For a change of pace, consider this deliciously different version. The warm flavor of curry goes so well with the saltiness of the ham. When mealtime arrives and you lift the lid on the slow cooker, you know you're in for a treat!

—**TRISHA KRUSE** EAGLE, ID

**PREP:** 10 MIN. • **COOK:** 7 HOURS
**MAKES:** 8 SERVINGS (2 QUARTS)

- 2 tablespoons butter
- 1 medium onion, chopped
- 4 garlic cloves, minced
- 3 teaspoons curry powder
- 1 package (16 ounces) dried green split peas
- 2 cups cubed fully cooked ham
- 1 cup sliced fresh carrots
- 4 cups reduced-sodium beef broth
- 2 cups water
- ½ teaspoon pepper

**1.** In a skillet, heat the butter over medium heat. Add the onion; cook and stir 3-4 minutes or until tender. Add the garlic and curry powder; cook 1 minute longer.

**2.** Transfer to a 4- or 5-qt. slow cooker. Add the remaining ingredients. Cook, covered, on low 7-9 hours or until peas are tender. Stir before serving.

**FREEZE OPTION** *Freeze cooled soup in freezer containers. To use, partially thaw in the refrigerator overnight. Heat through in a saucepan, stirring occasionally and adding a little water if necessary.*

**PER SERVING** *288 cal., 5 g fat (2 g sat. fat), 31 mg chol., 683 mg sodium, 39 g carb., 16 g fiber, 23 g pro.* **Diabetic Exchanges:** *3 lean meat, 2 starch, ½ fat.*

## EAT SMART · FAST FIX
# Greek Chicken & Artichokes

This 30-minute dinner was perennially popular with my friends when we were college students. I've tweaked it a bit on occasion by adding olives and onions.

—**CAITLIN CHANEY** TAMPA, FL

**START TO FINISH:** 30 MIN.
**MAKES:** 4 SERVINGS

- ¾ pound boneless skinless chicken breasts, cubed
- 1¼ teaspoons Greek seasoning
- 1 tablespoon olive oil
- 1 cup sliced fresh mushrooms
- 1 can (14½ ounces) no-salt-added diced tomatoes, undrained
- 1 can (14 ounces) water-packed quartered artichoke hearts, drained
- 2 cups cooked brown rice
- ¼ cup crumbled feta cheese

**1.** Toss the chicken with the Greek seasoning. In a large skillet, heat the oil over medium-high heat. Add the chicken; cook and stir until lightly browned. Add mushrooms; cook and stir 2 minutes longer.

**2.** Stir in the tomatoes and artichoke hearts. Bring to a boil. Reduce the heat; simmer, covered, 8-12 minutes or until the chicken is cooked through. Serve with brown rice. Top with crumbled feta cheese.

**PER SERVING** *309 cal., 7 g fat (2 g sat. fat), 51 mg chol., 704 mg sodium, 34 g carb., 4 g fiber, 25 g pro.* **Diabetic Exchanges:** *3 lean meat, 2 vegetable, 1½ starch, 1 fat.*

## EAT SMART · FAST FIX
# Sausage Spinach Salad

A light spinach salad instantly becomes a hearty entree when you toss in chunks of sausage. Enjoy the mustard dressing with smoked salmon and chicken, too.

—**DEBORAH WILLIAMS** PEORIA, AZ

**START TO FINISH:** 20 MIN.
**MAKES:** 2 SERVINGS

- 4 teaspoons olive oil, divided
- 2 fully cooked Italian chicken sausage links (3 ounces each), cut into ¼-inch slices
- ½ medium onion, halved and sliced
- 4 cups fresh baby spinach
- 1½ teaspoons balsamic vinegar
- 1 teaspoon stone-ground mustard

**1.** In a large nonstick skillet coated with cooking spray, heat 1 teaspoon oil over medium heat. Add sausage and onion; cook and stir until the sausage is lightly browned and the onion is crisp-tender.

**2.** Place the spinach in a large bowl. In a small bowl, whisk the vinegar, mustard and remaining oil. Drizzle over spinach; toss to coat. Add sausage mixture; serve immediately.

**PER SERVING** *244 cal., 16 g fat (3 g sat. fat), 65 mg chol., 581 mg sodium, 8 g carb., 2 g fiber, 17 g pro.* **Diabetic Exchanges:** *2 lean meat, 2 vegetable, 2 fat.*

## (?) Did you know?
The heart of the artichoke is revealed after the leaves are removed and the choke—the fuzzy inedible portion over the heart—is removed. Baby artichokes have not developed the fuzzy choke and are completely edible after some trimming.

CURRIED HAM & SPLIT PEA SOUP

## Meaty Slow-Cooked Jambalaya

**PREP:** 25 MIN. • **COOK:** 7 HOURS
**MAKES:** 12 SERVINGS (3½ QUARTS)

- 1 **can (28 ounces) diced tomatoes, undrained**
- 1 **cup reduced-sodium chicken broth**
- 1 **large green pepper, chopped**
- 1 **medium onion, chopped**
- 2 **celery ribs, sliced**
- ½ **cup white wine or additional reduced-sodium chicken broth**
- 4 **garlic cloves, minced**
- 2 **teaspoons Cajun seasoning**
- 2 **teaspoons dried parsley flakes**
- 1 **teaspoon dried basil**
- 1 **teaspoon dried oregano**
- ¾ **teaspoon salt**
- ½ **to 1 teaspoon cayenne pepper**
- 2 **pounds boneless skinless chicken thighs, cut into 1-inch pieces**
- 1 **package (12 ounces) fully cooked andouille or other spicy chicken sausage links**
- 2 **pounds uncooked medium shrimp, peeled and deveined**
- 8 **cups hot cooked brown rice**

**1.** In a large bowl, combine the first 13 ingredients. Place the chicken and sausage in a 6-qt. slow cooker. Pour the tomato mixture over top. Cook, covered, on low 7-9 hours or until the chicken is tender.

**2.** Stir in the shrimp. Cook, covered, 15-20 minutes longer or until shrimp turn pink. Serve with rice.

**PER SERVING** *387 cal., 10 g fat (3 g sat. fat), 164 mg chol., 674 mg sodium, 37 g carb., 4 g fiber, 36 g pro.* **Diabetic Exchanges:** *3 lean meat, 2½ starch.*

WALNUT-CRUSTED SALMON

MEATY SLOW-COOKED JAMBALAYA

Jazz up get-togethers the Louisiana way with a crowd-size pot of Meaty Slow-Cooked Jambalaya.
—**DIANE SMITH** PINE MOUNTAIN, GA

## Walnut-Crusted Salmon

When I find fillets on sale for a good price, I turn to this simple fish recipe featuring a walnut coating. Green beans and mashed potatoes make the perfect sides.
—**EDIE DESPAIN** LOGAN, UT

**START TO FINISH:** 25 MIN.
**MAKES:** 4 SERVINGS

- 4 **salmon fillets (4 ounces each)**
- 4 **teaspoons Dijon mustard**
- 4 **teaspoons honey**
- 2 **slices whole wheat bread, torn into pieces**
- 3 **tablespoons finely chopped walnuts**
- 2 **teaspoons canola oil**
- ½ **teaspoon dried thyme**

**1.** Preheat oven to 400°. Place salmon fillets on a baking sheet coated with cooking spray. Mix the mustard and honey; brush over salmon. Place bread in a food processor; pulse until coarse crumbs form. Transfer to a small bowl. Stir in walnuts, oil and thyme; press onto salmon.

**2.** Bake 12-15 minutes or until topping is lightly browned and fish just begins to flake easily with a fork.

**PER SERVING** *295 cal., 17 g fat (3 g sat. fat), 57 mg chol., 243 mg sodium, 13 g carb., 1 g fiber, 22 g pro.* **Diabetic Exchanges:** *3 lean meat, 1 starch, ½ fat.*

> Feta cheese gives Greek Sloppy Joes a distinctive flavor. I stuff any leftovers into pitas for lunch.
>
> —SONYA LABBE WEST HOLLYWOOD, CA

**GREEK SLOPPY JOES**

EAT SMART FAST FIX

## Greek Sloppy Joes

**START TO FINISH:** 25 MIN.
**MAKES:** 6 SERVINGS

- 1 **pound lean ground beef (90% lean)**
- 1 **small red onion, chopped**
- 2 **garlic cloves, minced**
- 1 **can (15 ounces) tomato sauce**
- 1 **teaspoon dried oregano**
- 2 **cups chopped romaine**
- 6 **kaiser rolls, split and toasted**
- ½ **cup crumbled feta cheese**

**1.** In a large skillet, cook the beef, onion and garlic over medium heat 6-8 minutes or until beef is no longer pink, breaking up beef into crumbles; drain. Stir in the tomato sauce and oregano. Bring to a boil. Reduce heat; simmer, uncovered, 8-10 minutes or until the sauce is slightly thickened, stirring occasionally.

**2.** Place the romaine on the bottoms of the rolls; top with the meat mixture. Sprinkle with feta cheese; replace the tops of rolls.

**PER SERVING** *337 cal., 10 g fat (4 g sat. fat), 52 mg chol., 767 mg sodium, 36 g carb., 3 g fiber, 24 g pro.* **Diabetic Exchanges:** *3 lean meat, 2 starch, 1 vegetable.*

EAT SMART FAST FIX

## Veggie Chowder

With five kinds of vegetables, this chowder is loaded with wholesome goodness but isn't too heavy. Pair it with your favorite sandwich, green salad or bread.

—VICKI KERR PORTLAND, ME

**START TO FINISH:** 30 MIN.
**MAKES:** 6 SERVINGS (1¾ QUARTS)

- 2 **cups cubed peeled potatoes**
- 2 **cups reduced-sodium chicken broth**
- 1 **cup chopped carrots**
- ½ **cup chopped onion**
- 1 **can (14¾ ounces) cream-style corn**
- 1 **can (12 ounces) fat-free evaporated milk**
- ¾ **cup shredded reduced-fat cheddar cheese**
- ½ **cup sliced fresh mushrooms**
- ¼ **teaspoon pepper**
- 2 **tablespoons bacon bits**

**1.** In a large saucepan, combine the potatoes, broth, carrots and onion; bring to a boil. Reduce heat; simmer, uncovered, 10-15 minutes or until the vegetables are tender.

**2.** Add the corn, milk, cheddar cheese, mushrooms and pepper; cook and stir 4-6 minutes longer or until heated through. Sprinkle with bacon bits.

**PER SERVING** *208 cal., 4 g fat (2 g sat. fat), 14 mg chol., 637 mg sodium, 34 g carb., 3 g fiber, 12 g pro.* **Diabetic Exchanges:** *2 starch, ½ fat.*

**VEGGIE CHOWDER**

Here in Michigan, the outdoor grilling season doesn't last long. I make the most of it with mouthwatering recipes like Grilled Pork with Spicy Pineapple Salsa.
—**DIANE NEMITZ** LUDINGTON, MI

GRILLED PORK WITH SPICY PINEAPPLE SALSA

EAT SMART FAST FIX
## Grilled Pork with Spicy Pineapple Salsa

**START TO FINISH:** 30 MIN.
**MAKES:** 8 SERVINGS (2 CUPS SALSA)

- 1 jar (16 ounces) chunky salsa
- 1 can (8 ounces) unsweetened crushed pineapple
- ½ cup port wine or grape juice
- ¼ cup packed brown sugar
- ¼ cup lime juice
- ¼ cup thawed orange juice concentrate
- 2 tablespoons Worcestershire sauce
- 1 teaspoon garlic powder
- ¼ teaspoon cayenne pepper

**PORK**
- 1 teaspoon ground cumin
- ½ teaspoon pepper
- ¼ teaspoon cayenne pepper
- 2 pork tenderloins (1 pound each) Lime wedges

**1.** In a large saucepan, combine the first nine ingredients. Bring to a boil; cook 20-25 minutes or until mixture is reduced by half, stirring occasionally.

**2.** Meanwhile, for pork, mix spices; rub over the tenderloins. Moisten a paper towel with cooking oil; using long-handled tongs, rub on grill rack to coat lightly. Grill pork, covered, over medium heat or broil 4 in. from heat 18-22 minutes or until a thermometer reads 145°, turning occasionally.

**3.** Let stand 5 minutes before slicing. Serve with salsa and lime wedges.

**PER SERVING** *220 cal., 4 g fat (1 g sat. fat), 63 mg chol., 318 mg sodium, 22 g carb., 1 g fiber, 23 g pro.* **Diabetic Exchanges:** *3 lean meat, 1½ starch.*

(5)INGREDIENTS EAT SMART FAST FIX
## Shredded Gingered Brussels Sprouts

Even people who normally don't care for Brussels sprouts will ask for a second helping of this ginger-spiced side dish.
—**JAMES SCHEND** PLEASANT PRAIRIE, WI

**START TO FINISH:** 20 MIN.
**MAKES:** 6 SERVINGS

- 1 pound fresh Brussels sprouts (about 5½ cups)
- 1 tablespoon olive oil
- 1 small onion, finely chopped
- 1 tablespoon minced fresh gingerroot
- 1 garlic clove, minced
- ½ teaspoon salt
- 2 tablespoons water
- ¼ teaspoon pepper

**1.** Trim Brussels sprouts. Cut sprouts lengthwise in half; cut crosswise into thin slices.

**2.** Place a large skillet over medium-high heat. Add the Brussels sprouts; cook and stir 2-3 minutes or until the sprouts begin to brown lightly. Add the oil and toss to coat. Stir in the onion, ginger, garlic and salt. Add the water; reduce heat to medium and cook, covered, 1-2 minutes or until vegetables are tender. Stir in pepper.

**PER SERVING** *56 cal., 2 g fat (trace sat. fat), 0 chol., 214 mg sodium, 8 g carb., 3 g fiber, 2 g pro.* **Diabetic Exchanges:** *1 vegetable, ½ fat.*

# Guilt-Free Sweets

Craving a treat? Go ahead and indulge! From a rich chocolate pie to yummy spritz cookies, these recipes will fit a healthier lifestyle.

**⑤INGREDIENTS** **EAT SMART** **FAST FIX** ▶

## Mocha Pumpkin Seeds

Roasted pumpkin seeds are a classic autumn snack. Perk them up a little with instant coffee and baking cocoa.

**—REBEKAH BEYER** SABETHA, KS

**START TO FINISH:** 25 MIN. • **MAKES:** 3 CUPS

- 6 **tablespoons sugar**
- 2 **tablespoons baking cocoa**
- 1 **tablespoon instant coffee granules**
- 1 **egg white**
- 2 **cups salted shelled pumpkin seeds (pepitas)**

**1.** Preheat oven to 325°. Place sugar, cocoa and coffee in a small food processor; cover and pulse until finely ground.
**2.** In a bowl, whisk egg white until frothy. Stir in pumpkin seeds. Sprinkle with the sugar mixture; toss to coat evenly. Spread in a single layer in a parchment paper-lined 15x10x1-in. baking pan.
**3.** Bake for 20-25 minutes or until dry and no longer sticky, stirring every 10 minutes. Cool completely in pan. Store in an airtight container.
**PER SERVING** *142 cal., 10 g fat (2 g sat. fat), 0 chol., 55 mg sodium, 10 g carb., 1 g fiber, 6 g pro.* **Diabetic Exchanges: 2 fat, ½ starch.**

MOCHA PUMPKIN SEEDS

FROZEN GREEK VANILLA YOGURT

**⑤INGREDIENTS** **EAT SMART**

## Frozen Greek Vanilla Yogurt

Making your own frozen Greek yogurt is easier than you may think. Kids will want to help—and taste the results!

**—TASTE OF HOME TEST KITCHEN**

**PREP:** 15 MIN.+ CHILLING • **PROCESS:** 15 MIN.+ FREEZING
**MAKES:** 2½ CUPS

- 3 **cups reduced-fat plain Greek yogurt**
- ¾ **cup sugar**
- 1½ **teaspoons clear vanilla extract**
- 1 **tablespoon cold water**
- 1 **tablespoon lemon juice**
- 1 **teaspoon unflavored gelatin**

**1.** Line a strainer or colander with four layers of cheesecloth or one coffee filter; place over a bowl. Place yogurt in prepared strainer; cover yogurt with sides of cheesecloth. Refrigerate 2-4 hours.
**2.** Remove the yogurt from cheesecloth to a bowl; discard strained liquid. Add the sugar and vanilla to yogurt, stirring until sugar is dissolved.
**3.** In a small microwave-safe bowl, combine cold water and the lemon juice; sprinkle with gelatin and let stand 1 minute. Microwave on high for 30 seconds. Stir and let the mixture stand 1 minute or until gelatin is completely dissolved.
**4.** Pour yogurt mixture into cylinder of ice cream freezer; freeze according to the manufacturer's directions, adding gelatin mixture during the last 10 minutes of processing.
**5.** Transfer the frozen yogurt to a freezer container. Freeze 2-4 hours or until firm enough to scoop.
**PER SERVING** *225 cal., 3 g fat (2 g sat. fat), 8 mg chol., 57 mg sodium, 36 g carb., trace fiber, 14 g pro.*

# Chocolate Eggnog Pie

**PREP:** 45 MIN. + CHILLING • **MAKES:** 8 SERVINGS

- ½ cup all-purpose flour
- ⅓ cup ground walnuts
- 3 tablespoons brown sugar
- 1 tablespoon baking cocoa
- ¼ cup reduced-fat butter, melted

**FILLING**
- ½ cup sugar
- 2 tablespoons cornstarch
- 2 cups reduced-fat eggnog
- 2½ teaspoons unflavored gelatin
- ½ cup cold water, divided
- 2 tablespoons baking cocoa
- ¾ teaspoon rum extract
- 2 cups reduced-fat whipped topping
- Additional reduced-fat whipped topping, optional
- Ground nutmeg, optional

**1.** Preheat the oven to 375°. In a small bowl, mix the flour, walnuts, brown sugar and cocoa; stir in butter. Lightly coat your hands with cooking spray; press the mixture into an ungreased 9-in. pie plate. Bake 8-10 minutes or until set. Cool completely on a wire rack.

**2.** For the filling, in a small heavy saucepan, mix sugar and cornstarch. Whisk in eggnog. Cook and stir over medium heat until thickened and bubbly. Reduce heat to low; cook and stir 2 minutes longer. Remove from heat.

CHOCOLATE EGGNOG PIE

For a light but luscious Christmastime dessert, try Chocolate Eggnog Pie. It won't disappoint!
—**KERI WHITNEY** SUNNYVALE, TX

**3.** In a microwave-safe bowl, sprinkle the gelatin over ¼ cup cold water; let stand 1 minute. Microwave on high 20 seconds. Stir and let stand for 1 minute or until gelatin is completely dissolved. Stir into eggnog mixture.

**4.** Divide the mixture in half. In a small bowl, whisk the baking cocoa and remaining water until blended; stir into one half of the eggnog mixture. Stir the rum extract into the remaining half. Refrigerate both mixtures, covered, until partially set.

**5.** Fold 2 cups whipped topping into rum-flavored portion; spoon into crust. Gently spread chocolate portion over top. Refrigerate, covered, at least 2 hours before serving. If desired, top with additional whipped topping and sprinkle with nutmeg.

**PER SERVING** *259 cal., 10 g fat (5 g sat. fat), 56 mg chol., 90 mg sodium, 39 g carb., 1 g fiber, 5 g pro.*

# Gluten-Free Spritz Delights

My daughter, who has Down syndrome, loves hosting parties for family and friends—especially on holidays. When she was diagnosed with celiac disease, I started baking gluten-free treats. These spritz cookies are my best discovery yet.
—**CHERYL COSTILOW** AMHERST, OH

**PREP:** 25 MIN. • **BAKE:** 10 MIN./BATCH + COOLING
**MAKES:** 8½ DOZEN

- 1 cup butter, softened
- ½ cup sugar
- 1 egg
- 1 teaspoon almond extract
- 2¼ cups gluten-free all-purpose baking flour
- 1½ teaspoons xanthan gum
- ½ teaspoon salt
- ¾ cup gluten-free vanilla frosting
- Food coloring, optional
- Gluten-free sprinkles

**1.** Preheat oven to 400°. In a large bowl, cream the butter and sugar until light and fluffy. Beat in the egg and extract. In another bowl, whisk the flour, the xanthan gum and salt; gradually beat into creamed mixture.

**2.** Using a cookie press fitted with the disk of your choice, press dough 1 in. apart onto ungreased baking sheets. Bake 6-8 minutes or until bottoms are light brown. Remove from pans to wire racks to cool completely.

**3.** In a microwave, warm the frosting to reach a drizzling consistency. If desired, tint with food coloring. Drizzle over the cookies; decorate with sprinkles. Let stand until set.

**NOTE** *This recipe was tested with King Arthur Gluten-Free Multi-Purpose Flour. Read all ingredient labels for possible gluten content prior to use. Ingredient formulas can change, and production facilities vary among brands. If you're concerned that your brand may contain gluten, contact the company.*

**PER SERVING** *38 cal., 2 g fat (1 g sat. fat), 7 mg chol., 30 mg sodium, 4 g carb., trace fiber, trace pro.*

## Feta Shrimp Skillet

**START TO FINISH:** 30 MIN.
**MAKES:** 4 SERVINGS

- 1 tablespoon olive oil
- 1 medium onion, finely chopped
- 3 garlic cloves, minced
- 1 teaspoon dried oregano
- ½ teaspoon pepper
- ¼ teaspoon salt
- 2 cans (14½ ounces each) diced tomatoes, undrained
- ¼ cup white wine, optional
- 1 pound uncooked medium shrimp, peeled and deveined
- 2 tablespoons minced fresh parsley
- ¾ cup crumbled feta cheese

**1.** In a large nonstick skillet, heat oil over medium-high heat. Add onion; cook and stir for 4-6 minutes or until tender. Add garlic and seasonings; cook 1 minute longer. Stir in tomatoes and, if desired, wine. Bring to a boil. Reduce heat; simmer, uncovered, 5-7 minutes or until sauce is slightly thickened.

**2.** Add the shrimp and parsley; cook 5-6 minutes or until the shrimp turn pink, stirring occasionally. Remove from the heat; sprinkle with the feta cheese. Let stand, covered, until the cheese is softened.

**PER SERVING** *240 cal., 8 g fat (3 g sat. fat), 149 mg chol., 748 mg sodium, 16 g carb., 5 g fiber, 25 g pro.* **Diabetic Exchanges:** *3 lean meat, 1 starch, 1 fat.*

## Apres-Ski Soup

*Aprés-ski* is French for "after skiing." This microwaved veggie-noodle soup is the ideal way to warm up after hitting the slopes—or enjoying any other fall or wintertime activities outdoors.

—**NANCY HAMLIN** LITTLETON, CO

**START TO FINISH:** 30 MIN.
**MAKES:** 6 SERVINGS (1½ QUARTS)

- 1 tablespoon butter
- 1¼ cups cubed acorn squash
- 1 carrot, thinly sliced
- 1 medium leek (white portion only), thinly sliced
- 3 cans (14½ ounces each) reduced-sodium chicken broth
- 1 small zucchini, halved and sliced
- ½ cup uncooked elbow macaroni
- 1 bay leaf
- ½ teaspoon dried basil
- ¼ teaspoon dried thyme
- ⅛ teaspoon salt
- ⅛ teaspoon pepper

**1.** Place butter in a 3-qt. microwave-safe bowl; microwave on high for 15-20 seconds or until melted. Add the squash, carrot and leek; stir to coat. Cook, covered, on high for 6 minutes.

**2.** Stir in the remaining ingredients; cook, covered, on high for 12-14 minutes or until the vegetables and macaroni are tender, stirring twice. Remove the bay leaf.

**NOTE** *This recipe was tested in a 1,100-watt microwave.*

**PER SERVING** *92 cal., 2 g fat (1 g sat. fat), 5 mg chol., 594 mg sodium, 15 g carb., 3 g fiber, 4 g pro.* **Diabetic Exchanges:** *1 vegetable, ½ starch, ½ fat.*

While on our honeymoon in Greece, my husband and I had a dish that was similar to Feta Shrimp Skillet. It brings back great memories every time I make it.
—**SONALI RUDER** NEW YORK, NY

FETA SHRIMP SKILLET

CARNE GUISADA

## Stuffed-Olive Cod

Head to the olive bar in your supermarket, then put a new spin on cod fillets for a simple, high-protein and low-fat entree.

—TRIA OLSEN QUEEN CREEK, AZ

**START TO FINISH:** 25 MIN.
**MAKES:** 4 SERVINGS

- 4 cod fillets (6 ounces each)
- 1 teaspoon dried oregano
- ¼ teaspoon salt
- 1 medium lemon, thinly sliced
- 1 shallot, thinly sliced
- ⅓ cup garlic-stuffed olives, halved
- 2 tablespoons water
- 2 tablespoons olive juice

**1.** Place cod fillets in a large nonstick skillet coated with cooking spray. Sprinkle with oregano and salt; top with lemon and shallot.
**2.** Scatter the garlic-stuffed olives around the cod fillets; add the water and olive juice. Bring to a boil. Reduce the heat to low; gently cook, covered, 8-10 minutes or until fish just begins to flake easily with a fork.

**PER SERVING** *163 cal., 3 g fat (trace sat. fat), 65 mg chol., 598 mg sodium, 4 g carb., trace fiber, 27 g pro.* **Diabetic Exchange:** *4 lean meat.*

## Carne Guisada

After moving from Texas to Michigan, my boyfriend and I grew homesick for Southwestern food. A spicy slow-cooked dinner of pork and potatoes was the cure! It goes really well with flour tortillas or rice, plus a twist of lime and chopped cilantro.

—KELLY EVANS DENTON, TX

**PREP:** 25 MIN. • **COOK:** 7 HOURS
**MAKES:** 12 SERVINGS (ABOUT 2 QUARTS)

- 1 bottle (12 ounces) beer
- ¼ cup all-purpose flour
- 2 tablespoons tomato paste
- 1 jalapeno pepper, seeded and chopped
- 4 teaspoons Worcestershire sauce
- 1 bay leaf
- 2 to 3 teaspoons crushed red pepper flakes
- 2 teaspoons chili powder
- 1½ teaspoons ground cumin
- ½ teaspoon salt
- ½ teaspoon paprika
- 2 garlic cloves, minced
- ½ teaspoon red wine vinegar
  Dash liquid smoke, optional
- 1 boneless pork shoulder butt roast (3 pounds), cut into 2-inch pieces
- 2 large unpeeled red potatoes, chopped
- 1 medium onion, chopped
  Whole wheat tortillas or hot cooked brown rice, lime wedges and chopped fresh cilantro, optional

**1.** In a 4- or 5-qt. slow cooker, combine the first 13 ingredients. If desired, stir in liquid smoke. Add pork, potatoes and onion; toss to combine. Cook, covered, 7-9 hours or until pork is tender.
**2.** Discard the bay leaf; skim fat from the cooking juices. Shred pork slightly with two forks. If desired, serve with tortillas, lime and cilantro.
**NOTE** *Wear disposable gloves when cutting hot peppers; the oils can burn skin. Avoid touching your face.*
**PER SERVING** *261 cal., 12 g fat (4 g sat. fat), 67 mg chol., 200 mg sodium, 16 g carb., 2 g fiber, 21 g pro.* **Diabetic Exchanges:** *3 medium-fat meat, 1 starch.*

STUFFED-OLIVE COD

## Greek-Style Chicken Skewers

This was a big hit with my son. It's the only chicken he doesn't want to put ketchup on! The great flavor from the seasonings does the tasty trick.

**—KATHY LEWIS-MARTINEZ**
SPRING VALLEY, CA

**START TO FINISH:** 30 MIN.
**MAKES:** 4 SERVINGS

- ¾ cup reduced-fat plain yogurt
- 1 tablespoon lemon juice
- 1 tablespoon olive oil
- 1 teaspoon poultry seasoning
- 1 teaspoon dried oregano
- ½ teaspoon salt
- ½ teaspoon grated lemon peel
- ¼ teaspoon onion powder
- ¼ teaspoon pepper
- 1 pound boneless skinless chicken breasts, cut into strips

**1.** In a large bowl, combine all of the ingredients, tossing lightly. Refrigerate chicken for 10 minutes or up to 8 hours.

GREEK-STYLE CHICKEN SKEWERS

**2.** Remove chicken from marinade; discard marinade. Thread chicken onto eight metal or soaked wooden skewers. Moisten a paper towel with cooking oil; using long-handled tongs, lightly coat the grill rack.

**3.** Grill the chicken, covered, over medium heat or broil 4 in. from the heat 5-7 minutes or until chicken is no longer pink, turning once.

**PER SERVING** *134 cal., 3 g fat (1 g sat. fat), 63 mg chol., 120 mg sodium, 1 g carb., trace fiber, 23 g pro.* **Diabetic Exchange:** *3 lean meat.*

## Cajun Beef & Rice

From a restaurant or store-bought mix, dirty rice can have a lot of sodium and fat. I trim it down for a guilt-free dinner.

**—RAQUEL HAGGARD** EDMOND, OK

**START TO FINISH:** 30 MIN.
**MAKES:** 4 SERVINGS

- 1 pound lean ground beef (90% lean)
- 3 celery ribs, chopped
- 1 small green pepper, chopped
- 1 small sweet red pepper, chopped
- ¼ cup chopped onion
- 2 cups water
- 1 cup instant brown rice
- 1 tablespoon minced fresh parsley
- 1 tablespoon Worcestershire sauce
- 2 teaspoons reduced-sodium beef bouillon granules
- 1 teaspoon Cajun seasoning
- ¼ teaspoon crushed red pepper flakes
- ¼ teaspoon pepper
- ⅛ teaspoon garlic powder

**1.** In a large skillet, cook beef, celery, green and red peppers, and onion over medium heat 8-10 minutes or until beef is no longer pink, breaking up beef into crumbles; drain.

**2.** Stir in the remaining ingredients. Bring to a boil. Reduce heat; simmer, covered, 12-15 minutes or until the rice is tender.

**PER SERVING** *291 cal., 10 g fat (4 g sat. fat), 71 mg chol., 422 mg sodium, 23 g carb., 2 g fiber, 25 g pro.* **Diabetic Exchanges:** *3 lean meat, 1 starch, 1 vegetable.*

SKILLET CASSOULET

## Skillet Cassoulet

Here's a skillet version of a traditional French dish. Chock-full of spicy kielbasa, ham and vegetables, it's a hearty meal in one that won't derail a healthy diet.

**—BARBARA BRITTAIN** SANTEE, CA

**START TO FINISH:** 30 MIN.
**MAKES:** 3 SERVINGS

- 2 teaspoons canola oil
- ¼ pound smoked turkey kielbasa, cut into ½-inch slices
- ¼ pound fully cooked boneless ham, cubed
- 2 medium carrots, sliced
- 1 celery rib, sliced
- ½ medium red onion, sliced
- 2 garlic cloves, minced
- 1 can (15 ounces) no-salt-added white kidney or cannellini beans, rinsed and drained
- 1 can (14½ ounces) no-salt-added diced tomatoes, undrained
- ¾ teaspoon dried thyme
- ⅛ teaspoon pepper

**1.** In a large skillet, heat the oil over medium-high heat. Add the kielbasa, ham, carrots, celery and onion; cook and stir until sausage is browned and vegetables are tender. Add garlic; cook 1 minute longer.

**2.** Stir in the remaining ingredients. Bring to a boil. Reduce heat; simmer, uncovered, for 4-5 minutes or until heated through.

**PER SERVING** *282 cal., 8 g fat (1 g sat. fat), 43 mg chol., 901 mg sodium, 33 g carb., 10 g fiber, 22 g pro.*

# Tuscan Turkey Soup

**START TO FINISH:** 30 MIN.
**MAKES:** 8 SERVINGS (2 QUARTS)

- 2 tablespoons olive oil
- 1 cup chopped onion
- 1 cup chopped celery
- 2 garlic cloves, minced
- 2 cans (14½ ounces each) reduced-sodium chicken broth
- 1 can (15 ounces) solid-pack pumpkin
- 1 can (15 ounces) white kidney or cannellini beans, rinsed and drained
- 2 cups cubed cooked turkey
- ½ teaspoon salt
- ½ teaspoon dried basil
- ¼ teaspoon pepper
  Grated Parmesan cheese, optional

**1.** In a large saucepan, heat the oil over medium-high heat. Add onion and celery; cook and stir until tender. Add garlic; cook 1 minute longer.

**2.** Stir in chicken broth, pumpkin, beans, turkey, salt, basil and pepper. Bring to a boil. Reduce heat; simmer, uncovered, 10-15 minutes or until heated through, stirring occasionally. If desired, serve with cheese.

**PER SERVING** *167 cal., 6 g fat (1 g sat. fat), 27 mg chol., 549 mg sodium, 14 g carb., 5 g fiber, 15 g pro.* **Diabetic Exchanges:** *2 lean meat, 1 starch, 1 fat.*

Use the leftovers from a Thanksgiving feast to prepare Tuscan Turkey Soup. It's so easy to fix, even novice cooks can serve up piping-hot bowlfuls in a flash.
—**MARIE MCCONNELL** SHELBYVILLE, IL

TUSCAN TURKEY SOUP

# Crispy Fish & Chips

A British pub classic becomes a crown jewel when you add Worcestershire, horseradish and panko bread crumbs.
—**LINDA SCHEND** KENOSHA, WI

**START TO FINISH:** 30 MIN.
**MAKES:** 4 SERVINGS

- 4 cups frozen steak fries
- 4 salmon fillets (6 ounces each)
- 1 to 2 tablespoons prepared horseradish
- 1 tablespoon grated Parmesan cheese
- 1 tablespoon Worcestershire sauce
- 1 teaspoon Dijon mustard
- ¼ teaspoon salt
- ½ cup panko (Japanese) bread crumbs
  Cooking spray

**1.** Preheat oven to 450°. Arrange fries in a single layer on a baking sheet. Bake on lowest oven rack 18-20 minutes or until light golden brown.

**2.** Meanwhile, place the salmon fillets on a foil-lined baking sheet coated with cooking spray. In a small bowl, mix the horseradish, Parmesan cheese, Worcestershire sauce, Dijon mustard and salt; stir in panko bread crumbs. Press mixture onto fillets. Spritz tops with cooking spray.

**3.** Bake the salmon on the middle oven rack 8-10 minutes or until fish just begins to flake easily with a fork. Serve with fries.

**PER SERVING** *419 cal., 20 g fat (4 g sat. fat), 86 mg chol., 695 mg sodium, 26 g carb., 2 g fiber, 32 g pro.* **Diabetic Exchanges:** *5 lean meat, 1½ starch.*

**top tip**

## Finished Fillets

Overcooked fish loses its flavor and becomes tough. Check fish fillets for doneness by inserting a fork at an angle into the thickest portion of the fillet and gently parting the meat. When the fish is opaque and flakes into sections, it is cooked completely.

Beef-Stuffed Cabbage Rolls satisfy big appetites without straying from a healthy eating plan.
—LYNN BOWEN GERALDINE, AL

BEEF-STUFFED CABBAGE ROLLS

## EAT SMART SLOW COOKER
## Beef-Stuffed Cabbage Rolls

**PREP:** 20 MIN. • **COOK:** 6 HOURS
**MAKES:** 6 SERVINGS

- 12 cabbage leaves
- 1 cup cooked brown rice
- ¼ cup finely chopped onion
- 1 egg, lightly beaten
- ¼ cup fat-free milk
- ½ teaspoon salt
- ¼ teaspoon pepper
- 1 pound lean ground beef (90% lean)

**SAUCE**

- 1 can (8 ounces) tomato sauce
- 1 tablespoon brown sugar
- 1 tablespoon lemon juice
- 1 teaspoon Worcestershire sauce

**1.** In batches, cook the cabbage in boiling water 3-5 minutes or until crisp-tender. Drain; cool slightly. Trim the thick vein from the bottom of each cabbage leaf, making a V-shaped cut.

**2.** In a large bowl, combine the brown rice, onion, egg, milk, salt and pepper. Add beef; mix lightly but thoroughly. Place about ¼ cup beef mixture on each cabbage leaf. Pull together cut edges of leaf to overlap; fold over filling. Fold in sides and roll up.

**3.** Place six cabbage rolls in a 4- or 5-qt. slow cooker, seam side down. In a bowl, mix the sauce ingredients; pour half of the sauce over the cabbage rolls in slow cooker. Top with remaining rolls and sauce. Cook, covered, on low for 6-8 hours or until a thermometer inserted in the beef reads 160° and the cabbage is tender.

**PER SERVING** *204 cal., 7 g fat (3 g sat. fat), 83 mg chol., 446 mg sodium, 16 g carb., 2 g fiber, 18 g pro.* **Diabetic Exchanges:** *2 lean meat, 1 starch.*

## EAT SMART FAST FIX
## Pecan-Crusted Chicken Nuggets

These baked nuggets are lighter than the original version I enjoyed as a child.
—HAILI CARROLL VALENCIA, CA

**START TO FINISH:** 30 MIN.
**MAKES:** 6 SERVINGS

- 1½ cups cornflakes
- 1 tablespoon dried parsley flakes
- ½ teaspoon garlic powder
- ½ cup panko (Japanese) bread crumbs
- ½ cup finely chopped pecans
- 3 tablespoons 2% milk
- 1½ pounds boneless skinless chicken breasts, cut into 1-inch pieces
- ½ teaspoon salt
- ¼ teaspoon pepper
  Cooking spray

**1.** Preheat oven to 400°. Place the cornflakes, parsley and garlic powder in a blender; cover and pulse until finely ground. Transfer to a shallow bowl; stir in the bread crumbs and pecans. Place milk in another shallow bowl. Sprinkle chicken with salt and pepper; dip in milk, then roll in crumb mixture to coat.

**2.** Place on a greased baking sheet; spritz the chicken with cooking spray. Bake 12-16 minutes or until chicken is no longer pink, turning once halfway through cooking.

**PER SERVING** *206 cal., 9 g fat (1 g sat. fat), 63 mg chol., 290 mg sodium, 6 g carb., 1 g fiber, 24 g pro.* **Diabetic Exchanges:** *3 lean meat, 1 fat, ½ starch.*

PECAN-CRUSTED CHICKEN NUGGETS

LEMON-BASIL GRILLED SHRIMP & COUSCOUS

**2.** Thread the shrimp onto metal or soaked wooden skewers. Moisten a paper towel with cooking oil; using long-handled tongs, rub on grill rack to coat lightly. Grill shrimp, covered, over medium-high heat 2-3 minutes on each side or until shrimp turn pink.

**3.** Remove the shrimp from skewers; toss with reserved dressing. Serve with couscous. Sprinkle with lemon peel and remaining basil.

**PER SERVING** *192 cal., 9 g fat (4 g sat. fat), 71 mg chol., 259 mg sodium, 3 g carb., 1 g fiber, 22 g pro.* **Diabetic Exchange:** *3 lean meat.*

## Southwest Steak & Potatoes

With bold seasonings, this meat-lover's dinner boasts a taste of the Southwest. Feel free to adjust the heat factor to your liking by using more or less chili powder.

—**KENNY FISHER** CIRCLEVILLE, OH

**START TO FINISH:** 30 MIN.
**MAKES:** 4 SERVINGS

- 4 **medium Yukon Gold potatoes**
- 2 **teaspoons cider vinegar**
- 1 **teaspoon Worcestershire sauce**
- 1 **beef top round steak (1 inch thick and about 1½ pounds)**
- 1 **tablespoon brown sugar**

- 1 **tablespoon chili powder**
- 1½ **teaspoons ground cumin**
- 1 **teaspoon garlic powder**
- 1 **teaspoon salt, divided**
- ⅛ **teaspoon cayenne pepper**
- ⅛ **teaspoon pepper**

**1.** Pierce the potatoes; place on a microwave-safe plate. Microwave, uncovered, on high 4-5 minutes or until almost tender, turning once. Cool slightly.

**2.** Meanwhile, mix the cider vinegar and Worcestershire sauce; brush over the steak. Mix the brown sugar, chili powder, cumin, garlic powder, ½ teaspoon salt and cayenne pepper until blended; sprinkle over both sides of the steak.

**3.** Cut the potatoes into ½-in. slices. Sprinkle with pepper and remaining salt. Grill potatoes and steak, covered, over medium heat 12-17 minutes or until the potatoes are tender and a thermometer inserted in the beef reads 145° for medium-rare, turning occasionally.

**4.** Cut steak into thin slices. Serve with potatoes.

**PER SERVING** *360 cal., 6 g fat (2 g sat. fat), 96 mg chol., 681 mg sodium, 34 g carb., 3 g fiber, 41 g pro.* **Diabetic Exchanges:** *5 lean meat, 2 starch.*

## Lemon-Basil Grilled Shrimp & Couscous

Fresh ingredients really make a difference in my grilled shrimp entree. The basil and lemon complement each other so nicely. Add a green salad for a complete meal.

—**TRISHA KRUSE** EAGLE, ID

**START TO FINISH:** 30 MIN.
**MAKES:** 6 SERVINGS

- 1½ **cups uncooked pearl (Israeli) couscous**
- ⅓ **cup lemon juice**
- ¼ **cup olive oil**
- 2 **tablespoons Dijon mustard**
- 3 **garlic cloves, minced**
- ½ **teaspoon salt**
- ¼ **teaspoon pepper**
- ½ **cup minced fresh basil, divided**
- 2 **pounds uncooked large shrimp, peeled and deveined**
- 2 **teaspoons grated lemon peel**

**1.** Cook the couscous according to the package directions; remove from heat. Meanwhile, in a large bowl, whisk the lemon juice, oil, Dijon mustard, garlic, salt and pepper until blended; stir in ¼ cup basil. Stir ¼ cup dressing into the cooked couscous; reserve the remaining dressing.

SOUTHWEST STEAK & POTATOES

# Honey-Lemon Chicken Enchiladas

**START TO FINISH:** 30 MIN. • **MAKES:** 6 SERVINGS

- ¼ **cup honey**
- 2 **tablespoons lemon or lime juice**
- 1 **tablespoon canola oil**
- 2 **teaspoons chili powder**
- ¼ **teaspoon garlic powder**
- 3 **cups shredded cooked chicken breast**
- 2 **cans (10 ounces each) green enchilada sauce, divided**
- 12 **corn tortillas (6 inches), warmed**
- ¾ **cup shredded reduced-fat cheddar cheese**
  **Sliced green onions and chopped tomatoes, optional**

**1.** In a large bowl, whisk the first five ingredients. Add the chicken and toss to coat. Pour 1 can enchilada sauce into a greased microwave-safe 11x7-in. dish. Place ¼ cup chicken mixture off center on each tortilla. Roll up and place in the prepared dish, seam side down. Top with the remaining enchilada sauce.

**2.** Microwave, covered, on high for 11-13 minutes or until heated through. Sprinkle with cheese. If desired, top with green onions and tomatoes.

**NOTE** *This recipe was tested in a full-size 1,100-watt microwave. If your microwave does not accommodate an 11x7-in. dish, bake casserole, covered, in a preheated 400° oven for 25-30 minutes or until heated through. Sprinkle with cheese and top as directed.*

**PER SERVING** *349 cal., 11 g fat (3 g sat. fat), 64 mg chol., 698 mg sodium, 39 g carb., 3 g fiber, 27 g pro.* **Diabetic Exchanges:** *3 lean meat, 2½ starch.*

My family devours a pan of Honey-Lemon Chicken Enchiladas. I've also used the filling for soft tacos.
—**KRISTI MOAK** GILBERT, AZ

HONEY-LEMON
CHICKEN ENCHILADAS

JALAPENO
JELLY-GLAZED
PORK CHOPS

# Jalapeno Jelly-Glazed Pork Chops

These golden chops get plenty of zip from jalapeno pepper jelly. My husband says there's less conversation at the table when I fix them because everyone's too busy eating!
—**SHANNON BRUCE** MOORESVILLE, IN

**START TO FINISH:** 25 MIN. • **MAKES:** 4 SERVINGS

- 1 **pound fresh green beans, trimmed**
- 2 **teaspoons olive oil**
- ¾ **teaspoon salt, divided**
- ⅛ **teaspoon plus ¼ teaspoon pepper, divided**
- 4 **boneless pork loin chops (¾ inch thick and 6 ounces each)**
- 4 **tablespoons jalapeno pepper jelly, divided**

**1.** Preheat oven to 425°. Place beans in a 15x10x1-in. baking pan coated with cooking spray; toss with oil, ¼ teaspoon salt and ⅛ teaspoon pepper. Roast 15-20 minutes or until tender and lightly browned, stirring occasionally.

**2.** Meanwhile, sprinkle the pork chops with the remaining salt and pepper. Place a large nonstick skillet coated with cooking spray over medium heat. Add pork chops; cook, uncovered, 4 minutes. Turn chops over; spread tops with half of the jalapeno jelly.

**3.** Cook, uncovered, for 2-3 minutes longer or until a thermometer reads 145°. Turn pork chops over; spread tops with remaining jalapeno jelly. Let stand 5 minutes. Serve with green beans.

**PER SERVING** *328 cal., 10 g fat (4 g sat. fat), 82 mg chol., 354 mg sodium, 27 g carb., trace fiber, 33 g pro.* **Diabetic Exchanges:** *4 lean meat, 1 starch, 1 vegetable, ½ fat.*

## top tip Dinner, Chop-Chop

One night, I cut up leftover pork chops and tossed them into the vegetable stir-fry I was preparing for supper. The meat added heartiness and a boost of savory flavor to our main course.
—**KAREN BULLARD** CASPER, WY

## Beef Pitas with Yogurt Sauce

EAT SMART | FAST FIX

I hope to someday tour the Mediterranean, but in the meantime, I enjoy a taste of that region by making beef pitas. The yogurt sauce not only tops them off, but also can be served as a dip for pita chips.

—**DANIEL ANDERSON** PLEASANT PRAIRIE, WI

**START TO FINISH:** 30 MIN. • **MAKES:** 4 SERVINGS

- 1  **cup (8 ounces) fat-free plain yogurt**
- ¼  **cup minced fresh parsley**
- 1  **garlic clove, minced**
- ⅛  **teaspoon plus ½ teaspoon salt, divided**
- 1  **pound beef top sirloin steak, cut into thin strips**
- 1  **teaspoon dried oregano**
- 1  **teaspoon minced fresh rosemary**
- ¼  **teaspoon pepper**
- 4  **teaspoons olive oil, divided**
- 1  **large sweet onion, sliced**
- 4  **whole pita breads, warmed**

**1.** In a small bowl, mix the plain yogurt, parsley, garlic and ⅛ teaspoon salt. Toss the beef with the herbs, pepper and remaining salt.

**2.** In a large nonstick skillet, heat 2 teaspoons oil over medium-high heat. Add onion; cook and stir 4-6 minutes or until tender. Remove from pan.

**3.** In same skillet, heat the remaining oil over medium-high heat. Add beef; cook and stir 2-3 minutes or until no longer pink. Serve in pitas; top with onion and sauce.

**PER SERVING** *405 cal., 10 g fat (2 g sat. fat), 47 mg chol., 784 mg sodium, 45 g carb., 2 g fiber, 33 g pro. **Diabetic Exchanges:** 3 starch, 3 lean meat, 1 fat.*

BEEF PITAS WITH
YOGURT SAUCE

SOUTHWESTERN CHICKEN
& LIMA BEAN STEW

EAT SMART | SLOW COOKER

## Southwestern Chicken & Lima Bean Stew

My spiced-up stew from the slow cooker is a popular choice when I have my daughter, son-in-law and grandkids over for dinner.

—**PAM CORDER** MONROE, LA

**PREP:** 20 MIN. • **COOK:** 6 HOURS • **MAKES:** 6 SERVINGS

- 4  **bone-in chicken thighs (1½ pounds), skin removed**
- 2  **cups frozen lima beans**
- 2  **cups frozen corn**
- 1  **large green pepper, chopped**
- 1  **large onion, chopped**
- 2  **cans (14 ounces each) fire-roasted diced tomatoes, undrained**
- ¼  **cup tomato paste**
- 3  **tablespoons Worcestershire sauce**
- 3  **garlic cloves, minced**
- 1½ **teaspoons ground cumin**
- 1½ **teaspoons dried oregano**
- ¼  **teaspoon salt**
- ¼  **teaspoon pepper**
    **Chopped fresh cilantro or parsley**

**1.** Place the first five ingredients in a 5-qt. slow cooker. In a large bowl, combine the tomatoes, tomato paste, Worcestershire sauce, garlic and dry seasonings; pour over the top.

**2.** Cook, covered, on low 6-8 hours or until the chicken is tender. Remove the chicken from slow cooker. When cool enough to handle, remove meat from bones; discard bones. Shred meat with two forks; return to slow cooker and heat through. If desired, sprinkle with cilantro.

**PER SERVING** *312 cal., 7 g fat (2 g sat. fat), 58 mg chol., 614 mg sodium, 39 g carb., 8 g fiber, 24 g pro. **Diabetic Exchanges:** 3 lean meat, 2 starch, 1 vegetable.*

MAKEOVER TURKEY BURGERS
WITH PEACH MAYO

## Makeover Turkey Burgers with Peach Mayo

Turkey burgers give the usual ground beef version some serious competition when you flavor the patties with teriyaki sauce and top them with a fruity mayo.

—**CHARLENE CHAMBERS**
ORMOND BEACH, FL

**START TO FINISH:** 25 MIN.
**MAKES:** 6 SERVINGS

- 1½ teaspoons canola oil
- 2 small peaches, peeled and chopped
- ½ teaspoon minced fresh gingerroot
- 4 teaspoons reduced-sodium teriyaki sauce, divided
- ¼ cup chopped red onion
- ½ teaspoon pepper
- ¼ teaspoon salt
- 1½ pounds lean ground turkey
- ⅓ cup fat-free mayonnaise
- 6 multigrain hamburger buns, split and toasted
  Optional toppings: lettuce leaves and slices of peaches, red onion and tomatoes

**1.** In a skillet, heat oil over medium-high heat. Add peaches and ginger; cook and stir until peaches are tender. Stir in 1 teaspoon teriyaki sauce; cook 1 minute longer. Transfer to a small bowl; cool slightly.
**2.** In a large bowl, combine the red onion, pepper, salt and remaining teriyaki sauce. Add the turkey; mix

lightly but thoroughly. Shape into six ½-in.-thick patties.
**3.** Moisten a paper towel with cooking oil; using long-handled tongs, rub on grill rack to coat lightly. Grill burgers, covered, over medium heat or broil 4 in. from heat for 5-6 minutes on each side or until a thermometer reads 165°.
**4.** Stir the mayonnaise into the peach mixture. Serve burgers on buns with peach mayo and toppings as desired.
**PER SERVING** *319 cal., 14 g fat (3 g sat. fat), 91 mg chol., 580 mg sodium, 25 g carb., 2 g fiber, 25 g pro.* **Diabetic Exchanges:** *3 lean meat, 2 starch, 1 fat.*

## Chicken and Black Bean Soup

This speedy soup is so good, your family may think it was simmering all day. And what a great way to use up tortilla chips!

—**LINDA LASHLEY** REDGRANITE, WI

**START TO FINISH:** 30 MIN.
**MAKES:** 6 SERVINGS (2 QUARTS)

- ½ pound boneless skinless chicken breasts, cut into 1-inch cubes
- 2 cans (14½ ounces each) reduced-sodium chicken broth, divided
- 2 cups frozen corn
- 1 can (15 ounces) black beans, rinsed and drained
- 1 can (10 ounces) diced tomatoes and green chilies, undrained
- 1 jalapeno pepper, seeded and chopped
- 2 tablespoons minced fresh cilantro
- 3 teaspoons chili powder
- ½ teaspoon ground cumin
- 1 tablespoon cornstarch
- 18 tortilla chips
  Shredded reduced-fat Mexican cheese blend, optional

**1.** Place a large nonstick saucepan coated with cooking spray over medium heat. Add the chicken; cook and stir 4-6 minutes or until no longer pink. Reserve 2 tablespoons chicken broth; add the remaining broth to pan. Stir in corn, beans, tomatoes, jalapeno pepper, cilantro, chili powder and cumin. Bring to a boil. Reduce heat; simmer, uncovered, 15 minutes.
**2.** Mix cornstarch and reserved broth until smooth; gradually stir into soup. Bring to a boil; cook and stir 2 minutes or until thickened. Top servings with crushed chips and, if desired, cheese.
**NOTE** *Wear disposable gloves when cutting hot peppers; the oils can burn skin. Avoid touching your face.*
**PER SERVING** *194 cal., 2 g fat (trace sat. fat), 24 mg chol., 752 mg sodium, 29 g carb., 5 g fiber, 17 g pro.* **Diabetic Exchanges:** *2 starch, 2 lean meat.*

CHICKEN AND
BLACK BEAN SOUP

RICOTTA-STUFFED
PORTOBELLO MUSHROOMS

With tomatoes and herbs, Ricotta-Stuffed Portobello Mushrooms are rich, creamy and fresh-tasting all at the same time. I like to add a side of grilled asparagus.

—**TRE BALCHOWSKY** SAUSALITO, CA

## Ricotta-Stuffed Portobello Mushrooms

**START TO FINISH:** 30 MIN.
**MAKES:** 6 SERVINGS

- ¾ **cup reduced-fat ricotta cheese**
- ¾ **cup grated Parmesan cheese, divided**
- ½ **cup shredded part-skim mozzarella cheese**
- 2 **tablespoons minced fresh parsley**
- ⅛ **teaspoon pepper**
- 6 **large portobello mushrooms**
- 6 **slices large tomato**
- ¾ **cup fresh basil leaves**
- 3 **tablespoons slivered almonds or pine nuts, toasted**
- 1 **small garlic clove**
- 2 **tablespoons olive oil**
- 2 **to 3 teaspoons water**

**1.** In a small bowl, mix ricotta , ¼ cup Parmesan, mozzarella, parsley and pepper. Remove and discard stems from mushrooms; with a spoon, scrape and remove gills. Fill caps with ricotta mixture. Top with tomato slices.

**2.** Grill, covered, over medium heat 8-10 minutes or until the mushrooms are tender. Remove from grill with a metal spatula.

**3.** Meanwhile, place basil, almonds and garlic in a small food processor; pulse until chopped. Add remaining Parmesan cheese; pulse just until blended. While processing, gradually add oil and enough water to reach desired consistency. Spoon over stuffed mushrooms before serving.

**NOTE** *To toast the nuts, spread them in a 15x10x1-in. baking pan. Bake at 350° for 5-10 minutes or until lightly browned, stirring occasionally. Or, spread in a dry nonstick skillet and heat them over low heat until lightly browned, stirring occasionally.*

**PER SERVING** *201 cal., 13 g fat (4 g sat. fat), 22 mg chol., 238 mg sodium, 9 g carb., 2 g fiber, 12 g pro.* **Diabetic Exchanges:** *1 ½ fat, 1 medium-fat meat, 1 vegetable.*

## Tapenade-Stuffed Chicken Breasts

My husband is a huge olive fan, so I put three different varieties in this tapenade. Sometimes I make just that part of the recipe and serve the spread with bread or crackers as an appetizer.

—**JESSICA LEVINSON** NYACK, NY

**START TO FINISH:** 30 MIN.
**MAKES:** 4 SERVINGS

- 4 **oil-packed sun-dried tomatoes**
- 4 **pitted Greek olives**
- 4 **pitted Spanish olives**
- 4 **pitted ripe olives**
- ¼ **cup roasted sweet red peppers, drained**
- 4 **garlic cloves, minced**
- 1 **tablespoon olive oil**
- 2 **teaspoons balsamic vinegar**
- 4 **boneless skinless chicken breast halves (6 ounces each)**
  **Grated Parmesan cheese**

**1.** Place the first eight ingredients in a food processor; pulse until tomatoes and olives are coarsely chopped. Cut a pocket horizontally in the thickest part of each chicken breast. Fill with olive mixture; secure with toothpicks.

**2.** Moisten a paper towel with cooking oil; using long-handled tongs, rub on the grill rack to coat lightly. Grill the chicken, covered, over medium heat or broil 4 in. from heat 8-10 minutes on each side or until a thermometer inserted in the stuffing reads 165°. Sprinkle with the Parmesan cheese. Discard toothpicks before serving.

**PER SERVING** *264 cal., 11 g fat (2 g sat. fat), 94 mg chol., 367 mg sodium, 5 g carb., 1 g fiber, 35 g pro.* **Diabetic Exchanges:** *5 lean meat, 1 fat.*

TAPENADE-STUFFED
CHICKEN BREASTS

**TATER
TOT-CHOS**
PAGE 271

# Kid-Friendly Foods

Youngsters will come running for the **child-pleasing choices** in this chapter. From cheesy main courses and nutritious snacks to sweet treats, these dishes are definitely **young at heart**.

**REFRESHING TROPICAL FRUIT SALAD**
*PAGE 270*

**WAGON WHEEL PASTA TOSS**
*PAGE 272*

**BANANA CUPCAKES**
*PAGE 273*

TURTLE BREAD

## FAST FIX
# Breakfast Spuds

Scrambled eggs, ham and sweet potato puffs all in one nutritious breakfast kids will eat—now that's worth celebrating!

—ANNIE RUNDLE MUSKEGO, WI

**START TO FINISH:** 30 MIN.
**MAKES:** 6 SERVINGS

- 1 package (20 ounces) frozen sweet potato puffs
- 8 eggs
- ⅓ cup 2% milk
- ¼ teaspoon salt
- ⅛ teaspoon pepper
- 1 cup cubed fully cooked ham
- 1 tablespoon butter
  Shredded cheddar cheese and sliced green onions

**1.** Bake sweet potato puffs according to package directions. In a large bowl, whisk eggs, milk, salt and pepper. Stir in ham.

**2.** In a large nonstick skillet, heat butter over medium heat. Add egg mixture; cook and stir until eggs are thickened and no liquid egg remains. Serve with potato puffs; sprinkle with cheese and green onions.

**PER SERVING** *294 cal., 14 g fat (4 g sat. fat), 302 mg chol., 752 mg sodium, 27 g carb., 2 g fiber, 15 g pro.*

BREAKFAST SPUDS

# Turtle Bread

My son Nick and his friends would always ask me to bake this turtle-shaped bread. Nick's brother and sister would join in to help me mix and knead the dough. That's when the flour really started flying!

—ELIZABETH INGARGIOLA GALLOWAY, NJ

**PREP:** 30 MIN. + RISING
**BAKE:** 35 MIN. + COOLING • **MAKES:** 1 LOAF

- 2¼ to 2¾ cups all-purpose flour
- 1 tablespoon sugar
- 1 package (¼ ounce) quick-rise yeast
- 1 teaspoon salt
- ½ cup water
- ⅓ cup milk
- 1 tablespoon butter
- 2 eggs
- 2 raisins

**1.** In a large bowl, combine 2 cups flour, sugar, quick-rise yeast and salt. In a small saucepan, heat the water, milk and butter to 120°-130°. Add to the dry ingredients; beat just until moistened. Add 1 egg; beat until smooth. Stir in enough remaining flour to form a soft dough.

**2.** Turn the dough onto a floured surface; knead until smooth and elastic, about 6-8 minutes. Cover and let rest for 10 minutes. Shape dough into one 2-in. ball, four 1½-in. balls, one 1-in. ball and one large round ball.

**3.** For the turtle shell, place the large dough ball in the center of a greased baking sheet. Place the 2-in. ball at the top for the head; position 1½-in. balls on either side for the feet. Shape the 1-in. ball into a triangle for the tail; place on opposite side of large ball from head.

**4.** Press all the edges together to seal. Add raisins for the eyes. Cover and let rise in a warm place until doubled, about 25 minutes.

**5.** Beat the remaining egg; brush over the dough. With a sharp knife, make shallow diamond-shaped slashes across top of turtle shell.

**6.** Bake at 350° for 35-40 minutes or until golden brown. Remove to a wire rack to cool.

**PER SERVING** *87 cal., 2 g fat (1 g sat. fat), 26 mg chol., 165 mg sodium, 15 g carb., 1 g fiber, 3 g pro.* **Diabetic Exchange:** *1 starch.*

## (5) INGREDIENTS
# Yogurt Ice Pops

My frozen pops get their smooth, creamy goodness from yogurt. Just about any fruit can be substituted in the recipe.
—**DENISE PATTERSON** BAINBRIDGE, OH

**PREP:** 20 MIN. + FREEZING
**MAKES:** 16 POPS

- 1 envelope unflavored gelatin
- 1 cup cold water
- ½ cup sugar
- 1½ cups (12 ounces) peach yogurt
- 2 cups sliced peeled fresh or frozen peaches
- 1 medium ripe banana, quartered
- 16 Popsicle molds or paper cups (3 ounces each) and Popsicle sticks

**1.** In a small saucepan, sprinkle the gelatin over cold water; let stand for 1-2 minutes. Stir in sugar. Cook and stir over low heat until gelatin and sugar are dissolved.

**2.** Transfer to a blender; add yogurt, peaches and banana. Cover; process until smooth. Fill each mold or cup with ¼ cup mixture; top with holders or insert sticks into cups. Freeze.

**PER SERVING** *63 cal., trace fat (trace sat. fat), 1 mg chol., 13 mg sodium, 14 g carb., 1 g fiber, 2 g pro.* **Diabetic Exchange:** *1 starch.*

YOGURT ICE POPS

Getting a little creative with food can make meals more appealing for children—and a lot easier for parents. A Hot Dog Speed Racer is sure to zoom off the plate!
—**JENNI SHARP** MILWAUKEE, WI

## FAST FIX ▶
# Hot Dog Speed Racer

**START TO FINISH:** 15 MIN.
**MAKES:** 1 SERVING

- 1 hot dog bun, split
- 6 pretzel sticks, divided
- 4 sweet pickle slices
- 4 slices ripe olives
- 2 hot dogs, cooked, divided
- 1 miniature pretzel
- 1 teaspoon prepared mustard
- ½ colossal ripe olive
- 2 slices miniature pepperoni

**1.** Place the hot dog bun on a plate, cut side up. For each wheel of the racecar, insert a pretzel stick partway into bun; attach a pickle slice and ripe olive slice for each wheel.

**2.** Cut a slit 1-in. from the end of a hot dog; insert miniature pretzel for the steering wheel. Place in bun.

**3.** Cut remaining hot dog in half for the driver (save remaining half for another use); insert a pretzel stick halfway into the cut end.

**4.** Place mustard in a food-safe plastic bag; cut a small hole in a corner of bag. Pipe the face onto driver. Insert driver behind steering wheel. Place olive half on driver for helmet.

**5.** Break the remaining pretzel stick in half; place on the steering wheel for the arms. Using mustard, attach the pepperoni slices for the headlights. Serve immediately.

**PER SERVING** *394 cal., 24 g fat (9 g sat. fat), 39 mg chol., 1,213 mg sodium, 31 g carb., 2 g fiber, 13 g pro.*

FAVORITE ICE CREAM TACOS

# Parmesan Chicken Nuggets

When my 3-year-old went through a stage where he'd eat very little besides chicken nuggets, I made these baked bites. They're so good, everyone at the table gobbled them up.

**—AMANDA LIVESAY** MOBILE, AL

**START TO FINISH:** 30 MIN. • **MAKES:** 8 SERVINGS

- ¼ **cup butter, melted**
- 1 **cup panko (Japanese) bread crumbs**
- ½ **cup grated Parmesan cheese**
- ½ **teaspoon kosher salt**
- 1½ **pounds boneless skinless chicken breasts, cut into 1-inch cubes**
    **Marinara sauce, optional**

**1.** Place butter in a shallow bowl. Combine the panko bread crumbs, Parmesan cheese and salt in another shallow bowl. Dip chicken in butter, then roll in crumbs.
**2.** Place in a single layer on two 15x10x1-in. baking pans. Bake at 375° for 15-18 minutes or until no longer pink, turning once. Serve with marinara sauce if desired.
**PER SERVING** *191 cal., 9 g fat (5 g sat. fat), 67 mg chol., 309 mg sodium, 5 g carb., trace fiber, 20 g pro.*

Favorite Ice Cream Tacos are fun for parties. Guests love adding the toppings!

**—NANCY ZIMMERMAN**
CAPE MAY COURT HOUSE, NJ

PARMESAN CHICKEN NUGGETS

# Favorite Ice Cream Tacos

**PREP:** 30 MIN. • **BAKE:** 10 MIN./BATCH + COOLING
**MAKES:** 16 TACOS

- ½ **cup packed brown sugar**
- ⅓ **cup butter, melted**
- ¼ **cup honey**
- ¾ **cup all-purpose flour**
- ½ **teaspoon water**
- 4 **to 5 drops green food coloring**
- 1 **cup flaked coconut**
- ½ **gallon chocolate ice cream**
- 1 **cup whipped topping**
    **Red, orange and yellow M&M's minis**

**1.** Using a pencil, draw two 3-in. circles on a sheet of parchment paper. Place the paper, pencil mark side down, on a baking sheet; set aside.
**2.** In a large bowl, beat the brown sugar, butter and honey until blended. Add the flour; mix well (batter will be thick). Spread 1 tablespoon of batter over each circle.
**3.** Bake at 350° for 6-7 minutes or until golden brown. Cool for 2 minutes. Loosen each cookie and curl around a rolling pin to form a taco shell. Cool completely before removing to a wire rack. Repeat with remaining batter.
**4.** In a small resealable plastic bag, combine the water and food coloring; add the coconut. Seal the bag and shake to tint. Fill taco shells with ice cream; garnish with whipped topping, coconut and M&M's.
**PER SERVING** *281 cal., 14 g fat (9 g sat. fat), 32 mg chol., 95 mg sodium, 38 g carb., 1 g fiber, 3 g pro.*

## Chili Cheese Dog Casserole

Children and dads alike will dive right into this hearty dish, thanks to the crispy cheese topping and corn bread crust.
—*TASTE OF HOME* TEST KITCHEN

**PREP:** 20 MIN. • **BAKE:** 30 MIN. • **MAKES:** 6 SERVINGS

- 1 package (8½ ounces) corn bread/muffin mix
- 1 cup chopped green pepper
- ½ cup chopped onion
- ½ cup chopped celery
- 1 tablespoon olive oil
- 1 package (1 pound) hot dogs, halved lengthwise and cut into bite-size pieces
- 1 can (15 ounces) chili with beans
- 2 tablespoons brown sugar
- ½ teaspoon garlic powder
- ½ teaspoon chili powder
- 1 cup (4 ounces) shredded cheddar cheese, divided

**1.** Prepare the corn bread batter according to the package directions. Spread half the batter into a greased 8-in. square baking dish; set aside.
**2.** In a large skillet, saute green pepper, onion and celery in oil until crisp-tender. Stir in the hot dogs; saute 3-4 minutes longer or until lightly browned. Stir in the chili, brown sugar, garlic powder and chili powder; heat through. Stir in ¾ cup cheddar cheese.
**3.** Spoon over corn bread batter; top with remaining corn bread batter. Sprinkle the remaining cheese over the top.
**4.** Bake, uncovered, at 350° for 28-32 minutes or until a toothpick inserted near the center comes out clean. Let stand for 5 minutes before serving.
**PER SERVING** *615 cal., 37 g fat (16 g sat. fat), 115 mg chol., 1,585 mg sodium, 49 g carb., 4 g fiber, 22 g pro.*

PIZZA TOTS

(5)INGREDIENTS FAST FIX

## Pizza Tots

Tater Tots, pizza sauce, mozzarella and pepperoni—it all adds up to the dinner of kids' dreams! And I like that it's ready in a snap.
—**ANNIE RUNDLE** MUSKEGO, WI

**START TO FINISH:** 30 MIN. • **MAKES:** 6 SERVINGS

- 4 cups frozen miniature Tater Tots
- ½ cup pizza sauce
- 1½ cups (6 ounces) shredded part-skim mozzarella cheese
- 12 slices pepperoni
- ¼ teaspoon Italian seasoning
  Crushed red pepper flakes, optional

**1.** Bake Tater Tots according to package directions on a 12-in. pizza pan.
**2.** Top with pizza sauce, cheese and pepperoni. Sprinkle with Italian seasoning and, if desired, pepper flakes. Bake 5-7 minutes longer or until cheese is melted.
**PER SERVING** *240 cal., 14 g fat (5 g sat. fat), 20 mg chol., 597 mg sodium, 23 g carb., 2 g fiber, 10 g pro.*

**top tip**

## Hot Dog Helper

When I have leftover mashed potatoes to use up, I slice cooked hot dogs lengthwise, cover them with the extra spuds, sprinkle on some shredded cheese and bake them until the cheese melts. It's fast, fuss-free and a hit with the whole family.
—**HEIDI PHILLIPS** GARDNERVILLE, NV

CHILI CHEESE DOG CASSEROLE

# d Waffle Fries

just about any meal better by adding
ffle fries topped with cheddar cheese,
reen onions and bacon bits. My version
is based on one from a local restaurant.
—**JEFFREY VICCONE** DECATUR, IL

**START TO FINISH:** 30 MIN.
**MAKES:** 4 SERVINGS

- 4 **cups frozen waffle-cut fries**
- ½ to 1½ **teaspoons steak seasoning**
- 1 **cup (4 ounces) shredded cheddar cheese**
- 2 **tablespoons chopped green onions**
- 2 **tablespoons real bacon bits**

**1.** Arrange the waffle fries in a greased
15x10x1-in. baking pan. Bake at 450°
for 20-25 minutes or until lightly
browned.
**2.** Sprinkle with steak seasoning; toss
to combine. Top with the remaining
ingredients. Bake 2-3 minutes longer
or until cheese is melted.
**NOTE** *This recipe was tested with
McCormick's Montreal Steak Seasoning.
Look for it in the spice aisle.*
**PER SERVING** *261 cal., 14 g fat (8 g sat.
fat), 33 mg chol., 404 mg sodium, 25 g
carb., 2 g fiber, 10 g pro.*

LOADED WAFFLE
FRIES

---

# Quick & Easy Turkey Sloppy Joes

When my husband
and I were newly
married and poor
college students,
I found this recipe
for sloppy joes and
tweaked it a little.
The vegetables lend a fresh taste.
—**KALLEE TWINER** MARYVILLE, TN

**START TO FINISH:** 30 MIN.
**MAKES:** 8 SERVINGS

- 1 **pound lean ground turkey**
- 1 **large red onion, chopped**
- 1 **large green pepper, chopped**
- 1 **can (8 ounces) tomato sauce**
- ½ **cup barbecue sauce**
- 1 **teaspoon dried oregano**
- 1 **teaspoon ground cumin**
- 1 **teaspoon chili powder**
- ¼ **teaspoon salt**
- 8 **hamburger buns, split**

**1.** In a large skillet, cook the turkey,
red onion and green pepper over
medium heat 6-8 minutes or until
the turkey is no longer pink and the
vegetables are tender, breaking up
turkey into crumbles.
**2.** Stir in the tomato sauce, barbecue
sauce and seasonings. Bring to a boil.
Reduce the heat; simmer, uncovered,
for 10 minutes to allow the flavors to
blend, stirring occasionally. Serve in
hamburger buns.
**PER SERVING** *251 cal., 6 g fat (2 g sat.
fat), 39 mg chol., 629 mg sodium, 32 g
carb., 2 g fiber, 16 g pro.* **Diabetic
Exchanges:** *2 lean meat, 1½ starch,
1 vegetable.*

# Honey-Banana Ice Cream Sandwiches

Lazy summer days call for extra-special,
cool-you-off treats like these delightful
sandwiches. With a homemade ice cream
filling between chocolate graham crackers,
they're irresistible to kids of all ages.
—**SUSAN ASANOVIC** WILTON, CT

**PREP:** 1 HOUR + FREEZING
**MAKES:** 10 SERVINGS

- 1 **cup whole milk**
- ½ **cup sugar**

---

- ⅓ **cup honey**
- 2 **ripe medium bananas**
- 2 **cups heavy whipping cream, divided**
- 1½ **teaspoons vanilla extract**
- ¼ **teaspoon almond extract**
- ⅛ **teaspoon salt**
- ½ **cup dried banana chips, chopped**
- 10 **whole chocolate graham crackers, halved**
- ¾ **cup finely chopped salted peanuts**
- ¼ **cup chocolate jimmies**

**1.** In a small heavy saucepan, heat
the milk and sugar until bubbles form
around the sides of the pan. Whisk in
the honey. Quickly transfer to a large
bowl; place in ice water and stir for
2 minutes.
**2.** Puree the bananas; add to the
cooled milk mixture with 1 cup heavy
whipping cream, extracts and salt.
Press waxed paper onto surface of
milk mixture. Refrigerate for several
hours or overnight.
**3.** In a small bowl, beat the remaining
heavy whipping cream until soft peaks
form; fold into the banana mixture.
Fill the cylinder of ice cream freezer
two-thirds full; freeze according to the
manufacturer's directions, adding the
dried banana chips during the last
minute. When the ice cream is frozen,
transfer to a freezer container; freeze
for 2-4 hours.
**4.** To assemble sandwiches, spread
ice cream onto each of 10 chocolate
graham cracker halves. Top with the
remaining graham crackers; press
down gently.
**5.** In a shallow dish, combine the
peanuts and jimmies. Roll the sides
of the ice cream sandwiches in peanut
mixture. Wrap in plastic wrap. Freeze
for at least 1 hour.
**PER SERVING** *459 cal., 28 g fat (14 g
sat. fat), 68 mg chol., 199 mg sodium,
48 g carb., 2 g fiber, 6 g pro.*

## ? Did you know?

Heavy whipping cream is a
rich cream that has 36-40% butterfat
and doubles in volume when it is
whipped. It's often labeled as either
heavy cream or whipping cream.

---

# Refreshing Tropical Fruit Salad

Youngsters will love this colorful medley for breakfast, lunch or any time at all.

—SHARON RICCI SPOONER, WI

**START TO FINISH:** 30 MIN.
**MAKES:** 12 SERVINGS (1 CUP EACH)

- 2 **large bananas, sliced**
- 2 **medium pears, cubed**
- ⅓ **cup fresh orange juice**
- ⅓ **cup unsweetened pineapple juice**
- 3 **cups cubed fresh pineapple**
- 1½ **cups sliced fresh strawberries**
- 1 **cup seedless red grapes, halved**
- 4 **medium kiwifruit, peeled and sliced**
- 2 **medium mangos, peeled and cubed**
- 2 **star fruit, sliced**

In a large bowl, combine the bananas, pears and juices. Add the pineapple, strawberries, grapes, kiwi and mangos; stir gently to combine. Arrange star fruit over top.

**PER SERVING** *120 cal., 1 g fat (trace sat. fat), 0 chol., 3 mg sodium, 31 g carb., 4 g fiber, 1 g pro.* **Diabetic Exchange: 2 fruit.**

---

**⑤ INGREDIENTS**

# Yummy Cracker Snacks

Simple cracker sandwiches dipped in milk chocolate candy coating are my family's all-time favorite treat. No matter how many I make, they're gone in a flash!

—D. WEAVER EPHRATA, PA

**PREP:** 1 HOUR + CHILLING
**MAKES:** 4 DOZEN

- 96 **butter-flavored crackers**
- 1 **cup creamy peanut butter**
- 1 **cup marshmallow creme**
- 2 **pounds milk chocolate candy coating, melted**
  **Holiday sprinkles, optional**

**1.** Spread half of the butter-flavored crackers with creamy peanut butter. Spread the remaining crackers with marshmallow creme; place creme side down over peanut butter crackers, forming a sandwich.

**2.** Dip the sandwiches in the melted chocolate candy coating, allowing excess to drip off. Place on waxed paper-lined pans; refrigerate for 15 minutes or until set. If desired, drizzle with additional candy coating and decorate with sprinkles. Store in an airtight container.

**PER SERVING** *170 cal., 10 g fat (6 g sat. fat), trace chol., 89 mg sodium, 19 g carb., 1 g fiber, 2 g pro.*

REFRESHING TROPICAL FRUIT SALAD

SOUTHWEST TUNA-NOODLE CASSEROLE

## Southwest Tuna-Noodle Casserole

My co-workers told me they had never tried tuna-noodle casserole. We live near the Mexican border, so they challenged me to develop a Southwest version. I took them up on it—and everyone who tasted my creation wanted the recipe!

—SANDRA CRANE LAS CRUCES, NM

**PREP:** 20 MIN. • **BAKE:** 30 MIN.
**MAKES:** 6 SERVINGS

- 1 package (16 ounces) egg noodles
- 2½ cups milk
- 1 can (12 ounces) light tuna in water, drained
- 1 can (10¾ ounces) condensed cream of chicken soup, undiluted
- 1 can (10¾ ounces) condensed cream of mushroom soup, undiluted
- 1 cup (4 ounces) shredded cheddar cheese
- 1 can (4 ounces) chopped green chilies
- 2 cups crushed tortilla chips

**1.** Cook noodles according to package directions. Meanwhile, in a large bowl, combine the milk, tuna, soups, cheese and chilies. Drain noodles; gently stir into tuna mixture.

**2.** Transfer to an ungreased 13x9-in. baking dish. Sprinkle with the tortilla chips. Bake, uncovered, at 350° for 30-35 minutes or until bubbly.

**PER SERVING** 673 cal., 22 g fat (9 g sat. fat), 117 mg chol., 1,241 mg sodium, 82 g carb., 4 g fiber, 36 g pro.

## Tater Tot-chos

When it comes to a child-pleasing dinner, it's hard to beat popular nacho ingredients combined with Tater Tots. Let kids load up their own plates for smiles all around.

—ELEANOR MIELKE MITCHELL, SD

**START TO FINISH:** 30 MIN.
**MAKES:** 6 SERVINGS

- 4 cups frozen miniature Tater Tots
- 1 pound ground beef
- 1 envelope reduced-sodium taco seasoning
- ⅔ cup water
- ½ cup shredded cheddar cheese
- 2 cups shredded lettuce
- ¼ cup sliced ripe olives, optional
- ¼ cup taco sauce
- ½ cup sour cream

**1.** Bake Tater Tots according to package directions.

**2.** Meanwhile, in a large skillet, cook beef over medium heat 6-8 minutes or until no longer pink, breaking into crumbles; drain. Stir in taco seasoning and water. Bring to a boil; cook and stir 2 minutes or until thickened.

**3.** To serve, top Tater Tots with beef mixture, cheese, lettuce and, if desired, olives. Serve with taco sauce and sour cream.

**PER SERVING** 375 cal., 23 g fat (9 g sat. fat), 70 mg chol., 828 mg sodium, 27 g carb., 2 g fiber, 18 g pro.

TATER TOT-CHOS

## (5) INGREDIENTS
# Frozen Chocolate Monkey Treats

**PREP:** 15 MIN. + FREEZING • **COOK:** 5 MIN. • **MAKES:** 1½ DOZEN

- 3 **medium bananas**
- 1 **cup (6 ounces) dark chocolate chips**
- 2 **teaspoons shortening**
  **Toppings: chopped peanuts, toasted flaked coconut and/or colored jimmies**

**1.** Cut each banana into six pieces (about 1 in.). Insert a toothpick into each piece; transfer to a waxed paper-lined baking sheet. Freeze until completely firm, about 1 hour.

**2.** In a microwave, melt chocolate and shortening; stir until smooth. Dip the banana pieces in chocolate mixture; allow excess to drip off. Dip in toppings as desired; return to the baking sheet. Freeze at least 30 minutes before serving.

**NOTE** *To toast coconut, spread in a 15x10x1-in. baking pan. Bake at 350° for 5-10 minutes or until golden brown, stirring frequently.*

**PER SERVING** *72 cal., 4 g fat (2 g sat. fat), 0 chol., trace sodium, 10 g carb., 1 g fiber, 1 g pro.*

Frozen Chocolate Monkey Treats make it fun and easy for children to get a little playful with their food.
—**SUSAN HEIN** BURLINGTON, WI

FROZEN CHOCOLATE MONKEY TREATS

WAGON WHEEL PASTA TOSS

## FAST FIX ▶
# Wagon Wheel Pasta Toss

Trying to come up with a quick dinner that would appeal to my daughter's selective palate, I combined saucy pasta with ground beef, pepperoni and mozzarella cheese. She loved it!
—**LORI DANIELS** BEVERLY, WV

**START TO FINISH:** 30 MIN. • **MAKES:** 4 SERVINGS

- 1½ **cups uncooked wagon wheel pasta**
- 1 **pound ground beef**
- 1 **cup sliced fresh mushrooms**
- ½ **cup chopped green pepper**
- 1 **can (15 ounces) tomato puree**
- ½ **cup diced pepperoni**
- 4½ **teaspoons sugar**
- 1 **teaspoon Italian seasoning**
- ½ **teaspoon salt**
- ½ **teaspoon garlic powder**
- ½ **teaspoon dried oregano**
- ¼ **teaspoon onion powder**
- 2 **cups (8 ounces) shredded part-skim mozzarella cheese**

**1.** Cook pasta according to package directions. Meanwhile, in a large skillet, cook beef, mushrooms and green pepper over medium heat until the meat is no longer pink, breaking meat into crumbles; drain. Add tomato puree, pepperoni, sugar and seasonings; cook and stir for 5 minutes.

**2.** Drain the pasta; stir into the meat mixture. Heat through. Sprinkle with cheese. Remove from the heat; cover and let stand until cheese is melted.

**PER SERVING** *618 cal., 31 g fat (14 g sat. fat), 118 mg chol., 995 mg sodium, 39 g carb., 3 g fiber, 44 g pro.*

## Banana Cupcakes

Whipping up these homemade cakes with from-scratch frosting is definitely worth the extra time and effort. Yum!

—**JANE DEARING** NORTH LIBERTY, IN

**PREP:** 25 MIN. • **BAKE:** 20 MIN. + COOLING • **MAKES:** 1½ DOZEN

- ½ cup shortening
- 1½ cups sugar
- 2 eggs
- 1 cup mashed ripe bananas (about 2 medium)
- 1 teaspoon vanilla extract
- 2 cups all-purpose flour
- ¾ teaspoon baking soda
- ½ teaspoon baking powder
- ½ teaspoon salt
- ½ cup buttermilk

**LEMON BUTTER FROSTING**

- 2 cups confectioners' sugar
- ⅓ cup butter, softened
- 3 tablespoons mashed ripe banana
- 1 tablespoon lemon juice

**1.** In a large bowl, cream the shortening and sugar until light and fluffy. Add the eggs, one at a time, beating well after each addition. Beat in bananas and vanilla. Combine the flour, baking soda, baking powder and salt; add to the creamed mixture alternately with buttermilk, beating well after each addition.

**2.** Fill paper-lined muffin cups two-thirds full. Bake at 375° for 18-22 minutes or until a toothpick inserted near center comes out clean. Cool for 10 minutes before removing from pan to a wire rack to cool completely.

**3.** In a small bowl, combine the frosting ingredients; beat until light and fluffy. Frost cupcakes.

**CHERRY BANANA CUPCAKES** *Fold ⅓ cup each chopped maraschino cherries and walnuts into the batter. In the frosting, substitute milk for lemon juice.*

**PER SERVING** *270 cal., 10 g fat (4 g sat. fat), 33 mg chol., 168 mg sodium, 44 g carb., 1 g fiber, 3 g pro.*

BANANA CUPCAKES

QUICK PIZZA ROLLS

## Quick Pizza Rolls

Here's a great way to fix pizzas for a slumber party or movie night. I freeze them, then take out as many as I need and bake.

—**DEBBIE GRAY** GILBERT, IA

**PREP:** 35 MIN. • **BAKE:** 10 MIN. • **MAKES:** 6 SERVINGS

- 1 pound ground beef
- ½ cup chopped green pepper
- ¼ cup chopped onion
- 1 can (8 ounces) tomato sauce
- 1 can (6 ounces) tomato paste
- ¼ cup water
- 1 garlic clove, minced
- 1 teaspoon sugar
- 1 teaspoon Italian seasoning
- ½ teaspoon salt
- 6 French rolls
- ¾ cup shredded cheddar cheese
- ¾ cup shredded part-skim mozzarella cheese

**1.** In a large skillet, cook the beef, pepper and onion over medium heat until meat is no longer pink, breaking meat into crumbles; drain. Add the tomato sauce, tomato paste, water, garlic, sugar, Italian seasoning and salt. Bring to a boil. Reduce heat; simmer, uncovered, for 10 minutes or until heated through.

**2.** Cut ¼ in. off the top of each roll; set aside. Carefully hollow out bottom of roll, leaving a ¼-in. shell (discard the removed bread or save for another use). Fill each roll with ½ cup meat mixture. Sprinkle with cheeses. Replace tops.

**3.** Place desired amount of sandwiches on a baking sheet. Bake at 350° for 10-15 minutes or until heated through. Individually wrap remaining sandwiches tightly in foil; freeze for up to 3 months.

**TO USE FROZEN SANDWICHES** *Thaw in the refrigerator overnight. Remove from the refrigerator 30 minutes before baking. Place foil-wrapped sandwiches on baking sheet. Bake at 350° for 30-35 minutes or until heated through.*

**PER SERVING** *415 cal., 16 g fat (8 g sat. fat), 60 mg chol., 903 mg sodium, 41 g carb., 4 g fiber, 27 g pro.*

GIANT MONSTER COOKIES

## Giant Monster Cookies

Who can resist a gigantic cookie loaded with chocolate chips, M&M's and peanut butter? If the appetites in your house aren't monster-size, scoop the dough by heaping tablespoonfuls instead.

**—JUDY FREDENBERG** MISSOULA, MT

**PREP:** 20 MIN. + CHILLING
**BAKE:** 15 MIN./BATCH
**MAKES:** ABOUT 2½ DOZEN

- 2 **cups creamy peanut butter**
- ⅔ **cup butter, softened**
- 1⅓ **cups sugar**
- 1⅓ **cups packed brown sugar**
- 4 **eggs**
- 2½ **teaspoons baking soda**
- 1 **teaspoon vanilla extract**
- 1 **teaspoon light corn syrup**
- 6 **cups old-fashioned oats**
- 1 **cup semisweet chocolate chips**
- 1 **cup milk chocolate M&M's**

**1.** In a large bowl, cream the peanut butter, butter, sugar and brown sugar until light and fluffy, about 4 minutes. Beat in the eggs, baking soda, vanilla and corn syrup. Add oats and mix well. Stir in chocolate chips and M&M's. Cover and refrigerate for 1 hour.
**2.** Drop by ¼ cupfuls 3 in. apart onto ungreased baking sheets. Bake at 350° for 14-18 minutes or until edges are lightly browned. Cool for 5 minutes before removing from pans to wire racks to cool completely. Store in an airtight container.

**PER SERVING** *318 cal., 17 g fat (6 g sat. fat), 37 mg chol., 217 mg sodium, 39 g carb., 3 g fiber, 8 g pro.*

## Peanut Butter & Jam Muffins

Selling youngsters on wholesome bran muffins is a breeze when peanut butter and jam are key ingredients.

**—JUDY VAN HEEK** CROFTON, NE

**PREP:** 20 MIN. • **BAKE:** 15 MIN.
**MAKES:** 1 DOZEN

- 1 **cup all-purpose flour**
- 1 **cup oat bran**
- ½ **cup packed brown sugar**
- 2 **teaspoons baking powder**
- ½ **teaspoon salt**
- ¼ **teaspoon baking soda**
- 1 **cup 2% milk**
- ½ **cup unsweetened applesauce**
- ⅓ **cup peanut butter**
- 1 **egg white**
- 2 **tablespoons honey**
- ¼ **cup seedless strawberry jam**

**1.** In a large bowl, combine the flour, oat bran, brown sugar, baking powder, salt and baking soda. In a small bowl, beat the milk, applesauce, peanut butter, egg white and honey on low speed until smooth; stir into the dry ingredients just until moistened.
**2.** Fill greased or foil-lined muffin cups half full. Drop 1 teaspoon jam into the center of each muffin; cover with remaining batter.

**3.** Bake at 400° for 15-20 minutes or until a toothpick inserted in muffin comes out clean. Cool for 5 minutes before removing from pan to a wire rack. Serve warm.
**PER SERVING** *161 cal., 5 g fat (1 g sat. fat), 2 mg chol., 244 mg sodium, 29 g carb., 2 g fiber, 5 g pro.* **Diabetic Exchanges:** *2 starch, ½ fat.*

⑤INGREDIENTS FAST FIX ▶

## ABC Melt

This baked, open-faced sandwich is ideal any time you need a quick lunch or dinner. The fresh apple slices, Canadian bacon and Swiss cheese on toasted English muffins satisfy everyone in a hurry.

**—BARBARA NOWAKOWSKI**
NORTH TONAWANDA, NY

**START TO FINISH:** 10 MIN.
**MAKES:** 2 SERVINGS

- 2 **English muffins, split and toasted**
- 2 **teaspoons prepared mustard**
- 4 **slices Canadian bacon**
- 1 **medium apple, thinly sliced**
- 4 **slices Swiss cheese**

Place the English muffin halves, cut side up, on an ungreased baking sheet. Spread with the mustard; layer with the Canadian bacon, apple slices and cheese. Bake at 350° for 5-6 minutes or until cheese is melted.
**PER SERVING** *446 cal., 19 g fat (12 g sat. fat), 77 mg chol., 1,104 mg sodium, 38 g carb., 3 g fiber, 29 g pro.*

ABC MELT

BAKED ELEPHANT EARS

additional ½ te
sugar. Roll dou
**5.** Place 2 in. a
coated with c
with the rem
7-9 minutes
Cool on wir

**PER SERVING** *109 c
fat), 18 mg chol., 76 mg sodium, 18 g
carb., trace fiber, 1 g pro.* **Diabetic
Exchanges:** *1 starch, ½ fat.*

## Yogurt Dill Dip

Let kids dip away as they eat nutritious
vegetables. It's a great snack that goes
over well with adults, too.

—**KRISANN DURNFORD** MUSKEGO, WI

**PREP:** 15 MIN. + CHILLING
**MAKES:** 2½ CUPS

- 1 **cup (8 ounces) plain yogurt**
- 1 **cup (8 ounces) reduced-fat sour
  cream**
- ½ **cup reduced-fat mayonnaise**
- 2 **tablespoons finely chopped onion**
- 2 **tablespoons minced fresh parsley**
- 2 **teaspoons dill weed**
- ½ **teaspoon salt**
- ¼ **teaspoon pepper**
  **Assorted fresh vegetables**

In a small bowl, combine the first eight
ingredients. Cover and refrigerate for
at least 1 hour. Serve with vegetables.
**PER SERVING** *44 cal., 3 g fat (1 g sat.
fat), 8 mg chol., 121 mg sodium, 2 g
carb., trace fiber, 1 g pro.* **Diabetic
Exchange:** *½ fat.*

YOGURT DILL DIP

## Baked Elephant Ears

My mother-in-law
handed down this
recipe from her
mother. The fun
elephant ears are
even better, I think,
than the ones at carnivals and festivals.

—**DELORES BAETEN** DOWNERS GROVE, IL

**PREP:** 35 MIN. + CHILLING • **BAKE:** 10 MIN.
**MAKES:** 2 DOZEN

- 1 **package (¼ ounce) active dry
  yeast**
- ¼ **cup warm water (110° to 115°)**
- 2 **cups all-purpose flour**
- 4½ **teaspoons sugar**
- ½ **teaspoon salt**
- ⅓ **cup cold butter, cubed**
- ⅓ **cup fat-free milk**
- 1 **egg yolk**

**FILLING**

- 2 **tablespoons butter, softened**
- ½ **cup sugar**
- 2 **teaspoons ground cinnamon**

**CINNAMON-SUGAR**

- ½ **cup sugar**
- ¾ **teaspoon ground cinnamon**

**1.** In a small bowl, dissolve the yeast
in warm water. In a large bowl, mix
flour, sugar and salt; cut in butter until
crumbly. Stir milk and egg yolk into
yeast mixture. Add to flour mixture;
stir to form a soft dough. Cover with
plastic wrap and refrigerate 2 hours.
**2.** Preheat oven to 375°. Punch down
the dough. Turn onto a lightly floured
surface; cover and let rest 10 minutes.
**3.** Roll the dough into an 18x10-in.
rectangle. Spread with softened butter.
Mix the sugar and cinnamon; sprinkle
over the butter. Roll up jelly-roll style,
starting with a long side; pinch seam
to seal. Cut crosswise into twenty-four
¾-in. slices. Cover slices with plastic
wrap until ready to flatten.
**4.** In a small bowl, mix cinnamon-sugar
ingredients. Sprinkle ½ teaspoon
mixture on a sheet of waxed paper; top
with a slice of dough. Sprinkle with an

**SEARED SALMON WITH STRAWBERRY BASIL RELISH** PAGE 281

# Table Traditions

**Gather 'round** for special stories and recipes. In this chapter, fellow cooks share the delicious ways they connect with loved ones through **memorable foods and get-togethers**.

**ZESTY COLESLAW**
*PAGE 283*

**COKECOLA CAKE**
*PAGE 285*

**TINA'S POT ROAST**
*PAGE 289*

# Cookoff With Dad

### A Washington reader's father surprised her with **secret ingredients**, and a **tradition was born**.

RECIPES & STORY BY **GINA MYERS** | SPOKANE, WA

You know you have a cool dad when you get home from school and discover that he's planned a father-daughter cook-off. That's what happened to me when I was a freshman in high school.

I'd become a huge fan of *Chopped*, a TV show featuring a group of chef contestants who have to transform the contents of "mystery baskets" into great food on the fly. One day, my dad had two mystery baskets waiting in the refrigerator, ready for a friendly competition.

The two of us had such a blast, we set up several more cook-offs. My mom and sister taste-tested our creations and acted as judges. When our family visited relatives in Ohio, my aunt even provided the commentary as Dad and I sliced and diced our way through the ingredients.

I was so inspired by these good-natured kitchen wars at home with Dad, I enrolled at The Culinary Institute of America in Hyde Park, New York. When I graduate, I hope to use my skills to work with people in impoverished nations, helping to establish healthy and environmentally friendly food systems.

So, who's the best cook in the family? When my dad and I competed, I always won! He was so cute about it, too. He would just smile and say, "Oh, I almost won. My dish was really good."

**BROWNED BUTTER ROASTED CAULIFLOWER**

## Browned Butter Roasted Cauliflower

This recipe is popular with my mother, who loves all kinds of vegetables. The briny capers, lemon juice and sweet raisins together allow the caramelized, nutty cauliflower to shine.

**PREP:** 50 MIN. • **BAKE:** 15 MIN. • **MAKES:** 4 SERVINGS

- 6 **garlic cloves, unpeeled**
- 3 **tablespoons unsalted butter**
- 1 **medium head cauliflower, broken into florets**
- ¼ **teaspoon salt**
- ¼ **teaspoon pepper**
- ¼ **cup golden raisins**
- ¼ **cup chopped fresh parsley**
- 1 **tablespoon capers, drained and coarsely chopped**
- 2 **teaspoons lemon juice**

**1.** Preheat oven to 400°. Cut stem ends off unpeeled garlic cloves. Wrap cloves in a piece of foil. Bake 25-30 minutes or until cloves are soft. Unwrap and cool to room temperature. Squeeze garlic from skins. Mash with a fork.

**2.** Meanwhile, in a small heavy saucepan, melt butter over medium heat. Heat for 5-7 minutes or until golden brown, stirring constantly. Remove from heat.

**3.** Place the cauliflower in a greased 15x10x1-in. baking pan. Drizzle with browned butter; sprinkle with salt and pepper. Toss to coat. Roast for 15-20 minutes or until cauliflower is golden brown and tender.

**4.** Transfer to a bowl. Add remaining ingredients and roasted garlic; toss to combine.

**PER SERVING** *148 cal., 9 g fat (5 g sat. fat), 23 mg chol., 260 mg sodium, 17 g carb., 4 g fiber, 4 g pro.*

COCOA-CRUSTED BEEF TENDERLOIN

(5) INGREDIENTS · EAT SMART · FAST FIX
## Cocoa-Crusted Beef Tenderloin

My beef tenderloin coated with baking cocoa and coffee earned me a sweet victory in one of my family's cooking competitions.

**START TO FINISH:** 30 MIN. • **MAKES:** 4 SERVINGS

- 4 **beef tenderloin steaks (1½ inches thick and 6 ounces each)**
- ½ **teaspoon salt**
- ½ **teaspoon coarsely ground pepper**
- 3 **tablespoons baking cocoa**
- 3 **tablespoons finely ground coffee**

**1.** Preheat broiler. Sprinkle steaks with salt and pepper. In a shallow bowl, mix cocoa and coffee. Dip steaks in cocoa mixture to coat all sides; shake off excess.

**2.** Place the steaks on a rack of a broiler pan. Broil 3-4 in. from heat 9-11 minutes on each side or until meat reaches desired doneness (for medium-rare, a thermometer should read 145°; medium, 160°; well-done, 170°).

**PER SERVING** *252 cal., 10 g fat (4 g sat. fat), 75 mg chol., 296 mg sodium, 1 g carb., trace fiber, 37 g pro.* **Diabetic Exchange:** *5 lean meat.*

EAT SMART · FAST FIX
## Kale Salad

The flavor and nutrition in this kale dish set it apart from the rest, and it's ready to put on the table in just 15 minutes.

**START TO FINISH:** 15 MIN. • **MAKES:** 8 SERVINGS

- 10 **cups sliced kale (about 1 bunch)**
- 1 **medium apple, thinly sliced**
- 3 **tablespoons olive oil**
- 2 **tablespoons lemon juice**
- 1 **teaspoon salt**
- ½ **teaspoon pepper**
- ¼ **cup crumbled feta cheese**
- ¼ **cup salted pumpkin seeds or pepitas**

**1.** Place kale in a large bowl. With clean hands, massage kale until the leaves become soft and darkened, about 2-3 minutes; stir in apple.

**2.** In a small bowl, whisk oil, lemon juice, salt and pepper until blended. Drizzle over salad; toss to coat. Sprinkle with cheese and pumpkin seeds.

**PER SERVING** *113 cal., 9 g fat (2 g sat. fat), 2 mg chol., 381 mg sodium, 6 g carb., 1 g fiber, 4 g pro.* **Diabetic Exchanges:** *2 fat, ½ starch.*

(5) INGREDIENTS
## Carrot Puree

Carrots pair beautifully with anything from roasted meat to grilled fish. Cook them fully to ensure a velvety smooth puree.

**PREP:** 20 MIN. • **COOK:** 40 MIN. • **MAKES:** 4 SERVINGS

- 2 **tablespoons olive oil**
- 2 **pounds carrots, chopped**
- 2 **shallots, chopped**
- 4 **garlic cloves, minced**
- 1 **teaspoon fresh thyme leaves**
- ½ **teaspoon salt**
- ¼ **teaspoon pepper**

**1.** In a Dutch oven, heat the oil over medium heat. Add the carrots and shallots; cook and stir 12-15 minutes or until the carrots are crisp-tender. Stir in the garlic and thyme; cook 1 minute longer. Add water to cover carrots; bring to a boil. Reduce heat; simmer, uncovered, 20-25 minutes or until carrots are very tender.

**2.** Drain; cool slightly. Place carrot mixture, salt and pepper in a food processor; process until smooth.

**PER SERVING** *172 cal., 7 g fat (1 g sat. fat), 0 chol., 455 mg sodium, 26 g carb., 7 g fiber, 3 g pro.*

CARROT PUREE

# Sunday Night Live

An Oregon home cook and recipe contest champ loves **inviting friends** to sample her new dishes every week. They cook, eat and **have a ball.**

RECIPES & STORY BY **STACY MULLENS** | GRESHAM, OR

When I had the opportunity to join a friend's Sunday dinner club, I jumped at the chance to get extra creative in the kitchen. There are things that my young daughter, Evelyn, doesn't like to eat that I wanted to experiment with. I also wanted to cook for other people who share my passion.

Before long, I started entering my best Sunday night creations in recipe contests—and was thrilled when I ended up winning some. My favorite plates start with crowd-pleasing flavors like bacon and cheddar cheese, but I also try to take chances with unexpected touches.

Now I'm into orange flower water, so I like to put a bit in my salad dressing. It's subtle because I don't want to bowl people over with an ingredient that sounds crazy. But I like food that breaks away from the ordinary and takes you on a little adventure.

The club is about more than just sampling new recipes. It's about friends celebrating together over their favorite dishes, like my Seared Salmon with Strawberry Basil Relish.

After years of weekly dinners, my Sunday crew is still my best test audience—next to Evelyn. She's very honest about the recipes she tries and isn't shy about saying, "This isn't my favorite, Mom. I don't think kids will like this." It's always fun to hear her ideas, and I hope I'm inspiring in her the same passion for cooking and sharing that I have.

MEDITERRANEAN EGGPLANT DIP

EAT SMART
## Mediterranean Eggplant Dip

The Mediterranean flavors in this appetizer are really vibrant. I surround the bowl with flatbread wedges and fresh vegetables, which we use to make our own mini sandwiches.

**PREP:** 20 MIN. • **BAKE:** 40 MIN.
**MAKES:** 16 SERVINGS (¼ CUP DIP EACH)

- 1 large eggplant (about 1½ pounds), peeled
- 1 small onion, coarsely chopped
- 6 garlic cloves, peeled
- 3 tablespoons olive oil
- 2 cups (16 ounces) reduced-fat sour cream
- 4 teaspoons lemon juice
- ¾ teaspoon salt
- ½ teaspoon pepper
- 10 drops liquid smoke, optional
  Minced fresh parsley
  Optional ingredients: Naan flatbread wedges, cherry tomatoes, celery sticks, julienned red pepper, baby carrots and Greek olives

**1.** Preheat oven to 400°. Cut eggplant crosswise into 1-in. slices; place on a greased 15x10x1-in. baking pan. Top with onion and garlic cloves. Drizzle with oil.
**2.** Roast 40-45 minutes or until the eggplant is very soft, turning and stirring vegetables once. Cool slightly.
**3.** Place eggplant mixture in a food processor; process until blended. Transfer to a large bowl; stir in sour cream, lemon juice, salt, pepper and, if desired, liquid smoke.
**4.** Sprinkle with parsley. Serve with flatbread wedges and vegetables as desired.
**PER SERVING** 77 cal., 5 g fat (2 g sat. fat), 10 mg chol., 132 mg sodium, 5 g carb., 2 g fiber, 3 g pro.

SEARED SALMON WITH
STRAWBERRY BASIL RELISH

## Seared Salmon with Strawberry Basil Relish

A honey-sweetened strawberry and basil relish over fish fillets? Yes! It's a deliciously different treatment for salmon.

**START TO FINISH:** 20 MIN. • **MAKES:** 6 SERVINGS

- 6 salmon fillets (4 ounces each)
- 1 tablespoon butter, melted
- ¼ teaspoon salt
- ⅛ teaspoon freshly ground pepper
**RELISH**
- 1¼ cups finely chopped fresh strawberries
- 1 tablespoon minced fresh basil
- 1 tablespoon honey
  Dash freshly ground pepper

**1.** Brush fillets with melted butter; sprinkle with salt and pepper. Heat a large skillet over medium-high heat. Add the fillets, skin side up, in batches if necessary; cook 2-3 minutes on each side or until fish just begins to flake easily with a fork.
**2.** In a small bowl, toss strawberries with basil, honey and pepper. Serve salmon with relish.
**PER SERVING** *215 cal., 12 g fat (3 g sat. fat), 62 mg chol., 169 mg sodium, 6 g carb., 1 g fiber, 19 g pro.* **Diabetic Exchanges:** *3 lean meat, ½ starch, ½ fat.*

## Mushroom & Peas Rice Pilaf

Just about anything can go in a rice pilaf, so toss in some peas and baby portobello mushrooms for extra color and texture.

**START TO FINISH:** 25 MIN. • **MAKES:** 6 SERVINGS

- 1 package (6.6 ounces) rice pilaf mix with toasted almonds
- 1 tablespoon butter
- 1½ cups fresh or frozen peas
- 1 cup sliced baby portobello mushrooms

**1.** Prepare the pilaf according to the package directions.
**2.** In a large skillet, heat butter over medium heat. Add peas and mushrooms; cook and stir 6-8 minutes or until tender. Stir in rice.
**PER SERVING** *177 cal., 6 g fat (2 g sat. fat), 10 mg chol., 352 mg sodium, 28 g carb., 3 g fiber, 5 g pro.* **Diabetic Exchanges:** *2 starch, ½ fat.*

## Creamy Fresh Asparagus Soup

With a twist of lemon and tarragon, my cool asparagus soup has springtime appeal. Add a garnish of grated peel and yogurt.

**PREP:** 20 MIN. • **COOK:** 20 MIN. • **MAKES:** 6 SERVINGS

- 2 tablespoons butter
- 2 pounds fresh asparagus, trimmed, peeled and coarsely chopped
- 1 large sweet onion, coarsely chopped (about 2 cups)
- 1 carton (32 ounces) reduced-sodium chicken broth
- 1 tablespoon lemon juice
- 1 teaspoon minced fresh tarragon
- ¾ teaspoon salt
- ⅛ teaspoon freshly ground pepper
- ¼ cup plain Greek yogurt
- ½ teaspoon grated lemon peel

**1.** In a Dutch oven, heat butter over medium-high heat. Add asparagus and onion; cook and stir 10-12 minutes or until asparagus is crisp-tender.
**2.** Add broth; bring to a boil. Reduce heat; simmer, covered, 6-8 minutes or until asparagus is tender. Remove soup from heat; cool slightly. Stir in juice, tarragon, salt and pepper.
**3.** Process in batches in a blender until smooth. Serve with yogurt and lemon peel.
**PER SERVING** *91 cal., 5 g fat (3 g sat. fat), 13 mg chol., 720 mg sodium, 9 g carb., 2 g fiber, 5 g pro.*

CREAMY FRESH ASPARAGUS SOUP

# Operation: Family Picnic

Sunday afternoons are perfect for **gathering the troops** to share stories—and **favorite foods** that make memories. Just ask this National Guard mom from Minnesota.

RECIPES & STORY BY **MICHELLE GAUER** | SPICER, MN

Summer at our house means bike rides, campfires and family get-togethers with food, food, food!

At gatherings like our after-church barbecues, we can't wait to dig into classic dishes from a long line of great cooks on both sides of the family. We always mix in a few new things, too.

Dr Spicy BBQ Pork is one of our more recent discoveries. A few years ago, my mom and I were experimenting with pulled pork recipes, and this was the winner. We piled it on homemade rolls, along with coleslaw, and served the sandwiches (about 375 of them) at my son Matt's graduation party with add-ons like cheese, French-fried onions, banana peppers and pickles. Now Matt is a private class soldier in the Army National Guard, and we couldn't be prouder of him and his service to our country.

Every dish has its own special story, too. The one behind Green Flop Jell-O is always good for a laugh. My mother-in-law thought she'd made a mistake with a new recipe because it separated into layers. She said, "It was a flop!" Well, Matt and my daughters, Megan and Moriah, absolutely loved it. We've been making it ever since.

Because we're all into food traditions, I created my own little cookbooks as gifts for everyone in the family. Relatives sent their signature recipes, then I added family photos and put everything into three-ring binders as keepsakes.

**RUSTIC GARDEN HERB BISCUITS**

## Rustic Garden Herb Biscuits

Rosemary butter takes warm biscuits to another level. I like to use herbs from the garden, but dried ones work, too.

**PREP:** 25 MIN. • **BAKE:** 25 MIN.
**MAKES:** 12 BISCUITS (¼ CUP ROSEMARY BUTTER)

- 3¾ cups all-purpose flour
- 6 tablespoons sugar
- 3 teaspoons baking powder
- 2 teaspoons dried minced onion
- 2 teaspoons minced fresh basil
- 2 teaspoons minced fresh parsley
- 1 teaspoon salt
- 1 teaspoon snipped fresh dill
- 1 garlic clove, minced
- ¾ teaspoon baking soda
- ½ teaspoon minced fresh rosemary
- 1 cup cold butter, cubed
- ¾ cup shredded Monterey Jack cheese
- 1½ cups buttermilk
- ¼ cup chopped roasted sweet red peppers

**ROSEMARY BUTTER**

- ¼ cup butter, softened
- 1 teaspoon honey
- ½ garlic clove, minced
  Dash minced fresh rosemary

**1.** Preheat oven to 350°. In a large bowl, whisk the first 11 ingredients. Cut in the butter until mixture resembles coarse crumbs. Stir in cheese. Add buttermilk and peppers; stir just until moistened.

**2.** Drop the mixture by ⅓ cupfuls into greased muffin cups. Bake 25-30 minutes or until golden brown. Cool 5 minutes before removing from pan to a wire rack.

**3.** In a small bowl, mix remaining ingredients until blended. Serve warm biscuits with rosemary butter.

**PER SERVING** *377 cal., 22 g fat (14 g sat. fat), 58 mg chol., 599 mg sodium, 39 g carb., 1 g fiber, 7 g pro.*

## Dr Spicy BBQ Pork

When I served this at my son's graduation party, I kept the meat warm in a slow cooker after roasting it in the oven. The pork is great by itself, stacked on buns or piled on a barbecue pizza.

**PREP:** 25 MIN. • **BAKE:** 4 HOURS
**MAKES:** 12 SERVINGS (⅔ CUP EACH)

- 1 **boneless pork shoulder roast (5 to 7 pounds)**
- 1 **teaspoon garlic powder**
- ½ **teaspoon salt**
- ½ **teaspoon freshly ground pepper**
- 6 **chipotle peppers in adobo sauce, finely chopped (about ⅓ cup)**
- 1 **large sweet onion, halved and sliced**
- 2 **tablespoons brown sugar**
- 2 **cans (12 ounces each) Dr Pepper**
- 1 **cup barbecue sauce**
- **French-fried onions, optional**

**1.** Preheat oven to 325°. Sprinkle roast with garlic powder, salt and pepper; rub with chipotle peppers. Place in a Dutch oven. Top with sweet onion; sprinkle with brown sugar. Pour Dr Pepper around roast. Bake, covered, 4 to 4½ hours or until meat is tender.

**2.** Remove the roast; cool slightly. Strain the cooking juices, reserving onion; skim fat from juices.

**3.** Shred pork with two forks. Return juices, onion and pork to Dutch oven. Stir in the barbecue sauce; heat through over medium heat, stirring occasionally. If desired, sprinkle with French-fried onions.

**PER SERVING** *372 cal., 20 g fat (7 g sat. fat), 112 mg chol., 466 mg sodium, 15 g carb., 1 g fiber, 33 g pro.*

DR SPICY BBQ PORK

ZESTY COLESLAW

## Zesty Coleslaw

I think my coleslaw tastes best when it's refrigerated for at least an hour. The mixture seems to get creamier as it sits.

**PREP:** 15 MIN. + CHILLING **MAKES:** 12 SERVINGS (⅔ CUP EACH)

- 1 **cup mayonnaise**
- ⅓ **cup sugar**
- 3 **tablespoons cider vinegar**
- 1 **teaspoon seasoned salt**
- ¾ **teaspoon pepper**
- ½ **teaspoon celery seed**
- 2 **packages (14 ounces each) coleslaw mix**
- 1 **small sweet red pepper, chopped**
- ½ **cup thinly sliced sweet onion**

In a large bowl, mix the first six ingredients. Add coleslaw mix, red pepper and onion; toss to coat. Refrigerate at least 1 hour before serving.

**PER SERVING** *180 cal., 15 g fat (2 g sat. fat), 7 mg chol., 247 mg sodium, 11 g carb., 2 g fiber, 1 g pro.*

**⑤INGREDIENTS**

## Green Flop Jell-O

Enjoy a bowlful of fluffy, creamy goodness! Make it with lime gelatin—which is what we prefer—or any flavor you like.

**PREP:** 15 MIN. + CHILLING • **MAKES:** 16 SERVINGS (¾ CUP EACH)

- 2 **cups lemon-lime soda**
- 2 **packages (3 ounces each) lime gelatin**
- 6 **ounces cream cheese, softened**
- 2 **cups lemon-lime soda, chilled**
- 1 **carton (12 ounces) frozen whipped topping, thawed**

**1.** Microwave 2 cups soda on high for 1-2 minutes or until hot. Place the hot soda and gelatin in a blender; cover and process until the gelatin is dissolved. Add cream cheese; process until blended.

**2.** Transfer to a large bowl; stir in chilled soda. Whisk in whipped topping. Pour into a 3-qt. trifle bowl or glass bowl. Refrigerate, covered, 4 hours or until firm.

**PER SERVING** *159 cal., 7 g fat (6 g sat. fat), 12 mg chol., 62 mg sodium, 21 g carb., 0 fiber, 2 g pro.*

# Parking Lot Potluck

**Pop the trunk!** For this Georgia mom, weekend tailgating is a tradition. Her family and plenty of pals hit the lot with **a spread of home cooking**.

RECIPES & STORY BY **HEIDI JOBE** | CARROLLTON, GA

Fall is my absolute favorite time of year. The weather's great, and my friends and I love tailgating.

We live in a town where football is a weekend-long event. Friday nights mean games at Carrollton High, my daughter Holley's school. I keep a tailgating kit ready for action at a moment's notice. Along with a tent, we set up tables, chairs, a grill and a slow cooker or two. Each meal has a theme, but our dessert is often CokeCola Cake—a real Southern staple.

College football is popular here, too, with the University of Georgia, Auburn and University of Alabama nearby. Girls dress up, wear the school colors and decorate coolers. We decorate our tents and even shake pompoms. That's Saturdays. Then come Sundays, which mean Atlanta Falcons NFL games and, of course, more great tailgating.

**(5) INGREDIENTS FAST FIX**

## Chicken Chili Wonton Bites

Everyone needs a go-to tailgate or picnic food. Wonton wrappers filled with chicken and spices are yummy and fun on the run.

**START TO FINISH:** 30 MIN. • **MAKES:** 3 DOZEN

- 36 wonton wrappers
- ½ cup buttermilk ranch salad dressing
- 1 envelope reduced-sodium chili seasoning mix
- 1½ cups shredded rotisserie chicken
- 1 cup (4 ounces) shredded sharp cheddar cheese
  Sour cream and sliced green onions, optional

**1.** Preheat oven to 350°. Press the wonton wrappers into greased miniature muffin cups. Bake 4-6 minutes or until lightly browned.

**2.** In a small bowl, mix salad dressing and seasoning mix; add chicken and toss to coat. Spoon 1 tablespoon filling into each wonton cup. Sprinkle with cheese.

**3.** Bake 8-10 minutes longer or until heated through and wrappers are golden brown. Serve warm. If desired, top with sour cream and green onions before serving.

**PER SERVING** 67 cal., 3 g fat (1 g sat. fat), 10 mg chol., 126 mg sodium, 6 g carb., trace fiber, 3 g pro.

## Game Day Gumbo

At Friday night high school games, our children and friends get together to share a delicious spread and plenty of team spirit. Gumbo is a Southern tradition that feeds our hungry crowd.

**PREP:** 20 MIN. • **COOK:** 40 MIN.
**MAKES:** 10 SERVINGS (3¾ QUARTS)

- 6 tablespoons butter, divided
- 1 pound boneless skinless chicken thighs, cut into 1-inch pieces
- 1 package (13½ ounces) smoked beef sausage, halved lengthwise and sliced
- 2 medium carrots, chopped
- 2 celery ribs, chopped
- 1 small sweet red pepper, chopped
- 3 garlic cloves, minced
- ¼ cup all-purpose flour
- 4 cups chicken stock
- 4 cups water
- 1 can (14½ ounces) no-salt-added diced tomatoes, undrained
- 1 package (8 ounces) jambalaya mix
- 1 package (8 ounces) dirty rice mix

**1.** In a Dutch oven, heat 2 tablespoons butter over medium-high heat. Add the chicken; cook and stir until browned. Remove from pan.

**2.** In same pan, brown sausage over medium heat; remove from pan and drain on paper towels.

**3.** Heat remaining butter in same pan over medium heat. Add carrots, celery and pepper; cook and stir until tender. Add garlic; cook 1 minute longer.

**4.** Stir in the flour until blended; gradually stir in chicken stock, water, tomatoes and rice mixes. Return chicken and sausage to pan. Bring to a boil. Reduce the heat; simmer, covered, 20-25 minutes or until rice is tender.

**PER SERVING** 433 cal., 20 g fat (9 g sat. fat), 69 mg chol., 1,385 mg sodium, 44 g carb., 1 g fiber, 19 g pro.

## Lemony Bacon-Artichoke Dip

Move over, spinach-artichoke dip—bacon adds way more flavor. You may want to fix a double batch. We never have leftovers!

**PREP:** 20 MIN. • **BAKE:** 25 MIN.
**MAKES:** 12 SERVINGS (¼ CUP EACH)

- 5 **thick-sliced bacon strips, chopped**
- 1 **can (14 ounces) water-packed quartered artichoke hearts, drained and chopped**
- 2 **garlic cloves, minced**
- 2 **packages (8 ounces each) reduced-fat cream cheese**
- ⅓ **cup sour cream**
- ½ **teaspoon onion salt**
- ¼ **teaspoon salt**
- ⅛ **teaspoon pepper**
- 2 **tablespoons lemon juice**
- ½ **cup grated Parmesan cheese**
  **Pita bread wedges, toasted**

**1.** Preheat oven to 400°. In a large skillet, cook bacon over medium heat until crisp, stirring occasionally. Remove with a slotted spoon; drain on paper towels. Discard drippings, reserving 2 teaspoons in pan. Add the artichoke hearts and garlic to drippings; cook and stir 1 minute.
**2.** In a large bowl, beat the cream cheese, sour cream, onion salt, salt and pepper until smooth. Beat in lemon juice. Fold in artichoke mixture and half of the bacon.
**3.** Transfer to a greased 2-qt. baking dish. Sprinkle with the remaining bacon; top with Parmesan. Bake, uncovered, for 25-30 minutes or until golden brown. Serve with pita wedges.
**PER SERVING** *141 cal., 11 g fat (7 g sat. fat), 35 mg chol., 421 mg sodium, 4 g carb., trace fiber, 6 g pro.*

LEMONY BACON-ARTICHOKE DIP

COKECOLA CAKE

## CokeCola Cake

We live in Coca-Cola country, where a popular dessert is a moist, chocolaty sheet cake made with that iconic soft drink.

**PREP:** 25 MIN. • **BAKE:** 30 MIN. • **MAKES:** 15 SERVINGS

- 2 **cups all-purpose flour**
- 2 **cups sugar**
- 1 **teaspoon baking soda**
- ½ **teaspoon salt**
- ½ **teaspoon ground cinnamon**
- 1 **can (12 ounces) cola**
- 1 **cup butter, cubed**
- ¼ **cup baking cocoa**
- 2 **eggs**
- ½ **cup buttermilk**
- 1 **teaspoon vanilla extract**

**GLAZE**

- 1 **can (12 ounces) cola**
- ½ **cup butter, cubed**
- ¼ **cup baking cocoa**
- 4 **cups confectioners' sugar, sifted**

**1.** Preheat oven to 350°. Grease a 13x9-in. baking pan.
**2.** In a large bowl, whisk the first five ingredients. In a small saucepan, combine the cola, butter and cocoa; bring just to a boil, stirring occasionally. Add to flour mixture, stirring just until moistened.
**3.** In a small bowl, whisk eggs, buttermilk and vanilla until blended; add to flour mixture, whisking constantly.
**4.** Transfer to prepared pan. Bake 25-30 minutes or until a toothpick inserted in center comes out clean.
**5.** About 15 minutes before cake is done, prepare glaze. In a small saucepan, bring cola to a boil; cook 12-15 minutes or until liquid is reduced to ½ cup. Stir in the butter and cocoa until butter is melted; remove from heat. Add confectioners' sugar; stir until smooth. Pour immediately over hot cake.
**PER SERVING** *491 cal., 20 g fat (12 g sat. fat), 74 mg chol., 346 mg sodium, 78 g carb., 1 g fiber, 4 g pro.*

# Cooking By Heart

Load up the table with meat and potatoes—and make room for **fond memories**, too. One New Yorker's Hanukkah dishes are as unforgettable as the **people who've shared them.**

RECIPES & STORY BY **ELLEN RUZINSKY** | YORKTOWN HEIGHTS, NY

I love to cook for anyone who likes to eat what I make, especially my sons. It's a trait I share with my mom, Enid, a home economics major who felt very much at home in the kitchen. When I got married, she gave me handwritten recipes for all the dishes I'd asked her to fix again and again.

While I prepare our Hanukkah menu each year, I think a lot about my mother and Ada, a woman who was like a grandmother to me. I make my mother's brisket, her potato kugel and my roasted Brussels sprouts, which my sons love. For dessert, I bake Ada's wonderful apple cake, a favorite in my family for decades.

For us, the holidays come to life thanks to flavors rooted in our past—a big reason we look forward to those times together. When I use an heirloom recipe, the memory of the person who first shared it makes the dish more special. I feel as if she's standing there with me as I work in the kitchen. And with that first bite, we're together again.

## Chunky Apple-Cinnamon Cake

This spiced dessert filled with fruit is a nice change from apple pie and is worthy of a special get-together. A big piece is good just as it is or with a scoop of vanilla ice cream.

**PREP:** 25 MIN. • **BAKE:** 45 MIN. + COOLING • **MAKES:** 15 SERVINGS

- 2¾ **pounds McIntosh, Jonathan or Granny Smith apples, peeled and thinly sliced (11 cups)**
- ½ **cup packed brown sugar**
- 3 **teaspoons ground cinnamon, divided**
- 1 **cup plus 1 tablespoon sugar, divided**
- 1 **cup canola oil**
- 4 **eggs**
- 3 **tablespoons orange juice**
- 2 **teaspoons vanilla extract**
- 2½ **cups all-purpose flour**
- 2 **teaspoons baking powder**
- ½ **teaspoon kosher salt**

**1.** Preheat oven to 425°. In a large bowl, toss apples with brown sugar and 2 teaspoons cinnamon.

CHUNKY APPLE-CINNAMON CAKE

**2.** In a large bowl, beat 1 cup sugar, oil, eggs, orange juice and vanilla until well blended. In another bowl, whisk flour, baking powder and salt; gradually beat into sugar mixture.

**3.** Transfer half of the batter to an ungreased 13x9-in. baking pan. Top with apples. Spread remaining batter over apples. Mix remaining sugar and cinnamon; sprinkle over top. Bake 10 minutes.

**4.** Reduce oven setting to 375°. Bake 35-45 minutes or until golden brown and apples are tender. Cool on a wire rack.

**PER SERVING** *349 cal., 17 g fat (2 g sat. fat), 56 mg chol., 138 mg sodium, 47 g carb., 2 g fiber, 4 g pro.*

POTATO KUGEL

## Potato Kugel

The secret to keeping the potatoes their whitest is by switching back and forth between the spuds and onion when grating them.

**PREP:** 20 MIN. • **BAKE:** 40 MIN. • **MAKES:** 12 SERVINGS

- 2 **eggs**
- ¼ **cup matzo meal**
- 2 **teaspoons kosher salt**
  **Dash pepper**
- 6 **large potatoes (about 4¾ pounds), peeled**
- 1 **large onion, cut into 6 wedges**
- ¼ **cup canola oil**

**1.** Preheat oven to 375°. In a large bowl, whisk eggs, matzo meal, salt and pepper.
**2.** In a food processor fitted with the grating attachment, alternately grate potatoes and onion. Add to egg mixture; toss to coat. In a small saucepan, heat the oil over medium heat until warmed. Stir into the potato mixture. Transfer to a greased 13x9-in. baking dish. Bake 40-50 minutes or until golden brown.
**PER SERVING** *210 cal., 6 g fat (1 g sat. fat), 35 mg chol., 515 mg sodium, 36 g carb., 3 g fiber, 5 g pro.*

## Braised Hanukkah Brisket

My mother always used the most marbled cut of brisket she could find so she'd get the most mouthwatering flavor.

**PREP:** 25 MIN. • **COOK:** 2½ HOURS
**MAKES:** 12 SERVINGS (4 CUPS VEGETABLES)

- 2 **tablespoons canola oil**
- 1 **fresh beef brisket (4 to 5 pounds)**
- 3 **celery ribs, cut into 1-inch pieces**
- 3 **large carrots, cut into ¼-inch slices**
- 2 **large onions, sliced**
- 1 **pound medium fresh mushrooms**
- ¾ **cup cold water**
- ¾ **cup tomato sauce**
- 3 **tablespoons Worcestershire sauce**
- 1 **tablespoon prepared horseradish**

**1.** In a Dutch oven, heat the oil over medium heat. Brown brisket on both sides. Remove from pan.
**2.** Add the celery, carrots and onions to same pan; cook and stir 4-6 minutes or until crisp-tender. Stir in the remaining ingredients.
**3.** Return brisket to pan, fat side up. Bring mixture to a boil. Reduce heat; simmer, covered, 2½ to 3 hours or until meat is tender. Remove beef and vegetables; keep warm. Skim fat from pan juices. If desired, thicken juices.
**4.** Cut brisket diagonally across the grain into thin slices. Serve with vegetables and pan juices.
**NOTE** *This is a fresh beef brisket, not corned beef.*
**PER SERVING** *247 cal., 9 g fat (3 g sat. fat), 64 mg chol., 189 mg sodium, 8 g carb., 2 g fiber, 33 g pro.* **Diabetic Exchanges:** *4 lean meat, 1 vegetable, ½ fat.*

## Roasted Brussels Sprouts with Cranberries

I toss dried cranberries into this quick-and-easy side dish, but you could replace them with raisins, walnuts...even sliced oranges.

**PREP:** 15 MIN. • **BAKE:** 20 MIN.
**MAKES:** 12 SERVINGS (½ CUP EACH)

- 3 **pounds fresh Brussels sprouts, trimmed and halved**
- 3 **tablespoons olive oil**
- 1 **teaspoon kosher salt**
- ½ **teaspoon pepper**
- ½ **cup dried cranberries**

Preheat oven to 425°. Divide sprouts between two greased 15x10x1-in. baking pans. Drizzle with oil; sprinkle with salt and pepper. Toss to coat. Roast 20-25 minutes or until tender, stirring occasionally. Transfer to a large bowl; stir in berries.
**PER SERVING** *94 cal., 4 g fat (1 g sat. fat), 0 chol., 185 mg sodium, 14 g carb., 5 g fiber, 4 g pro.* **Diabetic Exchanges:** *1 vegetable, 1 fat.*

ROASTED BRUSSELS SPROUTS WITH CRANBERRIES

# Help From My Friends

## When a family lost their home, their community **cooked up hope** and shared **best-loved dishes**.

STORY BY **MICHELLE COLLINS** | LAKE ORION, MI

A few years ago, our family came home to a real-life nightmare: Our house was engulfed in flames.

It seemed like an out-of-body experience. My husband, two young sons and I had been away from home for only about 40 minutes, and there were no appliances left on or candles burning. It was a freak accident, but we lost our dog and our possessions.

When you lose everything you own, all you can think is, where do I start? What do I do? That's when my friends sprang into action.

One friend, Jen Roncone, arrived with backpacks and lunches for the boys. She also put together an online meal calendar, where people signed up to make and deliver food to our family while we lived in a rental house.

For three months, every other day, someone took the time to bring over a meal. Everyone signed up. I almost felt guilty because people were making us such good dinners. It was winter, so we had plenty of hearty comfort food—chicken chili, lasagna, pot roasts, pot pies and more.

Many people told me to keep the casserole dishes and pots they'd used to bring dinner. My kitchen is now well stocked with treasured pieces attached to the memory of good friends and good food.

These special people had such an impact on our lives. We've since moved into our rebuilt home, but their support still brings tears to my eyes whenever I think of it. We'll always be thankful.

SAVORY BRAISED CHICKEN WITH VEGETABLES

**EAT SMART**

## Savory Braised Chicken with Vegetables

Here's one of my own family's favorite comfort dishes. It looks and tastes a lot more complicated than it actually is.

—**MICHELLE COLLINS** LAKE ORION, MI

**PREP:** 15 MIN. • **COOK:** 40 MIN. • **MAKES:** 6 SERVINGS

- ½ cup seasoned bread crumbs
- 6 boneless skinless chicken breast halves (4 ounces each)
- 2 tablespoons olive oil
- 1 can (14½ ounces) beef broth
- 2 tablespoons tomato paste
- 1 teaspoon poultry seasoning
- ½ teaspoon salt
- ½ teaspoon pepper
- 1 pound fresh baby carrots
- 1 pound sliced fresh mushrooms
- 2 medium zucchini, sliced
  Sliced French bread baguette, optional

**1.** Place the bread crumbs in a shallow bowl. Dip chicken breasts in bread crumbs to coat both sides; shake off excess.
**2.** In a Dutch oven, heat oil over medium heat. Add chicken in batches; cook 2-4 minutes on each side or until browned. Remove chicken from pan.
**3.** Add broth, tomato paste and seasonings to same pan; cook over medium-high heat, stirring to loosen browned bits from pan. Add vegetables and chicken; bring to a boil. Reduce heat; simmer, covered, 25-30 minutes or until vegetables are tender and a thermometer inserted in chicken reads 165°. If desired, serve with baguette.
**PER SERVING** *247 cal., 8 g fat (1 g sat. fat), 63 mg chol., 703 mg sodium, 16 g carb., 3 g fiber, 28 g pro.* **Diabetic Exchanges:** *3 lean meat, 2 vegetable, 1 fat, ½ starch.*

## Tina's Pot Roast

This kid-friendly pot roast is a satisfying, feel-good meal, so I decided it was a good one to share with Michelle's family. We like the flavorful gravy so much that we pour it over everything on the plate!

—**TINA MEYER** LAKE ORION, MI

**PREP:** 10 MIN. • **BAKE:** 2¾ HOURS • **MAKES:** 8 SERVINGS

- 1 tablespoon canola oil
- 1 boneless beef chuck roast (3 pounds)
- 1½ cups water
- 1 envelope brown gravy mix
- 1 envelope Italian salad dressing mix
- 1 envelope onion soup mix
- ½ teaspoon garlic powder
- ½ teaspoon pepper
- 3 pounds medium potatoes (about 9), peeled and quartered
- 1 pound medium carrots, cut into 2-inch pieces

**1.** Preheat oven to 325°. In a Dutch oven, heat the oil over medium heat. Brown roast on all sides.

**2.** In a small bowl, whisk the water, brown gravy mix, Italian salad dressing mix, onion soup mix, garlic powder and pepper until blended; add to the pan. Bring to a boil. Bake, covered, 1½ hours.

**3.** Add the potatoes and carrots; cook 1¼ to 1½ hours longer or until the meat and vegetables are tender. Skim fat if necessary.

**PER SERVING** *450 cal., 18 g fat (6 g sat. fat), 111 mg chol., 907 mg sodium, 33 g carb., 3 g fiber, 37 g pro.*

TINA'S POT ROAST

CHICKEN & EGG NOODLE CASSEROLE

## Chicken & Egg Noodle Casserole

After the house fire, my heart broke for the whole Collins family. Bringing over this chicken-noodle casserole for dinner was one thing I could think of to help out and let them know I was thinking of them.

—**LIN KRANKEL** OXFORD, MI

**PREP:** 20 MIN. • **BAKE:** 30 MIN. • **MAKES:** 8 SERVINGS

- 6 cups uncooked egg noodles (about 12 ounces)
- 2 cans (10¾ ounces each) condensed cream of chicken soup, undiluted
- 1 cup (8 ounces) sour cream
- ¾ cup 2% milk
- ¼ teaspoon salt
- ¼ teaspoon pepper
- 3 cups cubed cooked chicken breasts
- 1 cup crushed butter-flavored crackers (about 20 crackers)
- ¼ cup butter, melted

**1.** Preheat oven to 350°. Cook the noodles according to the package directions for al dente; drain.

**2.** In a large bowl, whisk cream soup, sour cream, milk, salt and pepper until blended. Stir in the chicken and noodles. Transfer to a greased 13x9-in. baking dish. In a small bowl, mix crushed crackers and butter; sprinkle over top. Bake 30-35 minutes or until bubbly.

**PER SERVING** *446 cal., 22 g fat (10 g sat. fat), 107 mg chol., 820 mg sodium, 37 g carb., 2 g fiber, 23 g pro.*

# Wintry Meal With Love

**Bring your family in from the cold** with big bowls of heartwarming soup, piled-high sandwiches and nutty treats from a **cozy Colorado home kitchen**.

RECIPES & STORY BY **CARA MCDONALD** | WINTER PARK, CO

When I met my husband, Igor, he was an expatriate Czech living in a Colorado Rockies valley dubbed "The Nation's Icebox." Like his tight-knit group of Czech friends, he had come to the state for the mountain lifestyle and winter sports.

Igor proposed to me one snowy day, and my evolution from single girl to wife began. On our honeymoon, we toured amazing castles in the Czech Republic, strolled cobblestoned squares while autumn winds blew leaves around us, and ate as if there were no tomorrow. Potato pancakes and Pilsner. Schnitzel, stew and full-fat dairy. My initial shock at the abundance of all things pork (ham-flavored potato chips, anyone?) soon faded in the culture of warmth and comfort.

I especially appreciate Igor's food heritage on ice-cold evenings when the snow piles high, the windows frost up and single-girl salads just won't cut it. Our go-to hearty dishes remind him of home—and now they remind me, too.

**FAST FIX**

## Ham & Potato Salad Sandwiches

These Czech classics originated in a deli in Prague, where they're a really popular winter party food. The little sandwiches with zingy toppings are super simple to pull together.

**START TO FINISH:** 15 MIN. • **MAKES:** 6 SERVINGS

- 1½ **cups deli potato salad**
- 6 **diagonally cut French bread baguette slices (½ inch thick)**
- 6 **ounces fully cooked ham, thinly sliced**
- 6 **slices tomato**
- 12 **dill pickle slices**
- 2 **hard-cooked eggs, sliced**
- 2 **slices red onion, separated into rings**

Spread ¼ cup potato salad on each baguette slice. Layer with ham, tomato, pickle, egg and onion.

**PER SERVING** *229 cal., 10 g fat (2 g sat. fat), 96 mg chol., 821 mg sodium, 25 g carb., 2 g fiber, 12 g pro.*

HAM & POTATO SALAD SANDWICHES

VANILLA CRESCENTS

## Vanilla Crescents

Buttery cookies shaped like crescent moons are fun for Christmas or any occasion. Dunk them into hot tea or coffee.

**PREP:** 20 MIN. • **BAKE:** 10 MIN./BATCH • **MAKES:** 4 DOZEN

- 1   cup unsalted butter, softened
- ½   cup sugar
- 1   teaspoon vanilla extract
- ⅛   teaspoon almond extract
- 2   cups all-purpose flour
- 1¼   cups ground almonds
- ½   teaspoon salt
  Confectioners' sugar

**1.** Preheat oven to 350°. In a large bowl, cream the butter and sugar until light and fluffy. Beat in extracts. In another bowl, whisk the flour, almonds and salt; gradually beat into creamed mixture.

**2.** Divide the cookie dough into four portions. On a lightly floured surface, roll each portion into a 24-in. rope. Cut crosswise into twelve 2-in. logs; shape each into a crescent. Place 1½ in. apart on ungreased baking sheets.

**3.** Bake 10-12 minutes or until set. Cool on pans 2 minutes before removing to a wire rack. Dust warm cookies with confectioners' sugar.

**PER SERVING** *75 cal., 5 g fat (3 g sat. fat), 10 mg chol., 25 mg sodium, 7 g carb., trace fiber, 1 g pro.*

## Ginger Butternut Squash Bisque

The couple who introduced us to this vegetarian soup prepared it on a freezing night, and we've been hooked ever since.

**PREP:** 25 MIN. • **BAKE:** 40 MIN. + COOLING • **MAKES:** 6 SERVINGS

- 1   medium butternut squash (about 3 pounds)
- 1   tablespoon olive oil
- 2   medium carrots, finely chopped
- 1   medium onion, chopped
- 2   garlic cloves, minced
- 2   teaspoons minced fresh gingerroot
- 2   teaspoons curry powder
- 1   can (14½ ounces) vegetable broth
- 1   can (13.66 ounces) coconut milk
- 1   teaspoon salt
- ½   teaspoon pepper
- 2   cups hot cooked brown rice
- ¼   cup flaked coconut, toasted
- ¼   cup salted peanuts, coarsely chopped
- ¼   cup minced fresh cilantro

**1.** Preheat oven to 400°. Cut the squash lengthwise in half; remove and discard seeds. Place squash in a greased shallow roasting pan, cut side down. Roast 40-45 minutes or until squash is tender. Cool slightly.

**2.** In a large saucepan, heat oil over medium heat. Add the carrots and onion; cook and stir until tender. Add the garlic, ginger and curry powder; cook and stir 1 minute. Add the vegetable broth; bring to a boil. Reduce the heat; simmer, uncovered, 10-12 minutes or until the carrots are tender.

**3.** Scoop the pulp from squash; discard skins. Add squash, coconut milk, salt and pepper to carrot mixture; bring just to a boil, stirring occasionally. Remove from heat; cool slightly. Process in batches in a blender until smooth.

**4.** Return to pan; heat through. Top servings with rice, coconut, peanuts and cilantro.

**NOTE** *To toast coconut, spread in a dry skillet; cook and stir over low heat until lightly browned.*

**PER SERVING** *386 cal., 21 g fat (14 g sat. fat), 0 chol., 749 mg sodium, 48 g carb., 10 g fiber, 7 g pro.*

GINGER BUTTERNUT SQUASH BISQUE

**OVERNIGHT
CINNAMON ROLLS**
*PAGE 300*

# Kitchen Techniques

**Let's cook!** Team up with *Taste of Home* Test Kitchen pros and fellow cooks for easy ways of making all sorts of **special recipes**, from homemade cinnamon rolls to from-scratch pasta.

**THREE-PEPPER GUACAMOLE**
*PAGE 299*

**HERB GARDEN LASAGNAS**
*PAGE 297*

**JUICY RASPBERRY PIE**
*PAGE 303*

# Nuts for Doughnuts

Share a batch of warm, fresh doughnuts straight from your very own kitchen. These golden goodies are easier to make than you may think—just follow the step-by-step guide here!

## Apple Cider Doughnuts

Cake doughnuts always remind me of our family vacations to South Dakota. We'd stop at Wall Drug for a dozen or so before heading off to go camping in the Badlands. What a sweet memory!

**—MELISSA HANSEN** MILWAUKEE, WI

**PREP:** 1 HOUR + CHILLING
**COOK:** 5 MIN./BATCH
**MAKES:** 1 DOZEN DOUGHNUTS PLUS DOUGHNUT HOLES

- 2 cups apple cider
- 3 cups all-purpose flour
- ½ cup whole wheat flour
- ⅔ cup packed brown sugar
- 2 teaspoons baking powder
- ¾ teaspoon salt
- ½ teaspoon baking soda
- ¼ teaspoon each ground cardamom, nutmeg, cinnamon and allspice
- 2 eggs
- 6 tablespoons butter, melted and cooled
  Oil for deep-fat frying
  Maple Glaze for Doughnuts or Chocolate Glaze for Doughnuts (recipes on page 295)

**1.** In a small saucepan, bring cider to a rapid boil; cook over high heat until the cider is reduced by half, about 12 minutes. Cool completely.

**2.** In a large bowl, whisk the flours, the brown sugar, baking powder, salt, baking soda and spices. In a small bowl, whisk eggs, melted butter and cooled cider; stir into the dry ingredients just until moistened (dough will be sticky). Refrigerate, covered, 1 hour or until firm enough to shape.

**3.** Divide dough in half. On a floured surface, pat each portion of dough to ½-in. thickness; cut with a floured 3-in. doughnut cutter.

**4.** In an electric skillet or deep fryer, heat oil to 365°. Fry doughnuts, a few at a time, 1 minute on each side or until golden brown. Fry doughnut holes, a few at time, 1 to 1½ minutes on each side or until golden brown and cooked through. Drain on paper towels; cool slightly. If desired, dip the tops of the doughnuts into glaze.

**PER SERVING** *335 cal., 15 g fat (5 g sat. fat), 46 mg chol., 338 mg sodium, 45 g carb., 1 g fiber, 5 g pro.*

---

**DOUGHNUTS, YOUR WAY**

**1. SHAPE**
All you need to flatten this dough are your hands. Just pat it down, then cut with a doughnut cutter. To keep the dough from sticking, wiggle your cutter in a little flour between cuts.

**2. SIZZLE**
Fry the doughnuts in batches for a minute on each side; let the oil reheat to 365° before starting the next round. Use heatproof tongs for flipping and transferring piping-hot doughnuts from the oil to paper towels.

**3. DIP**
Now it's time to dunk, drizzle and add all the tasty toppings of your dreams! Grab your glaze of choice and get ready to dip. For a translucent look, plunk your doughnut in the glaze while it's still warm. Want it more opaque? Let the doughnut cool a bit first. Feel free to double dunk!

**4. DRIZZLE**
If you like, drizzle a second glaze over already-dipped doughnuts. (Chocolate on maple? *Mmm!*)

APPLE CIDER DOUGHNUTS

MAPLE GLAZE FOR DOUGHNUTS

CHOCOLATE GLAZE
FOR DOUGHNUTS

## Chocolate Glaze for Doughnuts

If smooth, rich and decadent is your kind of glaze, you'll love this simple chocolate ganache. Want another yummy option? Follow the directions at the end of the recipe to make frosting instead.
—**KAREN MOORE** JACKSONVILLE, FL

**START TO FINISH:** 10 MIN.
**MAKES:** 1 CUP

- 6 **ounces semisweet chocolate, chopped**
- ½ **cup heavy whipping cream**
- 2 **tablespoons light corn syrup**
- 2 **teaspoons vanilla extract**

Place the chocolate in a small bowl. In a small saucepan, bring cream and corn syrup just to a boil. Pour over the chocolate; stir with a whisk until smooth. Stir in vanilla.

**TO MAKE CHOCOLATE FROSTING**
*Prepare the Chocolate Glaze for Doughnuts as directed; stir in 2 cups confectioners' sugar until smooth. Let stand 15 minutes or until the mixture thickens to a spreading consistency. Makes: 1¾ cups.*
**PER SERVING** *118 cal., 8 g fat (5 g sat. fat), 14 mg chol., 6 mg sodium, 11 g carb., 1 g fiber, 1 g pro.*

## Maple Glaze for Doughnuts

With syrup and three other ingredients, you can easily give your from-scratch goodies wonderful maple flavor.
—**BARBARA ELLIOTT** TYLER, TX

**START TO FINISH:** 5 MIN.
**MAKES:** 1 CUP

- 2 **cups confectioners' sugar**
- 3 **tablespoons 2% milk**
- 2 **tablespoons maple syrup**
- ½ **teaspoon maple flavoring**

In a small bowl, whisk all ingredients until smooth.
**PER SERVING** *89 cal., trace fat (trace sat. fat), trace chol., 3 mg sodium, 22 g carb., 0 fiber, trace pro.*

**top tip**

## Dressed Up

Top off glazed doughnuts with rainbow jimmies, chopped nuts, bits of bacon—any topper you prefer. Or, skip the glaze and coat plain doughnuts with yummy ginger sugar instead. In a bowl, combine ¾ cup sugar with 2-3 tablespoons ground ginger. Add the warm doughnuts and toss them until they're coated.

# Pasta 101

Start with some flour, a few eggs…and it's homemade pasta for dinner. One basic dough makes wonderful fettuccine or individual-size lasagnas.

RECIPES BY **KATHRYN CONRAD**
*TASTE OF HOME* SENIOR FOOD STYLIST

**CHICKEN & SPINACH LASAGNAS**

**(5) INGREDIENTS**

## Homemade Pasta Dough

Go for it. Once you make your own pasta from scratch, you'll be hooked!

**PREP:** 15 MIN. + STANDING
**MAKES:** 6 SERVINGS

- 2 **eggs**
- 1 **egg yolk**
- ¼ **cup water**
- 1 **tablespoon olive oil**
- ½ **teaspoon coarsely ground pepper**
- ¼ **teaspoon salt**
- 1½ **cups all-purpose flour**
- ½ **cup semolina flour**

**1.** In a small bowl, whisk the first six ingredients. On a clean work surface, mix all-purpose flour and semolina flour, forming a mound. Make a large well in the center. Pour egg mixture into the well. Using a fork or fingers, gradually mix flour mixture into egg mixture, forming a soft dough (the dough will be slightly sticky).

**2.** Lightly dust work surface with flour; knead dough gently five times. Divide into six portions; cover with plastic wrap. Let rest 30 minutes.
**TO MAKE FETTUCCINE** *Roll each ball into a 10x8-in. rectangle, dusting them lightly with flour. Roll each rectangle up jelly-roll style. Cut into ¼-in.-wide strips. Cook the pasta in boiling water 1-3 minutes.*
**PER SERVING** *363 cal., 13 g fat (6 g sat. fat), 135 mg chol., 343 mg sodium, 44 g carb., 3 g fiber, 19 g pro.* **Diabetic Exchanges:** *2½ starch, 2 medium-fat meat, 1 vegetable, ½ fat.*

## Chicken & Spinach Lasagnas

Personal-size lasagnas are as fun to put together and serve as they are to eat.

**PREP:** 45 MIN. + STANDING • **BAKE:** 30 MIN.
**MAKES:** 6 SERVINGS

**Homemade Pasta Dough (recipe at left)**

### FILLING

- 3 **cups shredded rotisserie chicken**
- 2 **cups chopped fresh baby spinach**
- 2 **teaspoons minced fresh thyme**
- 1½ **teaspoons grated lemon peel**
- 1 **teaspoon lemon juice**
- ¼ **teaspoon salt**
- 2¼ **cups (9 ounces) shredded fontina cheese, divided**
  **Grated Parmesan cheese and additional fresh thyme, optional**

**1.** Follow directions for Homemade Pasta Dough (recipe at far left).
**2.** In a large bowl, combine the first six filling ingredients; stir in 1½ cups fontina cheese. Grease six individual 12-oz. au gratin dishes; place on baking sheets. Preheat oven to 350°.
**3.** Fill a Dutch oven three-fourths full with salted water; bring to a boil. On a floured surface, roll each portion of dough into a 20x4-in. rectangle, dusting dough with additional flour as needed.
**4.** Add one noodle to boiling water; cook 1-2 minutes or until al dente. Place one-fifth of the noodle in bottom of a prepared dish; top with a scant ¼ cup chicken mixture. Fold noodle back to cover filling; repeat three times, topping and folding noodle each time. Repeat with remaining noodles and filling.
**5.** Sprinkle lasagnas with remaining fontina. Bake, covered, 30-35 minutes or until heated through. If desired, sprinkle with Parmesan and thyme.
**PER SERVING** *511 cal., 23 g fat (10 g sat. fat), 214 mg chol., 614 mg sodium, 36 g carb., 2 g fiber, 38 g pro.*

**MAKE FETTUCCINE**

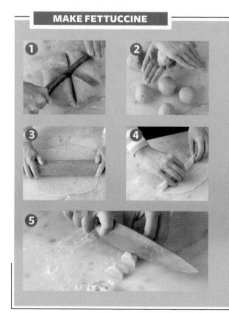

**1.** Cutting your own fettuccine is easy to do. First, divide your large ball of pasta dough into six wedges, like a pie.

**2.** Shape the wedges into balls. Cover them with plastic wrap and let them rest for 30 minutes.

**3.** Roll each ball of dough into a 10x9-in. rectangle, dusting lightly with flour as you go.

**4.** Roll up each rectangle jelly-roll style.

**5.** Cut each roll into ¼-in.-wide strips. Cook the fettuccine in boiling water 1-3 minutes.

# Herb Garden Lasagnas

I just love the taste and texture of these single-serving entrees. Fresh herbs lighten the flavor of the rich, cheesy dish.

**PREP:** 45 MIN. + STANDING • **BAKE:** 30 MIN.
**MAKES:** 6 SERVINGS

**Homemade Pasta Dough (recipe on page 296)**

**FILLING**

- 1 **cup whole-milk ricotta cheese**
- 1 **egg white, lightly beaten**
- 2 **tablespoons shredded carrot**
- 1 **tablespoon minced fresh basil**
- 1 **tablespoon thinly sliced green onion**
- 1 **teaspoon minced fresh mint**
- ¼ **teaspoon salt**
- 1 **cup crumbled queso fresco or feta cheese, divided**
- 4 **cups chopped tomatoes (about 6 medium), divided**
  **Optional toppings: thinly sliced green onion, fresh basil and fresh mint**

**1.** Follow directions for Homemade Pasta Dough (recipe on page 296).
**2.** In a small bowl, mix the first seven filling ingredients; stir in ½ cup queso fresco. Grease six individual 12-ounce au gratin dishes; place on baking sheets. Preheat oven to 350°.
**3.** Fill a Dutch oven three-fourths full with salted water; bring to a boil. On a floured surface, roll each portion of dough into a 20x4-in. rectangle, dusting dough with additional flour as needed.
**4.** Add one noodle to boiling water; cook for 1-2 minutes or until al dente. Place one-fifth of the noodle in the bottom of a prepared dish; top with 1 tablespoon of the ricotta mixture and 2 tablespoons tomato. Fold the noodle back to cover filling; repeat three times, topping and folding noodle each time.
**5.** Sprinkle lasagnas with remaining queso fresco and tomatoes. Bake, covered, 30-35 minutes or until heated through. If desired, sprinkle with additional herbs.

**PER SERVING** *363 cal., 13 g fat (6 g sat. fat), 135 mg chol., 343 mg sodium, 44 g carb., 3 g fiber, 19 g pro.* **Diabetic Exchanges:** *2½ starch, 2 medium-fat meat, 1 vegetable, ½ fat.*

**HERB GARDEN LASAGNAS**

**LASAGNA MAGIC**

Here's how to assemble individual lasagnas. One double-wide noodle is all it takes per serving. Place the end of a cooked noodle in a miniature casserole dish. Top with the filling, fold the pasta over and repeat—accordion-style. You can also nest your mini lasagnas in a 13x9-in. baking dish.

# Guacamole Mash-Up

Grab avocados and your favorite tortilla chips, then get scoopin'! These helpful Test Kitchen tips and techniques work like a charm on the three sensational guacamole recipes here.

**⑤ INGREDIENTS** **EAT SMART** **FAST FIX**

## Homemade Guacamole

My daughters sometimes refer to this as five-finger guacamole because it requires just five ingredients. It's so easy!

**—NANETTE HILTON** LAS VEGAS, NV

**START TO FINISH:** 10 MIN.
**MAKES:** 2 CUPS

- **3 medium ripe avocados, peeled and cubed**
- **¼ cup finely chopped onion**
- **¼ cup minced fresh cilantro**
- **2 tablespoons lime juice**
- **⅛ teaspoon salt**
  **Tortilla chips**

In a small bowl, mash the avocados with a fork. Stir in the onion, minced cilantro, lime juice and salt. Serve with tortilla chips.

**PER SERVING** *111 cal., 10 g fat (1 g sat. fat), 0 chol., 43 mg sodium, 6 g carb., 5 g fiber, 1 g pro.*

HOMEMADE GUACAMOLE

**1.** Cut into the ripe avocado stem to stern until you hit the seed. Repeat to cut the avocado into quarters.

**2.** Twist to separate.

**3.** Pull out the seed.

**4.** Pull back the skin on each piece like a banana peel. Then just slice as you like.

# Chunky Mango Guacamole

When serving a crowd, I double or even quadruple my mango-flavored appetizer.
—**DIANA NIENBERG** MCCOMB, OH

**START TO FINISH:** 15 MIN.
**MAKES:** 4 CUPS

- 3 **medium ripe avocados, peeled and chopped**
- 1 **large mango, peeled and chopped**
- 1 **large tomato, chopped**
- 1 **small red onion, chopped**
- ¼ **cup chopped fresh cilantro**
- 3 **tablespoons lime juice**
- 1 **teaspoon salt**
  **Assorted fresh vegetables and tortilla chips**

In a large bowl, combine the first five ingredients; stir in the lime juice and salt. Serve with vegetables and chips.
**PER SERVING** *67 cal., 5 g fat (1 g sat. fat), 0 chol., 151 mg sodium, 6 g carb., 3 g fiber, 1 g pro.* **Diabetic Exchanges:** *1 fat, ½ starch.*

# Three-Pepper Guacamole

If you're serious about guacamole, use a *molcajete*. This traditional Mexican tool is great for making the pepper paste in this recipe—and is fun for guests to try out at a fiesta.
—**LAURA LEVY** LYONS, CO

**START TO FINISH:** 25 MIN.
**MAKES:** 4 CUPS

- 3 **tablespoons plus ¼ cup minced fresh cilantro, divided**
- 4 **tablespoons finely chopped onion, divided**
- 3 **tablespoons minced seeded jalapeno pepper**
- 1 **tablespoon minced seeded serrano pepper**
- 2 **to 3 teaspoons chopped chipotle pepper in adobo sauce**
- 3 **garlic cloves, minced**
- ½ **teaspoon salt**
- 4 **medium ripe avocados, peeled and cubed**

THREE-PEPPER GUACAMOLE

- ⅓ **cup finely chopped tomatoes**
  **Tortilla chips**

In a large bowl, combine 3 tablespoons cilantro, 2 tablespoons onion, peppers, garlic and salt; mash together with a fork. Stir in avocados; fold in tomatoes and remaining cilantro and onion.

Serve immediately with chips.
**NOTE** *Wear disposable gloves when cutting hot peppers; the oils can burn skin. Avoid touching your face.*
**PER SERVING** *76 cal., 7 g fat (1 g sat. fat), 0 chol., 82 mg sodium, 4 g carb., 3 g fiber, 1 g pro.* **Diabetic Exchange:** *1½ fat.*

## KEEP IT GREEN!

Feel free to prepare guacamole ahead of time. To keep it nice and green, just cover it with a little water. The extra layer shields it from oxygen and helps prevent browning.

- In an airtight container, use a spoon to flatten the surface of your guacamole and remove any air pockets.
- Gently pour in about a half inch of water to cover the guacamole.
- Refrigerate, covered, up to two days. To serve, carefully pour off the water and stir the guacamole.

# Roll Models

After a bit of night-before prep, you'll wake up to risen sweet roll dough ready to shape in tempting ways. No kneading required!

RECIPES BY **CHRIS O'CONNELL** | SAN ANTONIO, TX

## ⑤ INGREDIENTS
### Easy Overnight Dough

Put this versatile dough in the fridge overnight. Then make cinnamon rolls, dinner rolls (I make Rudolph look-alikes) or wreaths. Or use the dough to mix and match: Use half for a dozen cinnamon rolls, 18 reindeer rolls or one wreath.

**PREP:** 15 MIN. + CHILLING

- 2 **packages (¼ ounce each) active dry yeast**
- 1½ **cups warm water (110° to 115°)**
- 2 **eggs**
- ½ **cup butter, softened**
- ½ **cup sugar**
- 2 **teaspoons salt**
- 5¾ to 6¼ **cups all-purpose flour**

**1.** In a small bowl, dissolve yeast in warm water. In a large bowl, combine eggs, butter, sugar, salt, yeast mixture and 3 cups flour; beat on medium speed until smooth. Stir in enough of the remaining flour to form a very soft dough (the dough will be sticky).
**2.** Do not knead. Cover with plastic wrap; refrigerate overnight.

### Overnight Cinnamon Rolls

Warm from the oven, these iced delights make the house smell absolutely heavenly. They're impossible to resist!

**PREP:** 20 MIN. + RISING • **BAKE:** 20 MIN.
**MAKES:** 2 DOZEN

- **Easy Overnight Dough (recipe above)**
- **CINNAMON FILLING**
- 1 **cup packed brown sugar**
- 4 **teaspoons ground cinnamon**
- ½ **cup softened butter, divided**
- **GLAZE**
- 2 **cups confectioners' sugar**
- ¼ **cup half-and-half cream**
- 2 **teaspoons vanilla extract**

**1.** Follow the directions for Easy Overnight Dough (recipe at left) through Step 2.
**2.** In a small bowl, mix brown sugar and cinnamon. Turn the dough onto a floured surface; divide in half. Roll one half into an 18x12-in. rectangle. Spread with ¼ cup butter to within ½ in. of the edges; sprinkle evenly with half of brown sugar mixture.
**3.** Roll up jelly-roll style, starting with a long side; pinch seam to seal.
**4.** Cut into 12 slices using a serrated knife or unflavored dental floss. Place in a greased 13x9-in. baking pan, cut side down. Repeat with the remaining dough and filling.
**5.** Cover with kitchen towels; let rise in a warm place until doubled, about 1 hour. Preheat oven to 375°.
**6.** Bake 20-25 minutes or until lightly browned. In a small bowl, mix the confectioners' sugar, cream and vanilla; spread over warm rolls.

### DARK CHOCOLATE FILLING
*Finely grate one 4-ounce bittersweet chocolate baking bar; gently stir in ½ cup sugar, 2 tablespoons baking cocoa and ½ teaspoon ground cinnamon. Sprinkle mixture evenly over butter in place of brown sugar-cinnamon mixture.*

### ORANGE-SPICE FILLING
*Mix 1 cup packed brown sugar, 2 tablespoons grated orange peel, 2 teaspoons ground cinnamon, 1 teaspoon ground ginger and ½ teaspoon each ground cloves, ground cardamom and ground allspice until blended. Sprinkle mixture evenly over butter in place of brown sugar-cinnamon mixture.*

**PER SERVING** *278 cal., 9 g fat (5 g sat. fat), 39 mg chol., 262 mg sodium, 47 g carb., 1 g fiber, 4 g pro.*

OVERNIGHT CINNAMON ROLLS

Once the dough is rolled into a log, use unflavored dental floss—or a serrated knife—to slice cinnamon rolls.

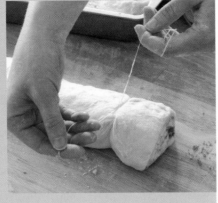

**OH, DEER!**

Time to call upon your inner artist. Transform a lump of plain dough into festive reindeer with scissors!

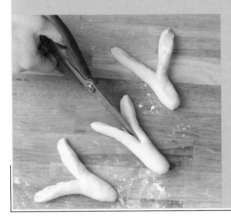

# Overnight Reindeer Rolls

Let the kids help you create an adorable team of reindeer. Pressing on a piece of candied cherry for Rudolph's red nose is sure to make any youngster smile! If you need a batch of traditional knot-shaped dinner rolls instead, simply follow the directions at the end of the recipe.

**PREP:** 50 MIN. + RISING • **BAKE:** 10 MIN.
**MAKES:** 3 DOZEN

**Easy Overnight Dough (recipe on page 300)**

**DECORATIONS**
- 1 egg
- 2 teaspoons water
- 36 raisins (about 2 tablespoons), halved
- 18 candied cherries, halved

**1.** Follow the directions for Easy Overnight Dough (recipe on p. 300) through Step 2.

**2.** Turn the dough onto a floured surface; divide and shape into 36 balls. Roll each ball into a 5-in. log. Cut each log halfway down the center. Pull the cut sections apart to form the antlers. Using kitchen shears, snip ½-in. cuts along the outer sides for the points of the antlers. Flatten the uncut half of the log for the face.

**3.** Place rolls 2 in. apart on greased baking sheets. Cover with kitchen towels; let rise in a warm place until doubled, about 30 minutes. Preheat oven to 400°.

**4.** In a small bowl, whisk the egg and water until blended; brush over the rolls. Press the raisin halves into the dough for the eyes; press the cherry halves into dough for the noses.

**5.** Bake 8-10 minutes or until golden brown. Serve warm.

**KNOT-SHAPED DINNER ROLLS**
*Shape dough into 36 balls. Roll each dough ball into a 6-in. rope; tie into a loose knot. Tuck ends under; place rolls 2 in. apart on greased baking sheets. Let rise and bake as recipe directs, increasing the baking time to 10-12 minutes.*

**PER SERVING** *116 cal., 3 g fat (2 g sat. fat), 24 mg chol., 155 mg sodium, 19 g carb., 1 g fiber, 3 g pro.*

OVERNIGHT REINDEER ROLLS

# Overnight Cinnamon Wreaths

Here's a lovely edible wreath to showcase on your dining table during the holiday season—or any time of year.

**PREP:** 20 MIN. + RISING • **BAKE:** 20 MIN.
**MAKES:** 2 WREATHS (12 SLICES EACH)

**Overnight Cinnamon Rolls (using cinnamon filling, recipe on page 300)**
**EGG WASH**
1 egg
2 teaspoons water

**1.** Follow directions for Overnight Cinnamon Rolls (recipe on p. 300) through Step 3.
**2.** Place one rolled-up log of dough on a parchment paper-lined 12-in. pizza pan or 15x10x1-in. baking pan, seam side down. Shape into a ring, pinching ends together to seal (The filling may leak slightly during baking; be sure to use rimmed baking pans.)
**3.** Using kitchen scissors, start at the outside edge of the ring and cut two-thirds of the way through the ring at 1-in. intervals. Separate the sections slightly and twist slightly to show the filling. Repeat with the remaining log of dough.
**4.** Cover the wreaths with kitchen towels; let rise in a warm place until almost doubled, about 1 hour. Preheat oven to 375°.
**5.** For the egg wash, in a small bowl, whisk the egg and water until blended; brush over the wreaths. Bake for 18-22 minutes or until golden brown.
**6.** Prepare the Overnight Cinnamon Rolls glaze; spread or drizzle over warm wreaths.

**PER SERVING** *281 cal., 9 g fat (5 g sat. fat), 48 mg chol., 265 mg sodium, 47 g carb., 1 g fiber, 4 g pro.*

**RING IT IN**

Shape rolled-up dough into a circle, pinching the ends together to seal. Then use clean scissors to snip partially through the ring.

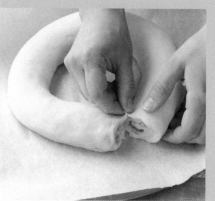

OVERNIGHT CINNAMON WREATHS

# All-Star Pie

Follow this helpful Test Kitchen guide, from roll-out to cool-down, for a showstopping homemade pie crust without the fuss.

## Juicy Raspberry Pie

This berry-packed delight looks stunning with a starry cutout design on top.

**—KAREN BERNER** GREENDALE, WI

**PREP:** 35 MIN. + CHILLING
**BAKE:** 55 MIN. + COOLING
**MAKES:** 8 SERVINGS

- 2½ cups all-purpose flour
- ½ teaspoon salt
- ⅔ cup cold unsalted butter, cubed
- ⅓ cup shortening
- 6 to 10 tablespoons ice water

**FILLING**
- 5 cups fresh raspberries
- 2 teaspoons lemon juice
- ¼ teaspoon almond extract
- 1 cup plus 1 teaspoon sugar, divided
- ⅓ cup all-purpose flour
- 1¼ teaspoons ground cinnamon, divided
- 1 tablespoon 2% milk

JUICY RASPBERRY PIE

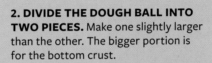
**PIE CRUST SECRETS**

**1. GO FOR BUTTERY FLECKS.** Create pea-size bits when cutting the butter into the dry ingredients. The flecks will melt in the oven and give off steam, creating flaky pockets.

**2. DIVIDE THE DOUGH BALL INTO TWO PIECES.** Make one slightly larger than the other. The bigger portion is for the bottom crust.

**3. GET ROLLING.** Start from the center and roll out to the edges.

**4. TIME TO FLUTE.** Your fingers and thumb are the only tools you need.

**1.** In a large bowl, mix the flour and salt; cut in the butter and shortening until crumbly. Gradually add the ice water, tossing with a fork until dough holds together when pressed. Divide dough in half. Shape each into a disk; wrap in plastic wrap. Refrigerate for 1 hour or overnight.

**2.** Preheat oven to 375°. For filling, place the raspberries in a large bowl; drizzle with lemon juice and almond extract. In a small bowl, mix 1 cup sugar, flour and 1 teaspoon cinnamon. Sprinkle over the raspberries and toss gently to coat.

**3.** On a lightly floured surface, roll one half of dough to a ⅛-in.-thick circle; transfer to a 9-in. pie plate. Trim the pastry even with rim. Add filling.

**4.** Roll the remaining dough to a ⅛-in.-thick circle; cut out stars using cookie cutters. Place over filling. Trim, seal and flute edge. If desired, decorate top with cutouts.

**5.** Bake 40 minutes. Mix remaining sugar and cinnamon. Brush top of pie with milk; sprinkle with cinnamon-sugar. Bake 15-20 minutes longer or until crust is golden brown and filling is bubbly. Cool on a wire rack.

**PER SERVING** *520 cal., 24 g fat (12 g sat. fat), 40 mg chol., 151 mg sodium, 70 g carb., 7 g fiber, 6 g pro.*

# General Index

This handy index lists every recipe by food category, major ingredient and/or cooking method, so you can easily locate recipes to suit your needs.

✓ *Recipe includes* EAT SMART

RECIPE INDEXES

# Alphabetical Index

This convenient index lists every recipe in alphabetical order, so you can easily find your favorite dishes.

✓ *Recipe includes* **EAT SMART**

Cinnamon-Walnut Sticky Buns, 145

✓Citrus Melon Mingle, 142

Citrus Steak Salad, 24

✓Cocoa-Crusted Beef Tenderloin, 279

Coconut Creme Chocolates, 90

Coconut Curry Chicken Soup, 205

Coconut-Pecan German Chocolate
    Pie, 103

✓Coconut Twice-Baked Sweet
    Potatoes, 50

Coconut-White Chocolate
    Cheesecake, 122

Coffee Milk, 199

CokeCola Cake, 285

✓Colorful Bean Salad, 20

Confetti Cake with Brown Sugar
    Buttercream, 110

Country Sausage & Egg Rolls, 148

Crab Cakes with Peanut Sauce, 173

Crab Rangoon Cheese Ball, 13

Cranberry Double-Nut Pie, 115

Cranberry-Orange Crumb Tart, 125

Cranberry Pineapple Upside-Down
    Cake, 106

Cranberry Swirl Loaf, 87

✓Cranberry-Walnut Sweet
    Potatoes, 157

Cream Cheese Bran Muffins, 78

✓Cream-of-the-Crop Veggies, 26

Creamy Cranberry Salad, 178

Creamy Fresh Asparagus Soup, 281

Creamy Lemon Milk Shakes, 8

Creamy Lime Pie with Fresh
    Berries, 107

Creamy Pastel Mints, 164

Creamy Pineapple Salad, 28

Creamy Root Veggie Soup, 41

✓Crispy Fish & Chips, 255

Crispy Mashed Potato & Stuffing
    Patties, 138

✓Crispy Potato Puffs, 180

Crumb-Coated Ranch Chicken, 61

Cumin-Chili Spiced Flank Steak, 72

Curried Fried Rice with
    Pineapple, 53

✓Curried Ham & Split Pea Soup, 246

### D

Dad's Famous Stuffies, 199

Dark Chocolate Raspberry Fudge, 98

Deep-Dish Apple Pie, 117

Deluxe Baked Macaroni and
    Cheese, 68

Devil's Food Cupcakes with
    Chocolaty Frosting, 176

Dill and Chive Bread, 79

Double-Crust Strawberry Pie, 111

Dr Spicy BBQ Pork, 283

### E

Easter Basket Cupcakes, 169

✓Easy Asian Chicken Slaw, 234

Easy Chicken Tamale Pie, 59

Easy Overnight Dough, 300

Easy Peanut Butter Truffles, 164

Easy Stuffed Shells, 61

Eggs Benedict Casserole, 149

✓Elegant Pork Marsala, 233

### F

Favorite Ice Cream Tacos, 266

✓Feta Shrimp Skillet, 252

5-Cheese Ravioli Marinara, 224

5-Ingredient Fudge, 92

Flaky Cheddar-Chive Biscuits, 82

Flank Steak with Cilantro & Blue
    Cheese Butter, 62

Folded Hazelnut Cookies, 98

Four-Cheese French Onion Soup, 33

Fourth of July Baked Beans, 171

Fresh Broccoli Salad with
    Lemon, 224

✓Fresh Green Beans & Garlic, 167

Frosted Pistachio Bars, 177

Frozen Chocolate Monkey
    Treats, 272

Frozen Grasshopper Pie, 107

✓Frozen Greek Vanilla Yogurt, 250

Frozen Key Lime Delight, 120

Fun-do Fondue, 215

### G

Game Day Gumbo, 284

✓Garlic Chicken Rigatoni, 243

Garlic Maple Dressing, 20

✓Garlic Mashed Rutabagas &
    Potatoes, 187

Garlicky Chicken Pizza, 234

German Apple Strudel, 174

German Beer Cheese Spread, 14

Giant Lemon Sugar Cookies, 213

Giant Monster Cookies, 274

Ginger Butternut Squash
    Bisque, 291

Ginger-Maple Roasted Pecans, 181

✓Ginger-Sesame Steamed Vegetable
    Salad, 240

Gingerbread People, 186

Gingerbread Scones, 141

Gingered Almond Truffle Tart, 125

Gingered Cranberry Pear Crisp, 127

Glazed Apple-Maple Blondies, 97

Glazed Gingerbread Cake, 113

✓Gluten-Free Spritz Delights, 251

Gobble-Up Strata, 217

Golden Danish Twists, 140

Golden Potato Soup, 38

Good Ol' Burger, 170

Great Garlic Bread, 85

✓Greek Chicken & Artichokes, 246

✓Greek Sloppy Joes, 248

✓Greek-Style Chicken Skewers, 254

Green Flop Jell-O, 283

Green Onion Tartar Sauce, 49

✓Grilled Brown Sugar-Mustard
    Chicken, 65

Grilled Eggplant Pita Pizzas, 74

Grilled Maple Pork Chops, 58

✓Grilled Nectarine & Cheese
    Crostini, 7

Grilled Pork Tenderloin &
    Veggies, 73

✓Grilled Pork with Spicy Pineapple
    Salsa, 249

Grilled Potatoes with Sour Cream
    Sauce, 51

Grilled Steak Salad with Tomatoes &
    Avocado, 161

Guinness Corned Beef and
    Cabbage, 71

### H

Ham & Cheese Bagels, 36

Ham & Cheese Grits Casserole, 197

Ham & Cheese Potato Casserole, 65

Ham & Potato Salad Sandwiches, 290